# Effective Product Control

Founded in 1807, John Wiley & Sons is the oldest independent publishing company in the United States. With offices in North America, Europe, Australia and Asia, Wiley is globally committed to developing and marketing print and electronic products and services for our customers' professional and personal knowledge and understanding.

The Wiley Finance series contains books written specifically for finance and investment professionals as well as sophisticated individual investors and their financial advisors. Book topics range from portfolio management to e-commerce, risk management, financial engineering, valuation and financial instrument analysis, as well as much more.

For a list of available titles, visit our Web site at www.WileyFinance.com.

# Effective Product Control

## Controlling for Trading Desks

PETER NASH

WILEY

This edition first published 2018
© 2018 Peter Nash

*Registered office*
John Wiley & Sons Ltd, The Atrium, Southern Gate, Chichester, West Sussex, PO19 8SQ,
United Kingdom

For details of our global editorial offices, for customer services and for information about how to apply
for permission to reuse the copyright material in this book please see our website at www.wiley.com.

Wiley publishes in a variety of print and electronic formats and by print-on-demand. Some material
included with standard print versions of this book may not be included in e-books or in
print-on-demand. If this book refers to media such as a CD or DVD that is not included in the version
you purchased, you may download this material at http://booksupport.wiley.com. For more information
about Wiley products, visit www.wiley.com.

Designations used by companies to distinguish their products are often claimed as trademarks. All
brand names and product names used in this book are trade names, service marks, trademarks or
registered trademarks of their respective owners. The publisher is not associated with any product or
vendor mentioned in this book.

Limit of Liability/Disclaimer of Warranty: While the publisher and author have used their best efforts
in preparing this book, they make no representations or warranties with respect to the accuracy or
completeness of the contents of this book and specifically disclaim any implied warranties of
merchantability or fitness for a particular purpose. It is sold on the understanding that the publisher is
not engaged in rendering professional services and neither the publisher nor the author shall be liable
for damages arising herefrom. If professional advice or other expert assistance is required, the services
of a competent professional should be sought.

*Library of Congress Cataloging-in-Publication Data*

Names: Nash, Peter, author.
Title: Effective product control : controlling for trading desks / by Peter Nash.
Description: Chichester, West Sussex, United Kingdom : John Wiley & Sons, 2018. | Includes index. |
Identifiers: LCCN 2017029434 (print) | LCCN 2017040992 (ebook) | ISBN 9781118939796 (Pdf) |
    ISBN 9781118939802 (epub) | ISBN 9781118939819 (cloth)
Subjects: LCSH: Financial institutions—Risk management. | Financial services industry—
    Risk management. | Portfolio management. | Stocks. | Investments.
Classification: LCC HG173 (ebook) | LCC HG173 .N27 2018 (print) | DDC 332.1068/1—dc23
LC record available at https://lccn.loc.gov/2017029434

A catalogue record for this book is available from the British Library.

ISBN 978-1-118-93981-9 (hardback)    ISBN 978-1-118-93979-6 (ePDF)
ISBN 978-1-118-93980-2 (ePub)    ISBN 978-1-118-93978-9 (obk)

10 9 8 7 6 5 4 3 2 1

Cover design: Wiley
Cover image: Top: ©Shai_Halud/Shutterstock, Bottom: ©Inozemtsev Konstantin/Shutterstock

Set in 10/12pt Times by Aptara Inc., New Delhi, India
Printed in Great Britain by TJ International Ltd, Padstow, Cornwall, UK

*I dedicate this book to my family, especially my children, who have forgone a great deal of Dad time for this book to come to life.*
*To Phoebe, Xani and Matilda.*
*Thank you.*

*In memory of Patrick Spratt, a product controller and friend who was larger than life.*

# Contents

# Preface

In 2003 I was working in a Dutch bank in a high rise overlooking the picturesque Sydney Harbour, when another junior external auditor sat beside me to review my work. This was the third new auditor in as many years and as they struggled to grasp what it was I did as a job, their lack of understanding generated in me mixed feelings of frustration and empathy for the person.

Their lack of knowledge wasn't their fault; product control is difficult to understand for an outsider and sending junior staff in to test controls is the model many audit firms use to carry out their audit assignments. Nevertheless, that exchange generated an idea to help close the gap between new auditors and product controllers and their more experienced colleagues.

Over the past 14 years I continued to work in product control in both Sydney and London, developing more experience, skills and friendships, which together have finally made possible the writing and publication of this book.

Due to the large numbers of sales and trading teams within banks, they remain the largest employer of product controllers. We will, therefore, aim the narrative of the book towards banks, but the content can also be applied to other contexts in which product control operates, such as hedge funds and corporate treasuries.

Whether you are embarking on your career or have years of experience in the field, this book will equip you with the building blocks necessary to be an effective product controller or effective in your review of product control. These building blocks cover both the core technical skills required in product control and the primary controls which product control are responsible for.

My hope is that through reading this book, your career is enhanced and more opportunities are afforded to you and your family.

Peter Nash

# Acknowledgements

**S**pecial thanks to Robert Phillips who encouraged me and helped develop the manuscript from its infancy.

Thank you also to the following people and organisations who have contributed to the content of this book:

Dooshyant Beekarry, Nico Botha, Paul Bradley, Paul Buchanan, Clive Budd, Matthew Burbedge, James Campbell, Lisa Chuilon (nee Able), James Clarke, CME, Brighton Cohen, COSO, Christine Cossor, Brent Davies, Delphi Derivatives, Kane Erickson, FCA, FINMA, Fitzgerald Jenkins Recruitment, Chad Foyn, Paul Galpin, Darren Gordois, Chris Harvell, James Hayden, Michael Hoppe, ICE, Sanjiv Ingle, Investing.com, Tim Jenkins, Steve Kelley, Thusitha Liyanage, Markit, Harkil Maru, Ruairi McHale, Denley Mirabueno, Mondrian Alpha Recruitment, Grant Moscowitz, Richard O'Flynn, Daniel Pass, Mark Proctor, SmartStream, Ben Tallentire, Thomson Reuters, TriOptima, TOM Recruitment, Treasury Services, Darren Wadhera, Peter Walsh, Ben Weekes, Matthew Wiles, Mark Williams and Keith Young.

Finally, thank you to my past managers who have shared their knowledge and experience throughout my career:

Scott Rissman, Ben Weekes, Geoff Simmonds, Callum Winchester, Craig Townsend, Sandy Coxon, Peter Roberts, Robert Phillips, Ron Antonelli, Diana Neo, Prash Patel, Pascal Loup, James Howard, Stephen Chippendale, Chad Foyn, Oliver Gee, Rob Jones, James Campbell, Ryan Evans, Nathan Harris and Kane Erickson.

# About the Author

**P**eter Nash is a qualified accountant who has spent almost two decades working in Product Control, controlling a wide range of sales and trading desks in Investment and Commercial banks. He is currently a director of FINSED (www.finsed.com), a financial services training and consulting firm specialising in Product Control.

# One

# Working in Product Control

The opening part of this book provides an introduction to what it's like to work in product control, beginning with a review of product control's emergence as a significant control function, before considering its purpose and the environment within which it operates. The book will then go on to explore the skills and experience required and consider what changes have impacted the function over the past decade.

# CHAPTER 1

# An Introduction to Product Control

## THE EMERGENCE OF PRODUCT CONTROL

Finance within banking is unlike finance in most other types of industries. In most non-banking companies, the finance team is separate from the producer. For example, in a manufacturing company the finance department is not on the shop floor, and in a retail company it is not in the stores. Most likely, finance is housed in the head office.

In these industries, the value of the product is not often in dispute. Usually the cost of sales and production, or margin per unit, is known and the revenues are the function of a simple calculation. There is also often a team of management accountants providing information to the product line managers on the results of their business and assisting in analytics on those results.

In banking, it is not that simple. Finance is more integral to the production because the products banks deliver are financial. In the 1990s, with increasing volumes of trading, a greater pool of financial instruments and higher levels of complexity, it was necessary for banks to establish a dedicated function within finance to control evolving sales and trading desks. With that, management accountants within finance morphed and grew into a function called product control, which came to dominate large swathes of finance, establishing footprints all over the developed world and later on, the developing world.

Over the past decade, these large swathes have been migrating from the more expensive financial centres such as London, New York, Tokyo, Hong Kong and Singapore, to cheaper locations such as India, Poland and the Philippines. This change has presented opportunities for aspiring workers in the developing nations and presented uncertain career paths for those remaining in the shrinking financial centres.

We will look at this trend in more detail in Chapter 2.

## THE PURPOSE OF PRODUCT CONTROL

Product control is the face of finance to the sales and trading desks in a bank. They provide financial control and transparency through (Figure 1.1):

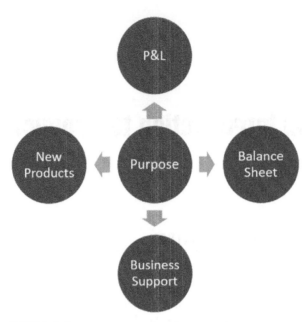

**FIGURE 1.1**    The purpose of product control

- Providing a profit and loss statement and balance sheet which is accurate and timely;
- Providing meaningful insight into the desk's financial results;
- Supporting the desk in the execution of their business strategy; and
- Evaluating and integrating new products into the financial environment.

Product control's purpose is executed through a series of controls across the P&L and balance sheet, many of which are performed daily. On top of these controls, product control's financial acumen and understanding of the bank's systems can be used to support the execution of the desk's business strategy. This includes providing insight into drivers of financial performance, reviewing the desk's use of legal entities within the banking group and assessing the efficiency of process workflows.

The centrepiece of the product control role is the daily P&L (Figure 1.2). If you aren't familiar with this term, it measures the income and expenses for the sales and trading desks. If the sum of the income from trading activities, client sales and trading expenses is greater than zero, a profit is reported, otherwise a loss is reported.

We will explore the controls that product control normally execute in greater detail throughout Parts III through VII of the book.

**FIGURE 1.2**    The P&L

## DIFFERENT TYPES OF PRODUCT CONTROL

Before we can explore the role of product control further we need to be aware that not every organization will share the same mandate for their product control function. Although there will be exceptions to this, we can broadly categorize the function into one of two types:

1. P&L only
2. P&L, balance sheet and financial reporting.

### P&L Only

The P&L-focused role is, as its name suggests, focused purely on the P&L. In firms across the industry this function may also be labelled as middle office. The review and substantiation of the balance sheet and financial reports are performed by a separate team(s) within finance.

There are benefits and drawbacks for any organizational structure. There are two main benefits to this model. First, it relies on a team with a narrower skill set, which can improve the control framework as the product controller does not have to be an expert in an excessive number of disciplines (accounting, risk management, financial reporting, etc.). Second, as the skill set is narrower it should be easier for the firm to hire and develop their talent.

The primary but manageable drawback to this structure is that a single team is not controlling all the financial aspects of the desk and weakness in the control framework arises when the roles and responsibilities of the different finance teams are not clearly defined and understood by all staff.

For example, the product controllers for the credit trading desk are aware of a late trade booking for 31 December (financial year end) that has missed the end of day report batches that are used to populate the P&L reporting system and general ledger (GL) for financial reporting. The product controller determines the trade has an immaterial impact on the P&L so decides not to adjust the P&L.

Although the trade had an immaterial impact on the P&L, it had a material impact on balance sheet usage, which the financial controllers will not be aware of. Consequently, the firm's year-end reporting misstates not only the balance sheet size and shape, but also the capital ratios, as the risk-weighted assets (RWAs) did not take this late trade into consideration.

This drawback can be compensated for by having clear roles and responsibilities and up-to-date standard operating procedures (SOPs) for each function. These documents make clear the control framework which the firm has in place for each desk.

Each task and responsibility should be documented extensively and refer to what is a control exception and when that exception should be escalated. In this example, the SOPs could require product control to adjust the month-end financials (both P&L and balance sheet) for every late trade.

### P&L: Balance Sheet and Financial Reporting Focus

A broader version of product control includes responsibilities which cover the P&L, balance sheet and some financial reporting for the bank.

This product controller is aware that changes in the balance sheet are the driver of P&L performance and as such it is critical that the balance sheet is reviewed, substantiated and understood.

This product controller will perform the same functions as the P&L-only controller in addition to the following tasks:

- Review and substantiation of the balance sheet
- Advising the desk on the accounting treatment for their transactions (if further expertise is not required from accounting policy)
- Assisting financial reporting in their review of the financial reports, including note disclosures
- Populating the GL with any necessary financial accounting entries.

As product control cover a substantial portion of the control framework assigned to finance, the bank benefits from a single team monitoring all aspects of the desk's financial performance (i.e., the P&L, balance sheet and financial reporting). This set-up should ensure both the P&L and balance sheet are aligned and that by seeing the full financial picture, issues are more readily identifiable.

The main drawbacks of this structure relate to the breadth of responsibilities being undertaken. As the product controller needs to be skilled in many more disciplines than the P&L-only function, it can be more difficult to recruit and develop talent. Additionally, so many responsibilities may cause some to be neglected.

As before, these drawbacks can also be compensated for by having clear roles and responsibilities and complete standard operating procedures.

For the purposes of this book we will focus on this type of product control function.

## SKILLS, QUALIFICATIONS AND EXPERIENCE

Product control has historically employed candidates with varying levels of experience but one of the most common recruitment styles of banks has been to employ candidates who, after completing three years of work experience in an accounting firm and passing their accounting exams, have qualified as chartered accountants. These chartered accountants would then be brought into the product control function and be trained up to control the sales and trading desks.

Over time, these candidates would gain the necessary experience to move through the product control ranks by becoming senior product controllers and then product control managers.

Accountants who, for various reasons, have decided not to train in accounting firms are also very prevalent in the product control ranks. These candidates commonly spend their qualifying period working within the financial services sector at banks, fund managers, credit rating agencies and so on. This means they have different, but equally valuable, experiences to bring to product control.

Once in product control both sets of candidates can further their qualifications and skills by taking postgraduate courses.

Table 1.1 lists the product control hierarchy and the typical experience, qualifications and skill sets that you could expect to see in any bank.

The depth and breadth of experience and skills, which product control provides, can open many opportunities within banking. Prior to the Jérôme Kerviel and Kweku Adoboli rogue trading events, these opportunities included transfers onto the trading desk. These transfers are

**TABLE 1.1** Qualifications, experience and technical skills

| Title and Position | | Qualifications and experience | | | | Technical skills | | | | |
|---|---|---|---|---|---|---|---|---|---|---|
| **Corporate Title** | **Position** | **Product Control Experience (Avg Years)** | **Bachelor's Degree** | **Qualified Accountant** | | **Accounting** | **Market Risk** | **Pricing** | **Control Framework** | |
| Managing Director (MD) | Global head of product control | 20 | X | X | | VH | VH | VH | VH | |
| Managing Director (MD) or Director (D) | Global head of business line product control (e.g. Credit) | 15 | X | X | | VH | VH | VH | VH | |
| Director (D) or Vice President (VP) | Regional head of business line product control | 10 | X | X | | H | H | H | H | |
| Vice President (VP) | Senior product controller | 6 | X | X | | M | M | M | H | |
| Assistant Vice President (AVP) | Product controller | 3 | X | X | | M | M | M | M | |
| Analyst | Junior product controller | 1 | X | Newly or part qualified | | L | L | L | L | |

Note: Corporate titles will vary across the industry

VH = very high, H = high, M = medium, L = low.

now very rare due to the risks they pose to the bank. More commonly, many product controllers transition into chief operating officers (COOs), chief financial officers (CFOs) and operational risk executives.

On the flip side, given the broad set of technical skills required to advance through the ranks in product control, it is more difficult to enter the field later in your career if you do not already have these skills.

## ORGANIZATIONAL STRUCTURE

Product control sits within the finance department and is aligned to support the business. Product control's most senior appointment is the global head who, in addition to setting the agenda for the work performed by their team, will interact directly with the bank's markets CEO, who is the head of the trading floor.

In addition to the overall global head of product control, the division has global heads responsible for each line of business and it is their responsibility to represent product control to the respective heads of those businesses.

Using Figure 1.3 as an example, there are heads of product control for credit, foreign exchange, rates, commodities and equities. These heads are responsible for supporting and controlling the business they are aligned to.

The teams of product controllers supporting and controlling the sales and trading desks for their business are usually consolidated into regional hubs where the traders are located. Sales staff, however, will be dotted all around the world as they are not limited to the regional hubs that exist for traders. The sales trades will be booked from the local offices and then risk managed in the regional hub by the trading desk.

In Figure 1.3 the regional hubs are Europe, the Middle East and Africa (EMEA), the Americas (both North and South America) and Asia.

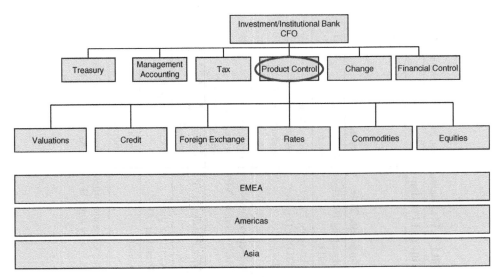

**FIGURE 1.3**   Finance and product control organizational structure

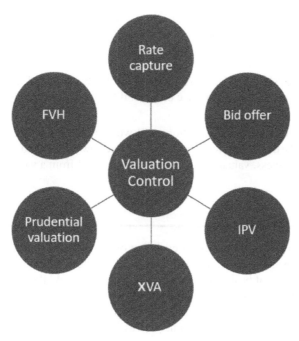

**FIGURE 1.4**   Remit of valuation control

The regional product control hubs will typically have managers for each line of business (e.g. credit, rates, etc.) in addition to a manager for the country (e.g. head of product control Singapore). The product control country manager will typically report directly into the country CFO (e.g. Singapore CFO) and will have an indirect reporting line to the global head of product control. They can also have indirect reporting lines to the heads of product control for each line of business.

There are exceptions to every rule and, in some cases, product control will not be based in the same location as their traders. For example, a small rates desk operating out of Sydney could be controlled by a regional product control team located in Singapore.

In addition to these teams, there is usually a separate product control team that is responsible for valuations. In rare cases, this team sits within market risk or alternatively may still sit within finance but report directly to the CFO or financial controller.

Valuations, or valuations control as they are also known, are responsible for a range of activities related to the valuation of financial instruments. Some of the common responsibilities for this team are illustrated in Figure 1.4 and they are outlined here:

- **Rate capture:** Rate capture is the sourcing of end of day rates which are used to revalue the desk's open positions. This doesn't always sit with valuations and can reside within the business, operations or in market risk.
- **Bid offer and XVA (comprehensive valuation adjustments):** Bid offer and XVA are the valuation adjustments required to bring the desk's portfolio to its fair value. We will look at valuation adjustments in more detail in Chapter 16.
- **Independent price verification (IPV):** IPV checks that the end of day prices align to fair value. We will look at IPV in Chapter 15.

- **Prudential valuation:** Prudential valuation is relatively new and isn't applicable in all jurisdictions. This work requires the valuations team to quantify additional valuation adjustments stipulated by the prudential supervisor, such as illiquidity and concentration risk.
- **Fair value hierarchy (FVH):** FVH allocates the bank's financial assets and liabilities into three levels depending upon price observability and market activity.

In addition to these activities, valuations will work with the line product controllers to review and validate the day 1 P&L for significant or exotic new trades. And when a new product is proposed by the business, valuations will assess the product from a valuations perspective.

## THE DESK

A bank maintains separate desks to cover each line of business (FX, rates, credit, etc.). This structure allows the bank to tailor skill sets and focus on the specific markets and financial instruments for each line of business, which benefits the clients and the bank.

For example, the FX desk will only be responsible for pricing client trades and taking discretionary positions in the FX market. These desks will likely be further segregated into sub-desks to facilitate further specialization, such as linear (vanilla) and non-linear (exotic), and time-zone requirements.

Although the financial markets are global in nature, within each of the underlying markets there will be trading start and finish times which the desk's working hours align to. Two of those markets are foreign exchange and the stock markets, which are illustrated in Figures 1.5 and 1.6.

Although product control aren't expected to work identical hours to the desk, they need to be primarily the same so the P&L and other deliverables are completed.

### The Trading Floor

The desk is located on a trading floor, which is a secure area of the bank and is strictly off limits to anyone who does not need to be there. In some firms, the trading floor seats a few dozen people and in others it seats hundreds of people.

As product control is the face of finance to the front office, to foster a closer working relationship it is important they are within close proximity to the desk. As trading floor space is priced at a premium, product control will be located on a different floor to the traders or in some cases a different building altogether.

The trading floor is a temperately warm area due to the numerous high-spec computers, multiple monitors and large number of data cables connecting the traders to the world. One of the most striking visual features of a trading floor is the proliferation of computer monitors. These screens enable the desk to view all the data it needs to make speedy and sound pricing and risk management decisions. These monitors contain:

- Live market data from suppliers such as Bloomberg and Reuters
- Live risk data from their risk management systems
- Client orders waiting to be filled

**Forex Market Hours**  Time: 26.01.14 15:59 GMT

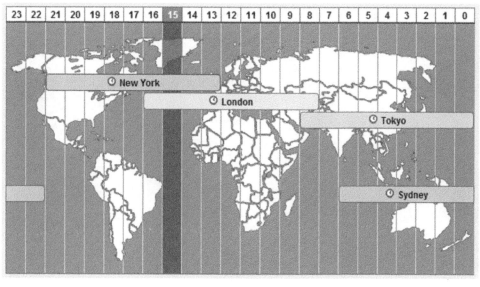

| 23 | 22 | 21 | 20 | 19 | 18 | 17 | 16 | 15 | 14 | 13 | 12 | 11 | 10 | 9 | 8 | 7 | 6 | 5 | 4 | 3 | 2 | 1 | 0 |

**Legend**

New York - Opens on Jan 27th, 2014

London - Opens on Jan 27th, 2014

Tokyo - Opens in 8 Hrs. 0 mins.

Sydney - Opens in 4 Hrs. 0 mins.

Market Open

Market Closed

**Overlaps:**

London & New York [13:00 - 17:00] GMT

Tokyo & London [08:00 - 09:00] GMT

Sydney & Tokyo [00:00 - 05:00] GMT

Overlapping trading hours contain the highest volume of traders.

**FIGURE 1.5** The foreign exchange market operating hours
Source: Courtesy, Investing.com www.investing.com

- Messaging services which contain information from key stakeholders and external clients – for example:
  - Product controllers provide the P&L report which requires approval.
  - Market risk provide market risk usage and limit reports which also require approval.
  - Middle office provide the day's trade blotter and trade amendments.

Those on the trading floor are connected to each other via dealer boards and turrets (called *squawk boxes*). These telecommunications devices also connect the traders with their external brokers. To adhere to regulatory requirements and provide evidence in the case of trade disputes, all telecommunication traffic on the trading floor is recorded.

In Figure 1.7 Sir Alex Ferguson is brokering a trade for charity. This desk configuration is similar to what you can expect to see for a trader on a bank's trading floor.

More recently, the trading floor environment has received a great deal of attention from regulators in multiple jurisdictions around the world. These regulators, for example, the Fed, FCA and APRA/ASIC, commenced reviews of all trader communications, including internal

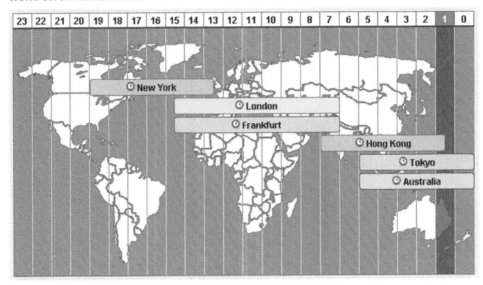

**World Stock Market Hours**                                    Time: 23.05.15 01:43 GMT

New York - Opens on May 26, 2015

London - Opens on May 26, 2015

Frankfurt - Opens on May 25, 2015

Hong Kong - Opens on May 26, 2015

Tokyo - Opens on May 25, 2015

Australia - Opens on May 25, 2015

○  Market Open

○  Market Closed

**Overlaps:**

New York & London [13:30 - 15:35] GMT

London & Hong Kong [07:00 - 08:00] GMT

Tokyo & Australia [00:00 - 06:00] GMT

**Overlapping trading hours contain the highest volume of traders.**

**FIGURE 1.6**  World stock market operating hours
Source: Courtesy, Investing.com www.investing.com

**FIGURE 1.7**  Sir Alex Ferguson brokering trades for charity in London
Source: ©PA Images

communications with colleagues and external communications with brokers and trading peers, in search of evidence to prove wrongdoing on the part of the trader.

This wrongdoing related mainly to the manipulation of key industry benchmarks such as LIBOR and BBSW, whose consensus yields were purported and in some cases proved, to be set at a level which illegally brought financial gain to the trader (at the expense of others).

These regulatory reviews prompted banks to conduct their own internal reviews of trader conduct, which not only focused on illegalities but also on other aspects of conduct such as trader language, client confidentiality and social activities related to work. The consequences now for traders exhibiting contrary behaviour can be severe and include financial penalties and termination of employment.

The effect of these reviews has been seen by some as bringing the trading floor into the 21st century by creating a more professional working environment, but it has also been viewed as creating a more sterile environment where traders are far more reluctant to "shoot from the hip". Gordon Gekko and Jordan Belfort need not apply to work in the City these days.

## Pressures of Supporting the Desk

The trading floor is a high-pressure environment, which raises the stress levels of traders and has a knock-on effect for product control. This pressure stems from the speedy and significant decisions traders need to make and the significant financial implications of these decisions.

As traders' pay is primarily based upon how much P&L they generate, traders can react badly when they incur trading losses, especially when they are behind budget. As product controllers, we need to be mindful of this, especially when you are the person reporting that loss. It's important not to take a trader's reaction personally.

As trading desks have great expectations placed on them, it is important that product control respond with appropriate urgency to their requests and to potential control issues. Financial markets have a way of inflicting damage on banks, so it's important that control issues and requests are dealt with in a timely manner.

This completes our introduction to product control. The remaining part of this book will examine the changes occurring within product control and introduce the role of product control's primary stakeholders.

CHAPTER**2**

# Changing Landscape of Product Control

P roduct control has undergone significant change over the past decade, all of which shows no
sign of reversing. In this chapter, we will explore what changes have occurred and consider
the drivers behind each of those changes. The primary changes are illustrated in Figure 2.1.

## OFFSHORING

Whilst banks have always tried to run lean operations, since the global financial crisis (GFC)
revenue pools have generally declined, capital requirements have increased, governments have
introduced new taxes on banks and more restrictive trading directives have been introduced by
regulators (e.g. Volcker).

All these factors make costs a critical issue and have necessitated that product control,
along with other functions within the bank, become leaner. This trimming has occurred through
a variety of methods, including outright job cuts, standardizing processes and transferring more
work to cheaper locations.

Standardization describes aligning multiple processes into a single or fewer processes.
The objective of standardization is to reduce complexity by simplifying operations, whilst
reducing operational risk and the bank's cost base. This shift has generated efficiencies for
the banks (i.e., cost savings), reduced complexity and been a key ingredient in the success of
moving work to cheaper locations.

This transfer of work to cheaper locations has been the biggest game changer for product
control over the past decade, as it has led to a significant reduction in roles based in New York,
London, Tokyo, Singapore and Hong Kong. We now see large swathes of product controllers
being employed in developing nations such as India, Philippines, Poland, Hungary, Brazil and
South Africa.

Figure 2.2 illustrates the offshoring options for a firm. The first decision for a firm is
whether the work will remain within its organization or be transferred to a third party organization. If the work remains within the organization, this is known as a *captive* model and if the
work is sent to a third party it is known as an *outsourced* model.

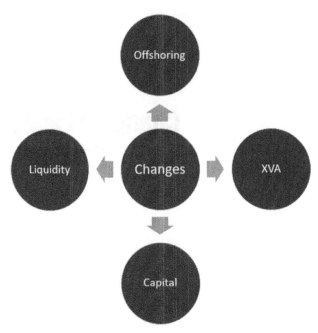

**FIGURE 2.1** Changes in product control

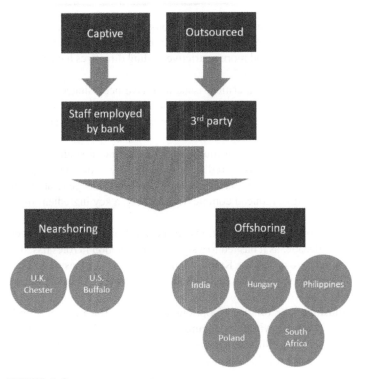

**FIGURE 2.2** Offshoring models

The current market is a mix of both models but has been more heavily skewed towards the captive model. My preference would be to use a captive model, as it gives you more control and influence over your workforce.

The next question, which may be less relevant if the work is outsourced, will be whether the work remains within the same country or not. Work sent to a cheaper location within the same country is known as *nearshoring* and work sent overseas is known as *offshoring.*

In 2013, recruitment firm Mondrian Alpha prepared a report that examined the offshoring/outsourcing and nearshoring activities undertaken by several large banks.[1] Many of their findings still provide a good overview of the changing landscape of product control. Highlights from the report include:

- The goal of the overall offshoring programme is to have a higher quality product control function at a significantly reduced cost. This is achieved through having simpler production type work performed in cheaper locations, leaving a thin layer onshore to provide advisory services to the front office.
- Top locations for offshoring include India, China, the Philippines, Brazil, South Africa, Poland, and Hungary.
- Offshoring becomes easier when:
  - **i)** Time zones are consistent e.g. London offshores to Budapest or Singapore offshores to Manila
  - **ii)** Systems and processes are properly embedded before offshoring commences
  - **iii)** The offshore team is seen as part of the one product control team and are wholly accountable for their work
  - **iv)** Turnover can be managed and there is depth of talent in the offshore location
- Nearshoring is an attractive option as it keeps teams within the same country but in less expensive cities. Nearshoring avoids some of the challenges of offshoring, such as inconsistent time zones, shallow offshore talent pools and clashes of cultures. All this ultimately results in closer cooperation within product control and the bank.

## My View

There is always a risk and reward trade-off for every investment and offshoring is no different. The main reward for a bank is a lower cost base, whilst the major risk is a weakened control framework. A bank needs to keep in mind that a weakened control framework is more prone to an operational risk event, which can cause losses that dwarf the benefit from the best cost-saving programmes. Rogue trading is just one of the operational risks that can be more difficult to detect when product control is offshored. Just think of the losses sustained by UBS ($2.3 billion)[2] and Société Générale (€4.9 billion)[3] through unauthorized trading! While the potential role of offshore product control in these cases is undetermined, when oversight is distanced from trading activity, the risk of rogue trading increases.

## Risky Choices

In my view, the control framework is most at risk of being weakened when the following choices are made.

**Unskilled Staff**   If the bank chooses to employ offshore staff with very little or no product control experience, the level of operational risk automatically increases. Banks may be forced to do this if they are establishing an office in a city where a product control talent pool does not exist or the working hours are unattractive for experienced controllers (e.g. 3 a.m. starts).

**Offshoring Is Rushed**   Offshoring cannot be rushed! The control framework, skills and experience of the incumbent team has taken many years to develop and this set-up cannot be replicated immediately by the new team.

Consequently, the transfer of work should occur methodically to enable the bank to learn lessons from each transfer phase. It also allows the bank to retain more of the onshore controllers after the first phase(s) has been executed, to assist with any negative fallouts.

## Benefits

In addition to cost savings, the other significant benefit of offshoring is the standardization of processes. Although a bank can standardize without offshoring, it often provides the catalyst for such change.

**Life Post-Offshoring for Onshore Product Controllers**   Offshoring can have benefits and drawbacks for the controllers left onshore. The most significant benefit for onshore controllers is the quantity of production work left onshore will be significantly less. This change should now free up time for onshore controllers to perform more analytical work.

The type of analytical work can vary at each bank, but typically the controller will analyse those components of the financials which can have a significant influence on the behaviour of the desk. This can vary quarter by quarter, but some examples include balance sheet usage, brokerage fees, capital, liquidity, return on assets, and so on.

Additionally, the controller will spend more time analysing the health of the control framework in finance to ensure the level of operational risk is not excessive. You could say that this role is becoming more akin to a CFO role.

The reality of a trading environment means additional work will always arise, yet cannot be anticipated. The main drawback for onshore staff post-offshoring is how to meet the demands of their new role with a reduced headcount.

As previously they were the controllers running reports and performing checks, but now they are receiving a finished product from their offshore colleagues and assessing its quality, this change throws up a need for onshore controllers to adapt and grow. This requires a different skill set and it can be quite frustrating at first, especially when the offshore person performing the work may have far less experience than they do. This change is a transitory period and the frustration should ease with time as respect and rapport between the onshore and offshore teams grows.

In addition to this, the question a bank must ask themselves is where will the next generation of onshore product controllers emerge from? From experience, I know that it can be difficult to manage a product control team effectively when you have no experience of the bank's systems and controls, let alone if you have no product control experience.

I expect the offshore and near shore controllers to grow in experience and take on more of the responsibilities that used to reside onshore. In this case, the onshore product control team as we now know it will become extinct and will be replaced by a pure CFO role.

## XVA

Another of the significant changes for product control centres around the valuation adjustments now being made to OTC derivatives and funding liabilities where the fair value option is elected.

XVA is the collective acronym used for valuation adjustments such as counterparty credit (CVA), own credit (DVA), funding uncollateralized derivatives (FVA), margin (MVA) and capital (KVA). This list continues to grow and VAs continue to be refined over time.

Although CVA and DVA were pricing considerations before the GFC, the GFC elevated their importance as the cost of credit risk rose significantly. This change affected both OTC derivatives and fair valued funding liabilities.

FVA emerged during the GFC when, also due to the spike in credit risk, OIS (overnight indexed swaps) and LIBOR (London Interbank Offered Rate) yields dislocated and their basis widened. Traders were forced to capture the cost or benefit of funding uncollateralized derivatives into their OTC derivatives.

In response to these developments, banks established trading desks dedicated to the pricing and risk management of CVA/DVA and FVA, often referred to as the XVA desk.

As the desk started to price these different costs and benefits into their transactions and manage the resulting risk, product control not only needed to understand these valuation adjustments, but were also required to embed the valuation adjustments in the finance layer. Such changes elevated the importance of the valuation controllers, whose technical skills were required to embed the new VAs successfully.

We will look at XVA further in Chapter 16.

## GREATER LEVELS OF CAPITAL

During the GFC it became very evident that banks were not maintaining enough capital to absorb trading losses caused by the significant fluctuations in financial markets and the credit events of companies such as Lehman Brothers. This capital deficiency resulted in many banks having to seek support from their governments to prevent their collapse.

Governments across the world were very aware of their need to protect the savings of investors and prevent the crisis from damaging real businesses (i.e., companies outside of financial services, such as manufacturers, retail, etc.) which require loans from banks to fund their working capital and investments. Consequently, the reaction from governments was significant. For example, in the United States the government passed legislation, the Emergency Economic Stabilization Act 2008, to support the purchase of up to $700 billion of troubled assets from banks (TARP). In Australia, the banks benefited from the government's guarantee on deposits and wholesale funding requirements for Australian deposit-taking institutions. Governments across Europe also effected similar measures.

As a result of this shock, the Bank for International Settlements (BIS) commenced with the design of Basel III, which sought to address the shortcomings in capital requirements that occurred during the GFC. If we fast-forward to today, we can observe that through Basel III, the Fundamental Review of the Trading Book (FRTB) and independent regulatory intervention, the levels of capital that banks now (and will) hold are higher than prior to the GFC. This has forced banks to be more deliberate about the size and quality of their assets, credit risk and the size and complexity of their market risk.

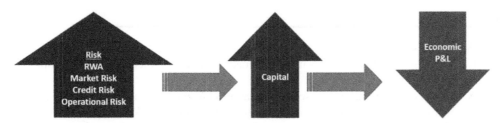

**FIGURE 2.3**    The impact of increased capital

The businesses Product Control support are now being evaluated not only on their accounting P&L, but also on their P&L performance after considering capital costs. There are various measurements used in the industry to assess capital adjusted returns, one measure is economic P&L. Economic P&L takes a business's net operating profit after tax (NPAT) and deducts a cost of capital.

Economic P&L = NPAT − (capital employed × cost of capital)

NPAT is the P&L product control report to the desk after being adjusted for tax and nontrading costs. The cost of capital is the cost of maintaining the necessary levels of debt and equity that comprise the capital base.

For example, if a bank has issued $1 billion of ordinary shares, the cost of this capital is the return shareholders require on their equity investment in the bank (i.e., dividends and capital growth). That return is market driven and may be a per annum amount of 10%, 12%, 15% and so on. For example, the rates desk used $200 million of capital to invest in sales and trading activities, which generated an NPAT of $80 million for the year. If the cost of capital is deemed to be 10%, the economic P&L for the year would be:

$$\begin{aligned} \text{Rates desk economic P\&L} &= \$80,000,000 - (\$200,000,000 \times 10\%) \\ &= \$80,000,000 - \$20,000,000 \\ &= \$60,000,000 \end{aligned}$$

As capital levels generally rise with increased risk, if a business increases risk, such as taking on more risk weighted assets, it will place downward pressure on economic P&L (as depicted in Figure 2.3).

This focus on capital has led to product control spending more time reviewing the balance sheet, identifying and explaining significant changes in risk-weighted assets (RWA) and partnering with the business to help reduce unwanted increases in the balance sheet.

## GREATER FOCUS ON LIQUIDITY

Like any company, a bank needs a certain level of cash to operate, but during the GFC, the financial markets experienced prolonged periods of illiquidity. During this time, Northern Rock, a British bank, could not continue operating as their interbank counterparts ceased providing loans, and retail depositors withdrew their money in vast sums. This is known as a *run on the bank*. As a result of this illiquidity, the banks, regulators and the BIS started to place greater emphasis on a bank's liquid assets and their funding profile. In Basel III, the BIS introduced two requirements:

1. Liquidity Coverage Ratio (LCR)

    "The objective of the LCR is to promote the short-term resilience of the liquidity risk profile of banks. It does this by ensuring that banks have an adequate stock of unencumbered high-quality liquid assets (HQLA) that can be converted easily and immediately in private markets into cash to meet their liquidity needs for a 30 calendar day liquidity stress scenario. The LCR will improve the banking sector's ability to absorb shocks arising from financial and economic stress, whatever the source, thus reducing the risk of spillover from the financial sector to the real economy."[4]

2. Net Stable Funding Ratio (NSFR)

    The objective of the NSFR is to "promote resilience over a long time horizon by creating additional incentives for banks to fund their activities with more stable sources of funding on an ongoing basis. The NSFR…supplements the LCR and has a time horizon of one year. It has been developed to provide a sustainable maturity structure of assets and liabilities."[5]

The function responsible for maintaining the appropriate levels of liquidity is treasury. To influence better funding behaviour by the trading desks, treasury started to penalize trading desks who were funding themselves ineffectively; for example, buying a 2-year corporate bond and funding that purchase using an overnight loan from treasury, which is known as a *tenor mismatch*. Conversely, the trading desk could be rewarded if they were overfunding their assets, as this excess term funding could be used to provide funding to other business. For example, borrowing $100 million for two years to fund the purchase of $90 million two-year government bonds.

As product control reports the financial impact of these penalties and rewards in the P&L, the business relied on product control to identify which positions (assets and liabilities) were driving these P&L entries. For product control to assist the business they needed to understand the business' balance sheet, specifically the size and tenor of the asset and liabilities, and how treasury viewed this construction from their funding paradigm.

## NOTES

1. Mondrian Alpha. 2013.
2. Harry Wilson, "UBS banker banned over $2.3bn rogue trading scandal," *The Telegraph*, 1 May 2014.
3. Alana Petroff and Pierre-Eliott Buet, "Rogue trader's fine to Société Générale cut by 99.98%," CNN Money, 23 September 2016.
4. Bank for International Settlements (BIS). Basel Committee on Banking Supervision, "Basel III: Liquidity The Liquidity Coverage Ratio and liquidity risk monitoring tools," January 2013, Introduction. http://www.bis.org/publ/bcbs238.pdf.
5. Ibid.

# CHAPTER 3

# Key Stakeholders

In the performance of their role, product control interact with numerous functions, each of which vary regarding their importance and frequency with which they interact. This chapter will introduce you to those functions which product control most commonly interact with.

Figure 3.1 illustrates the typical levels of interaction Product Control will have with each function.

## FRONT OFFICE: SALES AND TRADING DESK

The front office staff have three main objectives:

1. Provide the bank's clients with a suite of products to meet their investment and risk management needs.
2. Risk manage the bank's market and credit risk exposures to safeguard the bank from adverse market movements.
3. Participate in risk-taking (proprietary trading) to generate profits for the bank.

The front office are the most significant stakeholder who product control interact with. In most banks they are considered a client of product control whilst also being a function that product control must monitor and control. There is also a high level of interdependency between the two functions as the front office have a large vested interest in ensuring the P&L accurately reflects their performance.

The front office rely primarily on product control for the following:

- The provision of a daily P&L.
- The reconciliation of this P&L to the desk's P&L estimate (T+0 flash).
- The provision of a new trades report (as valued by the finance systems).
- The analysis of internal charges allocated to the desk and assistance in minimizing those charges.
- Ensuring their foreign currency P&L is sold down correctly at month-end.
- Assistance with the set-up of new traders and sales staff in the bank's systems (e.g., new trading books).

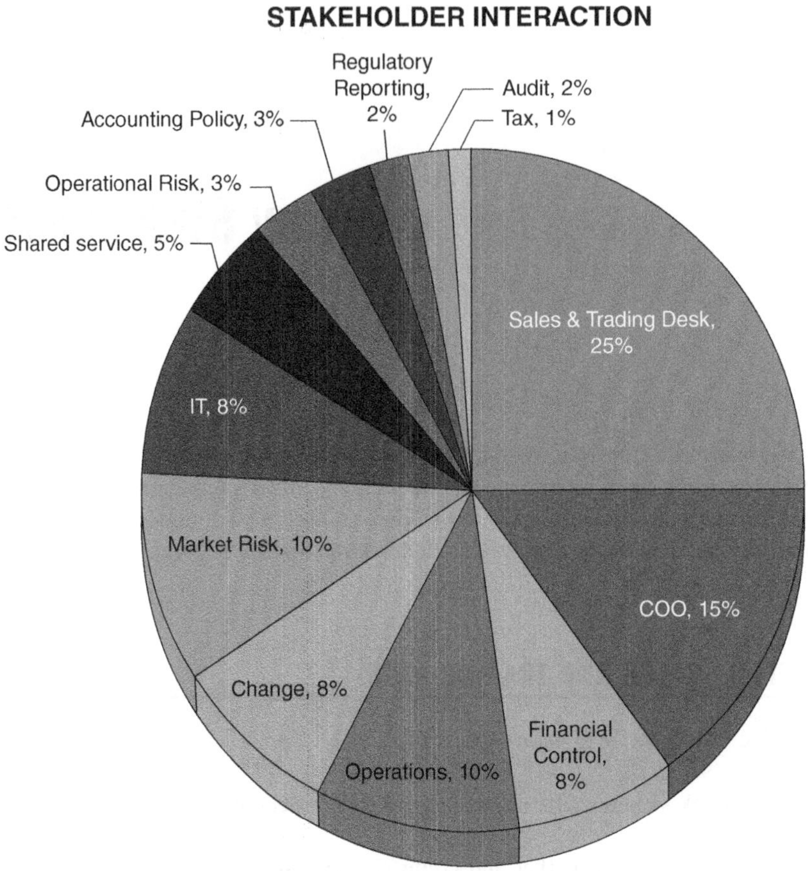

**STAKEHOLDER INTERACTION**

**FIGURE 3.1**  Stakeholder interaction with product control

- Assistance and advice when new products are implemented.
- Advice regarding the adoption of new accounting standards.
- The production of balance sheet reports and insight into the drivers of their balance sheet usage.

Product control also rely on the front office to perform their role effectively, which includes:

- Educating product control on the strategy of the desk.
- Providing insight into the markets which the desk are active in.
- Providing a T+0 flash.
- Approving the P&L.
- Explanation of exceptional day one and mark-to-market (MTM) P&L.
- Ensuring the risk management system (RMS) captures all the desk's trades.
- All trades are being valued correctly (includes both end of day marks and models).

## CHIEF OPERATING OFFICERS (COOs)

Chief operating officers (COOs), also known as *business managers*, assist the business in executing its strategy. Practically, this function brings together all the support functions in the end-to-end delivery of the business' products and services. Given this, product control will have a significant level of interaction with this function.

The COO can either report directly to the head of the business or to a global COO. For example, the rates COO could either report into the global head of the rates business or they could report into the global markets COO along with all the other COO's (e.g., credit, commodities, etc.).

The following describe some of the main functions COOs perform to fulfil their mandate.

### System Infrastructure

COOs will assist the business by establishing and maintaining the necessary system infrastructure to continue trading and marketing existing products as well as establishing new products. Their functions are, for example, to:

- Monitor system performance and follow up on the remediation of issues such as system failures or delays, which could impact the desk.
- Provide the desk with the necessary system access to book trades, monitor risk and so on.
- Create new books or portfolios so that trades can be recorded in the bank's systems.
- Request new nostros (bank accounts) to enable the firm to settle transactions executed by the desk.

### Onboarding New Products

When the business decide they want to trade or market a new product, the COO will launch new product proposals and facilitate the onboarding process. This can involve being the subject matter expert, or at the very least the point person that support functions can turn to for answers to any questions they have regarding the proposal.

### Daily Operational Effectiveness

The COO monitors the key performance indicators (KPIs), which are a measure of how well the desk is performing operationally. The purpose of these collective checks is to gauge the level of operational risk that the desk are running. By reviewing multiple indicators, the COO can make a more informed assessment of this risk.

These KPIs will usually assess the following factors:

- Trade booking accuracy (late trades and trade amendments).
- Timely and accurate T+0 Flash (no late, missing or inaccurate estimates).
- Timely and complete P&L and risk report sign-offs.
- Complete and accurate end of day remarking.

- That the desk are trading within their product and risk mandate.
- The size, number and age of P&L adjustments.
- The size, number and age of cash breaks.
- The number and age of missing trade confirmations.

### Forecasted Revenues, Costs, and Balance Sheet

The desk have targets for revenues, costs and balance-sheet usage. The COO will assist in developing these limits. Once created they will monitor the desk's relative performance against these levels.

### Operational Risk Incident (ORI)

An ORI is simply an event where the control framework has failed. A bank will have risk and financial thresholds which will determine whether an ORI has taken place. When there is an ORI, the COO will involve themselves in the write-up of the event and assist in rolling out any key recommendations published by the operational risk team.

### Implement Firm-Wide Changes

Often within banks, especially investment banks, the organization's structure can be changed in the hope that this brings with it higher operating profits. It is the COO who assists the desk in managing this change.

For example, the firm's senior management have decided to exit their structured-rates business; however, it is expected to take some time to exit all positions. To manage this effectively the firm has decided to create a legacy business unit. The structured rates desk will move from their current business unit into the legacy business unit. With this change comes the migration of all the static data (profit centres, trading books and any other organizational nodes), trades, P&L, balance sheet, costs and plans relating to structured rates. This change may sound simple but operationally it can be very difficult to execute.

## OPERATIONS

Operations are primarily responsible for confirming and settling transactions the business undertakes. Specifically, operations will carry out the following tasks illustrated in Figure 3.2.

Through these activities, operations are ensuring that the following activities occur:

- Executed trades are captured in the bank's systems
- Trades within the bank's systems are legally agreed with counterparties (confirmations)
- Cash flows and securities exchanges between counterparties are settled (cleared)
- Trades which fail to settle are identified and managed
- Trade life cycle events are executed correctly, for example corporate actions (e.g., share splits, dividends) and trade fixings (e.g., LIBOR, HSRA).

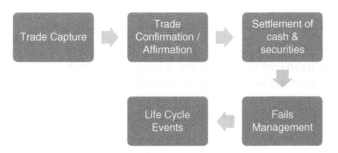

**FIGURE 3.2**   The role of operations

As operations are a cornerstone of the control framework, product control rely quite heavily on them for information regarding:

- Cash and security settlement issues, including outright and timing breaks that affect the nostro and security accounts
- Outstanding trade confirmations
- Failed trades (where settlement has not occurred)
- Trade event reports, for example, the trades involved in a tri-party compression exercise
- Fees and charges incurred, for example, brokerage and exchange fees.

By having this information, product control can report the desk's P&L and balance sheet more accurately.

## MIDDLE OFFICE

Middle office does not exist within every bank and, if it does, their roles and responsibilities will not be consistent across the industry.

As we touched on earlier in the book, product control can also be situated within middle office, but for the purposes of this chapter, we will cover those middle office tasks where product control are located within finance.

Middle office are closely aligned with the desk as they are responsible for:

- Trade bookings on behalf of the desk.
- Effecting the daily fixings for indices such as LIBOR.
- Saving down into the RMS (or equivalent) the desk's end of day marks which will be used to revalue their portfolio.

Product control rely on middle office for:

- Information on new and amended trade bookings, particularly those which generate significant day one P&L.

## MARKET RISK

Market risk is the risk that the desk's portfolio will rise or fall in value due to changes in market prices, which can lead to either profits or losses for the bank. As a bank wants to limit the losses incurred from market fluctuations, they will set an overall market risk limit for the group at board level. These group-level limits are then transformed into smaller business- and desk-level limits, which are applied across the various trading desks. Limits cover such things as:

- Maximum loss for moves in interest rates, foreign exchange rates, credit spreads or volatilities.
- Concentration limits on exposures in various maturities or even various countries.
- Types of products that can be traded.
- Daily P&L amounts.

The market risk function within a bank, sometimes known as market risk control, falls within the mandate of the chief risk officer, who is also responsible for the credit and operational risk of the firm.

Market risk is responsible for:

- Agreeing on, with the board and heads of business, the market risk limits that the trading desk can run.
- Quantifying, monitoring, and reporting the market risk exposures of the trading desk.
- Authorize short-term limit extensions or ask for positions to be closed to bring a desk back within agreed limits.
- Running stress-testing scenarios to highlight the bank's potential P&L in exaggerated market movements.
- Escalating market risk limit breaches to the senior management in market risk and the business.
- Model validation and approval.

As with any control function, it is important that market risk remain independent of the trading desk that they are aligned to.

Market risk rely on product control for the following:

- The official daily P&L which highlights what positions are generating the desk's P&L.
- A clean MTM P&L, which will be used for VaR back testing.
- Independently verifying the end of day marks (prices, rates and volatilities) used to revalue the desk's open positions.
- Advice on the availability of market prices when new products are proposed.

Product control (including valuation control) rely on market risk for:

- Market risk exposures (used for risk based P&L estimates).
- Approving and calibrating the financial models used to generate fair values.
- Assistance in quantifying financial model reserves.
- Assistance in determining the banking book and trading book classifications.

- Insights into the financial markets, particularly when quantifying prudential valuations for regulators.
- Allocating trading positions in the fair value hierarchy and determining fair value through the independent price verification process.

## FINANCIAL REPORTING

Historically, the role of financial reporting (which can also be known as *financial control*) in banking was a little secondary in finance. Reporting was not as stimulating as the front office facing product control and was regarded as a bit of a backwater by some. The key perspective in financial reporting is that of the legal entity and the governance around it is often set in law.

The role of financial reporting is in many ways at least as important, if not more so, as product control. The role was to report to an external body the results of the legal entity under the relevant rules or requirements. This would cover:

- Management reporting to the board of a legal entity.
- Financial reporting, audited financial statements and filing as part of the Companies Act requirements under IFRS and local GAAPs.
- Regulatory reporting to the local regulatory bodies – in the UK this is to the Prudential Regulatory Authority (PRA) and the European Banking Authority (EBA).
- Statistical reporting – in the UK typically this is the Bank of England (BoE).
- Other local filings and enquiries – for example, the Financial Conduct Authority (FCA), Office for National Statistics (ONS), and so forth.

The risks associated with financial reporting are high. The board members are personally responsible for shareholder or creditor loss if they knowingly act in a fraudulent or illegal manner. Regulators can impose fines, custodial sentences, and close the business down if they are not satisfied.

In recent years the importance of this has become particularly focused as the misdemeanours of the industry and lack of vigilance by the regulators have resulted in the media and politicians baying for blood and a large number of new requirements across the regulatory bodies.

The financial reporting team review and challenge the results presented to them, the role of product control is to provide an explanation and rationalization of the business results in the legal entity and thereby allow for onward explanation to stakeholders.

## MANAGEMENT REPORTING

The management reporting team, sometimes known as performance reporting, is responsible for providing a bank's management and external stakeholders with insight into the bank's performance.

At its core, this function will:

- Work with the businesses to establish budgets for revenue and expenses.
- Monitor the relative performance of the business against these budgets and obtain commentaries (usually from product control), which explain the performance drivers, on a weekly, monthly, quarterly and annual basis.

This function is heavily reliant on product control providing transparency into the business's performance through commentaries that describe both the outright performance and relative performance to plan (budget/forecast) or prior period (quarter, half or year).

The management reporting team expects that the performance data they are consuming (P&L and balance sheet) is accurate, rendering them completely reliant on product control executing the necessary controls over the business to ensure the data they are consuming is valid.

Where this function delivers added value is by providing senior management (e.g., group CFO) with transparency into the drivers of a business's performance in a clear and succinct manner. Consequently, this team's communication skills, both written and verbal, need to be of a very high quality.

## FINANCE CHANGE

The finance change function (which may exist within finance, IT or centralized within the COO) has a remit to support the run-the-bank (RTB) functions (also known as *business as usual* or *line* function) in delivering measured and clearly defined process, organization, technology, and sourcing enhancements and transformations.

This function is a critical resource to have when RTB functions need to scope out, execute, and manage changes of varying degrees. Finance change is predominantly deployed on larger-scale projects, such as implementing a new general ledger (GL), modifying the RMS feed into the GL, or establishing a fully functional legal entity from which the bank can trade.

The finance change function is so critical because they bring their project management skills to the table, which provide a solid control framework for managing change. Specifically, these skills assist the bank (and RTB) with determining:

- What will be changed
- How it will be changed
- How much it will cost to change
- How long it will take to change.

They also assist by managing the change and providing pre- and post-implementation support.

The interaction with RTB functions can be best reflected using a RACI matrix (Table 3.1). In this matrix, the following terms describe RTB's and Change's involvement in an activity.

R – Responsible

A – Accountable

C – Consumer

I – Informed

## IT

IT are a crucial function for a bank as they are responsible for the maintenance and development of the bank's technology platform. Product control, like all functions, are reliant upon

**TABLE 3.1** RACI matrix for run the bank and finance change teams

| Phase | Activities | RTB | Change |
|---|---|---|---|
| **Functional and Portfolio Management** | Portfolio Prioritization/Portfolio Management/Portfolio Financials | A | R/C |
| | Delivery of Domain Portfolios | C/I | R/A |
| | Ongoing RTB Stakeholder Engagement | I | R/A |
| | Systems Architecture | I | R/A/C |
| | Process Architecture | I | R/A |
| | Resource Management (Sourcing) | I | R/A |
| | Benefit Realization | A | R/I |
| **Initiating – Feasibility – Analysis** | Ongoing Sponsor Engagement | I | R/A |
| | Benefits Case | A | R/C |
| | Project Scope and Scope Prioritization | A | R/C |
| | Project Level Budgeting (Financial Management) | A | R/C |
| | Business Specifications | A | R/C |
| | Business Process Design | C | R/A/C |
| | Technical Analysis | I | R/A/C |
| | Technical Solution Design | I | R/A/C |
| **Design – Build – Implement – Post-Implementation** | Design – Technical | I | R/A/I |
| | Implementation (Development) | I | R/A/I |
| | Test Process Management | I | R/A/I |
| | System Test Design and Execution (including standard regression tests) | I | R/A/I |
| | User Test Design and Execution | A | R/A/I |
| | Deployment | I | R/A/I |
| | Go-live Sign-off | A | R/A/C |
| | Post-Implementation Support (Maintenance) | I | R/A/I |

many different IT systems operating effectively to perform their role. The following is a list of systems that product control would typically require to perform their role.

- Windows operating system
- Microsoft Excel, Access, Outlook, Word, PowerPoint and Internet Explorer
- RMS (e.g., Murex, Calypso, Wall Street, OpenLink)
- General Ledger
- P&L reporting tool
- Supervisory controls tool
- Bloomberg
- Reuters
- TLM.

IT will usually be segmented into several different groups of technicians, being the general help desk support, specialized system support and system development. Product control will most frequently deal with the specialized system support teams when issues arise with the RMS, GL and P&L reporting systems.

IT will generally have service level agreements (SLAs) in place to govern the way in which they support each of these systems. The time taken to respond to requests can be a key frustration for the controller so it is important that the IT function is made aware of the downstream impact an IT issue, such as a system outage, will have on the businesses concerned.

## OPERATIONAL RISK

Within each bank there is an operational risk control team whose job it is to monitor, report on and assist with the maintenance of a sound internal control framework across a bank.

As a bank has a myriad of different functions, there are usually different operational risk teams specializing in one or more of those functions. For example, there would be a single operational risk team for finance, which would cover product control, financial reporting and regulatory reporting.

For the day-to-day running of the business, the operational risk team will raise and administer operational risk incidents (ORIs) for material weaknesses and breakdowns in the control framework. When an ORI occurs, nine times out of ten the control breakdown results in a loss for a bank, which provides an incentive to remediate the control weaknesses which allowed the loss to occur.

They also monitor the effectiveness of the control framework and escalate and follow up on material breaches of the framework. Operational risk monitor the following categories:

- Material differences between the GL and the P&L reporting system.
- Material and aged unsupported items in the balance sheet.
- Material and aged cash breaks and system suspense items.
- Material differences in the intercompany balances and intra-entity accounts.

Each month or quarter, it is common for operational risk to meet with product control to go through items fitting into the above categories. This gives operational risk an opportunity to understand the level of risk that the bank is exposed to and what action plan is in place to address those risks. Operational risk can then report on and follow up on those material items which the bank is most at risk from.

On an annual basis, a bank will complete its full year Sarbanes–Oxley (SOX) reporting requirements (if applicable) and operational risk are usually the function responsible for administering this. Product control will be required to complete questionnaires that provide the operational risk team with transparency into which controls are and are not operating effectively. This information would then be used by the bank to determine which risks require remediating and forms the basis for the firm's submission to the regulator.

## REGULATORY REPORTING

Regulatory reporting is responsible for ensuring that any firm carrying on regulated business remains compliant with the regulations of the home state regulator (although these regulations are not necessarily set at the local level; for example, the Capital Requirements Regulation which applies in the UK is a European Union regulation).

The type of reporting typically includes the following information:

- **Capital base and capital requirements:** A firm must have a sufficiently large capital base to cover its capital requirements that are determined by the regulator.
- **Large exposures:** Firms must monitor exposures to groups of connected counterparties and report these to the regulators. If these limits are breached, they must trigger additional capital requirements.
- **Liquidity:** A firm must monitor and report its net liquidity position.
- **Statistical reporting:** Statistical reporting may also be required. This would cover balance sheet and P&L reporting as a minimum. It may also include detailed analysis of these including by country, currency, product and industry type. This is often used in published figures; for example, in the UK, the data produced feeds into balance of payments numbers plus a number of other sets of figures published by the Bank of England or the Office of National Statistics.
- **Periodic reporting:** Reports will be sent to the regulator on a periodic basis: weekly, monthly and quarterly. Additionally, daily monitoring may be required but is not necessarily reported to the regulator (e.g., daily capital requirement monitoring).
- **Regulatory monitoring:** Typically a team will also be responsible for monitoring the regulatory environment for potential legislative changes, and addressing the regulatory challenges that the development of new business, new securities/investment products and new markets bring.

Interaction with product control takes a number of forms:

- **Review of changes in balance sheet and P&L:** Regulatory reporting will often query moves in the balance sheet and P&L with controllers to gain an understanding of what is driving variances either in the disclosures on regulatory returns or the capital requirements that are being calculated. These queries may originate from regulatory reporting's own observations or from direct questions posed by the regulators.
- **Accounting journals:** Journals posted by product control will often not contain sufficient data attributes to either properly allocate their effect in a regulatory return or to adjust the capital requirements. The regulatory disclosures are often at a more granular level than the financials so regulatory reporting need to work with product control to get more details to produce accurate regulatory reports.
- **Daily P&L notifications:** Regulatory reporting need to be notified of the entities P&L on a daily basis, as material losses need to be deducted from an entities capital base.
- **Daily issue notification:** To produce accurate capital calculations, regulatory reporting need to be notified of any issues the controllers may have come across in their daily P&L preparation that may have a capital impact (e.g., a material misstatement of fair values).
- **Collaboration on new business initiatives and new and complex trades:** These new initiatives will often require input from regulatory reporting in terms of what is allowable either from a rules point of view or perhaps an assessment of the impact on the regulatory capital requirement.

## ACCOUNTING POLICY

Accounting policy (also known as technical accounting) is a specialist function located within the finance department. It has specialist knowledge on the accounting standards and technical expertise around the interpretation and application of such standards.

Accounting policy are responsible for accounting policy enforcement across the bank and ensures the bank's business activities are accounted for in conformity with Generally Accepted Accounting Principles (GAAP). Although part of the controller organization within finance, accounting policy is better described as an advisory function, advising key clients across the entire bank on accounting related items.

When new accounting standards become effective, it is up to accounting policy to provide the necessary guidance to the rest of finance so that the firm is compliant with the new standard.

The accounting policy function is generally responsible for:

- Leading implementation efforts for new accounting standards under the applicable GAAP.
- Preparing and delivering presentations to facilitate bank-wide education of new or changing accounting requirements to ensure that management understands the impact of new standards and regulations.
- Reviewing and approving new products and structured transactions, which usually forms part of an approval committee process. This includes working closely with product control to determine the appropriate booking methodology for new products and transactions to achieve the desired accounting outcome.
- Interaction with accounting standard setters (e.g., the International Accounting Standards Board) to provide banking industry input during the process of deliberating new standards.
- Participating in banking industry accounting committees to stay abreast of industry developments.
- Providing technical accounting advice to the front office, under the applicable GAAP, on proposed transactions and structures and to assist in identifying accounting solutions.
- Support finance, mainly product control, with technical accounting issues as they arise over a reporting period (e.g., year-end).

## TAX

Tax tend to reside in the finance department and reports to the CFO. Their main purpose is to ensure that the firm is applying the most appropriate tax treatment to its business activities around the globe. This usually includes most of the following activities:

- Establishing transfer pricing agreements (TPA) when necessary.
- Opining on the tax treatment for new products.
- Assisting the firm to adopt and apply new tax laws or changes in tax law that affect the business activities of the firm.
- Filing tax returns for the group's legal entities and ensuring that they pay the correct amounts of taxes.
- Ensuring that materially correct tax charges and balances are reported for both the group consolidation and subsidiary entity financial statements.

**TABLE 3.2** Sparta Bank FX revenues and costs by location

| FX – One Name Trading Revenues and Costs @ 31/01/2015 (USD equivalents) | | | | | |
|---|---|---|---|---|---|
| Location | Sales persons by location | Traders by location | Sales revenue by location | Trading revenue by location | Costs by location |
| Sydney, Australia | 2 | 0 | 1,200,000 | 0 | (33,333) |
| Singapore | 3 | 2 | 2,000,000 | 1,500,000 | (83,333) |
| New York, U.S. | 4 | 3 | 2,600,000 | 890,000 | (116,667) |
| London, U.K. | 4 | 5 | 3,250,000 | (500,000) | (150,000) |

The most frequent form of interaction between product control and tax occurs through transfer pricing agreements (TPAs). TPAs are required when the revenues for a business have not been recorded in the location(s) in which they were earned, or where costs are not recorded in the same location(s) as the revenues which they are deemed to be supporting.

Complex and judgmental calculations may be required to split the P&L between those locations, especially in cases where organizations operate a single book for a business that operates in multiple countries. Tax will establish the most appropriate TPA, which for most jurisdictions will mean referring to the OECD's (Organisation for Economic Co-operation and Development) guidance on transfer pricing. This may involve transferring a portion of costs to the locations where those costs have been used to help support revenue-generating activities, or transferring centrally booked revenues to the location(s) where they were effectively earned.

For example, Sparta Bank has decided to use One Name Trading (ONT) for their FX business. This decision results in all FX trades being booked into their London company, Sparta Bank London Limited.

Whether a trade is executed by traders or sales staff in Sydney, Singapore, London or New York, all counterparties to the firm's FX trades will face Sparta Bank London Limited (Table 3.2). This is illustrated in Figure 3.3.

For tax purposes, some of the revenues ought to be transferred to Sydney, Singapore and New York to reflect the work done (and perhaps the costs incurred) in those locations.

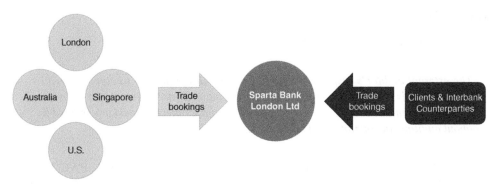

**FIGURE 3.3** Sparta Bank FX One Name Trading (Single book)

## AUDIT

Product control interact with two auditing functions, internal and external audit.

### Internal Audit

According to the Institute of Internal Auditors:

> *Internal auditing is an independent, objective assurance and consulting activity designed to add value and improve an organization's operations. It helps an organization accomplish its objectives by bringing a systematic, disciplined approach to evaluate and improve the effectiveness of risk management, control, and governance processes.*[1]

To maintain its independence from the business and functions they audit, internal audit reports directly to the board. Product control primarily interact with internal audit when they conduct reviews of the front to back (f2b) control framework for a business (e.g., foreign exchange).

To perform a detailed audit, internal audit will need evidence of controls performed across a series of random dates and it is off the back of these reviews that internal audit will issue its findings. If their findings are adverse, and there are varying degrees of adversity, product control will receive an audit point for every control issue. The audit point will detail the control(s) which internal audit have deemed unsatisfactory and will provide product control with a deadline to remediate the control(s). Audit points are taken very seriously by the bank so the timely remediation is very important.

To perform their roles effectively auditors can undertake training courses and/or get support from one of the big accounting practices (PWC, EY, KPMG or Deloitte) to form a view of what roles and responsibilities should exist in each of the bank's functions. They can also employ the services of an external trader, product controller, auditor, compliance officer, and so on to assist in their reviews. Internal audit also leverage off the reviews of significant frauds conducted by the regulatory bodies and big accounting firms.

### External Audit

According to the Institute of Chartered Accountants in Australia:

> *The external auditor's responsibility is to express an opinion on whether management has fairly presented the information in the financial statements. In an audit the financial statements are evaluated by the auditor, who is objective and knowledgeable about auditing, accounting, and financial reporting matters.*[2]

Given the size and complexity of banks, the big four accounting firms (EY, PWC, KPMG and Deloitte) are the most popular choice for external audit and, in my experience, product control has far more interaction with external audit than with internal audit.

Product control's main interaction with external audit occurs in the lead-up to year-end reporting and, to a lesser extent, during half-year-end reporting. During these periods external audit reviews the control framework and performs testing on a sample of controls.

For example, suppose product control have a policy to validate MTM P&L exceeding $50,000 using a risk-based P&L estimate. On a number of random days, where the MTM P&L exceeds $50,000 external audit will request evidence that this control has been performed.

## FINANCE SHARED SERVICE

In addition to these functions, a bank may choose to establish a finance shared service which, as its name suggests, is located within finance and provides services to all the other functions within finance. This function is a large production hub which facilitates a bank maintaining a thinner layer of staff in other finance functions, who are able to perform more analytical and advisory work.

For product control, the shared service will assist in the performance of the following controls:

- Monitoring the health of the finance systems (P&L reporting system and GL) which includes ensuring the overnight system batches are running correctly.
- System suspense accounts.
- Intercompany trade reconciliations.
- Intracompany control accounts.
- Internal settlement accounts.

## SUMMARY

As one function of many within a bank, product control cannot avoid its interdependency with these other functions we have just reviewed. Not only is managing our needs and those of our stakeholders a critical part of the role we perform, having the willingness to understand each other's needs is also a key ingredient to a successful operating environment.

## NOTES

1. The Institute of Internal Auditors, "Definition of Internal Auditing," 2016. https://na.theiia.org/standards-guidance/mandatory-guidance/Pages/Definition-of-Internal-Auditing.aspx.
2. The Institute of Chartered Accountants in Australia, "Addressing Unit 3BACF Accounting & Finance, The role and function of external auditors," Chartered Accountants Auditing & Assurance Handbook 2008 Institute of Chartered Accountants in Australia. http://www.charteredaccountants.com.au/Audit.

# Two

# Technical Skills

Although the core focus of this book is product control, it is also important to be cognizant of the core technical skills which a controller requires to be effective in their role. This part of the book will introduce four core technical skills which are central to being an effective product controller. These skills are accounting, market risk, pricing financial instruments and the control framework.

# CHAPTER 4

# Accounting Standards: Recognition and Measurement

**A** t the centre of a product controller's skill set is an understanding of how to account for the financial instruments they are controlling. This skill is necessary as accounting principles influence the P&L (the income statement), balance sheet (the statement of financial position) and the financial reporting of a bank.

As most banks have a global presence they will consequently have companies domiciled in multiple legal jurisdictions around the world. The jurisdiction is important as it will determine which Generally Accepted Accounting Principles (GAAPs) the bank will need to abide by when accounting for the sales and trading activities that it undertakes in those jurisdictions.

For example, an Australian subsidiary of a U.S. bank will produce financial statements using Australian GAAP for standalone financial reporting and U.S. GAAP for consolidated financial reports prepared by the bank's group.

Although each country will have its own set of GAAPs, there has been a global convergence of accounting standards. The International Accounting Standards Board (IASB) publishes international accounting standards which many countries have either adopted or aligned their local GAAP to.

For example, IFRS 13 Fair Value Measurement, as issued by the IASB, has been adopted by Australia with the issue of AASB 13 Fair Value Measurement by the Australian Accounting Standards Board.

IFRS is a consolidated set of accounting standards, developed and maintained by the IASB. The standards are intended to be applied globally and are used by over one hundred countries. By having consistent sets of accounting standards, investors and other users of financial statements can compare the financial performance of publicly listed companies on a like-for-like basis with their international peers.

Unfortunately, the most significant outlier in this global convergence of accounting standards is the United States, which never will agree to align their accounting standards to IFRS.

If you are a product controller who needs to adhere to the U.S. GAAP, this chapter will also include a summary of U.S. GAAP below each of the international standards we cover.

We will now explore those international accounting standards which are most relevant to product control.

The primary accounting standards for product control are:

- IAS 39:      Financial Instruments: Recognition and Measurement
- IFRS 9:     Financial Instruments (Effective January 1, 2018)
- IFRS 13:    Fair Value Measurement
- IAS 32:      Financial Instruments: Presentation (Chapter 21)
- IFRS 7:     Financial Instruments: Disclosures (Chapter 21)

In this chapter we will explore IAS 39, IFRS 9 and IFRS 13 in detail and we will cover the remaining accounting standards in the subsequent chapters listed above.

## IAS 39 FINANCIAL INSTRUMENTS: RECOGNITION AND MEASUREMENT

IAS 39 has been the pre-eminent accounting standard for most of my banking career but there will be a changing of the guard shortly as it is being fully replaced by IFRS 9, which becomes effective from January 1, 2018. This book contains both standards to aid controllers in the transition from the current standard to the new.

Figures 4.1 provides a high-level overview of IAS 39.

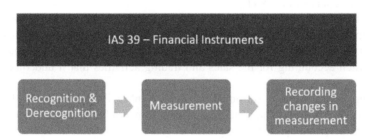

**FIGURE 4.1**   Overview of IAS 39
Note: Based upon IAS 39[1]

IAS 39 is a complex but important standard, as it guides product controllers in determining when to recognize (and de-recognize) financial assets and liabilities, how to measure them, and finally where changes in measurement should be recorded in the financial statements, for example in P&L or other comprehensive income.

### Recognizing a Financial Asset or Liability

Thousands of transactions are executed by a bank on any given trading day. Most of these transactions will be vanilla (or standard) in nature, whilst some will be structured (or exotic). For either type of transaction, it is imperative that a controller understands when they can recognize a financial asset or liability and start reporting a trade in the bank's P&L and balance sheet.

Under IAS 39, it is only when the entity has entered a contract, that the financial asset or liability can be recognized in the balance sheet (IAS 39:14).[2]

For product control, what this means is that the trade booked by the desk in the risk management system (RMS) should not be captured in P&L and balance sheet reporting unless the bank has entered a contract with the counterparty.

As product controllers go through their daily tasks, how do they know that the bank has become a party to a contract? The truth is that this is not an explicit question which a product controller typically considers. Why? The reason for this is that when we see a new trade appear in the bank's RMS we assume the bank has indeed entered a contract with the counterparty, as it is the role of operations and not product control to confirm that this has occurred. Operations perform this check via their confirmations process, where the bank's contract details are confirmed with the counterparty. If the counterparty does not recognize the trade, the desk will be informed that the trade is invalid and it will need to be removed from the bank's systems.

At this point it is important to consider outstanding contract confirmations as an operational risk to the bank, as if the counterparty doesn't recognize the trade, the bank is potentially reporting a fictitious P&L and balance sheet. It is therefore critical that when the bank is presenting financial information to the market at quarter end and year end, that unconfirmed trades are risk assessed by operations and finance consume this information to assess the potential impact on the financial reports.

**U.S. GAAP**   Under U.S. GAAP there are no significant differences for recognition.

**Trade Date Versus Settlement Date Accounting**   Firms can choose to apply trade date or settlement date accounting. Trade date accounting starts to account for financial instruments from the time they are traded, whereas settlement date accounting commences from the date they are settled.

For example, on T+0 (trade date) Bank ABC agrees to lend $10 million to Client A on T+3 (settlement date).

Under trade date accounting the loan would be accounted for in the P&L and statement of financial position from T+0. Under settlement date accounting the loan would only be accounted for from T+3.

Derivatives are not impacted by this choice, as they are automatically accounted for from trade date.

## Derecognizing a Financial Asset

IAS 39 provides guidance on when it is appropriate to derecognize a financial asset, which is summarized in Figure 4.2.

The asset can be derecognized if either the contractual rights to the cash flows of the financial asset have expired, or the asset is transferred and that transfer qualifies for derecognition (IAS 39:17).[3]

**Cash Flows Expire**   For example, once a bond reaches redemption (maturity) and the desk is repaid the principal and final coupon amount, the desk no longer have any rights to the cash flows of the asset. The asset will be derecognized.

**Transfer of An Asset**   If the asset has been transferred (i.e., sold) by the desk, to qualify as derecognition the transfer of risks and rewards and the transfer of control over the asset needs to be considered.

Product control would not typically consider whether risks and rewards have been transferred, as we assume derecognition occurs when a sale transaction is booked into the bank's systems.

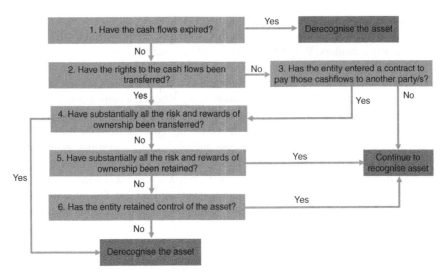

**FIGURE 4.2** Derecognizing an asset
Note: Based upon IAS 39:17.[4]

Within this part of the derecognition process, the desk can take into consideration instances where they remain as owner of the asset but have transferred the risks and rewards to a third party, or parties, via a new contract.

For example, the desk purchase a bond and enters a contract with a client to pay across the total return from that bond. This return would include all contractual cash flows of the bond (coupon and principal).

Although the bank is still the legal owner of the bond, it could be argued that all the risk and rewards of ownership have been passed to the client, which permits the desk to derecognize the bond from its balance sheet. This is known as "pass through" and is permitted under IFRS but not U.S. GAAP.

Repos are the most common transaction involving a financial instrument where derecognition needs to be considered.

Repo is the abbreviated name for a repurchase agreement, where one party (A) agrees to lend money to another party (B) in exchange for securities. The party who lends the money classifies the transaction as a reverse repo. By exchanging securities, the lender's risk of incurring a loss due to non-repayment by the borrower is lessened.

At the outset of the trade, both parties agree how much is being lent, what level of security is required for the loan and when the amounts will be repaid (usually overnight).

In Figure 4.3, Party A lends to Party B $10 million in exchange for bonds with a fair value of $10.5 million. When the borrowed funds are repaid by Party B, interest is included in the funds repaid to Party A. Party A also returns the bonds to Party B.

Although the legal ownership of the security passes from Party B to Party A on the near leg, as Party B still retains substantially all the risks and rewards of ownership, IAS 39 views this agreement (and the forward return obligation) as a secured financing transaction rather than an outright sale of an asset. Therefore, Party B continues to recognize the bonds on its balance sheet and recognizes a corresponding financial liability for the monies borrowed.

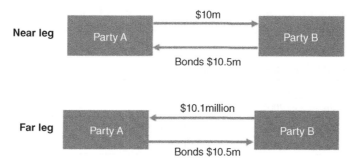

**FIGURE 4.3** Repurchase agreement

Table 4.1 illustrates the accounting for a repo. As Party B retains the risks and rewards of bond ownership they continue to recognize the bond as an asset. They also recognize the cash received from Party A ($10m) and a corresponding liability for the cash and interest they need to repay to Party A ($10.1m).

Party A, who has entered a reverse repo, recognizes the cash lent and interest owed as an asset ($10.1m), which is partially offset by a reduction in their cash balance ($10m).

**TABLE 4.1** Accounting for a repo transaction

| Balance Sheet (Party B) | | |
|---|---|---|
| Bonds | $10.5m | |
| Cash | $10.0m | |
| Repo | | $10.1m |

| Balance Sheet (Party A) | | |
|---|---|---|
| Reverse Repo | $10.1m | |
| Cash | | $10.0m |

**Lehman Brothers and Repo 105**  In the months leading up to its collapse, Lehman Brothers treated a number of significant repo transactions as outright sales of securities rather than secured borrowings.

Although they were legally able to do this under U.S. GAAP and had a legal opinion supporting them, it was a questionable practice which they didn't disclose in their financial statements. The bankruptcy examiner's report stated that "Lehman affirmatively misrepresented in its financial statements that the firm treated all repo transactions as financing transactions – i.e., not sales – for financial reporting purposes."[5]

It was known internally as Repo 105, as the collateral securing the loan was 5% greater than the loan consideration. For example, for every $100 borrowed, bonds worth $105 were exchanged with the lender.

The firm set about "selling" significant sums of inventory at quarter end to pay down liabilities and make their balance sheet look less leveraged than it was.[6]

According to the examiner's report into the bankruptcy of Lehman Brothers Holding Inc, the firm made significant use of Repo 105 on three occasions (Table 4.2):

**TABLE 4.2**   Repo 105 activities

| Reporting Date | Repo 105 activities |
|---|---|
| 4th quarter 2007 | $38.6 billion |
| 1st quarter 2008 | $49.1 billion |
| 2nd quarter 2008 | $50.38 billion |

Source: United States Bankruptcy Court Southern District of New York, Lehman Brothers Holdings Inc, Report of Anton R. Valukas, Examiner, Volume 3 of 9, Section Iii.A.4: Repo 105, Page 748

If we were to look at the difference between a balance sheet that treated the transactions as outright sales and one that treated the transactions as repos, we would see the following differences presented in Tables 4.3 and 4.4.

**TABLE 4.3**   Comparing two possible treatments of repo 105 transactions

| Balance Sheet Q2 2008 (Treated as outright sales) | | |
|---|---|---|
| Bonds | $0 | |
| Cash | $47.99bn | |

| Balance Sheet Q2 2008 (Treated as repos) | | |
|---|---|---|
| Bonds | $50.38bn | |
| Cash | $47.99bn | |
| Repo | | $47.99bn |

In this comparison, I have assumed that the Repo 105 balances provided in the examiner's report are the value of the securities ($50.38 billion), which means that Lehman Brothers would have received less cash, as the collateral needed to be 5% greater than the cash borrowed.

$$\text{Cash amount} = \frac{\$50.38bn}{1.05}$$
$$= \$47.98bn$$

If treated like a repo, the firm would not be able to reduce the value of its existing liabilities, as by entering a repo you are automatically recognizing a liability to repay the cash consideration you have received (and any applicable interest)

**U.S. GAAP**   Under U.S. GAAP, a financial asset can be derecognized when the contractual rights to the cash flows expire or the financial asset is transferred. For the transfer of the financial asset to qualify for derecognition, the focus is placed upon whether the entity has surrendered control of the asset.

There are three aspects of control that an entity needs to consider when determining if the transfer qualifies for derecognition. These are illustrated in Figure 4.4.

**FIGURE 4.4** Aspects of control within a transfer
Source: Based upon ASC 860-10-40-5[7]

1. **Legal ownership**

    The transferred financial assets need to have been placed beyond the reach of the transferor and its creditors.

    This needs to apply even in the event of bankruptcy or other receivership. A right to set-off is not an impediment to meeting this test (we will look at the right to set-off in Chapter 21) (ASC 860-10-40-5).[8]

2. **Right to use**

    The transferee needs to have the right to be able to transfer or pledge the financial asset to another party (ASC 860-10-40-5).[9]

3. **Effective control**

    The transferor cannot maintain effective control over the financial asset.

    Instances where the transferor maintains effective control can include:

    i) The transferor is entitled and obliged to repurchase or redeem the financial assets before maturity (ASC 860-10-40-5).[10]
       For example, a repo.
    ii) The transferor can cause the holder to return the financial assets and that ability provides more than an insignificant benefit (ASC 860-10-40-5).[11]
       For example, a call option.
    iii) The transferee requires the transferor to repurchase the transferred financial assets at a price so advantageous to the transferee that it is probable to occur (ASC 860-10-40-5).[12]
       For example, a put option.

## Derecognizing a Financial Liability

A financial liability can be removed from the balance sheet when the obligation is discharged, cancelled or expires (IAS 39:39).[13]

**U.S. GAAP** Under U.S. GAAP a financial liability is extinguished when the debtor pays the creditor or is released from their obligation (ASC 405-20-40-1).[14]

IAS 39 provides additional information on derecognition which I will not go into in this book. Please consult the standard or KPMG's insights into IFRS if you would like to know more.

## Measurement

**Initial Measurement** Once we have determined that the financial asset or liability can be recognized, we now need to determine how the asset or liability is to be measured.

Under IAS 39 all financial assets and liabilities are initially measured at fair value except for those financial assets and liabilities which are not classified as fair value through P&L (FVTPL). These non-FVTPL financial assets and liabilities are measured at fair plus transaction costs directly attributable to the acquisition of the financial asset or liability (IAS 39:43).[15]

You may be confused by how a loan or deposit, which is naturally accounted for at amortized cost, can be measured at fair value when it is initially recognized in the bank's books and records. For most of the loans and deposits you deal with, the fair value at initial measurement will be the transaction price agreed with the counterparty, unless this is an off-market rate.

For example, Bank Giro lends FINSED Pty Ltd $1,000,000 for one year at an interest rate of 10%. The initial fair value for this trade will be derived using a yield of 10%.

**Subsequent Measurement of Financial Assets and Liabilities**    After initial measurement, IAS 39 guides us on how to classify financial assets and liabilities. This is important as the classification influences the way in which we measure the financial assets and liabilities and how we account for changes in the unit of measure. You also need to keep in mind that financial assets and financial liabilities are treated differently under IAS 39.

The guidance in IAS 39 on subsequent measurement is particularly important for product control as it influences our financial accounting entries, P&L reporting and provides a framework for responding to measurement requests from the desk.

For example, a trader may demand that their loan is measured at fair value and changes in fair value are reported through P&L. To understand whether we are permitted to do this, we first need to consult with IAS 39.

We will first look at the subsequent measurement of financial assets before discussing liabilities.

**Subsequent Measurement of Financial Assets**    IAS 39 segregate financial assets into four categories:

*(a)* *Fair value through P&L;*
*(b)* *Held to maturity;*
*(c)* *Loans and receivables; and*
*(d)* *Available-for-sale (IAS 39:45).*[16]

Held to maturity is rarely used by trading desks due to restrictions placed on this category. Additionally, when IFRS 9 comes into full effect from January 1, 2018, held to maturity will no longer be an option for banks to select, so we will not look at this category in any detail.

From here, the standard guides us into how each of the financial asset categories will be measured.

Figure 4.5 illustrates the path IAS 39 takes us on from the recognition of a financial asset through to the subsequent measurement of that financial asset, which is influenced by which category is chosen.

***Fair Value through P&L***    Most of the financial assets that you will account for will be classified as fair value through P&L, where the financial asset is measured at fair value and changes in fair value are recorded in P&L. When your colleagues speak about *mark-to-market accounting*, they are actually referring to fair value through P&L.

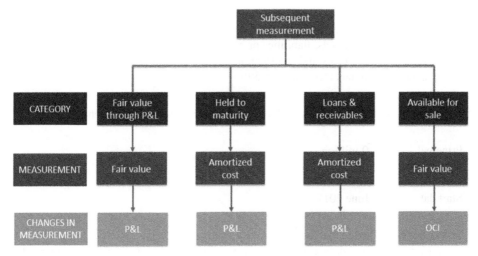

**FIGURE 4.5**    IAS 39's classification and measurement of financial assets
Source: Based upon IAS 39[17]

IAS 39 permits the bank to account for financial assets using fair value through P&L if:

1. They are classified as held for trading, or
2. They elect the fair value option.

*Classified as Held for Trading*    A financial asset is classified as held for trading if:

i) it is acquired to sell in the near term; and
ii) on initial recognition it is part of a managed portfolio with evidence of recent short-term profit-taking; or
iii) it is a derivative (IAS 39:9).[18]

For example, the trading desk purchases a corporate bond it intends to sell in the short term, which is included in a trading portfolio with other traded financial assets and liabilities.

> **Purchase details**
> Nominal            $1 million
> Purchase price    98.00
> Settle date        1st April
> Maturity            3 years

On 2nd April, the fair value of the bond increases to 98.05. This 5 basis-point increase in the fair value results in a profit of $500 and is recorded in P&L.

*Fair Value Option*    For financial assets which don't naturally reside in fair value through P&L, IAS 39 provides an option to elect this category if:

i) An embedded derivative exists which has a significant impact on the financial asset's cash flows; or

**ii)** when doing so results in more relevant information, because either:
- it eliminates or significantly reduces an accounting mismatch; or
- a group of financial assets, liabilities or both is managed and their performance evaluated on a fair value basis and information about the group is provided internally on a fair value basis to management (IAS 39:9).[19]

For example, Sparta Bank extends the following fixed rate loan to a client:

| | |
|---|---|
| Principal | $100 million |
| Interest rate | 7% |
| Term | 3 years |
| Start date | 1st June 2017 |

Sparta Bank will hedge the interest rate risk on this loan using an interest rate swap. As the interest rate swap is a derivative, it is measured at fair value with changes recorded in P&L. There will consequently be a mismatch in financial reporting for the bank. The bank may therefore elect the fair value option so that the loan is also measured at fair value, with changes in fair value being recorded in P&L.

In Table 4.4, the asymmetry in accounting for the loan at amortized cost and the derivative hedge at fair value through P&L results in a P&L of $633,333 for July 2017.

When the FVO is elected, changes in the loan's fair value offset changes in the fair value of the derivative hedge, resulting in a flat P&L.

***Loans and Receivables*** The next most common category that you will deal with is loans and receivables.

IAS 39 defines loans and receivables as:

- Not derivatives
- Have fixed or determinable payments
- Not quoted in an active market –
  - other than those which are either held for trading or classified as available for sale (IAS 39:9).[20]

**TABLE 4.4** The impact of electing the FVO

| Without electing FVO | | | |
|---|---|---|---|
| | Balance Sheet Jun-17 | Balance Sheet Jul-17 | P&L Jul-17 |
| Loan | $100,583,333 | $101,166,667 | $583,333 |
| Interest rate swap | $(125,000) | $(75,000) | $50,000 |
| Accounting mismatch | | | $633,333 |
| **Electing FVO** | | | |
| | Balance Sheet Jun-17 | Balance Sheet Jul-17 | P&L Jul-17 |
| Loan | $100,583,333 | $100,533,333 | $(50,000) |
| Interest rate swap | $(125,000) | $(75,000) | $50,000 |
| Accounting mismatch | | | $0 |

**TABLE 4.5**  A loan agreement

| Borrower | FINSED PTY LTD |
|----------|----------------|
| Principal | $1 million |
| Rate | 7% |
| Term | 1 year |
| Day count | 30/360 |

For this category, the financial assets are accounted for on an amortized cost basis using the financial asset's effective interest rate (EIR).

**Amortized cost is equal to:**

Initial cash paid or received

− principal repayments

+/− amortization or accretion (using the EIR)

− impairment

= Amortized cost

The EIR is the rate of return implicit in the contract and is typically the contractual rate adjusted for any discounts or premiums and deferred fees or costs which existed when the asset was originated or acquired.

For example, your bank enters the following loan agreement with FINSED, which is illustrated in Table 4.5.

In this agreement, your bank is lending FINSED $1 million for one year and is charging 7% for the loan. There are no deferred fees or costs at origination so the EIR for this loan will be 7%. In this example, the interest income after one month will be $5,833.33 which is calculated as follows:

$$\text{Interest Income} = \$1,000,000 \times \frac{30}{360} \times 7\%$$

Over the course of the loan, the bank earns $70,000 in interest (Table 4.6).

*Available-for-Sale (AFS)*  The final category we will look at is AFS. AFS financial assets are those financial assets which are NOT classified as:

- Fair value through P&L
- Loans and receivables
- Held to maturity (IAS 39:9).[21]

The reason AFS is chosen by the desk is to limit the amount of P&L noise from changes in the financial asset's fair value. As trading desks are buying and selling assets to make short-term trading gains, AFS is not a category which they will typically elect to use as changes in the financial asset's fair value is recorded in other comprehensive income (OCI) and only recycled (or reported) back through the P&L when the asset is derecognized (e.g., sold or matures). This category is more frequently used by non-trading areas such as treasury or structured finance.

**TABLE 4.6**   A loan agreement and its EIR

| Month | Loan Consideration | EIR | Days | Basis | Interest Income |
|---|---|---|---|---|---|
| January | $1,000,000 | 7% | 30 | 360 | $5,833.33 |
| February | $1,000,000 | 7% | 30 | 360 | $5,833.33 |
| March | $1,000,000 | 7% | 30 | 360 | $5,833.33 |
| April | $1,000,000 | 7% | 30 | 360 | $5,833.33 |
| May | $1,000,000 | 7% | 30 | 360 | $5,833.33 |
| June | $1,000,000 | 7% | 30 | 360 | $5,833.33 |
| July | $1,000,000 | 7% | 30 | 360 | $5,833.33 |
| August | $1,000,000 | 7% | 30 | 360 | $5,833.33 |
| September | $1,000,000 | 7% | 30 | 360 | $5,833.33 |
| October | $1,000,000 | 7% | 30 | 360 | $5,833.33 |
| November | $1,000,000 | 7% | 30 | 360 | $5,833.33 |
| December | $1,000,000 | 7% | 30 | 360 | $5,833.33 |
| Total |  |  |  |  | **$70,000.00** |

Under IAS 39, for AFS financial assets, the following items in Table 4.7 are recorded in OCI and P&L:

**TABLE 4.7**   AFS – allocating items into OCI or P&L

| Item | OCI | P&L |
|---|---|---|
| Fair value gains and losses | X |  |
| Dividends |  | X |
| Interest (EIR) |  | X |
| FX gains and losses |  | X |
| Impairment |  | X |

Source: Illustration based upon IAS 39[22]

Under IFRS 9, the AFS category will no longer exist; however, banks can make use of a new category: fair value through OCI.

In Table 4.8 the bank purchased the bond at a price of 98. Although the bank paid 98 for the bond, when the issuer redeems the bond in 1 year, your bank is going to receive 100%

**TABLE 4.8**   An AFS bond and its EIR

| Issuer | FINSED PTY LTD |
|---|---|
| Nominal | $1 million |
| Coupon | 7% |
| Maturity | 1 year |
| Price | 98.00 |
| Day count | 30/360 |

**TABLE 4.9**  Inputs into YTM calculation

| Trade price | 98 |
|---|---|
| Redemption | 100 |
| Purchase date | 30/06/2016 |
| Redemption date | 30/06/2017 |
| Coupon | 7% |
| Coupon payments p.a. | 1 |
| **YTM** | **9.1837%** |

of the nominal (or face value). What this means for your bank is that if the bond is held to redemption, it will yield a greater return than 7%.

What this also means, is the EIR will need to take this discount into account when determining the overall interest income to be recognized in the P&L. Using the data in Table 4.9 and the "yield" function in Microsoft excel, the EIR is 9.1837%.

You will notice that the coupon amounts in Table 4.10 equal the interest income in Table 4.6 as the coupon in this example is the same as the EIR in Table 4.6. The recognized interest income is calculated as follows:

$$\text{Interest Income (month)} = \text{Purchase consideration} \times \text{EIR} \times \frac{days}{basis}$$

$$= \$980,000 \times 9.1837\% \times \frac{30}{360}$$

$$= \$7,500$$

The accretion of the discount at purchase is then derived from the difference between the coupon income and the total interest income, which in this case is $7,500 less $5,833, which equals $1,667.

**TABLE 4.10**  Calculating interest income

| Month | Purchase Consideration | Coupon Income | Accretion of discount | Total Interest Income |
|---|---|---|---|---|
| January | $980,000 | $5,833 | $1,667 | $7,500 |
| February | $980,000 | $5,833 | $1,667 | $7,500 |
| March | $980,000 | $5,833 | $1,667 | $7,500 |
| April | $980,000 | $5,833 | $1,667 | $7,500 |
| May | $980,000 | $5,833 | $1,667 | $7,500 |
| June | $980,000 | $5,833 | $1,667 | $7,500 |
| July | $980,000 | $5,833 | $1,667 | $7,500 |
| August | $980,000 | $5,833 | $1,667 | $7,500 |
| September | $980,000 | $5,833 | $1,667 | $7,500 |
| October | $980,000 | $5,833 | $1,667 | $7,500 |
| November | $980,000 | $5,833 | $1,667 | $7,500 |
| December | $980,000 | $5,833 | $1,667 | $7,500 |
| Total | | **$70,000** | **$20,000** | **$90,000** |

***Investments in Equity Instruments and Related Derivatives*** Although not provided with its own category, if an equity investment does not have a quoted market price in an active market and its fair value cannot be reliably measured, it is to be measured at cost (IAS 39:46).[23]

The same conditions apply to any derivatives linked to and settled by delivery of unquoted equity instruments. (IAS 39:46)[24]

***Embedded Derivatives*** Some financial assets have embedded derivatives which must be separated and measured differently. These assets are separated into a host contract and the embedded derivative.

For example, a loan (host) with repayments linked to the performance of credit index (embedded derivative).

Where all of the following conditions are upheld:

**a)** the risk and economics of the host contract and derivative are not closely related;
**b)** another instrument with the same terms as the embedded derivative would be defined as a derivative; and
**c)** the fair value option hasn't been elected for the entire financial asset.

IAS 39 requires the embedded derivative to be separated from the host contract and measured at fair value through P&L. (IAS 39:10-11A)[25]

U.S. GAAP has similar requirements on embedded derivatives as IAS 39 in Topic 815 Derivatives and Hedging, Subtopic 15.

**Subsequent Measurement of Financial Liabilities** As Figure 4.6 illustrates, the classification and measurement of financial liabilities are much more simplistic than financial assets, as they are only allocated into one of two categories:

**1.** Fair value through P&L
**2.** Other liabilities.

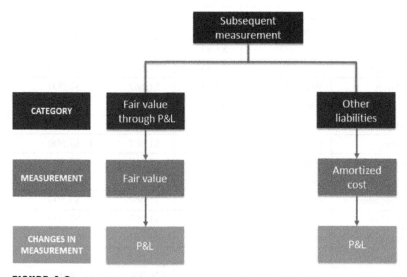

**FIGURE 4.6** Classification and measurement of financial liabilities under IAS 39
Note: Based upon IAS 39:47[26]

***Fair Value through P&L***   The conditions for this category are the same for financial assets and liabilities. The financial liability will be classified at fair value through P&L if it is:

A. *Classified as held for trading:* A financial liability is classified as held for trading if:
   i) It is incurred principally to repurchase in the near term; and
   ii) On initial recognition it is part of a managed portfolio with evidence of recent short-term profit-taking; or
   iii) It is a derivative (IAS 39:47).[27]
B. *Fair value option*: The entity elects the fair value option.

   The fair value option conditions for financial liabilities are the same as financial assets (IAS 39:9).[28]

   Financial liabilities in this category are measured at fair value with changes recorded in the P&L.

***Other Liabilities***   All other financial liabilities will be classified into this category and measured at amortized cost (using the EIR), with changes recorded in the P&L. The most common financial liabilities you will deal with in this category are borrowings and repos.

For derivative liabilities linked to, and which must be settled by, the delivery of an unquoted equity instrument, whose fair value can't be reliably measured, are measured at cost (IAS 39: 47).[29]

***U.S. GAAP***   U.S. GAAP is considerably different to IFRS with regards to classification and measurement of financial instruments and even has special guides for the type of entity being accounted for. For example, under U.S. GAAP, broker-dealer entities need to account for all their securities as held for trading, which means that the held to maturity and AFS categories are not available for selection. There is also the OCC (Office of the Comptroller of the Currency) BAAS (Bank Advisory Accounting Series) guide that provides explicit guidance for the accounting that bank chain entities need to follow.

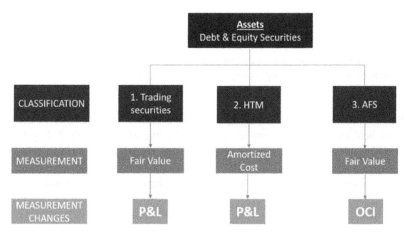

**FIGURE 4.7**   U.S. GAAP classification and measurement
Source: Based upon ASC 320 Investments – Debt and Equity Securities[30]

This chapter will now summarize the U.S. GAAP approach to classification and measurement.

U.S. GAAP classifies financial assets into the following categories which are illustrated in Figure 4.7 and 4.8.

*1) Held for Trading*   The desk can classify their debt and equity securities into this category if at inception, the desk intends to sell in the short term (ASC 320-10-25-1a).[31] These financial assets are measured at fair value, with changes being recorded in the P&L (ASC 320-10-35-1a).[32]

*2) Held to Maturity (HTM)*   To classify a security as held to maturity, the desk must have the intention and ability to hold the security until maturity. As equity securities do not mature, they cannot be classified as held to maturity (ASC 320-10-25-1c).[33] These financial assets are measured at amortized cost using the effective interest method, with changes being recorded in the P&L (ASC 320-10-35-1c).[34]

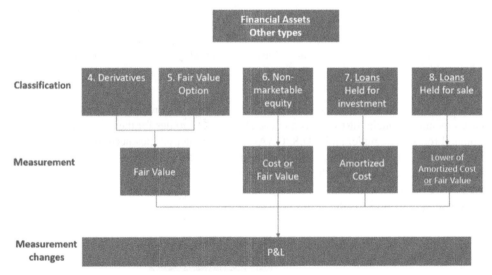

**FIGURE 4.8**   U.S. GAAP classification and measurement
Source: Based upon multiple topics within the Accounting Standards Codification[35]

*3) Available for Sale (AFS)*   Securities are classified as AFS if they are not classified as held for trading or held to maturity. Securities can only be classified as AFS if they have readily determinable fair values. A readily determinable fair value basically means that there are published quotes and transaction prices in the market for that asset (ASC 320-10-25-1b).[36] These financial assets are measured at fair value, with changes being recorded in OCI (ASC 320-10-35-1b).[37]

Under U.S. GAAP, the following items in Table 4.11 are recorded in P&L and OCI.

**TABLE 4.11**  AFS under U.S. GAAP: allocating items into OCI or P&L

| Item | OCI | P&L |
|---|---|---|
| Fair value gains and losses | X | |
| Dividends | | X |
| Interest (EIR) | | X |
| Realized gains and losses | | X |
| FX gains and losses | X | |
| Temporary impairment | X | |
| Other than temporary impairment (OTTI) | | X |

Source: Based upon ASC 320-10-35[38]

*4) Derivatives*   All financial instruments which meet the definition of a derivative are measured at fair value with changes recorded in P&L (ASC 815-10-35-1).[39] Examples of derivatives are interest rate swaps, credit swaps, futures, FX forwards, spot FX, cross currency swaps and equity options.

*5) Fair Value Option*   U.S. GAAP provides the flexibility to make an irrevocable election to measure a financial asset at fair value, which would not be naturally measured at fair value. Unlike IFRS, there are no criteria that need to be met. Changes in fair value are recorded in P&L (ASC 825-10-25).[40] A firm might elect to measure a loan or reverse repo at fair value when the interest rate risk on those assets is hedged using interest rate derivatives.

*6) Non-Marketable Equity Security*   Non-marketable equity securities are those without a readily determinable fair value and are measured at cost less impairment (for exchange seats and shares held in various government agencies in the U.S.) and fair value for all other instances (ASC 325-20-05).[41]

*7) Loans – Held for Investment*   Under U.S. GAAP, loans are either classified as held for investment or held for sale. If an entity wants to classify a loan as held for investment, it needs to have the intention and ability to hold the loan for the foreseeable future. These loans are measured at amortized cost using the effective interest method, with changes recorded in the P&L (ASC 310-10-35-47).[42]

*8) Loans – Held for Sale*   Loans are classified as held for sale if the entity intends to sell the loan. If the intention of the entity changes, they can reclassify the loans to held for investment. The loans are measured at the lower of amortized cost or fair value (ASC 310-10-35-48).[43]

***Impairment***   IAS 39 provides guidance on when an asset is deemed to be impaired and what actions should be taken to reflect that impairment in the financials. Unlike IFRS 9's expected loss model, IAS 39 operates on an incurred loss model, meaning a credit event needs to have already occurred to generate an impairment of the asset.

At each reporting date all financial assets measured at amortized cost, cost or classified as available for sale, need to be assessed to determine whether they are impaired. Impairment requires objective evidence resulting from one or more events occurring after the asset was initially recognized, which has had an impact on the estimated future cash flows of the financial asset (IAS 39:58-59).[44]

*Financial Assets Carried at Amortized Cost*   The impairment loss is the difference between the carrying amount and the present value of the estimated future cash flows using the original EIR when the financial asset was acquired. The loss is taken to P&L (IAS 39:63).[45]

If the asset recovers in value in a subsequent period, the impairment loss reversal can be recorded back through P&L (IAS 39:65).[46]

*Financial Assets Carried at Cost*   The impairment loss is the difference between the carrying amount and the present value of estimated future cash flows discounted at the current market rate of return for a similar financial asset. These impairment losses cannot be reversed (IAS 39:66).[47]

*Available for Sale*   When a decline in the fair value has been recognized directly in OCI and there is objective evidence that the asset is impaired, the cumulative loss recognized directly in OCI shall be removed from OCI and recognized in P&L (IAS 39:67).[48]

The amount to remove from equity and recognize in P&L is:

+ Fair value

− Acquisition cost

− Principal repayments

+/− amortization or accretion

− impairment losses already recognized in P&L (IAS 39:68).[49]

For all subsequent reversals of impairment losses, there must be an objective event which occurred after the impairment was recognized, which has caused the asset's value to increase. For equity AFS assets, impairment losses cannot be reversed through the P&L. However, for AFS debt assets, if in a subsequent period the asset increases in value, the impairment loss can be reversed through the P&L (IAS 39:69-70).[50]

**U.S. GAAP – Impairment**   Under U.S. GAAP, impairment also needs to be considered for financial assets.

*AFS and Held to Maturity*   These classifications have the same approach to impairment. There are two steps in determining whether a debt security is impaired, and if so, where is the impairment loss reported.[51]

Step 1 – Is the asset impaired?
    Impairment exists if the fair value is less than amortized cost (ASC 320-10-35-21).[52]
Step 2 – Is the impairment other than temporary (OTTI)?

OTTI is not intended to mean a permanent impairment; rather, the impairment is more than just a temporary loss of value (ASC 320-10-35-30).[53]

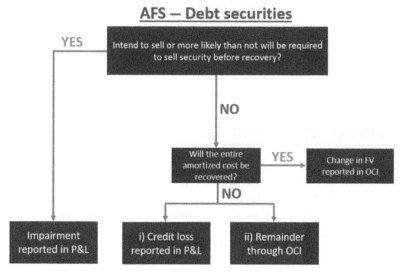

## AFS — Debt securities

**FIGURE 4.9**   Recording the impairment of AFS and held to maturity assets
Note: FV denotes fair value
Source: Based upon ASC 320-10-35[54]

Figure 4.9 details the steps in determining how to record the impairment of the AFS and held to maturity assets in the financials. Ultimately, where and how much of a loss is reported, is determined by:

a) the entity's intention and ability to hold the asset
b) the recoverability of the asset's carrying value (ASC 320-10-35-33A to 33C).[55]

When the entity does not intend to dispose of the asset but they expect to recover an amount which is less than the amortized cost value, the determination of what is recorded in OCI and P&L is a judgement-based decision.

*Loans Held at Amortized Cost*   A loan is impaired when, based upon current information and events, it is probable that a creditor will be unable to collect all amounts due under the loan agreement (ASC 310-10-35-16).[56] As with IAS 39, impairment under U.S. GAAP is concerned with past events which have caused the asset to be impaired (Topic 310-10-35-4a to 4b). [57]

The loss due to impairment can be estimated by the entity through means such as present valuing of future cash flows using the loan's EIR, taking the fair value of collateral (for collateral-dependent loans) and identifying the loan's observable market price (Topic 310-10-35-22). [58]

**Hedge Accounting**   On top of these classifications, a bank has the ability to account for financial instruments using hedge accounting. This accounting methodology is most commonly employed in a bank's Treasury or asset liability management (ALM) as it reduces P&L reporting volatility for portfolios which are matched (or hedged) from a cash flow or fair value perspective.

As most controllers will not come into contact with hedge accounting I will not be providing further detail on this method. Please refer to the accounting standard or your accounting policy team for further information and guidance.

## IFRS 9: FINANCIAL INSTRUMENTS

As I touched on earlier in the section on IAS 39, a new accounting standard, IFRS 9, has been introduced and will eventually fully replace IAS 39 for reporting periods commencing 1 January 2018. For product control, this means we need to understand what has changed from IAS 39 so that we can account for the financial assets and liabilities correctly.

In this section, I am going to go through those parts of IFRS 9 which are most relevant to product control.

### Recognition and De-recognition

There are no changes to the recognition and de-recognition of financial assets or liabilities.

### Classification and Measurement

There have been significant changes in classification and subsequent measurement, which will now be explored.

**Financial Assets**   IFRS 9 now has three classification categories and no longer includes the available for sale and held to maturity categories. The categories are:

1. Amortized cost (using the effective interest method)
2. Fair value through OCI
3. Fair value through P&L (IFRS 9: 4.1.1).[59]

IFRS 9 has introduced a business model and instrument test for determining how to account for debt instruments, which we will look at shortly.

A summary of IFRS 9 classification and measurement for financial assets is illustrated in Figure 4.10.

Figure 4.10 illustrates that IFRS 9 looks at two components when determining how to classify and measure a financial asset:

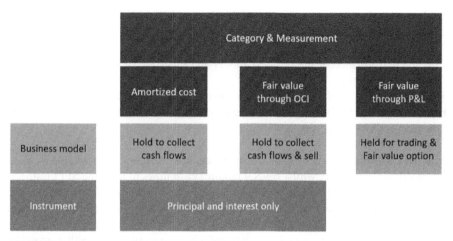

**FIGURE 4.10** IFRS 9: classification and measurement for financial assets
Source: Based upon IFRS 9 Chapter 4 Classification[60]

a) the business model for managing the financial asset; and
b) the characteristics of the financial asset's contractual cash flows (IFRS 9: 4.1.1).[61]

**Business Model** The business model test looks at whether the business is purchasing assets to:

- Sell;
- Collect their cash flows; or
- Both sell and collect cash flows (IFRS 9: 4.1.2-4.1.2A)[62]

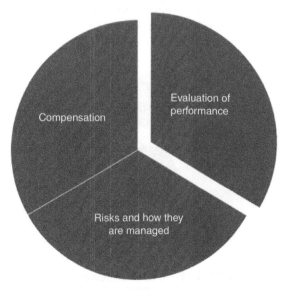

**FIGURE 4.11** Establishing the type of business model
Source: Based upon IFRS 9:B4.1.2B[63]

To determine the type of business model being used (Figure 4.11), an array of factors needs to be considered, such as:

■ How the performance of the business model and financial assets are evaluated and the frequency of reporting.
■ The risks affecting performance and how those risks are managed.
■ How managers of the business are compensated (e.g., on a fair value or contractual cash flow basis) (IFRS 9:B4.1.2B).[64]

**Contractual Cash Flows**   IAS 39's loans and receivables category required cash flows to be fixed or readily determinable, whilst IFRS 9 requires cash flows to meet the SPPI test.

The contractual cash flow test establishes whether the instrument is making payments solely of principal and interest (SPPI). Principal is considered to be the fair value of a financial asset when it is initially recognized (IFRS 9:4.1.3).[65]

Interest can incorporate several components which are consistent with a basic lending agreement. These include items such as the time value of money, credit risk, liquidity risk, a profit margin and administration costs, which are illustrated in Figure 4.12 (IFRS 9:B4.1.7A).[66]

IFRS 9 provides guidance regarding whether an instrument's features prevent it from being defined as SPPI. Some of these features are considered below.

**Tenor Mismatch**   For example, a 5 year loan has a floating coupon that is reset every year using the market 5 year swap rate. Even after 4 years, the reference swap rate used is 5 years rather than 4 years.

This feature doesn't preclude the loan from meeting the SPPI test, but the entity does need to consider whether the tenor mismatch is causing a significant difference in cash flows throughout the life of the loan (IFRS 9:B4.1.9A-9C).[67]

To make this assessment, the entity would compare the undiscounted cash flows using a benchmark yield (e.g., 1 year) to the undiscounted cash flows of the loan (e.g., 5 years). If the difference is significant, then the financial asset would fail the SPPI test.

**FIGURE 4.12**   IFRS 9: interest components
Source: Based upon IFRS 9:B4.1.7A[68]

**Regulated Interest Rates**   Some governments and regulatory bodies set the interest rates at which lending is conducted in their country. To meet the SPPI test we need to establish that the regulated interest rate considers the time value of money, doesn't compensate the investor for other risks and doesn't create volatility in the contractual cash flows that's inconsistent with a basic lending agreement (IFRS 9:B4.1.9E).[69]

**Leverage**   As leverage increases the variability of the financial asset's contractual cash flows, it causes financial assets to fail the SPPI test (IFRS 9:B4.1.9).[70]

**Non-Recourse Financing**   Non-recourse financing is not precluded from meeting the SPPI test, but the lender does need to look through to the underlying assets or cash flows. If the financing agreement gives rise to additional cash flows or limits cash flows in a way that is inconsistent with payments only of principal and interest, this type of arrangement fails the SPPI test (IFRS 9:B4.1.17).[71]

For example, a non-recourse loan, backed by a train line to London's Heathrow airport, is made from the investor to the train line owner. If the agreement requires increased contractual cash flows if more passengers use the train line, the agreement fails the SPPI test.

With all these features, there are two considerations for an entity:

a) *De minimis* If the magnitude of the feature's impact is too trivial or minor, then the feature does not prevent the instrument from being defined as solely payments of principal and interest (IFRS 9:B4.1.18).[72]
b) **Non-genuine** If the feature is significant (i.e., not *de minimis*), but it is very unlikely to occur, then the feature does not prevent the instrument from being defined as solely payments of principal and interest (IFRS 9:B4.1.18).[73]

**Embedded Derivatives**   Where the fair value option wasn't elected, IAS 39 required an embedded derivative to be separated from the host contract and measured at fair value through P&L. Under IFRS 9, because the embedded derivative would cause a financial asset to fail the SPPI test, the entire asset is measured at fair value, with changes recorded in P&L.

For example, a firm buys a note issued from a bank, which has a pay off linked to the performance of a commodity index. The entire note would be accounted for at fair value through P&L.

**Amortized Cost**   This category is measured at amortized cost using the effective interest method.

This category is used if the following criteria are met:

■ The financial asset is held within a business model whose objective it is to hold financial assets to collect their contractual cash flows; and
■ The financial asset gives rise to cash flows on specific dates which are solely payments of principal and interest (IFRS 9:4.1.2).[74]

Sales can still be made in this business model, but they should be incidental to the overriding objective, which is to collect contractual cash flows. For example, sales may be required when a single asset's credit risk becomes too risky or credit concentration exceeds the business' appetite (IFRS 9:B4.1.3B).[75]

**Fair Value through Other Comprehensive Income**    This category is measured at fair value, with changes recorded in OCI. Financial assets are measured at fair value through OCI if:

a) The financial asset resides in a business model which achieves its objective by holding financial assets to collect their contractual cash flows, and by selling financial assets; and
b) The financial asset gives rise to cash flows on specific dates which are solely payments of principal and interest (IFRS 9:4.1.2A).[76]

This category can expect to have higher levels of inventory turnover than the amortized cost category. As with IAS 39's AFS category, the items recorded in P&L and OCI remain the same, which are illustrated in Table 4.7.

**Recycling**    When the financial asset is derecognized, the cumulative balance in OCI is recycled to the P&L for debt instruments only (IFRS 9:5.7.10).[77] An equity instrument's OCI balance is not recycled through P&L upon derecognition.

**Fair Value through P&L**    Under IFRS 9, any financial assets which aren't measured at amortized cost or fair value through OCI are measured at fair value through P&L (IFRS 9:4.1.4).[78] Another way to look at this category is illustrated in Figure 4.13, which is congruent with IAS 39 apart from the fair value option, whose scope has been narrowed under IFRS 9.
    Under IFRS 9, the fair value option now only includes the accounting mismatch criteria for financial assets (IFRS 9:4.1.5).[79] Table 4.12 lists the fair value changes under IFRS 9.

**Equity Investments**    Under IFRS 9, upon initial recognition, an entity can irrevocably elect to account for an investment in an equity instrument at fair value through OCI, which would otherwise by accounted for at fair value through P&L (IFRS 9:4.1.4).[80]

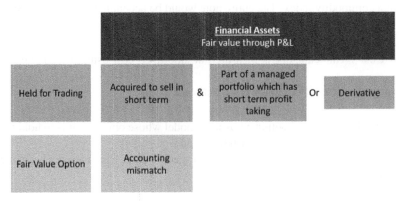

**FIGURE 4.13**    IFRS 9 – Fair value through P&L
Note: Based upon IFRS 9: Appendix A and IFRS 9:4.1.5[81]

**TABLE 4.12**   Fair value option: IFRS 9 versus IAS 39

| Fair value option | IFRS 9 | IAS 39 |
|---|---|---|
| **Financial assets** | | |
| Accounting mismatch | X | X |
| Performance managed and evaluated on a fair value basis | | X |
| **Financial liabilities** | | |
| Accounting mismatch | X | X |
| Performance managed and evaluated on a fair value basis | X | X |

**Impairment**   Finally, we come to impairment. IFRS 9 requires assets measured at fair value through OCI and amortized cost to be considered for impairment.

During the global financial crisis (GFC), IAS 39's incurred loss impairment model was criticized for its backward-looking focus, which without a past credit event, limited a bank's ability to write down the value of their investments in a timely manner.

Under IFRS 9, an entity doesn't need to wait until a credit event has occurred to recognize a credit loss.[82] IFRS 9's new impairment model aims to provide more useful information about an entity's expected credit losses on financial instruments, as it requires an entity to recognize expected credit losses at all times and update expected credit losses at each reporting date.[83]

The impairment measurement approach depends on whether an asset has experienced a significant increase in credit risk since initial recognition. For those assets where the credit risk has significantly increased since initial recognition, a lifetime expected credit loss approach is taken, whilst for assets where the credit risk has not increased significantly since initial recognition, only a 12-month expected credit loss approach is required (IFRS 9:5.5.3-5.5.5).[84] This is illustrated in Figure 4.14.

*U.S. GAAP*   Under U.S. GAAP, impairment will migrate from an incurred loss model to an expected loss model in 2021, with the bigger banks adopting the change in 2020.

**FIGURE 4.14**   IFRS 9: Impairment
Note: Based upon IFRS 9:5.5.3–5.5.5[85]

**Financial Liabilities**    Under IFRS 9, there is one change affecting financial liabilities. When the fair value option is elected for a financial liability, changes in fair value due to own credit are now recorded in OCI rather than P&L and if the liability is extinguished before maturity, the amount in OCI is *not* recycled through P&L and is instead reclassified to retained earnings.[86]

This component of the standard was introduced off the back of the volatility in bank earnings during the GFC. During the GFC, banks that elected to fair value their funding liabilities were adding billions of dollars to their P&L when the bank's credit spreads widened (deteriorated) and billions of dollars were being wiped from the P&L when their credit spreads tightened (improved). This created unnecessary financial reporting noise which IFRS 9 deals with.

Firms do not have to wait until 2018 to implement this part of the standard; they can early adopt this component of the standard.

The FASB has also made this change to own credit in U.S. GAAP, which becomes effective in 2018. This can also be early adopted, which the majority of big banks have done in 2016.

**Hedge Accounting**    Under IFRS 9 hedge accounting has been simplified. As most product controllers will not come into frequent contact with hedge accounting, I will not be devoting content to it within this book.

## IFRS 13: FAIR VALUE MEASUREMENT

In 2013 a new accounting standard, IFRS 13 Fair Value Measurement, was introduced which:

**a)** Defines what fair value is;
**b)** Establishes a framework for measuring fair value; and
**c)** Require certain disclosures about fair value measurements (IFRS 13:1).[87]

IFRS 13 applies when other IFRS' require or permit fair value measurements or disclosures about fair value measurements (IFRS 13:5).[88]

As IAS 39 and IFRS 9 require or permit financial assets and liabilities to be measured at fair value, IFRS 13 needs to be referred to, to determine the fair value for those items.

### Defining Fair Value

Fair value is defined by IFRS 13 as:

*The price that would be received to sell an asset or paid to transfer a liability in an orderly transaction between market participants at the measurement date. (IFRS 13:9)*[89]

The abbreviated term used to describe this definition in the market is the "exit price." We will now explore the IFRS 13 definition in more detail.

**Market Participant**    Fair value is a market-based measurement rather than an entity-specific measurement. (IFRS 13:2)[90] As fair value is a market-based measurement, it is important for the buyer or seller to be:

1. Independent of the entity: Unless there is evidence that the transaction price is on market terms, the source of fair value cannot be a counterparty who is a related party to the entity (IFRS 13:Appendix A).[91] For example, Sparta Bank London trading with Sparta Bank Australia.
2. They have a reasonable understanding of the asset or liability (IFRS 13: Appendix A).[92]
3. The party is able and willing, but not forced, to enter a transaction (IFRS 13: Appendix A).[93] The party does not have to trade, they only need to be able and willing to trade on the measurement date.

**Orderly Transaction**   Fair value is estimated assuming the transaction is an orderly transaction and one that is not forced (IFRS 13:Appendix A).[94]

For example, Sparta Bank experienced a depositor run and was haemorrhaging vast amounts of cash very quickly. To strengthen its liquidity profile, the bank was forced to sell their entire bond inventory to the market. The transaction prices of the bond sales, which were most probably heavily discounted, may not be reflective of fair value, as they were essentially forced liquidations.

**Intention to Hold**   An entity's intention to hold the asset or liability past the measurement date is irrelevant, meaning fair value needs to be estimated at the measurement date regardless of whether the entity intends to hold or exit their position (IFRS 13:3).[95]

For example, the fixed income desk purchases a bond at a price of 91 on T+0 and on T+5 the market price drops to 89.50. Even if the desk has no intention of selling the bond on T+5, the fair value of the bond is still 89.50.

**Blockage Factors**   As fair value focuses on the characteristics of the asset or liability, it cannot be adjusted for entity specific blockage factors such as large holdings, where the market's daily turnover is too low to absorb the entity's holding without affecting the price (IFRS 9:69).[96]

For example, the desks owns 80% or $8 million of a FINSED bond issuance. The market is currently providing executable quotes at the following levels for market parcels of $100,000:

Bid   97
Ask   98

As the desk holds most of the issuance and the daily volume for these bonds is typically $1,000,000 (e.g., 10 trades with a face value of $100,000), they will not be able to exit their entire holding at these prices. In this case, the fair value would be estimated using a transaction based on a face value of $100,000 and a bid price of 97.

**Bids and Offers**   Within financial markets, participants publish prices where they are willing to purchase (bid) or sell (offer or ask) a financial instrument. Bid prices are typically quoted below offer or ask prices, which can be seen in Figure 4.15 for spot FX contracts.

The reason bid prices are lower than ask prices is that if you are purchasing an asset, you will typically want to pay less than what the seller wants to receive.

Although IFRS 13 instructs entities to apply the price within the bid-offer spread which most reflects fair value,[97] the approach most banks take to determining fair value is to source bid prices for assets and ask prices for liabilities. We will look at bid-offer valuation adjustments in Chapter 16.

| Quote List | | | Bid | Ask | Time | Date | Contributor |
|---|---|---|---|---|---|---|---|
| EUR= | Euro | | 1.0967 | 1.0969 | 18:36 | 25/05/2015 | CBA |
| GBP= | British Pound | | 1.5483 | 1.5487 | 18:36 | 25/05/2015 | RBS |
| CHF= | Swiss Franc | | 0.9428 | 0.9440 | 18:36 | 25/05/2015 | DANSKE BANK |
| JPY= | Japanese Yen | | 121.62 | 121.64 | 18:36 | 25/05/2015 | RBS |
| AUD= | Australian Dollar | | 0.7822 | 0.7826 | 18:36 | 25/05/2015 | RBS |
| NZD= | New Zealand $ | | 0.7302 | 0.7308 | 18:36 | 25/05/2015 | RBS NY |
| CAD= | Canadian Dollar | | 1.2293 | 1.2299 | 18:36 | 25/05/2015 | RBS |

**FIGURE 4.15**   Bid and Ask quotes for spot FX rates
Source: Thomson Reuters

## Arriving at Fair Value

When determining the fair value of a financial asset or liability, there are three main steps, which are illustrated in Figure 4.16. We will now look in detail at each of these steps.

**Unit of Account**   At what level should fair value be measured? Is it on an individual asset and liability level or can we group assets and liabilities together before determining fair value?

The default level to measure fair value is on an individual asset or liability level; however, the entity can apply for an exception to this and measure fair value based upon a group of financial assets and liabilities.

The exception is permitted if the entity:

- Manages the group of financial assets and liabilities based upon its net exposure to either market risk or credit risk in accordance with a documented risk or investment strategy.
- Provides information about the group on that basis to key management personnel.
- Is measuring that group at fair value on a reoccurring basis in the statement of financial position (IFRS 13:48-49).[98]

Within the group, the entity cannot net market risk which is not substantially the same. For example, the interest rate risk associated with a financial asset cannot be combined with the FX risk from a financial liability, as the combination of the two items would neither reduce the interest rate or FX risk (IFRS 13:54).[99]

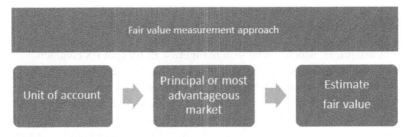

**FIGURE 4.16**   IFRS 13: Determining fair value

Where a financial asset and liability are exposed to the same type of market risk, such as interest rate risk, but the type of interest rate risk they are exposed to is not identical, the basis between the two types must be reflected in the fair value of the group (IFRS 13:54).[100]

For example, a desk may have a financial asset; for example, a U.S. Treasury bond, which is exposed to changes in U.S. Treasury yields, and a financial liability; for example, an interest rate swap, which is exposed to changes in LIBOR. The basis between the U.S. Treasury yields and LIBOR must be reflected in the fair value of that group of financial assets and liabilities.

The duration of the market risk exposure also needs to be substantially the same amongst the group (IFRS 13:55).[101]

For example, the 2-year interest rate risk on a U.S. interest rate swap cannot be netted with the 10-year interest rate risk on a U.S. Treasury bond. In this case, the 2-year risk on the interest rate swap can only be netted with the 2-year risk on the U.S. Treasury bond.

**Principal or Most Advantageous Market**   The next component of the fair value process is to consider which market should be the source of the exit price. Fair value measurement assumes the transaction takes place in the principal market or in the absence of a principal market, the most advantageous market for the asset or liability (IFRS 13:16).[102]

As each entity may have access to a different market, the determination of the principal and most advantageous market needs to be determined from the perspective of the entity (IFRS 13:19).[103] Without evidence to the contrary, the market which the entity would normally transact in can be presumed to be the principal market, or in the absence of a principal market, the most advantageous market (IFRS 13:17).[104]

In practice, the principal and most advantageous market are usually one in the same and although we can use this assumption to expedite our search for fair value, it is still important that we understand what defines a principal and most advantageous market. The principal market is that market which has the greatest volume and activity for the asset and liability, whilst the most advantageous market is that market which maximizes the amount received to sell an asset or minimizes the price paid to transfer a liability, after taking transportation and transaction costs into account (IFRS 13:Appendix A).[105]

Table 4.13 provides transaction data relating to trading in FINSED shares. There are three markets which enable market participants to buy and sell shares. As Market B has the greatest volume (500 million) and level of activity (900), this is the principal market.

Let's assume that our entity has 100 FINSED shares and they do not have access to Market B. We now need to establish which is the most advantageous market. As we are long shares

**TABLE 4.13**   Market transactions for FINSED shares

| Market | A | B | C |
|---|---|---|---|
| Volume per annum | 100,000,000 | 500,000,000 | 250,000,000 |
| Trades per month | 500 | 900 | 600 |
| Bid price | $28 | $28.50 | $28.25 |
| Ask price | $29 | $29.50 | $30.50 |
| Transaction costs | $0.25 | $0.25 | $0.75 |

**TABLE 4.14**  Fair value of FINSED shares

| Market | A | C |
|---|---|---|
| Bid price | $28 | $28.25 |
| Transaction costs | $ 0.25 | $ 0.75 |
| Amount received | $27.75 | $27.50 |

we need to identify the price which a market participant would purchase those shares from us, which would be expressed through the bid price.

When identifying the most advantageous market we also need to factor in transaction costs and transportation costs as these amounts will affect the amount we receive. As shares don't require transportation to the market, this factor is irrelevant in this example. Transaction costs will be incurred if we trade, so this cost needs to be factored in to determine the amount we will receive for our shares.

In Table 4.14, the amount we would receive from transacting in markets A and C is derived using the bid price less the transaction costs. As market A yields a greater amount than market C, Market A is the most advantageous market.

Now that we know which market to source fair value from, we now need to establish the fair value for the shares in Market A. The fair value of the shares is not based upon a price of $27.75; it is based upon a price of $28, as although transaction costs are taken into consideration when determining the most advantageous market, they are not considered when determining fair value. However, if transportation costs were a factor in this example, they would need to be considered when determining fair value.

When determining fair value, it is important to remember that the entity doesn't need to transact in the market, it only needs to have access to the market on the measurement date (IFRS 13:20).[106]

**Estimate Fair Value**  When a price for an identical asset or liability is not observable, such as for an interest rate swap or illiquid corporate bond, an entity estimates fair value using a valuation technique. This valuation technique must reflect the assumptions market participants would make and it must also maximize the use of observable pricing inputs and minimize the use of unobservable inputs (IFRS 13:3).[107]

It is within this step that IFRS 13 lays out three approaches for estimating fair value:

1. Market approach
2. Cost approach
3. Income approach.

In product control or Valuation Control, the controllers use their collective experience to arrive at what they think is the best estimate of fair value for an asset or liability. To shape that judgement process, it is helpful to understand the approaches IFRS 13 takes to using valuation techniques in determining fair value.

**Market Approach**  The market approach is often used to value businesses, where prices and other relevant information generated by market transactions, are fed into a valuation technique which may generate fair values based upon market multiples (IFRS 13:B5-B6).[108]

The market approach also incorporates matrix pricing, which is a mathematical valuation technique where the fair value of an instrument, such as a bond, is derived by relying on the bond's relationship to a quoted benchmark bond (IFRS 13:B7).[109] We will look at an example of this approach in Chapter 16.

**Cost Approach**   Product control does not typically interact with the cost approach, which reflects the amount currently required to replace the service capacity of an asset (IFRS 13:B8).[110]

**Income Approach**   Product control makes frequent use of the income approach. The income approach converts future amounts, such as cash flows or income and expenses, into a single discounted amount. As the future amounts of these assets or liabilities are typically unknown, the valuation technique estimates what these future amounts could be, based upon current market expectations (IFRS 13:B10).[111]

Two examples of this approach are present value techniques and option pricing models (IFRS 13:B11).[112] Present value techniques are used to estimate the fair value of derivatives such as interest rate swaps. Swap yield curves are used to estimate future cash flows and these cash flows are then discounted back to today into a net present value (NPV). The NPV is the estimated fair value of the interest rate swap.

Option pricing models, such as Black–Scholes and variations thereof, take multiple pricing inputs to estimate the fair value of options such as calls and puts.

## U.S. GAAP and Fair Value Measurement

Under U.S. GAAP, Topic 820 Fair value measurement, has no significant differences to IFRS 13.

That completes our primary review of IFRS and U.S. GAAP technical accounting. We will look further at the accounting standards in Chapters 20 and 21 when we explore financial accounting entries and financial reporting.

## NOTES

1. ©IFRS Foundation. IAS 39 Financial Instruments: Recognition and Measurement.
2. ©IFRS Foundation. IAS 39 Financial Instruments: Recognition and Measurement, paragraph 14.
3. ©IFRS Foundation. IAS 39 Financial Instruments: Recognition and Measurement, paragraph 17.
4. ©IFRS Foundation. IAS 39 Financial Instruments: Recognition and Measurement, paragraph 17.
5. United States Bankruptcy Court Southern District of New York, Lehman Brothers Holdings Inc, Report Of Anton R. Valukas, Examiner, Volume 3 Of 9, Section III.A.4: Repo 105, page 735.
6. United States Bankruptcy Court Southern District of New York, Lehman Brothers Holdings Inc, Report Of Anton R. Valukas, Examiner, Volume 3 Of 9, Section III.A.4: Repo 105, page 737.
7. Financial Accounting Standards Board, Accounting Standards Codification®, Topic 860 Transfers and Servicing, Subtopic 10, Section 40, paragraph 5.
8. Financial Accounting Standards Board, Accounting Standards Codification®, Topic 860 Transfers and Servicing, Subtopic 10, Section 40, paragraph 5.
9. Financial Accounting Standards Board, Accounting Standards Codification®, Topic 860 Transfers and Servicing, Subtopic 10, Section 40, paragraph 5.

10. Financial Accounting Standards Board, Accounting Standards Codification®, Topic 860 Transfers and Servicing, Subtopic 10, Section 40, paragraph 5.

11. Financial Accounting Standards Board, Accounting Standards Codification®, Topic 860 Transfers and Servicing, Subtopic 10, Section 40, paragraph 5.

12. Financial Accounting Standards Board, Accounting Standards Codification®, Topic 860 Transfers and Servicing, Subtopic 10, Section 40, paragraph 5.

13. © IFRS Foundation. IAS 39 Financial Instruments: Recognition and Measurement, paragraph 39.

14. Financial Accounting Standards Board, Accounting Standards Codification®, Topic 405 Liabilities, Subtopic 20, Section 40, paragraph 1.

15. © IFRS Foundation. IAS 39 Financial Instruments: Recognition and Measurement, paragraph 43.

16. © IFRS Foundation. IAS 39 Financial Instruments: Recognition and Measurement, paragraph 45.

17. © IFRS Foundation. IAS 39 Financial Instruments: Recognition and Measurement.

18. © IFRS Foundation. IAS 39 Financial Instruments: Recognition and Measurement, paragraph 9.

19. © IFRS Foundation. IAS 39 Financial Instruments: Recognition and Measurement, paragraph 9.

20. © IFRS Foundation. IAS 39 Financial Instruments: Recognition and Measurement, paragraph 9

21. © IFRS Foundation. IAS 39 Financial Instruments: Recognition and Measurement, paragraph 9.

22. © IFRS Foundation. IAS 39 Financial Instruments: Recognition and Measurement.

23. © IFRS Foundation. IAS 39 Financial Instruments: Recognition and Measurement, paragraph 46(c).

24. © IFRS Foundation. IAS 39 Financial Instruments: Recognition and Measurement, paragraph 46(c).

25. © IFRS Foundation. IAS 39 Financial Instruments: Recognition and Measurement, paragraphs 10–11A.

26. © IFRS Foundation. IAS 39 Financial Instruments: Recognition and Measurement, paragraph 47.

27. © IFRS Foundation. IAS 39 Financial Instruments: Recognition and Measurement, paragraph 47.

28. © IFRS Foundation. IAS 39 Financial Instruments: Recognition and Measurement, paragraph 9.

29. © IFRS Foundation. IAS 39 Financial Instruments: Recognition and Measurement, paragraph 47.

30. Financial Accounting Standards Board, Accounting Standards Codification®, Topic 320 Investments – Debt and Equity Securities.

31. Financial Accounting Standards Board, Accounting Standards Codification®, Topic 320 Investments – Debt and Equity Securities, Subtopic 10, Section 25, Sub paragraph 1a.

32. Financial Accounting Standards Board, Accounting Standards Codification®, Topic 320 Investments – Debt and Equity Securities, Subtopic 10, Section 35, Sub paragraph 1a.

33. Financial Accounting Standards Board, Accounting Standards Codification®, Topic 320 Investments – Debt and Equity Securities, Subtopic 10, Section 25, Sub paragraph 1c.

34. Financial Accounting Standards Board, Accounting Standards Codification®, Topic 320 Investments – Debt and Equity Securities, Subtopic 10, Section 35, Sub paragraph 1c.

35. Financial Accounting Standards Board, Accounting Standards Codification®.

36. Financial Accounting Standards Board, Accounting Standards Codification®, Topic 320 Investments – Debt and Equity Securities, Subtopic 10, Section 25, Sub paragraph 1b.

37. Financial Accounting Standards Board, Accounting Standards Codification®, Topic 320 Investments – Debt and Equity Securities, Subtopic 10, Section 35, Sub paragraph 1b.

38. Financial Accounting Standards Board, Accounting Standards Codification®, Topic 320 Investments – Debt and Equity Securities, Subtopic 10, Section 35.

39. Financial Accounting Standards Board, Accounting Standards Codification®, Topic 815 Derivatives and Hedging, Subtopic 10, Section 35, paragraph 1.

40. Financial Accounting Standards Board, Accounting Standards Codification®, Topic 825 Financial Instruments, Subtopic 10, Section 25.

41. Financial Accounting Standards Board, Accounting Standards Codification®, Topic 325 Investments-Other, Subtopic 20, Section 5.

42. Financial Accounting Standards Board, Accounting Standards Codification®, Topic 310 Receivables, Subtopic 10, Section 35, paragraph 47.

43. Financial Accounting Standards Board, Accounting Standards Codification®, Topic 310 Receivables, Subtopic 10, Section 35, paragraph 48.

44. ©IFRS Foundation. IAS 39 Financial Instruments: Recognition and Measurement, paragraphs 58-59.

45. ©IFRS Foundation. IAS 39 Financial Instruments: Recognition and Measurement, paragraph 63.

46. ©IFRS Foundation. IAS 39 Financial Instruments: Recognition and Measurement, paragraph 65.

47. ©IFRS Foundation. IAS 39 Financial Instruments: Recognition and Measurement, paragraph 66.

48. ©IFRS Foundation. IAS 39 Financial Instruments: Recognition and Measurement, paragraph 67.

49. ©IFRS Foundation. IAS 39 Financial Instruments: Recognition and Measurement, paragraph 68.

50. ©IFRS Foundation. IAS 39 Financial Instruments: Recognition and Measurement, paragraphs 69–70.

51. Joanne M Flood's *Wiley GAAP 2016* provides guidance on impairment considerations for equity securities.

52. Financial Accounting Standards Board, Accounting Standards Codification®, Topic 320 Investments – Debt and Equity Securities, Subtopic 10, Section 35, paragraph 21.

53. Financial Accounting Standards Board, Accounting Standards Codification®, Topic 320 Investments – Debt and Equity Securities, Subtopic 10, Section 35, paragraph 30.

54. Financial Accounting Standards Board, Accounting Standards Codification®, Topic 320 Investments – Debt and Equity Securities, Subtopic 10, Section 35.

55. Financial Accounting Standards Board, Accounting Standards Codification®, Topic 320 Investments – Debt and Equity Securities, Subtopic 10, Section 35, Sub paragraphs 33A to 33C.

56. Financial Accounting Standards Board, Accounting Standards Codification®, Topic 310 Receivables, Subtopic 10, Section 35, paragraph 16.

57. Financial Accounting Standards Board, Accounting Standards Codification®, Topic 310 Receivables, Subtopic 10, Section 35, Sub paragraphs 4a to 4b.

58. Financial Accounting Standards Board, Accounting Standards Codification®, Topic 310 Receivables, Subtopic 10, Section 35, paragraph 22.

59. ©IFRS Foundation. IFRS 9 Financial Instruments, paragraph 4.1.1.

60. ©IFRS Foundation. IFRS 9 Financial Instruments, Chapter 4 Classification.

61. ©IFRS Foundation. IFRS 9 Financial Instruments, paragraph 4.1.1.

62. ©IFRS Foundation. IFRS 9 Financial Instruments, paragraph 4.1.2–4.1.2A.

63. ©IFRS Foundation. IFRS 9 Financial Instruments, paragraph B4.1.2B.

64. ©IFRS Foundation. IFRS 9 Financial Instruments, paragraph B4.1.2B.

65. ©IFRS Foundation. IFRS 9 Financial Instruments, paragraph 4.1.3.

66. ©IFRS Foundation. IFRS 9 Financial Instruments, paragraph B4.1.7A.

67. ©IFRS Foundation. IFRS 9 Financial Instruments, paragraphs B4.1.9A–9C.

68. ©IFRS Foundation. IFRS 9 Financial Instruments, paragraph B4.1.7A.

69. ©IFRS Foundation. IFRS 9 Financial Instruments, paragraph B4.1.9E.

70. ©IFRS Foundation. IFRS 9 Financial Instruments, paragraph B4.1.9.

71. ©IFRS Foundation. IFRS 9 Financial Instruments, paragraph B4.1.17.

72. ©IFRS Foundation. IFRS 9 Financial Instruments, paragraph B4.1.18.

73. ©IFRS Foundation. IFRS 9 Financial Instruments, paragraph B4.1.18.

74. ©IFRS Foundation. IFRS 9 Financial Instruments, paragraph 4.1.2.

75. ©IFRS Foundation. IFRS 9 Financial Instruments, paragraph 4.1.3B.

76. ©IFRS Foundation. IFRS 9 Financial Instruments, paragraph 4.1.2A.

77. ©IFRS Foundation. IFRS 9 Financial Instruments, paragraph 5.7.10

78. ©IFRS Foundation. IFRS 9 Financial Instruments, paragraph 4.1.4.

79. ©IFRS Foundation. IFRS 9 Financial Instruments, paragraph 4.1.5.

80. ©IFRS Foundation. IFRS 9 Financial Instruments, paragraph 4.1.4.

81. ©IFRS Foundation. IFRS 9 Financial Instruments, Appendix A and paragraph 4.1.5.
82. ©IFRS Foundation. IFRS 9 Financial Instruments, paragraph IN9.
83. ©IFRS, "Financial Instruments—Phase II: Impairment," http://www.ifrs.org/current-projects/iasb-projects/financial-instruments-a-replacement-of-ias-39-financial-instruments-recognitio/impairment/Pages/Financial-Instruments-Impairment-of-Financial-Assets.aspx.
84. ©IFRS Foundation. IFRS 9 Fair Value Measurement, paragraphs 5.5.3–5.5.5.
85. ©IFRS Foundation. IFRS 9 Fair Value Measurement, paragraphs 5.5.3–5.5.5.
86. ©IFRS Foundation. IFRS 9 Financial Instruments, paragraph B5.7.9.
87. ©IFRS Foundation. IFRS 13 Fair Value Measurement, paragraph 1.
88. ©IFRS Foundation. IFRS 13 Fair Value Measurement, paragraph 5.
89. ©IFRS Foundation. IFRS 9 Financial Instruments, paragraph 9.
90. ©IFRS Foundation. IFRS 13 Fair Value Measurement, paragraph 2.
91. ©IFRS Foundation. IFRS 13 Fair Value Measurement, Appendix A.
92. ©IFRS Foundation. IFRS 13 Fair Value Measurement, Appendix A.
93. ©IFRS Foundation. IFRS 13 Fair Value Measurement, Appendix A.
94. ©IFRS Foundation. IFRS 13 Fair Value Measurement, Appendix A.
95. ©IFRS Foundation. IFRS 13 Fair Value Measurement, paragraph 3.
96. ©IFRS Foundation. IFRS 13 Fair Value Measurement, paragraph 69.
97. ©IFRS Foundation. IFRS 13 Fair Value Measurement, paragraph 70.
98. ©IFRS Foundation. IFRS 13 Fair Value Measurement, paragraphs 48–49.
99. ©IFRS Foundation. IFRS 13 Fair Value Measurement, paragraph 54.
100. ©IFRS Foundation. IFRS 13 Fair Value Measurement, paragraph 54.
101. ©IFRS Foundation. IFRS 13 Fair Value Measurement, paragraph 55.
102. ©IFRS Foundation. IFRS 13 Fair Value Measurement, paragraph 16.
103. ©IFRS Foundation. IFRS 13 Fair Value Measurement, paragraph 19.
104. ©IFRS Foundation. IFRS 13 Fair Value Measurement, paragraph 17.
105. ©IFRS Foundation. IFRS 13 Fair Value Measurement, Appendix A.
106. ©IFRS Foundation. IFRS 13 Fair Value Measurement, paragraph 20.
107. ©IFRS Foundation. IFRS 13 Fair Value Measurement, paragraph 3.
108. ©IFRS Foundation. IFRS 13 Fair Value Measurement, paragraphs B5–B6.
109. ©IFRS Foundation. IFRS 13 Fair Value Measurement, paragraph B7.
110. ©IFRS Foundation. IFRS 13 Fair Value Measurement, paragraph B8.
111. ©IFRS Foundation. IFRS 13 Fair Value Measurement, paragraph B10.
112. ©IFRS Foundation. IFRS 13 Fair Value Measurement, paragraph B11.

# CHAPTER 5

# Market Risk

**M**arket risk is an important technical skill which a product controller requires to be effective in their role. This chapter will highlight what market risk is, how a bank measures it and what interaction product control have with market risk.

## WHAT IS MARKET RISK AND HOW IS IT GENERATED?

Market risk is the risk that the desk's portfolio will rise or fall in value due to changes in market prices, which can lead to either profits or losses for the bank. Market risk is generated whenever the desk hold a position in a financial instrument, which could have originally been driven by a client wanting to execute a trade, the desk engaging in proprietary trading or the desk making markets in a financial instrument. The desk can mitigate market risk through hedging their risk exposures either fully or partially. As market risk is not static (i.e., it can change throughout the trading day), the desk need to rebalance their portfolio on an ongoing basis to maintain their desired risk exposure.

Figure 5.1 illustrates the generation of market risk via the arrows leading into the bank and the mitigation of risk via the arrows leading away from the bank.

When a client trades with the bank, they are usually hedging their own risk and passing that risk on to the bank. The bank can then choose to hedge that risk, by passing it on to the market, or it can retain the risk and hope the market moves in its favour.

When the desk makes a market in a financial instrument, it is publishing bid and ask prices into the market. The risk for the desk is that they will get hit on the bid and the market moves against them before the ask is hit (or vice versa). We will look further at market making in Chapter 16.

Proprietary trading is where the bank uses its own money (capital) to place bets on the market. For example, the bank expects the Federal Reserve to unexpectedly cut their target federal funds rate from 0.75% to 0.50% at the next board meeting, so they buy 30-day federal funds futures contracts to profit from this change, if it does occur.

As 30-day federal funds futures contracts are quoted at a price of 100 less the federal funds yield, the desk purchase futures at a price of 99.25 (100 less 0.75). If the Fed cuts the target rate to 0.50% the futures price will rise to 99.50 (100 less 0.50), leading to a profit for the desk.

Market risk is inextricably linked to an instrument's pricing inputs, which means that if a trader considers an input to be relevant for pricing, then that input will also generate market

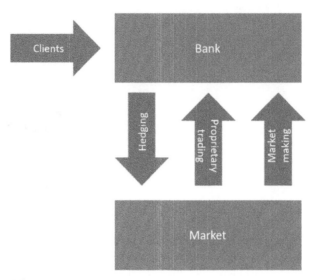

**FIGURE 5.1**   Generating and laying off market risk

risk for the bank. This market risk exposes the bank to gains or losses as the underlying market prices oscillate. For example, a trader who considers interest rates as an input into the price of a financial instrument, such as an interest rate swap, will be aware that they are generating interest rate risk for the bank. If the trader's book is not perfectly hedged, as interest rates change, P&L is generated for the bank. This relationship is depicted in Figure 5.2 for an interest rate swap.

Figure 5.2 depicts an interest rate swap being priced using a swap yield curve, which generates a market risk exposure that is sensitive to changes in the swap yield curve. As the yields in this curve change, either up or down, these changes will generate profits or losses for the bank. As each financial instrument is unique, so too are the pricing inputs and market risk it is generating.

Table 5.1 lists the market risks which are attributable to each financial instrument. I have ignored counterparty credit risk.

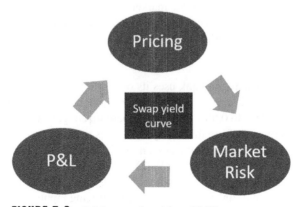

**FIGURE 5.2**   Pricing, market risk and P&L

**TABLE 5.1** Financial instruments and their market risks

| Financial instrument | Type of market risk | | | | |
|---|---|---|---|---|---|
| | Interest Rates | Credit | FX | Volatility | Equity |
| FX SPOT | | | X | | |
| FX FORWARD | X | | X | | |
| FX SWAP | X | | | | |
| FX OPTION | X | | X | X | |
| INTEREST RATE SWAP | X | | | | |
| CROSS CCY SWAP | X | | X | | |
| OVERNIGHT INDEX SWAP | X | | | | |
| FORWARD RATE AGREEMENT (FRA) | X | | | | |
| SWAPTION | X | | | X | |
| STOCKS | | | | | X |
| GOVERNMENT BONDS AND PAPER | X | X | | | |
| CORPORATE BONDS AND PAPER | X | X | | | |
| CREDIT DEFAULT SWAP (CDS) | X | X | | | |

If the market risk box is checked it means the financial instrument's value is sensitive to that market risk factor. For example, an FX forward has both FX and interest rate risk, which means that its fair value can vary if there are changes in either FX spot rates and or yields (in the form of FX swap points).

In this table I have omitted the market risk of time, which measures the gain or loss a bank will experience as time gets one day closer to maturity. Most derivatives will be sensitive to changes in time; however, it is short-dated options that are most sensitive.

## HOW IS MARKET RISK MEASURED BY A BANK?

Greeks, value-at-risk (VaR) and stress testing are the most common parameters used by a bank to measure market risk. Each of these measurements is used for different purposes and not all will be used by product control. However, it is still important that you are aware of these measurements and what they indicate for the bank.

### The Greeks

A trading desk will have thousands of open trades on their books, which are generating different types and amounts of market risk. These risks need to be managed by the desk in the context of financial markets whose prices can change in less than a second. With this in mind,

**TABLE 5.2**   The main risk parameters (Greeks)

| Symbol | Greek | Description |
|--------|-------|-------------|
| Δ | Delta | Measures the change in the asset's value due to changes in the underlying asset's price |
| Γ | Gamma | Measures the change in delta due to changes in the underlying asset's price |
| Θ | Theta | Measures the change in an asset's value due to changes in time |
| V | Vega | Measures the changes in an asset's value due to changes in the volatility of the underlying asset |

the desk need access to concise yet specific parameters which can measure the market risk they are exposed to.

The Greeks are the desk's solution to this requirement and are also the most common risk parameter that product control interact with. Product control use the Greeks to validate the P&L from existing positions. Table 5.2 lists the main Greeks which product control will interact with.

Not every Greek is relevant for each financial instrument. For example, vega will only be applicable for financial instruments with optionality, which includes both explicit options and other types of financial instruments that contain an element of optionality. For example, convertible bonds have default optionality depending of the value of the equity. Table 5.3 lists a sample of financial instruments and the Greeks which are relevant for each one.

Where appropriate, the Greeks will be presented by tenor or in the case of vega, by delta or strike. This breakdown across tenor is necessary from a pricing and risk management perspective as yields, for example, will not typically be congruent across an entire yield curve and nor will their oscillations. For example, the 1-month yield of 0.60% could rise by one basis point whilst the 3-year yield of 0.80% could fall by three basis points as the yield curve flattens. The same will be true for delta/strike for a volatility surface.

A desk, such as a rates desk, which has interest rate exposures as its primary form of market risk, will want a single view of their interest rate exposure across their entire portfolio, which is depicted in Figure 5.3.

**TABLE 5.3**   Financial instruments and their market risk parameters (Greeks)

| Parameter | Financial Instruments | | | | |
|-----------|-----------------------|---|---|---|---|
| Greek | Spot FX | Stock | Interest rate option | Interest rate swap | Credit default swap |
| Delta | FX | Equity price | Interest rates | Interest rates | Credit spreads |
| Gamma | N/A | N/A | Change in Interest rate delta | Change in interest rate delta | Change in credit delta |
| Vega | N/A | N/A | Interest rate volatility | N/A | N/A |
| Theta | N/A | N/A | Yes | Yes | Yes |

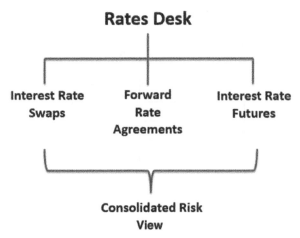

**FIGURE 5.3**   Consolidating interest rate risk

The financial instruments listed in Figure 5.3 will have a mix of single and multiple points of interest rate risk. For example, a 3x6 FRA is exposed to a single investment period that commences in 3 months' time, for a duration of 3 months. If the FRA was dealt on 1st January, it would be exposed to the 3-month LIBOR fixing on 1st April. The market risk on the FRA is therefore the risk that the 3-month LIBOR rate fixing in 3 months' time will change. This is illustrated in Figure 5.4. If we link this information back to the dv01 risk in Table 5.5, the 3-month (3M) risk would include the interest rate risk from this FRA contract.

For an interest rate future, there is also only a single period of interest rate risk, which exists at the settlement date of the futures contract. Futures and FRAs operate in a similar manner. For an interest rate swap, the desk would be exposed to multiple periods of interest rate risk. We will use the interest rate swap listed in Table 5.4 to provide an example of this.

The interest rate swap in Table 5.4 is a fixed for floating swap which matures in two years.

Figure 5.5 illustrates, via vertical lines, those points along the interest rate swap's life where it is exposed to the 3-month LIBOR fixing (1st January, 1st April, 1st July, 1st October). As interest is settled in arrears, the final payment is in December of year two, three months after the final fixing date. Once the fixing is known, this final cash flow will be treated as a fixed cash flow and present valued each day until settlement. If we link this information back

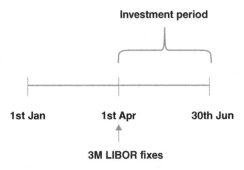

**FIGURE 5.4**   Market risk arising from a FRA

**TABLE 5.4**   Interest rate swap

| | |
|---|---|
| Notional | $5 mln |
| Currency | USD |
| Pay | LIBOR 3M |
| Receive | 1.13% |
| Payment frequency | Qrtly |
| Start date | 1st January |
| Maturity | 2 yrs |
| CSA | No |

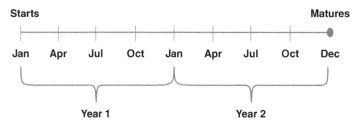

**FIGURE 5.5**   Interest rate risk for an interest rate swap

to the dv01 risk in Table 5.5, the 3M, 6M, 9M, 1Y and 2Y buckets would all include risk from this interest rate swap contract.

   This interest rate delta will then be presented as a dv01 for the desk to manage. dv01 is the P&L sensitivity for 1 basis point (0.01%) shift up or down in yields. Often a bank will derive a dv01 from shifting the yields both up and down by 1 basis point, so that convexity is taken into account. For simplicity, the examples in this book will view interest rate sensitivities as the P&L impact from a 1 basis point shift up in yields.

   Let's assume that the trades within the rates portfolio generate the interest rate risk which is presented in Table 5.5. What this means is that for every 1 basis point increase in yields

**TABLE 5.5**   Bucketed USD dv01 (per 1bp shift up)

| Tenor | dv01 |
|---|---|
| O/N | $7,000 |
| 1M | $(3,500) |
| 2M | $9,000 |
| 3M | $22,500 |
| 6M | $50,000 |
| 9M | $40,000 |
| 1Y | $25,000 |
| 2Y | $(50,000) |
| **Total** | **$100,000** |

**TABLE 5.6** FX exposures

| Currency | FX delta | Spot FX Rates |
|---|---|---|
| AUD | −1,000,000 | 0.7822 |
| CAD | 3,500,000 | 1.2293 |
| EUR | 800,000 | 1.0967 |
| GBP | 380,000 | 1.5483 |
| JPY | −200,600,000 | 121.62 |

(across the entire yield curve), the desk can expect to profit $100,000, and for every 1 basis point fall in yields, the desk can expect to lose $100,000.

As we stated earlier, the yield curve will not typically change by the same amount across the entire curve, which means we need to quantify the shift in yields for each tenor. If the 3M yield increased by 1 basis point, the desk would expect to gain $22,500 (1 × $22,500) whilst if the 1Y yield fell by 2.5 basis points, the desk would expect to lose $62,500 ($25,000 × −2.5). Product control will apply this methodology when validating the P&L from the desk's existing positions.

The process which we have followed for interest rate exposures could be replicated for other market risks. Below are examples of market risk exposures to FX and credit. Table 5.6 lists the FX exposures which the desk is running. These exposures can be applied to the changes in market rates to determine the P&L impact. For example, if GBP strengthens from 1.5483 to 1.55 the desk could expect to gain $646.

$$\text{FX P\&L} = £380,000 \times (1.55 - 1.5483)$$
$$= \$646$$

Moving on to credit, Table 5.7 lists the credit exposures which the desk has against Microsoft. The exposures are presented as a cs01, which is the P&L sensitivity for a 1 basis point widening in the CDS spreads. CDS spreads are a measure of the riskiness of the reference entity, in this case Microsoft, and represent the riskiness of the company in relation to a risk free investment.

If Microsoft's 5-year CDS spread widened by 2 basis points, the desk would expect to gain $12,000.

$$\text{Credit P\&L} = 6,000 \times (75 - 73)$$
$$= \$12,000$$

**TABLE 5.7** Credit delta for Microsoft

| Tenor | cs01 | CDS spreads |
|---|---|---|
| 1Y | (1,000) | 66 |
| 2Y | 500 | 67 |
| 3Y | 2,500 | 70 |
| 5Y | 6,000 | 73 |

**TABLE 5.8**   Time decay for a swaps portfolio

|  | T+0 | T−1 |
|---|---|---|
| Swap yield | 3% | 3% |
| Day count | 364 | 365 |
| Df | 0.9710 | 0.9709 |
| Future cash flow | NPV | NPV |
| 1,000,000 | 970,951 | 970,874 |
| − 1,000,000 | − 970,951 | − 970,874 |

**Theta**   Theta, or time decay, is another important risk and the P&L attribute that product control interact with, in linear and non-linear portfolios. Theta can fluctuate significantly and be difficult to model for non-linear financial instruments.

Theta measures the change in the value of the portfolio due to changes in time. Theta can be sourced from the sub-attribution P&L or be derived using sensitivities generated by risk models. For example, in Table 5.8 is the NPV of two future cash flows, +$1million/–$1million, occurring 365 days in the future.

When time progresses one day forward, the maturity of those future cash flows is now 364 days into the future. As a result of a one day change (and no other changes), the NPV of the portfolio has increased for both cash flows by $77. That $77 effect is measured via theta or time decay.

In Chapter 10 we will look at how product control uses the Greeks to validate the P&L from existing positions.

## VaR

Value-at-risk (VaR) is a measure of market risk that is used to monitor the risk in trading portfolios and determine how much regulatory capital a bank needs to set aside for market risk exposures.

Given a certain confidence level, VaR tells senior management what maximum losses they can expect to incur if the market prices were to move adversely against the firm's positions.

There are three main methods which a bank can use to calculate VaR:

1. Variance and covariance
2. Historic simulation
3. Monte Carlo simulation.

The primary method used by banks to calculate VaR is historical simulation, which has several components that need to be considered.

**Simulation Set**   A bank will need to identify its simulation set, which are those open trading positions the bank held at the close of business on the previous day.

**History Set**   A bank will then source historical price movement data, which for most banks entails sourcing two to three years of data, but sometimes more. When historic simulation is run, a population of P&L scores will be returned; for example, +$1.5 million, –$0.5 million, and so forth. As the simulation set (i.e., open positions) remains the same under all simulations, it is the price movements that cause the change in P&L scores.

**Confidence Level**    A bank needs to know how often a maximum loss can be expected to be exceeded, which is achieved through a confidence level. If the population is normally distributed, a confidence level of 99% will capture between two and three standard deviations of P&L scores. The less frequently a P&L score occurs, the further away from the mean (average) it will sit.

Confidence levels and standard deviations are interconnected, with higher standard deviations resulting in greater confidence levels. This relationship is illustrated in Figure 5.6. By setting a larger threshold for P&L returns (higher standard deviation and greater confidence level), you are more certain that these P&L scores will be exceeded less often.

Most banks will use a confidence level of 99%, which if a bank has a VaR of $100 million, it can expect not to lose more than $100 million on all but two to three business days each year [(1–99%) × 250 business days].

**Holding Period**    Finally, the bank will need to specify a holding period. A holding period defines how long the bank expects to hold the positions before being able to close them out. If the market is assumed to be moving adversely against your positions, the longer the holding

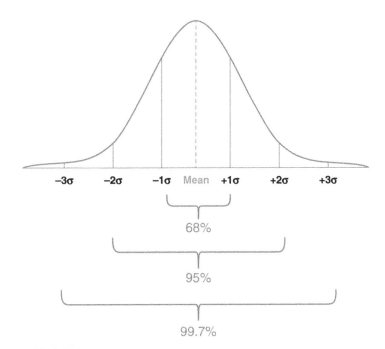

**FIGURE 5.6**    The standard deviation of P&L scores

period, the larger the VaR will be. Most banks use a holding period of one day, although many regulators also wish to see the result with a 10-day holding period as well.

**Product Control and VaR**   Although product control will deal mainly with the Greeks, it is also important that they understand VaR for several reasons.

(1) It is the main measure of market risk used in the bank. As VaR limits are set at board level and cascaded down to each business and desk, it is a high profile measurement.

(2) When product control is notified that VaR limits have been increased for their desk, they should be on notice that there could be a subsequent increase in the size of the desk's market risk exposures. This also means that the market moves P&L could start to become larger as the desk increases their risk taking positions.

(3) Market risk performs VaR back testing, where the P&L predicted using the VaR model is compared to the actual market moves P&L published by product control. This control is very significant for the bank as it confirms to the regulator that the bank's internal risk models are operating effectively and are appropriate for calculating the market risk component of regulatory capital.

For this control to operate effectively product control needs to keep the market moves P&L clean from any P&L that is not related to true market moves changes, such as new trades, amended trades, and so on. These components of the P&L need to be reported separately.

(4) VaR has a direct impact on the amount of capital a bank needs to maintain. Product controllers working with their business to minimize capital levels would need to be aware of material fluctuations in VaR and the corresponding impact they have on the bank's capital and economic profit calculations.

**Changes Regarding VaR**   It is worth pointing out that the regulatory community, via the Basel Committee on Banking Supervision (BCBS), is currently reconsidering the role of VaR in the measurement of market risk for capital. This review is and has been conducted through the fundamental review of the trading book (FRTB).

During the GFC many banks reported daily P&L results which were more excessive and more frequent than the maximum losses being returned by VaR, as the VaR models failed to consider that the market could swing as wildly as it did. As prices changed beyond the confidence levels used by the banks in their VaR calculations, the tails in the distribution curves became evidently larger than what had been predicted. This is known as "fat tails".

Although VaR tells you how often the maximum losses will be exceeded, it fails to tell you how much you could lose if the market moves beyond that confidence level into the tails of the distribution curve.

For example, if Sparta Bank produced a $100 million VaR using a confidence level of 99%, VaR does not tell the board and senior management what the losses will be if the price movements cause the P&L scores to move beyond the 99% confidence level. Sparta Bank may lose $600 million if that were to occur, but the problem with VaR is that it cannot provide this information.

Through FRTB, the expected shortfall (ES) model is going to replace VaR, as ES will tell senior management and the board how much they could expect to lose if the market does swing out into the tails.

## Stress Testing

Stress testing is the final component of market risk measurement that we will look at. Stress testing involves "shocking" or "stressing" pricing inputs and quantifying the P&L impact under each stressed scenario. Banks perform periodic stress testing for their own analysis and for regulatory reasons, as it is an indicator of how much capital the bank needs to hold to withstand losses during periods of significant market volatility.

Banks who fail regulatory stress tests are asked to raise additional capital to create a larger buffer to withstand future periods of significant stress. As of the writing of this book, the European Central Bank (ECB) has been conducting a review of the eurozone bank's capital base.

> *The ECB and European Banking Authority are carrying out separate sets of tests in the biggest review of the health of Europe's banking sector ever undertaken. The eurozone's banks have rushed to fill a €35bn black hole this year ahead of an unprecedented test of their ability to withstand financial shocks. However, the European Central Bank (ECB) is expected to fail several of these lenders when it releases the results of its stress tests later this month.[1]*

That completes our look at market risk as a technical skill. We will look at how product control apply market risk to their role in Chapter 10.

## NOTE

1. Titcomb, James, "Eurozone banks rush to fill black hole ahead of stress tests, Banks have raised more in 2014 so far than in the last two years to prepare for unprecedented tests of their financial resilience." *The Telegraph.* http://www.telegraph.co.uk/finance/newsbysector/banksandfinance/11155339/Euro zone-banks-rush-to-fill-black-hole-ahead-of-stress-tests.html ©Telegraph Media Group Limited 2014.

# CHAPTER 6

# Pricing Financial Instruments

Although product control is not responsible for pricing client trades or risk managing the trading portfolio, we need to understand how to source or construct a price for each type of financial instrument that we interact with. This understanding assists controllers in the execution of the many controls which product control undertakes. This chapter intends to guide you on how to approach pricing which will be illustrated through examples for several financial instruments.

## HOW TO APPROACH THE PRICING OF A FINANCIAL INSTRUMENT

When faced with a financial instrument that we are unfamiliar with, there are a series of steps that we can progress through to understand how to source or construct a price. Although quite basic, these steps provide a solid approach to understanding the pricing of the financial instrument. Figure 6.1 outlines these steps.

Before jumping straight into where and how you source a price for a financial instrument, it is important to first consider the nature of the financial instrument. The simple question of "what is it" brings to the fore three questions regarding the nature of the instrument:

1. **Cash flows.** There are two aspects to consider regarding cash flows:
    a) The first is to consider what cash flows occur during the life of the instrument. Some of the most common forms of cash flows are as follows:

    Principal – Are principal amounts exchanged between both parties (cross currency swap) or are they just notionally exchanged (interest rate swap)?

    Coupons – Are coupons exchanged throughout the life of the financial instrument (semi-annual coupon paying bond) or is the coupon included in the redemption value of the security (zero coupon bond)?

    Fees – Are there one-off payments that are either paid or received.

    Premiums – Is there a premium attached to the purchase of an option or a credit default swap (CDS) contract? Is this premium a one-off payment (option) or is there an ongoing payment schedule (CDS)? (A premium can also be considered a type of fee.)

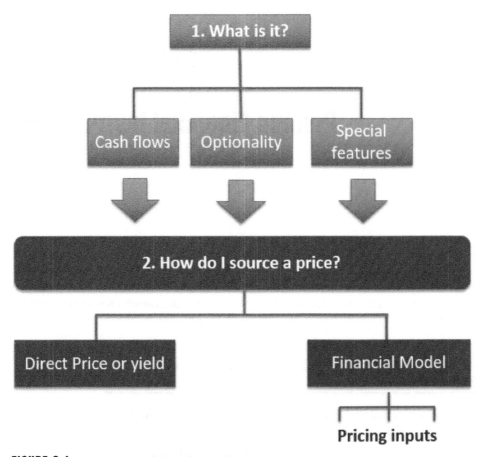

**FIGURE 6.1** Approach to pricing a financial instrument

**b)** The second aspect to consider is when those cash flows occur. Due to the time value of money, a dollar in a year's time is not worth the same amount as a dollar today. In a positive sloping yield curve environment, where yields farther into the future are higher than shorter dated yields, cash flows farther out will be worth less today than shorter dated cash flows.
**2. Optionality.** Does the instrument contain optionality? Optionality usually gives one party the right, but not the obligation, to exercise a feature within the financial instrument. For a financial instrument which is an option, the rights inferred by the option form the centerpiece of the financial instrument. For example, Sparta Bank buys the following equity option listed in Table 6.1.

In Table 6.1, Sparta Bank has the right, but not the obligation, to buy 1,000 Microsoft shares at a price of $65 in one year's time.

Optionality can also be embedded within a financial instrument, also conferring rights to one party, yet it is not the centerpiece of the financial instrument. For example, a company issues a three-year bond into the market that has an embedded call option, which gives the

**TABLE 6.1**   Equity option

| Nominal | 1,000 shares |
|---|---|
| Underlying shares | Microsoft common stock |
| Buy/Sell | Buy |
| Call/Put | Call |
| Strike | $65 |
| Expiry | 1 year |
| Expiry type | European |
| Premium | $5,000 |
| Current share price | $60 |

company the right to redeem the bond after one year. This type of optionality also needs to be considered from a pricing point of view.

## Special Features

Does the instrument contain any special features which could have an impact on pricing? For example, in a cross currency swap does the principal amount in the non-dollar leg reset to the current FX spot rate at the start of each new coupon period? These factors all need to be considered when considering the price of the underlying financial asset or liability.

For over-the-counter (OTC) derivatives, there is an additional and significant pricing consideration post the GFC which concerns whether the trade is subject to a credit support annex (CSA). We will cover CSAs in Chapter 16.

Now that we are more informed regarding the components of the financial instrument, we can now go about sourcing a price or yield (collectively "price"). There are two methods for sourcing a price. First, you can source the price directly from the market, such as in the case of liquid stocks, where prices are quoted on an exchange, or liquid bonds, where prices are quoted through brokers or traders publishing prices on Bloomberg and Reuters.

Alternatively, prices can be derived through a financial model, such as the Black–Scholes option pricing model, where a number of pricing inputs are consumed by the model and a price or value for the financial instrument is derived. It is important to be aware that this modelled price is only theoretical and that it is the market which determines whether the theoretical price is accurate.

Because of this, models used in banks will always be calibrated to market prices to ensure they are accurate. This calibration is usually performed by front office staff with doctorates in mathematics (i.e., *quants*) and validated by market risk staff with equivalent skills.

## PRICING EXAMPLES

We will now look in detail at pricing examples for some of the main financial instruments you will encounter in your roles. We cannot cover all the financial instruments as there are just too many.

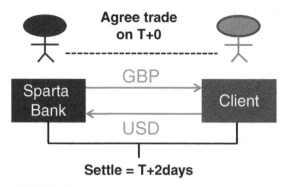

**FIGURE 6.2**   Spot FX trade

## Spot FX

A spot FX contract is a derivative, which trades in the OTC market and is one of the simplest financial instruments you will encounter. Spot FX involves the exchange of one currency in return for another on spot date (T+2 business days for most currencies).

Clients will typically use Spot FX contracts to hedge an underlying FX exposure or to convert immediate foreign currency receipts/outgoings into their local currency. Traders will use these contracts to hedge FX exposures and to take a directional position in the hope of making trading profits. In Figure 6.2, Sparta Bank has agreed to sell British pounds in exchange for U.S. dollars, which will settle two days after today.

**How Do I Source a Price?**   As the spot FX market trades trillions of dollars in contracts each business day, prices are readily available in the market via data services such as Bloomberg and Reuters.

In Figure 6.3 are bid and ask quotes for each currency against U.S. dollars (USD). A bid quote indicates the level at which the market participant is willing to buy and an ask quote is the level at which the market participant is willing to sell. For example, RBS are prepared

| Quote List | | | | | | |
|---|---|---|---|---|---|---|
| Menu ▾   ↑ Q ▾ | ● Search Related ▾ Trade ▾   ● ● 🔳 Go to ▾ Templates ▾  ✕ | | | | | |
| | Name | | Bid | Ask | Time | Date | Contributor |
| EUR= | Euro | 🔳 ↑ | 1.0967 | 1.0969 | 18:36 | 25/05/2015 | CBA |
| GBP= | British Pound | 🔳 ↓ | 1.5483 | 1.5487 | 18:36 | 25/05/2015 | RBS |
| CHF= | Swiss Franc | 🔳 ↓ | 0.9428 | 0.9440 | 18:36 | 25/05/2015 | DANSKE BANK |
| JPY= | Japanese Yen | 🔳 ↑ | 121.62 | 121.64 | 18:36 | 25/05/2015 | RBS |
| AUD= | Australian Dollar | 🔳 ↑ | 0.7822 | 0.7826 | 18:36 | 25/05/2015 | RBS |
| NZD= | New Zealand $ | 🔳 ↓ | 0.7302 | 0.7308 | 18:36 | 25/05/2015 | RBS NY |
| CAD= | Canadian Dollar | 🔳 ↓ | 1.2293 | 1.2299 | 18:36 | 25/05/2015 | RBS |

**FIGURE 6.3**   Spot FX quotes in the market
Source: Thomson Reuters

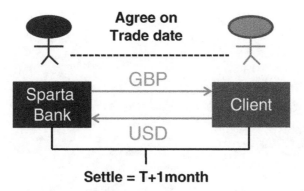

**FIGURE 6.4**  FX forward trade

to buy British pounds and sell U.S. dollars at a FX spot rate of 1.5483. Conversely, RBS are prepared to sell British pounds and buy U.S. dollars at an FX spot rate of 1.5487.

## FX Forward

An FX forward contract is a derivative which trades in the OTC market. Parties exchange one currency in return for another and the transaction settles on a date other than spot. I deliberately do not limit an FX forward trade to only settling after the spot date for two reasons. Firstly, the pricing of trades settling today or tomorrow are priced akin to trades settling after spot. Secondly, the FX forwards desk will manage the risk on these trades and those settling after spot.

Clients, such as importers and exporters, will use FX forwards to hedge future dated foreign currency receipts or outgoings. Traders will use FX forwards to hedge interest rate risk or take a directional position in the hope of making trading profits (includes arbitrage opportunities using the money markets). The trader can hedge the FX risk on this contract using an FX spot trade.

In Figure 6.4, Sparta Bank has agreed to sell British pounds in exchange for U.S. dollars, which will settle in one month.

### How Do I Source a Price?

There are two sources of FX forward prices.

 i) The outright FX forward rate
ii) Spot FX rate and one-month FX forward points (also known as swap points). The forward points represent the interest rate differential between the two currencies being exchanged.

In Figure 6.5 are bid and offer quotes for GBP/USD spot and forward contracts. Using the data provided by Thomson Reuters in Figure 6.5 (rounded to 4 decimal places), the one-month outright FX forward offered rate is 1.4638. If we subtract the offered spot price 1.4641 from the forward rate, we derive forward points of $-3.00$ $((1.4638 - 1.4641) \times 10,000)$[1]. After rounding, this agrees to the offered swap points illustrated in the Reuters screen shot.

As the exchange of currencies doesn't take place at the spot date, the interest rates for each currency play a part in the pricing of the instrument. This is what the swap points in the Reuters screen are representative of. With this in mind, an alternate method for pricing an FX

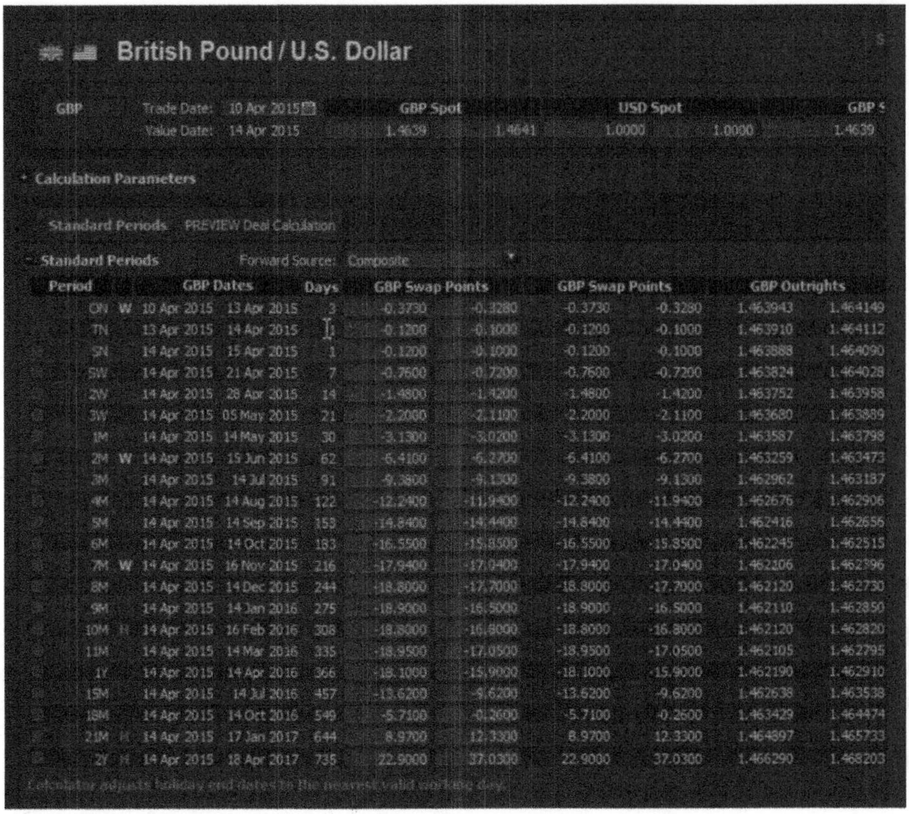
British Pound / U.S. Dollar

| GBP | Trade Date: 10 Apr 2015 | GBP Spot | | USD Spot | | GBP S |
|---|---|---|---|---|---|---|
| | Value Date: 14 Apr 2015 | 1.4639 | 1.4641 | 1.0000 | 1.0000 | 1.4639 |

Calculation Parameters

Standard Periods PREVIEW Deal Calculation

Standard Periods Forward Source: Composite

| Period | | GBP Dates | | Days | GBP Swap Points | | GBP Swap Points | | GBP Outrights | |
|---|---|---|---|---|---|---|---|---|---|---|
| ON | W | 10 Apr 2015 | 13 Apr 2015 | 3 | -0.3730 | -0.3280 | -0.3730 | -0.3280 | 1.463943 | 1.464149 |
| TN | | 13 Apr 2015 | 14 Apr 2015 | 1 | -0.1200 | -0.1000 | -0.1200 | -0.1000 | 1.463910 | 1.464112 |
| SN | | 14 Apr 2015 | 15 Apr 2015 | 1 | -0.1200 | -0.1000 | -0.1200 | -0.1000 | 1.463888 | 1.464090 |
| SW | | 14 Apr 2015 | 21 Apr 2015 | 7 | -0.7600 | -0.7200 | -0.7600 | -0.7200 | 1.463824 | 1.464028 |
| 2W | | 14 Apr 2015 | 28 Apr 2015 | 14 | -1.4800 | -1.4200 | -1.4800 | -1.4200 | 1.463752 | 1.463958 |
| 3W | | 14 Apr 2015 | 05 May 2015 | 21 | -2.2000 | -2.1100 | -2.2000 | -2.1100 | 1.463680 | 1.463889 |
| 1M | | 14 Apr 2015 | 14 May 2015 | 30 | -3.1300 | -3.0200 | -3.1300 | -3.0200 | 1.463587 | 1.463798 |
| 2M | W | 14 Apr 2015 | 15 Jun 2015 | 62 | -6.4100 | -6.2700 | -6.4100 | -6.2700 | 1.463259 | 1.463473 |
| 3M | | 14 Apr 2015 | 14 Jul 2015 | 91 | -9.3800 | -9.1300 | -9.3800 | -9.1300 | 1.462962 | 1.463187 |
| 4M | | 14 Apr 2015 | 14 Aug 2015 | 122 | -12.2400 | -11.9400 | -12.2400 | -11.9400 | 1.462676 | 1.462906 |
| 5M | | 14 Apr 2015 | 14 Sep 2015 | 153 | -14.8400 | -14.4400 | -14.8400 | -14.4400 | 1.462416 | 1.462656 |
| 6M | | 14 Apr 2015 | 14 Oct 2015 | 183 | -16.5500 | -15.8500 | -16.5500 | -15.8500 | 1.462245 | 1.462515 |
| 7M | W | 14 Apr 2015 | 16 Nov 2015 | 216 | -17.9400 | -17.0400 | -17.9400 | -17.0400 | 1.462206 | 1.462396 |
| 8M | | 14 Apr 2015 | 14 Dec 2015 | 244 | -18.8000 | -17.7000 | -18.8000 | -17.7000 | 1.462120 | 1.462730 |
| 9M | | 14 Apr 2015 | 14 Jan 2016 | 275 | -18.9000 | -16.5000 | -18.9000 | -16.5000 | 1.462110 | 1.462850 |
| 10M | H | 14 Apr 2015 | 16 Feb 2016 | 308 | -18.8000 | -16.8000 | -18.8000 | -16.8000 | 1.462120 | 1.462820 |
| 11M | | 14 Apr 2015 | 14 Mar 2016 | 335 | -18.9500 | -17.0500 | -18.9500 | -17.0500 | 1.462105 | 1.462795 |
| 1Y | | 14 Apr 2015 | 14 Apr 2016 | 366 | -18.1000 | -15.9000 | -18.1000 | -15.9000 | 1.462190 | 1.462910 |
| 15M | | 14 Apr 2015 | 14 Jul 2016 | 457 | -13.6200 | -9.6200 | -13.6200 | -9.6200 | 1.462638 | 1.463538 |
| 18M | | 14 Apr 2015 | 14 Oct 2016 | 549 | -5.7100 | -0.2600 | -5.7100 | -0.2600 | 1.463429 | 1.464474 |
| 21M | H | 14 Apr 2015 | 17 Jan 2017 | 644 | 8.9700 | 12.3300 | 8.9700 | 12.3300 | 1.464897 | 1.465733 |
| 2Y | H | 14 Apr 2015 | 18 Apr 2017 | 735 | 22.9000 | 37.0300 | 22.9000 | 37.0300 | 1.466290 | 1.468203 |

**FIGURE 6.5** GBP/USD FX forward rate
Source: Thomson Reuters

forward is by using the Spot FX rate and the money market rates for each currency. This is illustrated in the following equation.

$$Forward\ FX\ Rate = \frac{Spot\ rate \times (1 + r_t t)}{1 + r_b t}$$

Where:

$r_t$ is the term currency's interest rate, which is usually the currency that is quoted last (in this case USD)

$r_b$ is the base currency's interest rate, which is usually the currency that is quoted first (in this case GBP)

$t$ is time e.g., for one-month FX forward would be 30/360 for USD and 30/365 for GBP.

Let's assume the money market rate for one-month terms for GBP and USD are 0.44% and 0.19% respectively. We then enter this data into the equation as follows:

$$\text{GBP/USD 1 month} = 1.4641 \times \frac{\left(1 + \left(0.19\% \times \frac{30}{360}\right)\right)}{\left(1 + \left(0.44\% \times \frac{30}{365}\right)\right)}$$

By solving the formula above, you arrive at an FX forward rate of 1.4638 which agrees to the outright FX forward rate published in Reuters. Theoretically, interest rate parity tells us that the swap points and interest rates should always match as if there was a different FX forward rate derived through the money markets, a trader could theoretically arbitrage the difference in the two markets. However, because in an FX forward or FX swap[2] you are not investing or borrowing in a single currency, you will find that the implied foreign money market yield is generally higher than that seen in the money market. This is because an FX forward contains a currency swap basis, where a spread is added to the foreign yield. For example, for an AUD/USD cross currency swap, the party who is paying AUD interest and receiving USD interest, may pay the AUD Bank Bill Swap Rate (BBSW) plus a spread of 0.05% whilst receiving USD LIBOR flat (no spread).

It is also worth remembering that if the FX forward points are negative, it indicates that the right-hand-side currency (term currency) has a lower interest rate than the left-hand-side currency (base currency) and vice versa if the points are positive.

## Bonds

A bond is a debt security which is primarily traded in the OTC market but there are also instances where bonds are listed and traded on exchanges. Bonds are issued by companies and governments to raise funds from investors and in return for purchasing a bond, the investor usually receives a periodic payment of interest, known as a coupon, which can be set as fixed or floating. If the coupon is floating it will reference a market index such as LIBOR, plus or minus a spread.

The purchaser of the bond is only entitled to a coupon from when the bond purchase settles. If a bond is traded part of the way through a coupon period, the buyer will pay a clean price for the bond plus the accrued coupon up to, but not including, the day the purchase settles.

The bond can be issued for varying lengths of time and when the bond does finally mature (or redeem), the investor receives back their principal (usually par or 100) plus the final coupon payment.

Zero coupon bonds (e.g., commercial paper and bank bills) are slightly different in that they are issued at a discount to par (when interest rates are positive) and redeem the full face value (or par) at redemption. This means they do not pay intermittent coupons and instead return both principal and an implicit coupon upon redemption of the bond.

For example, FINSED issues $1 million 90-day commercial paper (CP) at a price of 98.00. When the investor purchases the CP they pay $980,000 (98% × $1,000,000). 90 days after issuance, the CP will redeem and the investor will receive back $1,000,000. This means that over the 90-day investment period the investor has earned $20,000 in interest.

In Figure 6.6, Sparta Bank has purchased a 2-year bond at par (or 100) which settles on T+3. The bond pays a fixed coupon of 4% per annum on a semi-annual basis which means that every six months we can expect to receive a payment of $2 $\left(\$100 \times \frac{4\%}{2}\right)$. When the bond reaches maturity, which is two years after the issue date, we expect to receive $102, namely, our initial principal $100 plus the final coupon $2.

**How Do I Source a Price?**    Liquid bonds will have quoted prices from brokers and traders, which the bank can use to derive the fair value of the bond. Pricing providers such as Bloomberg and Reuters are a good source for such market prices.

Most bonds are traded on a clean price in the market, which means that if the bond is part way through a coupon period, the accrued coupon is not included in the clean price. If the accrued coupon was included in the price it would be known as a dirty price.

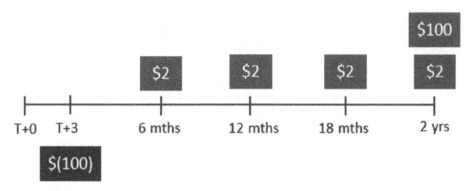

**FIGURE 6.6**   Bond cash flows

For illiquid bonds and private placements, it may be more difficult to identify a collection of prices in the market to determine the fair value. When this is the case, how would you go about deriving the fair value or market price for the bond? Let's first look at the bond pricing formula, which has the following inputs:

**a)** Coupon (Cpn)
**b)** Market yield (r)
**c)** Number of payments per annum (n)
**d)** Final Principal (M)
**e)** $i$th payment number (i)
**f)** Final payment number (N), which is $n \times$ number of years

$$P = \frac{\frac{Cpn}{n}}{\left(1+\frac{r}{n}\right)^1} + \frac{\frac{Cpn}{n}}{\left(1+\frac{r}{n}\right)^2} + \cdots \frac{\frac{Cpn}{n}}{\left(1+\frac{r}{n}\right)^i} + \frac{M+\frac{Cpn}{n}}{\left(1+\frac{r}{n}\right)^N}$$

Using our example in Figure 6.6, we are already aware of all the pricing inputs apart from (b), the market yield. The market yield will be the risk-free yield (e.g., U.S. Treasury bonds for U.S. bonds) plus a credit spread for the bond issuer. The reason we price in the credit risk of the issuer is to factor in the risk of the issuer defaulting on its obligation to repay the investor their principal and coupons.

For example, if the two-year treasury yield was 3% and the two-year CDS is 100 basis points for that issuer, the market yield to insert into the bond formula would be 4% (ignoring any basis between CDS and bond spreads for funding). Assuming these yields were also semi-annual, the theoretical price of the bond we purchased would be:

$$P = \frac{\frac{4}{2}}{\left(1+\frac{4\%}{2}\right)^1} + \frac{\frac{4}{2}}{\left(1+\frac{4\%}{2}\right)^2} + \frac{\frac{4}{2}}{\left(1+\frac{4\%}{2}\right)^3} + \frac{100+\frac{4}{2}}{\left(1+\frac{4\%}{2}\right)^4}$$

$$P = 100$$

**TABLE 6.2**   Bond purchase

| Issuer | Wanganui Construction |
|---|---|
| Coupon | 10% semi annual |
| Maturity | 5 years |
| Industry | Construction |
| Credit rating | BBB+ |

The price for this bond is equal to 100 as the market yield equates to the coupon on the bond. If the market yield increased to 4.5%, due either to an increase in U.S treasury yields or credit spreads, the price on the bond would fall below par to 99.05, as investors could enter the market and purchase an equivalent bond with a higher paying coupon.

Another way of looking at this is to refer back to the bond pricing formula. As the market yield is the denominator, if that pricing input increases it will cause the bond price to decrease and conversely, as we saw when the market yield falls below the coupon of our bond, the bond price will increase. As a rule of thumb:

If coupon > market yield −> price > 100

If coupon < market yield −> price < 100

Another common method used to price illiquid bonds is to identify a similar bond in the market and use that as a proxy. For example, let's say we have purchased the bond in Table 6.2.

To determine the fair value of the bond we could reference another bond in the market which has quoted prices. For example, we could look for a bond issued by a construction firm, with a five-year maturity and a credit rating of BBB+. Under IFRS 13, this is known as the market approach.

As with any price discovery, you will start your search hoping to find an exact replica of your bond, but there is strong possibility that you will not find such a bond. When this occurs you will need to start building in assumptions regarding the difference between your bond and the proxy.

For example, say that we have been able to find a five-year bond issued by a construction firm but that firm has a credit rating of A-, which is a higher credit quality than your bond. To use that bond's yield to derive the fair value for your bond, you will need to estimate what yield adjustment needs to be made from A–to BBB+ (e.g., perhaps there is a 50 basis points increase in yield). Once you have done this, you have the market yield which can be used as a fair value proxy for your bond.

## Interest Rate Swap

An interest rate swap (IRS) is a derivative contract which trades in the OTC market. An IRS has two legs, where parties swap the interest obligations on one index for another index throughout the life of the trade. The most common type of IRS traded is a fixed for floating swap, where one party pays (or receives) fixed interest and in return receives (or pays) floating interest over the life of the trade.

Although an IRS has principal amounts, they are referred to as notionals, as they are not exchanged and are only used to calculate interest. The start date represents when interest will start to get calculated from and interest is usually settled in arrears.

**TABLE 6.3**   Interest rate swap

| | |
|---|---|
| Trade date | 30th March |
| Start date | 3rd April |
| Trader | Nicole Greenwood |
| Counterparty | FINSED Pty Ltd |
| Notional | $10 million |
| Ccy | USD |
| Payment frequency | Semi-annually |
| Pay | 6 mth LIBOR |
| Receive | 3% |
| Settlement | Arrears |
| Maturity | 2 years |
| Day count | ACT/365 |
| CSA | No |

Table 6.3 is an example of an IRS, where, using a notional of $10 million, Sparta Bank is paying FINSED 6 month LIBOR and is receiving a fixed rate of 3% every 6 months.

Figure 6.7 is a graphical illustration of the trade in Table 6.3 from both the bank's view and the client's view. The floating LIBOR legs are represented by a "?" as the fixing rates are not yet known.

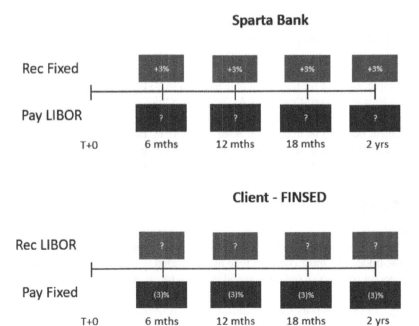

**FIGURE 6.7**   Interest rate swap

An interest rate swap can also be constructed using two floating legs, where each party exchanges interest referencing a different tenor, which is known as a basis swap. For example, Bank A pays 1 month LIBOR plus a *spread* and receives 6-month LIBOR. As there is a basis between the two tenors, a *spread* is built into the price to account for this.

As market participants would prefer to receive interest earlier rather than later, to receive the interest leg with the shorter duration a party will have to accept a lower yield. For example, for a 1-month/6-month basis swap, the 1 month yield is lower than the 6 month yield.

Normally $(1 + R\_1m \times 1/12)^6 = (1 + R\_6m \times 6/12)$. But because we have a basis, the equality would not hold. The amount you add to R_1m to make the equality hold is your basis. For example, a home loan bank may have a very large number of clients who fix their mortgage rates monthly, yet the bank draws funds from the capital markets using 3 month borrowings. The bank therefore wishes to pay 1 month and receive 3 month in an IRS to hedge this basis risk. Depending on how aggressive the bank is to shift this basis risk will determine the basis between 1 month vs 3 month $((1m + x) \, vs \, 3m)$

Clients enter an IRS to hedge interest rate risk or to convert the yield of an asset from fixed to floating (known as an asset swap). Traders will also use an IRS for the same reasons and to take a directional position in the hope that they can make trading profits.

As an IRS is an OTC agreement, each component of the trade is open for negotiation. This means that the notional, tenor, reference indices, compounding and payment frequencies and day count conventions can be tailored to a party's needs. Notionals, for example, can amortize (reduce in amount), accrete (increase in amount) or roller coaster (increase and decrease in amount) over the life of the trade.

The most common reference index for an IRS is LIBOR (London Interbank Offered Rate), which is the cost of unsecured borrowing between interbank counterparties in London. LIBOR is published each business day in five currencies (USD, GBP, CHF, JPY, EUR) and seven tenors (i.e., overnight, one week, one month, two months, three months, six months, and one year).[3]

The day count of an IRS influences the interest calculation for each coupon period. There are multiple conventions that a trader can use which can include selections such as:

1. 30/360: Assumes 30 days every month, even when there are actually 31 days or 28/29 days in the month (e.g., for March: notional × r% × 30/360).
2. ACT/360: Uses the actual number of days each month, e.g., 31 for March and 30 for April (e.g., for March: notional × r% × 31/360).
3. ACT/365: Uses the actual number of days each month, e.g., 31 for March and 30 for April (e.g., for March: notional × r% × 31/365).

The currency being traded has an influence over which convention is used, with most Commonwealth currencies using a base of 365 days whilst the remaining currencies (particularly EUR and USD) using 360 as their basis.

**How Do I Source a Price?**   As an IRS is a bespoke financial instrument, whose terms are agreed between two counterparties (or three if a broker is used), the price for an identical IRS is not published in the market. Consequently, a financial model needs to be used to derive its price or value.

To derive the price or value of an IRS, two swap yield curves need to be used:

1. **Forecast swap curve:** This curve is used to estimate the future cash flows for the floating leg(s).
2. **Discount swap curve:** This curve is used to present value the future cash flows of both legs back to today to derive a net present value (NPV).

**Forecast Swap Curve**    The forecast swap curve is used to estimate what the future interest rate fixings will be for the floating leg(s) of the swap. A forecast swap curve is not required for the fixed leg as we already know what the fixed cash flows will be.

The forecast curve will need to be able to provide the estimated future fixings for every coupon of the IRS. So, if you have a 20-year IRS with semi-annual fixings, your curve will need semi-annual yields covering all 40 rate fixings.

The swap yield curve is constructed using multiple financial instruments and tenors, extending as far as the bank requires and can be constructed differently at each bank. Table 6.4 and Figure 6.8 illustrate a typical swap yield curve. Although the financial instruments used to derive the yields are not congruent across the curve, they all represent unsecured interbank funding yields (i.e., same credit quality).

Within an IRS portfolio there will be trades with different compounding frequencies (e.g., 3-month, 6-month, etc.). For the risk management system (RMS) to accurately estimate the

**TABLE 6.4**    Swap yield curve construction

| Tenor | Rate type |
| --- | --- |
| Overnight | Interbank lending |
| 1-month | Interbank lending |
| 2-month | Interbank lending |
| 3-month | Interbank lending |
| 6-month | Futures or FRAs* |
| 1-year | Futures or FRAs* |
| 18-months | Futures or FRAs* |
| 2-years | Swap |
| 3-years | Swap |
| 5-years | Swap |
| 10-years | Swap |
| 12-years | Swap |
| 15-years | Swap |
| 20-years | Swap |
| 25-years | Swap |
| 30-years | Swap |
| 50-years | Swap |

*forward-rate agreement

## US Dollar Swaps Curve

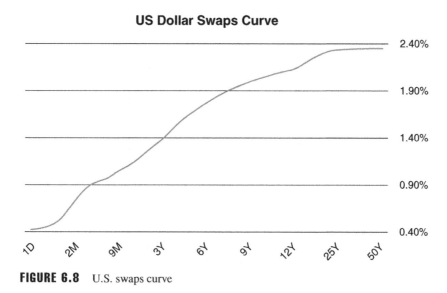

**FIGURE 6.8**   U.S. swaps curve

future rate fixings, it needs a rate with the matching compounding frequency. For example, a trade with 3-month floating fixings needs 3-month forecasted yields for each fixing date to estimate the floating cash flows.

The two methods to deal with this are:

1. Publish a swap curve for each type of compounding frequency.
2. Maintain a primary swap curve and tenor basis curves.

For example, the primary swap curve for the bank is constructed using yields with quarterly compounding (3-month LIBOR). Your trader has entered a two-year IRS with one-month rate fixings. To forecast the floating cash flows accurately, the RMS will use the base swap curve plus the "1's/3's" basis (i.e., one-month versus three-month yield basis) to derive accurate floating rate fixings out to two years. This tenor basis is quoted by brokers in the swap market.

**Discounting Swap Curve**   The discount swap curve (also known as the *cost of funds curve*) is used to present value the future cash flows of both legs, which derives the trade's NPV.

Prior to the global financial crisis (GFC), the discount and forecast curves were one in the same, but since the GFC there are multiple cost of funds curves. The discount curve a bank applies depends upon whether the trade is collateralized or not. If a trade is collateralized, the bank will use a yield curve that reflects the cost of collateral stipulated in the credit support annex (CSA).

The cost will vary between CSAs, as some CSAs permit the cheapest collateral to be delivered, whilst other CSAs are more vanilla. The cost of most collateral though, can be captured in the overnight index swap (OIS) rate.

Alternatively, if the trade does not come under a CSA, then you will need to use a swap curve that reflects the cost of unsecured funding. The market tends to use a curve based on

**TABLE 6.5**   Interest rate swap trade details

| Notional | $10mln |
|---|---|
| Currency | USD |
| Pay | LIBOR 3M |
| Receive | 1.13% |
| Payment frequency | Qrtly |
| Start date | T+5 |
| Maturity | 3 yrs |
| CSA | No |
| Day count | 30/360 |

LIBOR, as these yields reflect the cost of unsecured interbank lending. This approach isn't congruent across the market and some banks use a curve which reflects the cost of longer-term borrowing, such as the levels at which they issue debt into the market. We will now use the IRS in Table 6.5 to explore the application of forecasting and discounting.

*Leg 1 – Receive Fixed*   Forecasting: As the receive leg cash flows are known for the entire life of the swap, there is no need to forecast these amounts. These future cash flows are reflected in the cash flow column of Table 6.6. As all IRS (apart from OIS) use a simple interest formula to calculate interest, the cash flow calculation is:

$$\text{Cash flow} = \text{Notional} \times \text{rate} \times \frac{\text{days}}{\text{day count}}$$

**TABLE 6.6**   Interest rate swap – Leg 1

| Start | End | Rate | Days | Day count | Notional | Cash flow | Discount factor | NPV |
|---|---|---|---|---|---|---|---|---|
| Tue 05/04/16 | Tue 05/07/16 | 1.13% | 91 | 360 | 10,000,000 | 28,564 | 0.9972 | 28,483 |
| Tue 05/07/16 | Wed 05/10/16 | 1.13% | 92 | 360 | 10,000,000 | 28,878 | 0.9943 | 28,713 |
| Wed 05/10/16 | Thu 05/01/17 | 1.13% | 92 | 360 | 10,000,000 | 28,878 | 0.9914 | 28,631 |
| Thu 05/01/17 | Wed 05/04/17 | 1.13% | 90 | 360 | 10,000,000 | 28,250 | 0.9887 | 27,930 |
| Wed 05/04/17 | Wed 05/07/17 | 1.13% | 91 | 360 | 10,000,000 | 28,564 | 0.9859 | 28,161 |
| Wed 05/07/17 | Thu 05/10/17 | 1.13% | 92 | 360 | 10,000,000 | 28,878 | 0.9831 | 28,389 |
| Thu 05/10/17 | Fri 05/01/18 | 1.13% | 92 | 360 | 10,000,000 | 28,878 | 0.9803 | 28,309 |
| Fri 05/01/18 | Thu 05/04/18 | 1.13% | 90 | 360 | 10,000,000 | 28,250 | 0.9776 | 27,617 |
| Thu 05/04/18 | Thu 05/07/18 | 1.13% | 91 | 360 | 10,000,000 | 28,564 | 0.9749 | 27,846 |
| Thu 05/07/18 | Fri 05/10/18 | 1.13% | 92 | 360 | 10,000,000 | 28,878 | 0.9721 | 28,073 |
| Fri 05/10/18 | Mon 07/01/19 | 1.13% | 94 | 360 | 10,000,000 | 29,506 | 0.9694 | 28,602 |
| Mon 07/01/19 | Fri 05/04/19 | 1.13% | 88 | 360 | 10,000,000 | 27,622 | 0.9668 | 26,704 |
|  | Total |  |  |  |  | 343,708 |  | 337,458 |

**TABLE 6.7**   Interest rate swap – Leg 2

| Start | End | Rate | Days | Day count | Notional | Cash flow | Discount factor | NPV |
|---|---|---|---|---|---|---|---|---|
| **Tue 05/04/16** | Tue 05/07/16 | 1.13% | 91 | 360 | 10,000,000 | (28,564) | 0.9972 | (28,483) |
| **Tue 05/07/16** | Wed 05/10/16 | 1.15% | 92 | 360 | 10,000,000 | (29,389) | 0.9943 | (29,221) |
| **Wed 05/10/16** | Thu 05/01/17 | 1.16% | 92 | 360 | 10,000,000 | (29,644) | 0.9914 | (29,391) |
| **Thu 05/01/17** | Wed 05/04/17 | 1.16% | 90 | 360 | 10,000,000 | (29,000) | 0.9887 | (28,672) |
| **Wed 05/04/17** | Wed 05/07/17 | 1.17% | 91 | 360 | 10,000,000 | (29,575) | 0.9859 | (29,158) |
| **Wed 05/07/17** | Thu 05/10/17 | 1.18% | 92 | 360 | 10,000,000 | (30,156) | 0.9831 | (29,646) |
| **Thu 05/10/17** | Fri 05/01/18 | 1.19% | 92 | 360 | 10,000,000 | (30,411) | 0.9803 | (29,812) |
| **Fri 05/01/18** | Thu 05/04/18 | 1.19% | 90 | 360 | 10,000,000 | (29,750) | 0.9776 | (29,084) |
| **Thu 05/04/18** | Thu 05/07/18 | 1.19% | 91 | 360 | 10,000,000 | (30,081) | 0.9749 | (29,325) |
| **Thu 05/07/18** | Fri 05/10/18 | 1.20% | 92 | 360 | 10,000,000 | (30,667) | 0.9721 | (29,812) |
| **Fri 05/10/18** | Mon 07/01/19 | 1.21% | 94 | 360 | 10,000,000 | (31,594) | 0.9694 | (30,626) |
| **Mon 07/01/19** | Fri 05/04/19 | 1.22% | 88 | 360 | 10,000,000 | (29,822) | 0.9668 | (28,831) |
| | **Total** | | | | | **(358,653)** | | **(352,060)** |

For the first coupon period the calculation is:

$$\text{Cash flow} = \$(10,000,000) \times 1.13\% \times \frac{91}{360}$$
$$= \$(28,564)$$

Discounting: As there is no CSA in place, a LIBOR-based swap curve will be used.

$$\text{NPV} = \text{Cash flow} \times \text{discount factor}$$

For the first coupon period, the calculation is:

$$\text{NPV} = \$28,654 \times 0.9972$$
$$= \$28,483$$

*Leg 2 – Pay Floating*   Forecasting: The floating leg of the swap needs to estimate the future fixings for every quarterly investment period. A quarterly LIBOR-based swap curve is used to estimate the rate fixings, which are listed in the "Rate" column of Table 6.7.

**Overall Result**   Summing the NPV values of both legs results in an NPV of $(14,602), which is illustrated in Table 6.8. This would result in an unrealized loss being reported in the P&L and a derivative liability being reported on the balance sheet.

## FX Option

An FX option is the right, but not the obligation, to buy or sell a currency (in exchange for another currency) at a predetermined FX rate.

**TABLE 6.8**    Summary of NPVs

| Start | End | Leg1 | Leg2 | Total |
|---|---|---|---|---|
| Tue 05/04/16 | Tue 05/07/16 | 28,483 | (28,483) | 0 |
| Tue 05/07/16 | Wed 05/10/16 | 28,713 | (29,221) | (508) |
| Wed 05/10/16 | Thu 05/01/17 | 28,631 | (29,391) | (760) |
| Thu 05/01/17 | Wed 05/04/17 | 27,930 | (28,672) | (742) |
| Wed 05/04/17 | Wed 05/07/17 | 28,161 | (29,158) | (997) |
| Wed 05/07/17 | Thu 05/10/17 | 28,389 | (29,646) | (1,256) |
| Thu 05/10/17 | Fri 05/01/18 | 28,309 | (29,812) | (1,503) |
| Fri 05/01/18 | Thu 05/04/18 | 27,617 | (29,084) | (1,466) |
| Thu 05/04/18 | Thu 05/07/18 | 27,846 | (29,325) | (1,479) |
| Thu 05/07/18 | Fri 05/10/18 | 28,073 | (29,812) | (1,739) |
| Fri 05/10/18 | Mon 07/01/19 | 28,602 | (30,626) | (2,025) |
| Mon 07/01/19 | Fri 05/04/19 | 26,704 | (28,831) | (2,127) |
| | **Total** | **337,458** | **(352,060)** | **(14,602)** |

When purchasing an FX option, a premium is paid from the buyer to the seller, which usually settles on T+2. Whilst the premium is the maximum amount the buyer can lose from purchasing the option, the seller's losses are unlimited, which makes selling an option far riskier. There are different varieties of FX options. Here are some of the most common:

**European options:** Most FX options have a European expiry, which means that the option can only be exercised on the expiry date and not before.

**American options:** American options can be exercised at any time up to and including the expiry date.

**Asian options:** Asian options are average rate options, where instead of referencing the underlying asset's price on a specific date, the underlying asset's price is observed and averaged over a period. Oil options are often of this type.

**Bermudan options:** A Bermudan option is not an American option and it is not a European option, it lies somewhere in between. Bermudans can be exercised on multiple dates throughout the option's life.

**Digital options:** Digital options are binary options, where the payout is 1 or 0. If a specific condition is met, then the buyer of the option receives a monetary pay out rather than an FX position.

**Barrier options:** There are two types of barrier options, knock in and knock out. A knock in option does not exist until the barrier is triggered and if it is triggered the knock in option converts into a vanilla option. Conversely, a knock out option ceases to exist when the barrier is triggered. Barrier options can have one or more barriers.

For example, in Table 6.9 the FX options desk has traded a 50-delta option. In this example, the trader has purchased right to buy AUD10m and sell USD7.5m in 1 year. This option has cost the trader $300,000 which is payable to the counterparty on T+2.

**TABLE 6.9** AUD/USD FX option

| Trader | Ben Sherman |
|---|---|
| Buy/Sell | Buy |
| Call/Put | AUD Call USD Put |
| Notional | A$10,000,000 |
| Strike | $0.75 |
| Expiry | 1 yr |
| Exercise type | European |
| Premium | $300,000 |
| Delta | 50% |

**How Do I Source a Price?** The price for an identical FX option is not published in the market, which means that a financial model is used to derive its price or value. The financial model takes the following pricing inputs into account:

1. FX spot (S): The AUD/USD spot rate.
2. Strike (K): $0.75, which is the rate at which the option can be exercised.
3. Volatility ($\sigma$): The volatility of the AUD/USD FX spot rate.
4. Time (T): 1 year, which is the time to expiry.
5. Interest rates ($r_f$ and $r_d$): The interest rates of AUD and USD for a term of 1 year.

Statistically, volatility is measured using the annualized standard deviation of the daily FX spot rate changes. When pricing FX options, the market uses *implied volatility*, which is the market's expectation of future volatility, rather than historic volatility which is derived from the fluctuation in past prices. Volatility is quoted over a surface which is a matrix of tenor and delta or strike. So, for the option in Table 6.9 the trader would be referencing the volatility for a 1-year, 50-delta option from Figure 6.9, which is 11.50%.

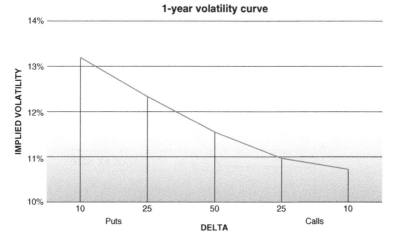

**FIGURE 6.9** AUD/USD FX volatility

**TABLE 6.10**   Moneyness of a long call option

| Moneyness | Delta |
|-----------|-------|
| In the money | > 50 |
| At the money | 50 |
| Out of the money | < 50 |

Delta is an important consideration as it represents the *moneyness* of an option (the strike rate in relation to the spot rate). The three categories of moneyness for a long call option are listed in Table 6.10, along with the corresponding deltas. Deltas can be positive or negative depending upon whether the option has been purchased (long) or sold (short) and whether it is a call or put. Purchased call options have positive deltas and purchased put options have negative deltas, whilst the opposite is true if those options have been sold rather than purchased.

As the FX spot rate changes, so too does the delta of the option. For example, for a purchased call option, if the spot FX rate increases, so too would the delta of the option and vice versa if the spot FX rate falls. If delta does change, it impacts which volatility will be used to price the option. For example, if the delta increased to 75, the volatility applied from Figure 6.9 is 12.33%. This is sourced from the left-hand side of the figure using the 25 put delta point as a reference. We can do this as we know that for vanilla European options, a long call delta less a long put delta equals one (= 1).

Options in general can come in structures, like risk reversals, straddles or butterflies, which may be presented as one overall package but constructed of one or more underlying trade bookings. To understand the overall impact on the desk's risk and P&L it is very helpful to consult the Greeks arising from the trade.

It can also be helpful to understand what the payoff is for the overall structure of the FX option. If you are unsure of what the combined payoff is, you can always define the payoff for each trade in the structure which, when combined, provide the overall structure's payoff.

Figure 6.10 illustrates how the value of the option in Table 6.9 grows as the spot FX rate increases. The trade does not start to yield a profit until the spot FX rate exceeds the strike rate of $0.75. As the option has been purchased, there is a floor on how much the trader can lose, which is the premium outlaid.

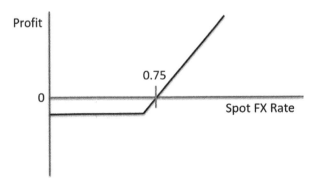

**FIGURE 6.10**   The payoff for a long AUD/USD call option

**TABLE 6.11**    Pricing add-ons

| Pricing add-on | Reason |
|---|---|
| CVA | To factor in the credit risk of the counterparty |
| DVA | To factor in the credit risk of your firm |
| FVA | To factor in the cost or benefit from uncollateralized funding |

## Pricing Add-ons

For OTC derivatives, there are a number of pricing add-ons that the front office need to consider when setting a price. The most developed of these adjustments are listed in Table 6.11.

We will be looking at these add-ons in Chapter 16.

That completes our review of how to approach the pricing of a financial instrument. This approach is a basic one, but once you have this basic grasp of the financial instrument, you will be in a good place to delve more deeply into the pricing drivers.

## NOTES

1. The convention is to quote the value as forward points. Most currencies use a factor of (or 10,000) to calculate the forward points, which is similar to basis points for interest rate swaps. As some currencies follow a different convention to calculate the forward points, such as for Japanese yen, its important to check the convention for the given currency pair.
2. An FX swap contains a spot FX transaction and an FX forward transaction.
3. A number of traders and brokers were and are being accused of manipulating the LIBOR fixings going back a number of years. As a result of this, the responsibility for setting LIBOR each day was moved from the BBA to ICE in 2014 to enhance the integrity of the published rate fixings. In Australia, the administration of BBSW was transferred from AFMA to the ASX in 2017.

# CHAPTER 7

# Internal Control

Internal control is the final technical skill that we will explore in Part II of the book. In this chapter, we review how the market defines internal control and what influences the type of internal control framework a bank establishes. We finish the chapter with a glance at a typical set of front to back controls for a trading desk.

A good product controller will understand the internal controls which they are responsible for, whilst exceptional product controllers will understand the entire internal control framework for a trading desk.

## WHAT IS INTERNAL CONTROL?

Each bank will maintain vast quantities of internal controls which are governed by an internal control framework. The framework provides a structure for identifying, maintaining and monitoring this often complex web of internal controls. An effective framework is necessary as ineffective frameworks provide limited defences against risks and can result in severe consequences for the bank, investors, creditors and the general public.

We have witnessed breakdowns in internal control through events like the global financial crisis (GFC), where banks gambled beyond their means and underestimated the negative fallout from those bets. There has also been a breakdown in controls over the submissions of quotes for the fixing of LIBOR and FX rates, where traders and brokers got greedy and manipulated the fixings in their favour. We have also witnessed a breakdown in internal control through rogue trading incidents where traders engaged in unauthorized trading and lost vast amounts of money and damaged the credibility of their bank's brand and that of their management.

Internal control is therefore vital to the success of a bank, but how can we define it?

**COSO**  The Committee of Sponsoring Organizations of the Treadway Commission (COSO) is a joint initiative of American Accounting Association, American Institute of CPAs, Financial Executives International, The Association of Accountants and Finance Professionals in Business and The Institute of Internal Auditors. COSO provides thought leadership through the development of frameworks and guidance on enterprise risk management, internal control and fraud deterrence.[1]

COSO has established a widely respected and applied framework of internal control, which defines internal control as:

> *A process, effected by an entity's board of directors, management, and other personnel, designed to provide reasonable assurance regarding the achievement of objectives relating to operations, reporting and compliance.*[2]

COSO splits an organization's objectives into three core parts, being operations, reporting and compliance.

1. **Operations:** Is the entity achieving its operational and financial performance objectives? These objectives could include earnings and balance sheet usage targets as well as the entity's target environmental footprint.
2. **Reporting:** Is the entity preparing internal and external reporting in a timely manner and are these reports reliable and transparent?[3]

    Reporting encompasses both financial reporting and non-financial reporting. For a bank, the critical external reports it wants to "get right" are its external financial reporting to the market as well as its submissions to regulatory bodies.

    As a CEO makes decisions using internal reports, the bank also needs to ensure their internal reporting is timely, reliable and transparent to ensure the best decisions are made by management.
3. **Compliance:** Is the entity complying with the laws and regulations that they are subject to?[4]

COSO's internal control framework is illustrated in the COSO cube in Figure 7.1. In this cube are the three objectives we have just listed, along with five components of control that can be applied across four different aspects (or views) of the organization, being entity, division, operating unit and function.

Within each of the five components of control are 17 principles, which represent the fundamental concepts associated with each component. The principles supporting the components of internal control, adapted from COSO,[5] are as follows:

**Control Environment**
1. Strong ethics and integrity.
2. Independent board of directors provides oversight.
3. Clearly established reporting structure that supports the achievement of objectives.
4. Commitment to professional development and to attracting and retaining staff.
5. Culture of accountability.

**Risk Assessment**
6. Clear and specific objectives that support risk identification.
7. Strong risk identification, analysis and management.
8. Consideration and understanding of fraud risk.
9. System for assessing factors that influence internal control.

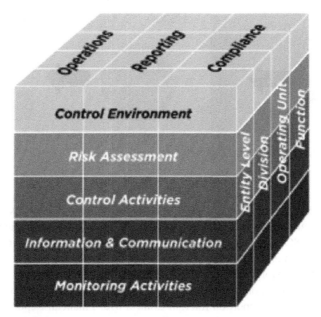

**FIGURE 7.1**   COSO Integrated Control Framework
Source: Committee of Sponsoring Organizations of the
Treadway Commission (COSO), © 2013. Used by permission.

**Control Activities**
10. Control activities that support risk mitigation.
11. Control activities that integrate technology appropriately.
12. Policies and procedures that clarify control activities.

**Information and Communication**
13. Use and generation of relevant internal control information.
14. Internal communication of internal control objectives and responsibilities.
15. External communication with third parties of internal control information.

**Monitoring Activities**
16. Evaluation performance to determine efficacy of internal control functions.
17. Timely communication of internal control problems to accountable parties, senior management and board of directors.

Carrying on from COSO's guidance on internal control, Figure 7.2 illustrates the interconnectedness between a bank's internal control framework and the achievement of its objectives. Within this illustration you can see that a bank faces risks emanating from both within and outside the organization. Internal risks consider potential losses arising from failures in people and processes, whilst external risks consider losses arising from external events such as price movements in financial instruments (market and credit risk), vendor failure, terrorism, natural disaster and political/regulatory intervention.

**FIGURE 7.2** Objectives and internal control

Using its desired risk appetite, a bank can then design internal controls to identify and manage those risks and assess the effectiveness of those controls on a periodic basis.

By using the COSO framework as a guide in the design of an internal control framework, a bank can design, implement and operate an effective framework in the pursuit of its objectives. Major banks, such as JP Morgan, HSBC and UBS all evidence their adherence and application of COSO in their annual reports. These attestations are usually contained in the "Directors' Report" or "Management's Report on Internal Control over Financial Reporting." It is worth reviewing this section of their annual reports, if only once, to comprehend the importance of the COSO control principles.

## ESTABLISHING AN INTERNAL CONTROL FRAMEWORK

Imagine that you have been approached by a brand new investment bank that wants to hire you to establish and manage their product control function. This is a big step in your career and you are eager to pursue this opportunity. You have made it to interview stage and are meeting with the bank's CFO. During this meeting the CFO asks you this simple question:

*If you were my product control manager, what internal controls would you embed?*

How would you answer this simple yet broad question?

If you have only ever worked in one bank and therefore only ever experienced one internal control framework, how do you know that type of framework is the most appropriate for your potential new employer?

Before deciding on the individual controls that you would want to embed, let's take a step back and consider some of the factors which will influence your decision:

1. The board and senior management
2. Regulatory requirements
3. Market practice
4. Type of business.

We will now look at each of these points in further detail.

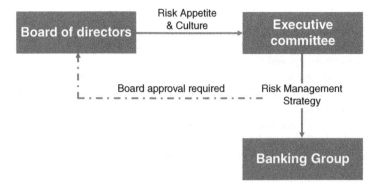

**FIGURE 7.3** Establishing a risk culture and risk management framework

## The Board and Senior Management

The board of directors are responsible for establishing the risk appetite and risk culture of the bank which provides senior management with a guide in establishing a risk management framework (a risk management framework and an internal control framework are one and the same). This relationship is illustrated in Figure 7.3.

This appetite and culture significantly influences the type of internal control framework which your bank will embed within its operations. Risk appetite, or risk tolerance, is broader than just market and credit risk limits, it also considers operational risk. Operational risk is the risk associated with a breakdown in processes and controls within the bank. Whilst operational risk cannot be eliminated completely, the board and senior management will typically want the risk reduced to manageable levels to provide a sound risk and reward profile for the bank.

A bank with a large risk appetite will be prepared to consume higher levels of market, credit and operational risk. Although greater levels of risk may generate higher earnings, for example if the bank positions itself on the right side of the market or employs fewer staff to execute controls, it also reduces the level of assurance the board possesses regarding the achievement of their firm's objectives. Higher risk also increases the regulatory capital a firm needs to maintain.

For example, the CFO of a London-based bank has decided to offshore their product control function to reduce their cost base. Two locations have been short listed for approval, Antarctica and Mumbai (Table 7.1).

A bank with a large risk appetite may choose Antarctica which, although is the cheapest alternative, is also a very risky choice as it elevates the level of operational risk within product control. Although this is not a serious example, it highlights the choices available to the bank.

**TABLE 7.1** Offshoring review

|  | **Antarctica** | **Mumbai** |
|---|---|---|
| Cost | Extremely low | Medium |
| IT connectivity | Very poor | Very good |
| Talent pool | Very poor | Very good |
| Geographical and political stability | Very poor | Good |

Another example of risk appetite relates to trade booking protocols. For example, the structured rates desk has an opportunity to execute a trade with a client which will generate a day1 profit of $10 million. The drawback for the desk and the bank is that the risk management system (RMS) cannot accept and process the trade booking.

The choice for the bank is to either execute the trade, earn the $10 million profit and manage the trade booking in an offline system such as Microsoft Excel. Alternatively, the bank can decline the trade.

Before making this decision, management would need to understand what level of operational risk the bank would be fostering if the trade was booked offline and balance this against the reward from the trade (which would need to align with the board's risk appetite).

**The Lines of Defence**   One of the ways senior management seek to manage operational risk is by establishing three lines of defence within their organization (Figure 7.4). Under this model, all staff are responsible for risk management and staff are segregated into three lines. Whilst each line cooperates with the others, they also retain their independence. When viewed together, these functions form an integrated control blanket which is designed to reduce the level of operational risk to acceptable levels.

**Line 1 – The Business and Operations**   The vast majority of staff within a bank will reside in level one, as this level captures staff who own risk and are responsible for managing that risk.

For example, the Trading Desk own the market risk generated by their trading activity and are responsible for managing this market risk within their desk level limits.

Operations own the settlement of cash and securities and are responsible for ensuring the settlement takes place correctly.

Product Control own the P&L and balance sheet for the sales and trading desks and are responsible for ensuring these reports are on time, complete and accurate. Although the Desk and Product Control are categorized into the same line of defence, Product Control are still required to maintain their independence.

It is important to reflect on the principle that the Desk is responsible for internal control as much as Product Control. Throughout my career, I have witnessed ill-discipline and laziness from the Trading Desk, who have expected Product Control to tidy up their books, which can include adjusting the P&L for mismarked positions or inaccurate, untimely and incomplete

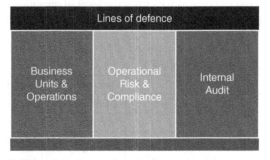

**FIGURE 7.4**   Lines of defence

bookings. An understanding of the three lines of defence enables Product Control to hold the Desk to account for the tasks they are responsible for performing.

**Line 2 – Corporate Risk Management**   The second line of defence is comprised of staff within corporate risk management, who oversee the design and operation of controls in the first line. Corporate risk management include functions such as operational risk and compliance.

**Line 3 – Internal Audit**   The third line of internal defence is Internal Audit, who provide the Board with independent assurance that key risks are being managed and controls are designed and operating effectively to manage these risks.

**Alternative Forms of the Three Lines of Defence**   As banking continues to evolve and further crises come to pass, there will inevitably be introspection regarding the suitability of the three-lined defence model. The Bank for International Settlements, for example, recently published a paper titled *The four lines of defence model for financial institutions*. In this paper the authors propose that a fourth line of defence should be created, comprising external audit and regulators, which aims to:

> …*assign a specific role to external parties (namely, external auditors and banking supervisors) in relation to the design of the internal control system, acknowledging that, although they remain outside the organisation's boundaries, they constitute a vital element of assurance and governance systems.*
>
> *As the four-lines-of-defence model intends to enhance coordination between external parties and internal auditors, greater communication is at the basis of its success.*[6]

Figure 7.5 illustrates external audit and regulators interacting with Internal Audit to form a fourth line of defence.

## Regulatory Requirements

When establishing a framework, the most pertinent consideration is to ensure that the framework complies with all relevant laws and regulations for the bank's entities that you have responsibility for. Failure to do this can result in fines, imprisonment and reputational damage for the bank and its officers.

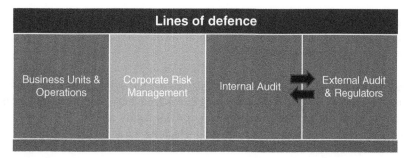

**FIGURE 7.5**   Four lines of defence

Each legal jurisdiction which a bank operates within will have its own regulatory supervisors and legal codes. For the purposes of this book, we will look at some of the regulatory requirements in the U.S.

**Sarbanes–Oxley (SOX)**   One of the primary regulatory pieces of the modern era that shapes a bank's internal control framework is the Investor Protection Act, or more commonly, the Sarbanes–Oxley Act (SOX). SOX legislation was passed into law by the U.S. government in 2002 in response to the collapse of Enron and WorldCom, whose demise damaged investor confidence in the internal control framework of publicly listed companies.

These collapses also damaged the integrity of those external auditors assigned to audit the control frameworks, resulting in the set-up of the Public Company Accounting Oversight Board to oversee the activities of the auditing profession.

SOX broadly applies to U.S. public companies, accounting firms and to non-U.S. companies issuing and registering securities in the U.S. Section 404 of the Act places an annual requirement on management regarding internal controls and procedures for financial reporting. Management are required to:

1. Accept responsibility for internal controls and procedures for financial reporting.
2. Assess their effectiveness.

In order to know what they are responsible for and need to assess, the great majority of companies and all CPA firms use COSO's definition of internal control.[7]

**Impact on Product Control**   As product control execute a series of controls which form part of the internal control framework, the effectiveness of these controls needs to be assessed each year. The operational risk team within the bank will require product control to confirm whether these controls are effective, which requires product control to evidence the existence and effectiveness of these controls. Ineffective controls will be risk assessed by the operational risk team and, where necessary, remediation undertaken.

External auditors who prepare or issue audit reports for the respective company are required to attest to and report on the assessment made by the management. These attestations will also appear in the bank's annual report.

**Dodd–Frank and the Volcker Rules**   Another primary regulatory piece of the modern era is the Dodd–Frank Wall Street Reform and Consumer Protection Act, which was made into law in 2010 as a result of the enormous financial and job losses that resulted from the GFC.

The main components of the Act that impact trading desks are:

1. Outlawing excessive risk taking in banks.
2. Taking away the risk of a bank being too big to fail.
3. Ending government bailout of banks.[8]

Section 619 of the Act, which is known as the *Volcker rule*, is focused on the first of those bullet points. It achieves this through prohibiting banks from engaging in proprietary trading or having an ownership interest in a hedge fund or private equity fund.[9]

There are a number of exemptions to the rule which for a trading desk include:

- Underwriting and market making activities: Inventory held must not exceed near-term demand of customers.

- Hedging of specific risks.
- Trading in government obligations: This includes trading in US government, agency, state and municipal obligations. Limited exemptions apply to foreign sovereigns or their political subdivisions.
- Certain trading activities of foreign banking entities: Foreign banking entities are not prohibited from trading, so long as the entities' trading decisions are made outside the U.S. and the principal risks are held beyond U.S. borders.
- Other exemptions: Repurchase and reverse repurchase agreements and transactions relating to liquidity management.[10] Spot foreign exchange and spot physical commodity transactions are also exempt.[11]

These rules came into effect on a staggered basis from 2014, with larger banks having to start complying earlier than smaller banks. The impact on banks from the Volcker rule has been substantial and has resulted in a significant reduction in proprietary trading within affected banks.

**Impact on Product Control**   The Volcker rule has a compliance and reporting regime which requires companies to report on the following metrics each month. This part of the rule directly impacts product control.

The metrics to be reported on are:

1. Risk
   - Limits and usage
   - Risk predict P&L
   - VaR
2. P&L attribution by
   - Existing positions
   - New trades
   - Other P&L

   The volatility of earnings also requires reporting.[12]
3. Customer facing trades
   - Inventory turnover
   - Ageing of positions
   - Customer vs. non-customer trade and value ratios.[13]

Product control are responsible for providing the regulator with the P&L attribution reports each month and will assist the business in providing data pertaining to customer facing trades.

As trading desks will have different activities such as client trading, proprietary trading, market making and hedging, in order to comply with the Volcker rule and make use of the available exemptions, the desk will need to establish different trading books/portfolios to segregate each type of activity. These additional books will need to be incorporated into product control's reporting, control and analysis.

This segregation of activities is especially important for market risk as they will be required to establish Volcker risk limits, generate Volcker risk reports and monitor overall compliance with the rule.

## Market Practice

The internal control framework a bank establishes is often influenced by the best practices which exist in the market. As product controllers rotate from one bank to another, particularly the heads of product control, it facilitates the sharing of knowledge about what controls have worked well in other banks. When a bank gets experience from several peers it can establish a framework based upon the best of those experiences.

In addition to this, as regulators review the internal control frameworks of banks in their jurisdiction, those frameworks which are seen to be working well can be used as a benchmark for the industry. For example, in Australia one of the prudential standards a bank needs to adhere to is CPS 220 Risk Management. One aspect of this prudential standard is that every three years a bank is required to perform a comprehensive review of their risk management framework. During this review a bank is required to compare its framework to that of an identified better practice, if one exists.

## Type of Business

A framework cannot be applied as a one-size-fits-all; it needs to be tailored to the business it is controlling. For example, a high-volume spot FX desk has very different characteristics to that of a structured credit desk. Consequently, the framework for each business needs to be tailored to its nature.

Table 7.2 illustrates the attributes for both a Spot FX and structured credit desks.

As you can see from Table 7.2, the desks are vastly different and require different internal control frameworks. For the spot FX desk, product control would focus on:

- **Trend in daily volumes** As the FX market is mature and competitive, the margins are very narrow. The notional transacted is seen as a big driver of P&L.
- **Exceptional new trades** New trades with a larger than usual trading spread and day one P&L would be validated.
- **Open risk** P&L from the desk's spot FX exposure would be validated using the FX delta on existing positions and the change in market rates. The drivers behind changes in the market rates would also be analysed.

For the structured credit desk, the following criteria are important for product control:

- **Trade bookings are complete.** As the name suggests, when this desk trades there are multiple trade bookings which covers both the trade with the client and the hedging transactions. Before the P&L can be reported all the trades need to be booked, which is not always a given.

**TABLE 7.2**  Comparing two trading desks

| Attribute | Spot FX | Structured credit |
|---|---|---|
| Volume | High | Low |
| Complexity | Low | High |
| Day 1 P&L | Low | High |
| Packaged trades | No | Yes |
| Technical skills required | Low | High |

- **Trade bookings are accurate.** Sometimes all of the risks (trade features) in a structured trade cannot be recorded in the RMS. Product control will check the RMS trade booking back to the trade's term sheet (similar to a confirmation) to ensure that the trade booking is accurate.
- **Un-modelled risk.** Although all the attributes of the trade booking are accurate, sometimes the trade will have a feature which cannot be valued accurately by the RMS. Product control need to be aware of this as they may need to make a model valuation adjustment.
- **Observable market data.** The curves and surfaces used to revalue the structured trade need to be reviewed to understand whether the pricing inputs are observable. If the pricing inputs are unobservable, product control may need to take a day one P&L reserve (under IFRS, not U.S. GAAP) and allocate the asset to level 3 of the fair value hierarchy.

As you can deduce from this comparison, each desk needs a tailored framework rather than a one size fits all model.

## EXAMPLE OF FRONT TO BACK INTERNAL CONTROLS

In this final part of the chapter we will look at an example of front to back internal controls for a trading desk. Whilst this example will not be a panacea and cover every single control, it does provide you with a flavour for what types of controls exist for a trading desk and which functions perform them.

In Figure 7.6 are four swimming lanes, with each swimming lane representing a function(s) of the bank and the activities they are responsible for performing. Each of the controls has a number (e.g., 1.1), and there is a description of the controls in Tables 7.3 and 7.4.

As you can see from Figure 7.6, within a bank there can be many systems which interact with each other in some shape or form. Along each of these flows are a series of controls which help the bank maintain an effective internal control framework. A good product controller is also a good "plumber" as they are familiar with the bank's "plumbing," which describes the flow of data between systems.

**TABLE 7.3**   Key to Table 7.4

| Abbreviation | Division |
|---|---|
| CR | Credit risk |
| FO | Front office |
| FR | Financial reporting |
| FSS | Finance shared service |
| MO | Middle office |
| MR | Market risk |
| OPS | Operations |
| PC | Product control |
| QRC | Qualitative risk control |
| RR | Regulatory reporting |

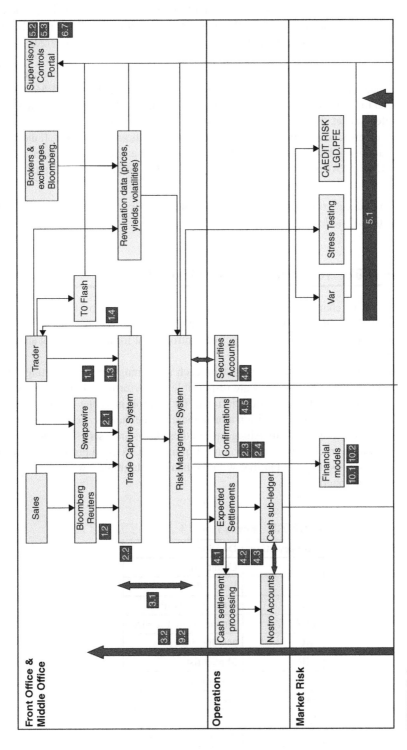

**FIGURE 7.6** Front to back controls

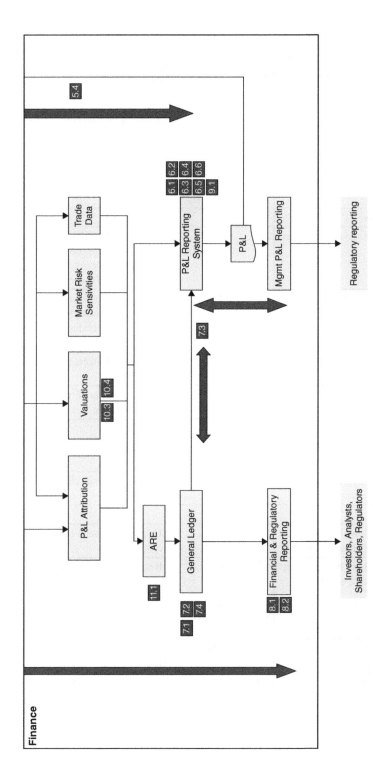

**FIGURE 7.6** *(Continued)*

**TABLE 7.4** Control framework

| Core controls within the front to back trade flow | | | |
|---|---|---|---|
| **1. Trade Capture** | **ID** | **Function** | **Description** |
| Trade input controls | 1.1 | MO | Direct trades approved by Middle Office |
| | 1.2 | FO | Trader approval for new trades captured manually or input by others |
| | 1.3 | MO | Trader Blotter checked by Middle Office |
| | 1.4 | FO | Trader authorization for booking amendments |
| **2. Trade Checks** | | | |
| Trade processing service providers | 2.1 | MO | MarkitSERV trades are matched between counterparties. (MarkitSERV is a trade processing and confirmation service for OTC derivatives.) |
| Internal trade generation | 2.2 | MO | Trade generation on internal trades is checked to ensure there are no one sided internal trades |
| Trade terms confirmed with counterparties | 2.3 | OPS | Broker reconciliation – confirm trade details and brokerage amounts with brokers |
| | 2.4 | OPS | Counterparty confirmation of documentation |
| **3. Inter System Checks** | | | |
| Trade Capture – RMS | 3.1 | FO IT | Integrity of feeds checked and confirmed |
| RMS – Operations, Risk Control and Finance Layers | 3.2 | ALL | Integrity of feeds checked and confirmed |
| **4. Settlements** | | | |
| Reconcile cash flows in RMS to cash flows in settlement system | 4.1 | OPS | Daily rec between expected and actual cash |
| Reconcile cash flows in settlement system to real world nostro balances | 4.2 | OPS | Reconciliation of actual cash entries on the external nostro, to settlement entries in the cash sub-ledger |
| | 4.3 | OPS | Cash breaks (nostro vs. settlement system) are identified and aged |
| Reconcile securities positions in RMS to real world clearer | 4.4 | OPS | Euroclear/Clearstream Settlement Reconciliation |
| Confirm coupon payments with counterparties | 4.5 | OPS | Counterparty confirmation on settlements |

*(continued)*

**TABLE 7.4** *(Continued)*

| Core controls within the front to back trade flow | | | |
|---|---|---|---|
| **1. Trade Capture** | **ID** | **Function** | **Description** |
| **5. Risk Control** | | | |
| Quantify market and credit risk exposures | 5.1 | MR/CR | Publish market and credit risk exposure reports |
| Front Office approve risk reports | 5.2 | FO | Trader approves market risk reports confirming they are accurate |
| Front Office approve risk limit breaches | 5.3 | FO | Front Office Mgmt approve/reject Market Risk limit breaches |
| Reconcile estimated MTM P&L using VaR to Actual MTM P&L | 5.4 | MR | Reconcile VaR to Product Control MTM P&L |
| **6. P&L** | | | |
| P&L is decomposed into the underlying attributes for validation | 6.1 | PC | Product Control consumes reports which attribute P&L to Trading Activity, MTM, Valuation Adjustments, Fees and charges |
| Trading activity P&L is reviewed and validated | 6.2 | PC | New and amended trades exceeding agreed thresholds are reviewed in order to validate the P&L |
| MTM P&L is reviewed and validated | 6.3 | PC | MTM P&L exceeding agreed thresholds are validated using a risk based P&L approach |
| Other P&L is reviewed and validated | 6.4 | PC | Funding, Valuation adjustments, Fees and charges are reviewed in order to validate the P&L |
| Actual P&L is reconciled to the T0 Flash | 6.5 | PC | Daily reconciliation between the Desk's T0 Flash & Product Control's actual P&L |
| Daily P&L commentary | 6.6 | PC | Daily P&L commentary is produced for those P&L attributes which have exceeded agreed thresholds |
| P&L is approved by the Front Office | 6.7 | FO | The Front Office approve the P&L published by Product Control |
| **7. Reconciliations** | | | |
| Balance sheet substantiations | 7.1 | PC | The balance sheet is substantiated periodically |
| | 7.2 | PC | Unsupported balances are aged and escalated according to agreed thresholds |
| P&L reconciliations | 7.3 | PC | The P&L is reconciled between the GL – P&L reporting system – Management reporting system (if applicable) |
| Intercompany reconciliations | 7.4 | FSS | Open trades and receivables/payables are reconciled within the Group |

*(continued)*

**TABLE 7.4** *(Continued)*

| Core controls within the front to back trade flow | | | |
|---|---|---|---|
| **1. Trade Capture** | **ID** | **Function** | **Description** |
| **8. Financial and Regulatory Reports** | | | |
| Financial reports are reviewed | 8.1 | FR | The financial reports are reviewed and analysed to ensure their content is accurate |
| Regulatory reports are reviewed | 8.2 | RR | The regulatory reports that are submitted to various regulatory bodies are reviewed and analysed to ensure their content is accurate |
| **9. Other** | | | |
| P&L adjustments | 9.1 | PC | P&L adjustments are reported, escalated and approved |
| New products and change requests | 9.2 | ALL | New products and change requests are submitted by the Front Office for approval by relevant stakeholders prior to trading |
| **10. Valuation** | | | |
| Financial model approval | 10.1 | QRC | Financial models which derive fair value of open trades are approved |
| Financial model validation | 10.2 | QRC | Financial models which derive fair value of open trades are recalibrated periodically |
| Independent price verification | 10.3 | PC | Independent Price Verification of market data used to derive fair value of open trades |
| Valuation adjustments | 10.4 | PC | Valuation adjustments are quantified and reported and approved by Trading Desk (Bid-Offer, Model, Day 1, FVA, CVA/DVA) |
| **11. Financial Accounting** | | | |
| Financial Accounting | 11.1 | FR | Single source of financial accounting rules stored in the Accounting Rules Engine (ARE) |

There are times when these internal controls fail, both within product control and in other functions, and this can have serious and even deadly consequences for a bank. In Chapter 23, we will examine instances where this has occurred.

# NOTES

1. The Committee of Sponsoring Organizations of the Treadway Commission. All rights reserved. https://www.coso.org/Pages/default.aspx.

2. The Committee of Sponsoring Organizations of the Treadway Commission. All rights reserved. COSO, Internal Control – Integrated Framework – Executive Summary, May 2013, page 3. https://www.coso.org/Documents/990025P-Executive-Summary-final-may20.pdf.
3. Ibid.
4. Ibid.
5. Committee of Sponsoring Organizations of the Treadway Commission (COSO). "Internal Control – Integrated Framework – Executive Summary," May 2013, page 3. https://www.coso.org/Documents/990025P-Executive-Summary-final-may20.pdf.
6. Isabella Arndorfer and Andrea Minto. "The 'four lines of defence model' for financial institutions: Taking the three-lines-of-defence model further to reflect specific governance features of regulated financial institutions," Financial Stability Institute, Bank for International Settlements, Occasional Paper No 11, December 2015, page 10, http://www.bis.org/fsi/fsipapers11.pdf.
7. The Institute of Internal Auditors. "SARBANES-OXLEY SECTION 404: A Guide for Management by Internal Controls Practitioners." 2nd Edition, January 2008. https://global.theiia.org/standards-guidance/Public%20Documents/Sarbanes-Oxley_Section_404_–_A_Guide_for_Management_2nd_edition_1_08.pdf.
8. White House website. "Economy: Middle Class, Dodd-Frank Wall Street Reform," Accessed January 2017. https://www.whitehouse.gov/economy/middle-class/dodd-frank-wall-street-reform.
9. United States Congress. Dodd-Frank Wall Street Reform and Consumer Protection Act. "Summary: H.R.4173 – 111th Congress (2009–2010)" (United States). https://www.congress.gov/bill/111th-congress/house-bill/4173.
10. U.S. Securities and Exchange Commission, Press Release, Agencies Issue Final Rules Implementing the Volcker Rule, 2013-258, 10 December 2013, https://www.sec.gov/News/PressRelease/Detail/PressRelease/1370540476526.
11. Norton Rose Fulbright. "Implications of the Volcker Rule for Foreign Banking Entities," March 2014. http://www.nortonrosefulbright.com/knowledge/publications/113806/implications-of-the-volcker-rule-for-foreign-banking-entities.
12. Morrison & Foerster LLP. "A User's Guide to The Volcker Rule," February 2014, page 28. http://www.iflr.com/pdfs/A-users-guide-to-the-Volcker-Rule.pdf.
13. Ibid.

# Three

# Profit and Loss Controls

O ne of the primary responsibilities of product control is to publish a P&L report for the sales and trading desk. Before this report can be published, product control need to have a high level of assurance that the results are an accurate reflection of the Desk's performance. This assurance is gained through the execution of a series of controls which we will look at in Part Three of this book.

Figure 8.1 illustrates the core P&L controls which we will review in this part of the book. As we step into each control, we will review how these controls are typically performed and explore why they are necessary to safeguard the P&L.

# CHAPTER 8

# System Feeds, End of Day Rates and Profit and Loss Estimates

**B** efore product control can commence reporting the desk's P&L, they require access to complete, timely and accurate data. In this chapter we will look at three sets of data which are critical to reporting the P&L. These are system feeds, end of day rates and the front office P&L estimate.

## SYSTEM FEEDS

Successful and timely feeds of data from upstream systems into the P&L reporting system is critical for product control to be able to report the P&L. In Figure 8.1 I have illustrated an optimal flow of trades and data which will be used for P&L reporting.

The starting point in Figure 8.1 is the capture of trades booked by sales and trading staff into a trade booking system (also known as a trade capture system). Banks may have multiple trade booking systems to suit the needs of each business.

Once a trade is captured in the booking system it then feeds the risk management system (RMS) which values the trade and quantifies its risk using end of day rates and financial measurement and risk models. A bank may use several RMSs such as Murex, Calypso, OpenLink, Wall Street or in-house software.

The RMS then feeds the general ledger (GL) (usually via an accounting rules engine), where the data is converted into financial accounting entries which generate a P&L and balance sheet for each business.

The P&L reporting system then takes this data and prepares reports for product control to use for P&L reporting. The P&L will usually be decomposed (or attributed) into several main components:

  **i)** P&L from new and amended trades
 **ii)** P&L from market movements (MTM), which measures the change in value of existing positions
**iii)** Other P&L, which will capture items such as fees and funding.

The MTM P&L is further attributed into its product and pricing drivers, such as credit, rates, FX, volatility, and so forth. This is illustrated in Figure 8.2.

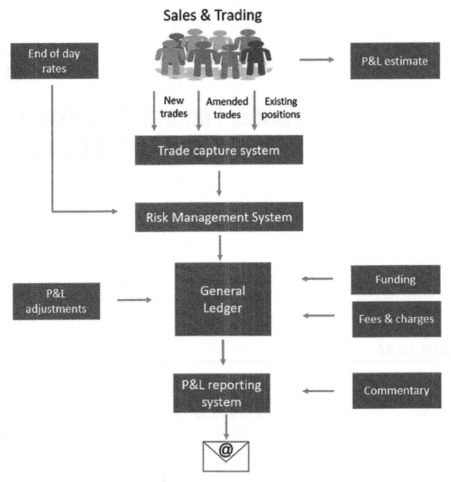

**FIGURE 8.1** Optimal controls over the P&L[1]

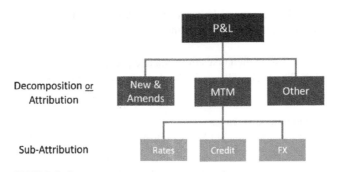

**FIGURE 8.2** Decomposing or attributing the P&L

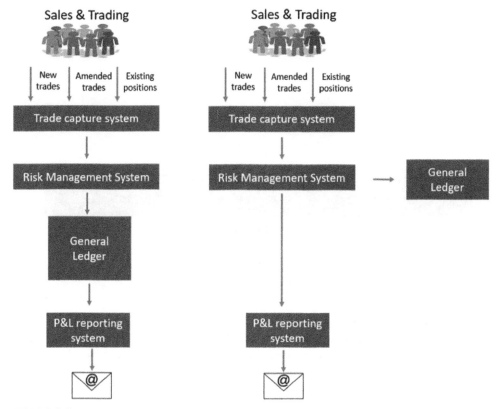

**FIGURE 8.3** Alternative P&L reporting feeds

Now, not every bank will take a feed from the GL into a P&L reporting system, as most banks will use a sub-optimal approach by taking a direct feed from the RMS into the P&L reporting system. This alternative approach is illustrated on the right-hand side in Figure 8.3. Under this approach, the RMS still feeds the GL but the GL does not feed the P&L reporting system. As the financial reports for the bank will be prepared using data in the GL, this approach requires product control to spend additional time reconciling the GL and P&L reporting system, which is known as a FOBO (front office to back office) reconciliation.

## END OF DAY

The trade capture, RMS and GL systems will have a time at which they perform an end of day cut-off. The end of day cut-off is necessary as it enables each system to run batches which produce end of day reports that are used by multiple functions including product control. Any trades, amendments, prices and so on, which are entered after the cut-off will no longer be captured in the reporting for that business day.

When product control is using this data in P&L reporting, it needs to know if the data is complete and accurate. The following functions assist with this awareness, which is illustrated in Figure 8.4.

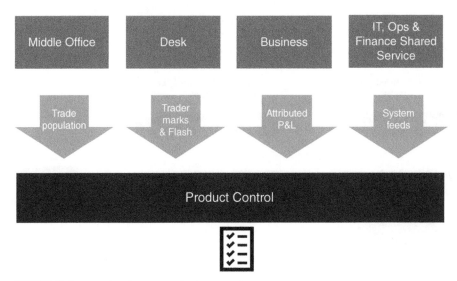

**FIGURE 8.4**   Supply of data and checks to product control

**Middle office** should ideally provide product control with an *end of day checkout*, which acts like the passing of a baton in a team relay. It is through this checkout that product control is made aware of whether there are any issues with trade bookings. This can include existing trades which:

- Missed the end of day cut-off
- Been booked with inaccuracies
- Contain valuation issues.

**The desk** is responsible for ensuring all open positions have a current price that can be used to revalue open position in the RMS, which can be a mix of trader and independent prices. The broader business is responsible for providing an attributed P&L from the RMS for new trades (sales and trading margins) and existing trades (market moves).

**IT** are responsible for ensuring that the end of day system batches (RMS, P&L reporting system, GL and any other pertinent systems) are run successfully for delivery of data at the pre-agreed times. In addition to this, **IT, Operations and the Finance Shared Service** have a joint responsibility for ensuring the integrity of the interconnectedness in the front to back (f2b) systems (e.g., RMS » GL).

It is imperative that the inter-system feeds are monitored and any breaks or cut-off issues are reported to product control so that this can be factored into their review of new trades and the broader P&L.

## END OF DAY RATES

Each day a bank needs to source yields, prices, volatilities, correlations, basis spreads, credit spreads (collectively "rates") to revalue open trades measured at fair value. A bank will source

**FIGURE 8.5** Sourcing end of day rates

rates from their trading desk and third party providers. Most banks will have a mix of rate sources, with investment banks typically having a higher proportion of trader-marked rates than those of commercial banks (Figure 8.5).

Product control's valuation control team will perform some, but not all, of the checks for end of day rates. I will however elaborate on all the checks performed over the end of day rates.

## Externally Sourced Rates

For rates which are sourced externally, the bank will have a rates validation team which can be located in product control (valuation control), operations or market risk. I think it is sensible for the function performing independent price verification (IPV) to also be responsible for collecting the external rates, as this set-up makes it easier to ensure that all non-independent rates are being captured through the IPV process.

Rates can be sourced from providers such as:

- Bloomberg
- Reuters
- ICE data services (IDS purchased IDC and SuperDerivatives)
- Brokers
- Markit.

Figure 8.6 illustrates the SuperDerivatives pricing process. As not every data point a bank needs can be observed in the market, a certain amount of modelling may be required.

When the rates are imported each day, the following three typical checks are performed, which are illustrated in Figure 8.7.

**Completeness** The first check the rates validation team perform is to confirm that all the necessary rates have been sourced. This is a very simple check as it will be obvious if a rate has not been populated. If this occurs, the team will use contacts in product control, market risk and the desk to establish an alternative rate source.

It is important to have governance around establishing new rate sources or making changes to existing ones. Most banks will bring such events to the attention of their valuation committee for either approval or noting.

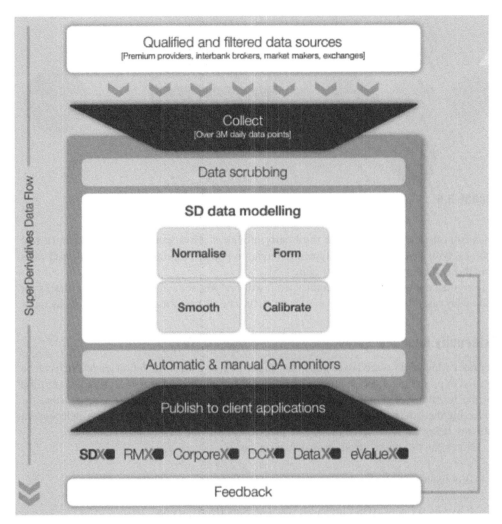

**FIGURE 8.6** SuperDerivatives pricing service
Source: SuperDerivatives Inc

**Stale Rates** The second and third checks are based around the daily change in rates. A stale rate is a rate which has not changed for a period of time. Stale rate checks indicate that there could be a problem with the rate source not updating correctly.

As some rates genuinely don't change daily (e.g., central bank target cash rates), an unchanged rate for three weeks can be genuine. Such factors need to be considered when establishing the number of days a rate is unchanged before labelling it as stale.

**Significant Changes** If a rate changes significantly from one day to the next, it could indicate there is a problem with the rate source. Banks will establish movement thresholds (e.g., +/– 5%), and changes above this threshold will be considered exceptions which require investigation.

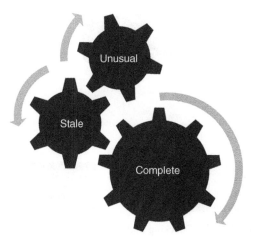

**FIGURE 8.7**  External rate checks

It is important to consider that just because a rate has been sourced from a third party, that provider's independence is not always a guarantee of quality. Independent rates need to be reviewed to ensure they are reflective of fair value. This is especially pertinent for illiquid rates.

---

**EXAMPLE**

An independent rate provider is required to provide the bank with a volatility surface out to 10 years for the currency pair GBP/ZAR. This will be used to revalue any FX options the bank holds in this currency pair. Let's assume the market is only quoting volatility out to 5 years, which means the rate provider has to engineer a volatility surface beyond 5 years.

To do this, they may make assumptions about the difference in volatility between the last known observable tenor, 5 years and 6, 7, 8, 9 and 10 years. The assumption may be a simple spread of +1% for each year or something more complex.

---

It is important that product control is cognizant of these assumptions as valuation adjustments may be required to bring related financial assets and liabilities to their fair value.

## Trader Sourced Rates

Trader sourced rates are also checked for completeness and accuracy and undergo the following checks, which are illustrated in Figure 8.8.

**Completeness**  Trader marks need to be updated daily, with the desk head and COO being notified of exceptions. A trader who repeatedly fails to update their rates can expect to face disciplinary action.

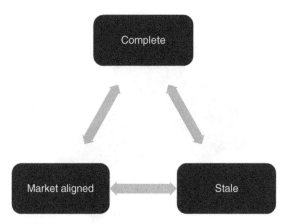

**FIGURE 8.8**   Checking trader marks

A lot of banks have also implemented the concept of "one instrument–one price". This concept aims to prevent multiple prices being used to revalue the same financial instrument across two or more desks within the bank. Under this arrangement, a financial instrument will be assigned an owner from the trading desk. It is the owner's responsibility to set the rate that is used for end of day revaluation.

For example, the scenario in Table 8.1 can occur where the bank has not elected to maintain a single price for a financial instrument. In this example, three different desks are trading the same GE bond, and have all set different prices to revalue their positions.

**Stale Rates**   Trader prices are also monitored to ensure prices are published every day that reflect the current market and are not the prior day's rates which have been rolled forward due to error, laziness or fraud. Again, their management should monitor these statistics and review breaches seriously.

**Market Aligned**   There are three types of checks performed by product control to verify that the trader's marks are aligned to the market.

i) IPV. At the end of every month, and sometimes during the month, the valuations team will independently verify, via the IPV process, that trader rates are aligned to fair value (fair value is the market's price for the financial instrument). We will look at IPV in Chapter 15.

ii) Benchmarking. Where readily observable prices are available from the market, product control can conduct *benchmarking*, which compares trader marks to market prices. Benchmarking is less detailed and accurate than IPV as it uses fewer price sources than IPV, tolerates

**TABLE 8.1**   Multiple prices for one financial instrument

| Trader | Desk | Financial Instrument | Position | Price |
|---|---|---|---|---|
| Mike Jones | Asia Credit | GE 7% S/A 2020 | $10m | 99.10 |
| Adam Reynolds | Global Strategic Trading | GE 7% S/A 2020 | $20m | 99.11 |
| Kylie James | Americas Credit | GE 7% S/A 2020 | $(2)m | 99.095 |

larger price variances and has fewer and less technical staff reviewing price variances. However, it still provides assurance that the trader mark is aligned to the market.

iii) Implicit IPV. When prices move significantly and this has a material impact on the P&L, product control review external market data and related news to understand whether the changes are reasonable. This process can be referred to as *implicit IPV*.

## P&L ESTIMATE

The front office P&L estimate, also known as *the flash*, is an important process that is run by the desk on T+0. The purpose of the flash is to provide senior management and other key stakeholders (including product control) with a timely estimate of how much P&L the desk generated on the day.

As the flash is intended to reflect the full day's P&L, it is produced at the end of the trading day (T+0) and should capture P&L from:

- New trades
- Trade amendments
- MTM P&L from the existing portfolio
- Funding
- Fees and charges
- Changes in reserves (valuation adjustments).

Basically, the flash should capture ALL components of the P&L that will be included in the official P&L reported by product control. An example of a flash is included in Table 8.2.

**TABLE 8.2**  Example of a trader flash

| FX desk P&L | |
|---|---|
| **Attribute** | **T0 Flash** |
| New trades | $70,000 |
| Modified trades | −$11,000 |
| | |
| **MTM P&L** | **−$572,000** |
| AUD | $6,000 |
| CAD | −$18,000 |
| GBP | −$560,000 |
| | |
| Funding | −$7,000 |
| Fees and charges | −$6,000 |
| Reserves | $0 |
| | |
| **Total P&L** | **−$526,000** |

When the P&L is material, the flash should include a commentary which highlights the P&L drivers. For example, using the flash in Table 8.2, the traders provide the following blurb on the trading results:

*Long GBP and market sold off 2 cents on fears regarding Brexit vote*

As the flash is an indication of the desk's earnings, it needs to be compared to the P&L produced by product control. We will look at this control in Chapter 14.

That concludes our review of the tasks and activities that are necessary for product control to commence work on P&L reporting.

## NOTE

1. People icons sourced from http://free-illustrations.gatag.net/tag/%E4%BB%B2%E9%96%93-%E3%83%81%E3%83%BC%E3%83%A0.

# CHAPTER 9

# Review of New and Amended Trades

The review of new and amended trades forms a key part of the control framework within a bank. This chapter will look at why these controls are necessary and examine how they are executed.

## NEW TRADES

### Why New Trades Are Generated

Each day the sales and trading desks accept client orders and trades in the market to generate profits and hedge risk for their bank (Figure 9.1).

When a client trades with a bank, the bank's sales desk will earn a fee that is usually included in the trade price rather than as an explicit payment. This fee is known internally within the bank as margin, spread, edge or sales credits. In Figure 9.2 the sales desk has earned a margin of $0.20 by purchasing a bond at $1.00 from the trading desk and selling it on to the client for $1.20.

The sales desk will attempt to make as much margin as possible without being so large that the client withdraws its business from the bank (banks will maintain policies regarding this). As margins earned on a vanilla trade will typically be consistent from one day to the next, to increase sales revenue the sales person needs to either increase their client base or the frequency with which his clients trade. The trading desk may also add their own margin to the client transaction which is retained in their P&L.

The trading desk can also profit from trading off the client flow, with larger volumes providing greater opportunities for profits to be extracted. Traders like receiving client orders from opposite directions (buy and sell) as they can provide a price to both clients without having to cross the bid offer spread, which is a cost in trading.

In addition to trading off the flow, the trading desk will use their expertise to take directional positions in the market and hope the market moves in their favour. This is known as proprietary trading. The size of these directional positions will be limited by their market risk limits, which have become more restrictive since the Volcker rule was introduced.

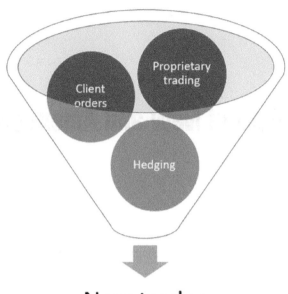

# New trades

**FIGURE 9.1**   Drivers of new trades

**FIGURE 9.2**   Drivers of new trades
Note: You will not always see a separate trade between sales and trading.
This is more commonly seen for FX trading and when selling to clients
through a subsidiary

## Reviewing New Trades

Reviewing new trades is an important control, as once a new trade passes inception, it becomes one of thousands of trades within a portfolio. Day one therefore provides a unique opportunity to identify unusual or exceptional trades. Figure 9.3 provides an overview of the process required to perform a review of new trades.

**Step 1 – Extracting the New Trade Data**   The review of new trades begins with the extraction of data from either the risk management system (RMS), P&L reporting system or general

**FIGURE 9.3**   Steps in the new trade process

**TABLE 9.1** New trades

| Trade | 1 | 2 |
|---|---|---|
| Salesperson | Kathleen Marcella | Nick Woodward |
| Trader | David Blair | Dean Jones |
| Trade Date | 16/01/2015 | 16/01/2015 |
| Time traded | 07:59:00 | 09:05:00 |
| Financial Instrument | GE 3.50% S/A 31/12/2017 | Interest Rate Swap |
| Buy/Sell | Buy | Receive 2.00% Pay EURIBOR |
| Trade Price | 91.50 | 2.00% |
| Entry Mkt Price | 91.60 | 1.99% |
| Closing Mkt price | 91.65 | 1.97% |
| Nominal | 10,000,000 | 100,000,000 |
| Delta (shift up in yields) | (1,000) | (10,000) |
| Currency | USD | EUR |
| Value Date | 18/01/2015 | 31/01/2015 |
| Maturity Date | 31/12/2017 | 31/01/2018 |
| Day count | 30/360 | 30/360 |
| Calculation frequency | N/A | Quarterly |
| Payment frequency | Semi annually | Quarterly |
| Counterparty | Boost Hedge Fund | Treasury |
| Counterparty type | External | Internal |
| Collateralized | N/A | No |
| Sales margin | 5,000 | – |
| **Trade entry P&L** | **10,000** | **10,000** |
| Intraday MTM | 5,000 | 20,000 |
| **Total P&L** | **15,000** | **30,000** |

ledger (GL), whichever is the most detailed, complete and consistent set of data within the firm. Consistency in this context refers to having the same end of day population of trades and market values as would be consumed by the GL for external reporting.

The new trade data extraction is automatically performed via overnight system batches, which produce and deliver reports to product control each morning. Alternatively, product control may have to log into the RMS each morning to manually extract the data.

The data that can be extracted to perform the new trade review is dependent upon the functionality within the RMS. For example, the market price at trade execution is not always available, as the RMS will need to have a live feed of market prices to capture this data. Assuming there are no limitations on what the RMS can provide, the fields in Table 9.1 are a good baseline to commence with.

The following is a description of these fields.

■ Legal entity: The legal entity is the company within the banking group that has been used to execute the trade.

- Trader: Knowing who on the trading desk is responsible for the trade provides a contact point should any issues arise.
- Trade date: The day the trade was executed. A bank can elect to financially account for trades on a trade or settlement date basis.
- Time traded: The time the trade was executed. This field assists in attributing the new trade P&L to changes in intraday market movements.
- Financial instrument: This indicates what the desk has traded.
- Buy/Sell (or alternatively Pay/Rec): This field indicates the direction of the trade.
- Trade price: Trade price is the level at which the trade was executed.
- Notional or nominal or face value: Notional indicates the size of the trade.
- Delta: Delta is a risk sensitivity generated by the bank's internal risk models. For linear financial instruments, it is the main form of market risk. This field assists product control with attributing new trade P&L. [delta × (closing price *less* traded price)]
- Currency: This is the currency in which the trade is denominated.
- Value date: The value date, also known as the effective, start date or settlement date, is when the purchase or sale settles (security and cash are exchanged) and when interest periods commence.
- Maturity date: The maturity date determines when the trade will be derecognized and is the final day a trade should be on the bank's books.
- Day count: The day count determines how interest is calculated on the financial instrument. (See Chapter 6.)
- Counterparty and counterparty type: These fields indicate who the desk has traded with, which determines if the trade is deemed external, intra-company or inter-company.
- Collateralized: This field indicates whether a credit support annex (CSA) is in place between the bank and the counterparty for OTC derivatives. These fields impact the trade's valuation as it determines which yield curve should be used to discount future cash flows.
- Sales margin: Sales margin records how much money the sales desk earned from the client trade and will be zero if trading internally or with an interbank counterparty.
- Trade entry P&L: This field quantifies the P&L resulting from the difference between the trade price and the market price when the trade reaches the RMS. [Position × (market price@entry *less* traded price).] A bank would need a live price feed to generate this data.

For trade number one, the trading desk have generated an entry profit of $5,000, which is the total trade entry P&L of $10,000 less the sales margin of $5,000.

**Step 2 – Identifying Which Trades Should Be Reviewed in More Detail**   As hundreds of thousands of new trades will enter a bank each day, product control cannot perform a detailed review of every one of these trades, nor is it necessary. Product control need to adopt predefined criteria that highlights only a small population of trades for further review.

The exception criteria can be simple or dynamic, but should avoid being too simplistic as it may fail to consider the characteristics of each business whilst also avoid being too complicated, as it risks human error in its application.

Where sales trades can be distinguished from the trading desk (e.g., for an FX business), it is appropriate for the criteria to be tailored for a sales environment. For example, as sales desks do not have any responsibility to run or hedge the risk from client trades, they should not be incurring any losses. So, for new trades executed by the sales desk, a lower threshold for losses would be appropriate (such as zero) compared to the trading desk.

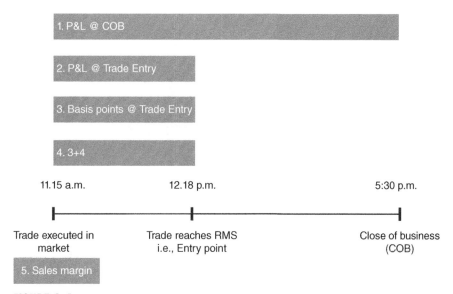

**FIGURE 9.4** New trade threshold criteria

There are several criteria that a bank can employ to highlight exceptional trades. Figure 9.4 illustrates some of these criteria, which we will review in more detail.

The first four criteria will be relevant for trading desks, whilst the fifth will be relevant for sales desks only.

**1. P&L Measured at Close of Business (COB)** The P&L at the COB is the P&L resulting from the difference between the COB price (end of day price and COB price are one and the same) and the traded price.

The primary benefit of this criterion is its simplicity, whilst its drawback is that the COB values will include intraday mark-to-market (MTM) P&L, which is not new trade P&L in its strictest sense, but rather P&L from market movements.

For example, a British client who exports goods to the U.S. wants to buy GBP and sell USD through their bank. In Figure 9.5 the sales desk sells GBP/USD at a price of 1.55 to the client, earning a margin of 0.0005 or 5 pips. The trading desk have decided to run a short GBP and long USD spot FX exposure.

Let's assume this trade was executed at 9:30 a.m. when the market price was 1.5495 and subsequent price fluctuations are illustrated in Figure 9.6.

At the end of day, the price used to revalue the open trading position is 1.5480, which generates an intraday MTM profit of 0.0010 or 10 pips [-1 × (1.5485 less 1.5495)] for the

**FIGURE 9.5** New trade threshold criteria

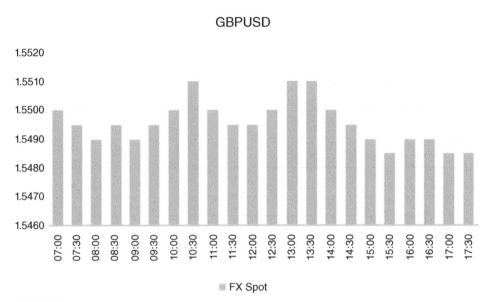

**FIGURE 9.6**   Intraday GBP/USD Spot FX prices

trader's short GBP position. This is illustrated in Table 9.2. Even though the trading desk generated zero entry P&L on the new trade, the day one P&L will include the intraday MTM profit of 10 pips, which is not new trade revenue in the strictest sense.

**2. P&L Generated at Point of Entry**   The trade entry P&L is very useful data as it is generated by valuing the new trade when it is first recorded in the RMS using a live market data feed. The product controller needs to be made aware of any delays in booking the trade in the RMS as this will affect the entry level P&L. For example, in Figure 9.4 the trade was executed at 11.15 a.m. but the RMS did not receive the trade until 12.18 p.m. Due to this delay, the entry P&L will reflect the market rates at 12.18 p.m. rather than 11.15 a.m. If the P&L on the trade is material, product control will need to review the market price range between the two times to validate the entry level P&L.

The main benefit of this approach is that the P&L will not be corrupted by intraday MTM noise. I don't see a significant drawback to this approach.

**TABLE 9.2**   New trade P&L

| Desk | Trade | Position | Trade price | Market price @ entry | Trade entry P&L (pips) | Market price @ close | Day 1 P&L (pips) |
|------|-------|----------|-------------|----------------------|------------------------|----------------------|------------------|
| Trading | 1 | −1 | 1.5495 | 1.5495 | 0 | 1.5485 | 10 |
|  |  |  |  |  |  |  |  |
| Sales | 2 | 1 | 1.5495 | 1.5495 | 0 | 1.5485 | −10 |
| Sales | 3 | −1 | 1.55 | 1.5495 | 5 | 1.5485 | 15 |
|  |  |  |  | Sales Total | 5 |  | 5 |

**TABLE 9.3**   EUR OIS bid offer spreads

| Product – Overnight Index Swaps (OIS) | | |
|---|---|---|
| **Currency** | **Tenor** | **Spread (bps)** |
| EUR | 3m | 0.20 |
| | 9m | 0.35 |
| | 1y | 0.35 |
| | 2y | 0.50 |
| | 3y | 0.50 |
| | 4y | 1.00 |
| | 5y | 1.00 |
| | 10y | 1.00 |
| | 15y | 2.00 |
| | 20y | 2.00 |

**3. Basis Points at Point of Entry**   The basis point margin generated at point of entry is derived by comparing the market price, at the time of entry, to the traded price. This is useful data as it can be used to identify those trades which have traded off market

When using this criterion, you need to be aware of pricing inputs included in the trade price but not included in the RMS revaluation price. This may include pricing add-ons such as bid offer, CVA, DVA and FVA.

As most RMS revalue derivatives using mid-prices, using the bid offer spread to set acceptable basis point variances is one approach a bank may use. For example, a one-year EUR OIS trade generated entry P&L of +0.40 basis points. Using Table 9.3, the basis points attributable to half the bid offer spread (i.e., mid vs. bid or mid vs. offer) is only 0.175 basis points. As the trade exceeds this by 0.225 basis points, a more detailed review of the trade is required to establish the reasons for the variance.

The main benefit to this approach is that it can identify exceptions that a monetary threshold never could. The flip side to this is that P&L size is not considered in highlighting exceptional trades. This means that trades with negligible P&L will also be highlighted for review, which is not conducive to a risk/reward paradigm. For example, if a new EUR OIS one-year trade generated a 45 basis point profit but P&L of only $275.00, the criteria would flag this deal up for review. However, if the average new trade P&L is $25,000 and the average daily P&L for the desk is $750,000, it makes little sense to spend time reviewing this trade. Additionally, as each financial instrument will have differing bid offer spreads, a significant amount of work is required to establish appropriate thresholds.

**4. The Basis Points and P&L Generated at Point of Entry**   This in my opinion is the most useful criteria to identify trades that require a more detailed review. I have this view as it incorporates both an instrument level pricing threshold (basis points) and a materiality threshold ($).

The only drawback to this approach, which in my view is worth it, is that it will take additional time to set up and maintain the basis point thresholds as the margins will need to be periodically recalibrated to the market.

**TABLE 9.4** Possible review criteria for sales trades

| | | % of Notional for Profits only | |
|---|---|---|---|
| **Financial instrument** | **P&L threshold** | **G10** | **Emerging Markets** |
| Spot FX | $(0)k or $20k | 0.200% | 0.350% |
| Interest rate swaps | $(0)k or $50k | 0.300% | 0.400% |
| Corporate bonds | $(0)k or $50k | 0.015% | 0.040% |
| Government bonds | $(0)k or $20k | 0.010% | 0.030% |

**5. Sales Desk – P&L and Percentage of Notional** The margins earned by the sales desk should be fairly consistent on a day to day basis. Additionally, as the sales desk don't run market or credit risk they should never incur a loss on a client trade unless they are providing a new client with a short-term incentive to trade with the bank. It is with these points in mind that product control can construct criteria to catch and review those sales trades which fall outside the norm.

To develop appropriate criteria to review sales trades, product control need to understand how sales margins are applied across each of the business areas and products. P&L and percentage of notional can be appropriate criteria to use when controlling a sales desk. Similar to the OIS bid–offer matrix, a matrix can be established by financial instrument type and or market. Table 9.4 is an example of such a matrix.

Unlike new trade P&L for the trading desk, the point at which sales revenue is measured will always be the same; namely, the point of entry. The P&L will always be the difference between the client price and the price taken from the trading desk.

The main benefit to this approach is that it is tailored to individual markets and instruments, which should mean that it highlights genuine exceptions. For example, in Table 9.4 any new interest rate swaps in a G10 currency that have a loss will be reviewed, as will profits greater than $50,000 where the margin exceeds 30 basis points. Note that losses only have a monetary threshold.

The main drawback is the time investment required to establish the thresholds and periodically recalibrate them. Additionally, it can be helpful to quantity the P&L on all trades with a counterparty. For example, on [a given date], a sales desk executed 20 Spot FX trades with counterparty ABC, each of which generated a $10,000 margin. Individually these trades wouldn't be flagged for review, but collectively they represent material counterparty P&L which is worth understanding.

Even on trading books it would be helpful to review the total P&L per counterparty and drill down into specific trades if it's deemed necessary.

**Step 3 – How to Review a New Trade** Now that we have determined how to identify trades that require further review, we are now going to look at how to review an exceptional new trade. The purpose of this step is to:

- Determine whether the P&L can be reported.
- Determine whether any valuation adjustments are required before reporting the P&L.
- Understand how the desk generated the P&L.

Figure 9.7 presents a decision tree that illustrates the typical high-level steps that product control will consider in their review of new trades. Although I do not present it in this flow

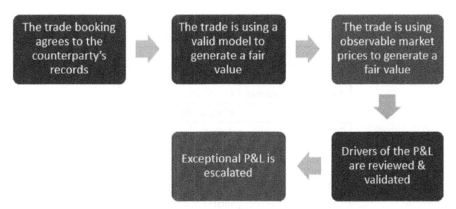

**FIGURE 9.7** Considerations in a new trade review

diagram, some banks will have an extra decision point where the product controller is required to consider whether the trade is exotic. If the trade is considered exotic, there are usually additional reviews and approvals required from valuations, market risk, accounting policy and the head of the trading desk or business, before the P&L is reported.

**The Trade Booking Agrees to the Counterparty's Records**  In Chapter 4 we learnt that a trade should only be recognized if the bank has entered a contract with a counterparty. With this in mind, the first step in determining whether the new trade's P&L is valid, is to confirm that the trade is a true reflection of a legally enforceable contract between the bank and the counterparty.

Product control should be made aware, via an end of day check out from operations or middle office, as to whether the RMS booking is an accurate reflection of the trade agreed with the counterparty.

Operations will check, via trade confirmations, whether the counterparty agrees with the trade particulars booked by the desk. If there are discrepancies, the desk need to either correct the error or get the counterparty to amend their records. If the RMS booking is incorrect, operations and the desk need to make product control aware of what trade features require amending, which can be used to determine the necessary adjustments to the P&L, balance sheet and note disclosures.

In some banks this end of day checkout may not actually occur, which means that product control rely on negative communication; namely, if they aren't advised, the trades booked are assumed to be accurate and complete.

You should be aware that during the confirmation process, counterparties may not respond immediately, which can lead to a confirmation remaining outstanding for days. Secondly, trades with a deferred start date may not be confirmed by operations until a few days before the start date. For example, if the start date is T+11, the confirmation process may not commence until T+8. Rogue traders like to use deferred settlement trades to conceal their actual P&L.

**The Trade is Using a Valid Model to Generate a Fair Value**  As discussed in Chapter 6, where there isn't an explicit price to derive the fair value of a financial instrument, the firm will use financial models to achieve this.

**TABLE 9.5**   OIS trade example

| | |
|---|---|
| Sales | Scott Quinnell |
| Trader | George Smith |
| Notional | £1,000,000 |
| Financial Instrument | Overnight Index Swap |
| Counterparty | Garfield PLC |
| Maturity | 1 year |
| Pay/Rec | Receive 0.31%<br>Pay SONIA |
| Payment frequency | Monthly |
| Currency | GBP |
| Collateralized | No |

In most banks, quantitative risk control (QRC) will ensure the most appropriate models are being used to value each financial instrument and will perform a periodic recalibration of the financial models. This involves comparing the valuation produced by the models to the market's valuation and if there are differences, the model will be recalibrated (adjusted).

Product control (or valuation control) need to be familiar with which models are used to revalue the trading portfolio in the event the desk decide to deviate to a new model or trade a new product. When this occurs, product control should consult QRC to ensure the model is appropriate for the desk's use. In some cases a model valuation adjustment is required, which we will look at in Chapter 16.

**The Trade is Using Observable Market Prices to Generate a Fair Value**   Before we can report the new trade P&L, we need to ensure that the trade's valuation aligns to fair value. As the RMS end of day prices will not usually incorporate bid–offer and other valuation adjustments, it is unusual for the RMS end of day prices to align to fair value.

To understand these valuation adjustments, we will look at them from a trade pricing perspective. Chapter 16 provides further details on valuation adjustments.

Table 9.5 illustrates a client trade where the desk receives a fixed yield of 0.31% and pays a floating yield referencing SONIA (Sterling Overnight Index Average). The base price is 0.21% for this financial instrument and excludes margin and possible valuation adjustments.

*Bid–Offer*   A bid is the price the market is willing to pay whilst an offer is the price the market is willing to receive. The bid–offer spreads differ by financial instrument and tenor and are seen as a cost for the trading desk.

When a client trades with the bank, the bank will price the trade inclusive of the cost to exit the position, which will include crossing the bid–offer spread. For example, in Table 9.5 (Figure 9.8), the desk executes the following transaction with a client: If the desk were to

**FIGURE 9.8**   Client transaction

**TABLE 9.6** OIS bid–offer quotes

| Tenor | Pay (bid) | Mid | Receive (offer) |
|---|---|---|---|
| 1 year | 0.31% | 0.315% | 0.32% |

**FIGURE 9.9** Crossing the bid–offer to hedge risk

hedge the risk on this transaction with an interbank counterparty, they would need to cross the bid–offer spread and pay fixed and receive floating. The bid–offer spreads for this instrument are listed in Table 9.6.

If the desk hedge the risk on the client trade, they will need to pay 0.32%. This is because the pay and receive quotes are from the market's view, not the bank's.

Figure 9.9 illustrates Sparta Bank trading with the client and hedging the market risk with an interbank counterpart. As the desk have not incorporated the bid–offer spread into the client price, they are incurring a one basis point loss on the trade.

To avoid this loss, the desk needs to incorporate the cost of the bid offer into the client's price, which is illustrated in Table 9.7 and Figure 9.10.

*Credit Value Adjustment (CVA) and Debit Value Adjustment (DVA)* CVA is the valuation adjustment required to account for counterparty credit risk whilst DVA is the valuation adjustment required to account for the bank's own credit risk. CVA and DVA are only relevant for OTC derivatives and the firm's funding liabilities where the fair value option is elected.

As the trade in Table 9.5 is an OTC derivative, CVA and DVA are both relevant. The CVA and DVA on an uncollateralized trade will be far more significant than a collateralized trade, as there is no collateral providing protection against default. These adjustments will be factored into the price the desk gives the client, which means the trade valuation used in P&L reporting will also need to incorporate these amounts.

In this example, let's assume the desk is earning a client margin of 2 basis points. As the counterparty's credit worthiness is significantly inferior to the bank's, the xVA desk (which

**TABLE 9.7** OIS trade example adjusted for bid offer

| Price component | Amount |
|---|---|
| OIS 1 year base rate | 0.31% |
| Bid offer | 0.01% |
| **Total** | **0.32%** |

**FIGURE 9.10** Transaction price now incorporates the cost of crossing the bid–offer

**TABLE 9.8**   OIS trade example adjusted
for bid–offer, margin and CVA

| Price component | Amount |
|---|---|
| OIS 1-year base rate | 0.310% |
| Bid–offer | 0.010% |
| Margin | 0.020% |
| CVA | 0.005% |
| **Total** | **0.345%** |

**FIGURE 9.11**   Transaction price now incorporates bid–offer, margin and CVA

manages CVA and DVA risk) has advised that a net CVA adjustment of 0.5 basis points is
appropriate, which will be factored into the price given to the client.

To factor the margin and CVA adjustment into the client transaction, the fixed rate needs
to increase from 0.32% to 0.345%. This is illustrated in Table 9.8 and Figure 9.11.

Product control need to ensure the trade's valuation incorporates CVA otherwise, trade
valuation and P&L will be overstated by two basis points.

*Funding Value Adjustment (FVA)*   FVA is the valuation adjustment required to account for
the cost or benefit of funding uncollateralized derivatives. The xVA desk (which manages
FVA risk) will provide the desk with a quote for this amount. As the trade is generating an
uncollateralized expected positive exposure for the bank, the xVA desk has advised that the
desk needs to charge the client an extra 0.25 basis points to capture the cost of FVA. This
results in the fixed rate becoming 0.3475%, which is illustrated in Table 9.9 and Figure 9.12.

**TABLE 9.9**   OIS trade example adjusted
for bid–offer, margin, CVA and FVA

| Price component | Amount |
|---|---|
| OIS 1-year base rate | 0.3100% |
| Bid–offer | 0.0100% |
| Margin | 0.0200% |
| CVA | 0.0050% |
| FVA | 0.0025% |
| **Total** | **0.3475%** |

**FIGURE 9.12**   Transaction price now incorporates bid–offer, margin, CVA and FVA

Product control need to ensure the trade's valuation incorporates FVA otherwise the trade valuation and P&L will be overvalued by 0.25 basis points.

### Other End of Day Price Considerations

**Material IPV variances:** If the financial instrument that is generating exceptional new trade P&L has had material IPV variances in the most recent IPV exercise, product control need to consider whether the trader's marking is aligned to fair value. Product control can check market data sources, such as Bloomberg and Reuters, to assess whether the trader's mark is reasonable or not. For complex financial instruments, the valuations team can be brought in to assist.

**Observability:** Observability is another key consideration for both independent and trader sourced marks, as if the new trade P&L is generated using unobservable pricing inputs, a day one reserve may be required to report an accurate P&L. A day one reserve is not required for U.S. GAAP. We will look at day one reserves in Chapter 16.

Consideration should also be given to the fair value hierarchy when assessing observability, as significant unobservable pricing inputs should lead to a financial asset or liability being allocated to level three of the hierarchy. See Chapter 21.

**Drivers of the P&L are Reviewed and Validated** Once it has been established, through the above steps, that the RMS valuation and P&L are accurate, product control now need to establish how the desk generated this P&L. This step requires an understanding of three primary drivers of new trade P&L:

1. Margin
2. Volume
3. Market movements.

*Margin* One of the main drivers of new trade P&L is going to be the margin that the bank earns from the client. Margin won't normally exist on run-of-the-mill interbank trades. Product control should consider if the size of the margin was unusual and if so, engage the desk to understand how they generated a margin of this size.

Some of the reasons for unusual margin could be the following:

- The trade was part of a structured or corporate finance transaction which required more work than usual and, hence, generated a larger margin.

    For example, the bank helped its U.S. client issue a bond in Australia. Off the back of this issuance, the bank executed a cross currency swap with the client to convert the AUD proceeds into USD.
- The negative margin resulted from providing a beneficial rate to the client to generate more future business.
- The loss on the trade is offset with the profit generated from the cancellation of an existing trade.
- The desk wanted to exit an aged position and were willing to take a small loss to do so.

When product control review the response from the desk, they should apply professional scepticism and not just accept the answer at face value. After all, they are a control function.

**FIGURE 9.13**   Selling CDS protection to a client

*Volume*   Volume is another driver of new trade P&L. If a client is charged the same margin every time they trade with the bank, the way the desk can increase their P&L is through increasing trading frequency or increasing the size of the transaction. Where the volumes are unusually large, product control should seek to understand the business rationale for the increase.

*Market Movements*   The final driver of new trade P&L is the P&L emanating from changes in market rates after the trade has been executed. As most banks measure their new trade P&L using the end of day marks, the P&L will include both margin and intraday market movements. Even if the market risk on a trade is hedged, the hedging is executed via a separate trade, which results in product control seeing gross market moves P&L on both the client trade and the hedge. The challenge in this scenario is to identify which hedging trades relate to the client trade so that the net P&L can be assessed.

For example, in Figure 9.13, the desk sold CDS protection on HSBC to the client, Lighting Inc., and hedged the risk in the interbank market. The desk has earned a margin of 5 basis points (83 basis points less 78 basis points).

Although the desk has hedged their market risk, the P&L on each new trade will usually be reported separately. Table 9.10 lists the market moving from 83 basis points at the time of the trade, to 85 basis points at COB. This results in an apparent $20,000 loss on the client trade and a $70,000 profit on the interbank hedge. This example highlights the importance of reviewing the overall result for a client trade.

Where the trader has not hedged the market risk on the trade, if the market moves P&L is material, product control need to validate the P&L. One of the ways you can do this is through looking at the change in the market from the time of execution until the end of day. Bloomberg and Reuters both provide intraday pricing functionality to assist with this task.

*Requesting Information on P&L Drivers from the Desk*   When engaging the desk to understand the driver of new trade P&L, the time it takes to source feedback should be as quick as possible, but it isn't always the case. Ideally, the answers would be sourced on T+1 but at times there can be delays due to a number of factors including time-zone differences, holidays, sick leave and high workloads. If the trade's P&L was so large that it was a material driver of the overall P&L then the commentary cannot be delayed past T+1 and the matter should be escalated.

**TABLE 9.10**   Day 1 P&L for CDS trading

| Trade | CS01 | Trade price | CDS Spread (COB) | Day 1 P&L |
|---|---|---|---|---|
| A | (10,000) | 0.83% | 0.85% | $(20,000) |
| B | 10,000 | 0.78% | 0.85% | $70,000 |
| Total | 0 | | | $50,000 |

**TABLE 9.11** New trade commentary requests

| Point of contact | T+1 | T+2 | T+3 | T+4 |
|---|---|---|---|---|
| Trader/Sales person<br>Product Control Line Manager | X | X | X | X |
| Regional Desk Head + Regional COO<br>Product Control – Regional Head of Business Line | | X | X | X |
| Global Desk Head and Global COO<br>Product Control – Global Head of Business line | | | X | X |
| Global Head of Business<br>Product Control – Global Head | | | | X |

For less material new trade P&L, it may be worthwhile providing your product control team with an escalation matrix that advises them what action to take and when. This matrix also encourages the desk to respond to requests in a timely manner as failing to do so may get them into strife with their superiors. Table 9.11 shows an example of such a matrix.

In Table 9.11, for every day that passes where the desk have not responded to product control's request, the escalation proceeds up one layer of the organizational hierarchy. By including more senior people as the request ages, product control are increasing the pressure on the trader or sales person to respond to their request. Additionally, management is being made aware of potential issues for those traders or sales people that continually have aged exceptions.

Another method for extracting commentary from the desk is to withhold all day one P&L until the commentary is provided. As the desk's remuneration is based on the P&L they generate, you may find that this approach is very effective. However, this should only be done in accordance with your bank's policy.

**Escalation of Significant New Trade P&L**   We have criteria to identify new trades which require further review, but we should also have criteria for escalating new trades with significant P&L, an example of which is included in Table 9.12. Escalating significant new trades adds an additional layer of control as more senior staff are given the responsibility to review the trade which can help detect issues if they may exist. This is also a key rogue trading control.

**TABLE 9.12** Escalation of significant new trade P&L

| Escalation of material new trade P&L | | | | |
|---|---|---|---|---|
| Contact | $500k–$1mln | $1mln–$5mln | $5mln–$10mln | >$10mln |
| Trader/Sales Line Manager<br>Product Control Line Manager | X | X | X | X |
| Regional Desk Head + Regional COO<br>Product Control – Regional Head of Business Line | | X | X | X |
| Global Desk Head and Global COO<br>Product Control – Global Head of Business line | | | X | X |
| Global Head of Business<br>Product Control – Global Head | | | | X |

When the trade's P&L is escalated, management should be informed regarding:

▪ Which desk and trader/sales person executed the trade.
▪ The business rationale for the client executing the trade (including their name) or, for interbank trades, the desk's rationale.
▪ The economics of the trade, are there any special or non-standard features?
▪ How the desk generated the day one P&L.

In addition to the product controller performing this review, it is also important that the line product control manager performs a supervisory review of the reasons for the exceptions.

## Presentation of New Trade P&L

In P&L reporting, the P&L from new trades needs to be reported separately so that management can understand the contribution new trades are making to the bank's financial performance. It is also important to report it separately from market movements P&L, as if it is included it will cause a breach in the VaR backtesting results and a variance in the risk tie run by product control.

In Table 9.13, the new trade P&L is split into Entry P&L and Intraday MTM P&L. The sum of these two fields is the value of the trades at COB on T+0. Not all banks will have this split and may only have one column, which is the new trade P&L as of COB on T+0.

## AMENDED TRADES

Each business day there will be a population of trades that will be cancelled or amended. A trade is cancelled if it is removed entirely from the bank's books, whilst a trade is amended if it is altered but remains on the bank's books.

When a trade is amended, one or more fields are updated to reflect the new version of the trade. The amendment may take place on the same day as the initial booking, known as an intraday amendment, or it can take place in the days following the initial booking. I will refer to cancellations and amendments collectively as amendments.

As per new trades, product control will have a threshold (usually based upon a dollar value) which helps to identify those exceptional amendments which require further review. When reviewing exceptional amendments, product control should apply professional judgement in their approach. Three questions to ask yourself are:

1. What has been amended?
2. Why has it been amended?
3. Does the P&L arising from the change make sense?

### Why Are Trades Amended?

Trades are amended for three primary reasons:

1. Input error
2. Change of circumstance
3. Rogue trading.

**TABLE 9.13**  Presentation of new trade P&L

**Daily P&L**

| | Trading Activity | | | | Market Moves | Other | | | | Grand Total |
| --- | --- | --- | --- | --- | --- | --- | --- | --- | --- | --- |
| | New Trades Entry P&L | Intraday Market Moves | Amendments | Total Trading Activity | | Funding | Valuation adjustments | Fees and charges | Total Other | |
| Trading | 125,000 | 55,000 | 17,000 | 197,000 | 729,000 | –23,000 | –1,000 | 15,000 | –9,000 | 917,000 |
| Sales | 630,000 | 0 | | 630,000 | 0 | 0 | 0 | 0 | 0 | 630,000 |
| Total | 755,000 | 55,000 | 17,000 | 827,000 | 729,000 | –23,000 | –1,000 | 15,000 | –9,000 | 1,547,000 |

**TABLE 9.14**   Types of amendments

| Item | Reason for amendment |
|------|----------------------|
| **Input error** | |
| 1 | Front office input error |
| **Change in circumstance** | |
| 2 | Counterparty not known at the time of booking |
| 3 | Trade compression exercise |
| 4 | Close out or partial close out of a trade |
| 5 | Novation of the trade to a different counterparty |
| 6 | Novation of the trade to a central clearing counterparty (CCP) |
| 7 | Change of book |
| **Rogue trading** | |
| 8 | Rogue trading |

Table 9.14 lists the most common instances where amendments are required under each of the three categories:

We will now look at each of the amendments in Table 9.14 in more detail.

**1. Front Office Input Error**   Trade booking errors occur when the trader or sales person books a trade which is different to what was agreed with the counterparty. These errors are usually picked up by operations, who have the task of confirming the trade with the bank's counterparty.

In Figure 9.14 is an example of a trade amendment. The trader booked a buy of stock at $10 but the price should have been $10.50. This error was picked up by operations on T+1 and the trader duly updated his booking.

Due to this change, a loss of $0.50 was recorded in the amendments P&L on T+1.

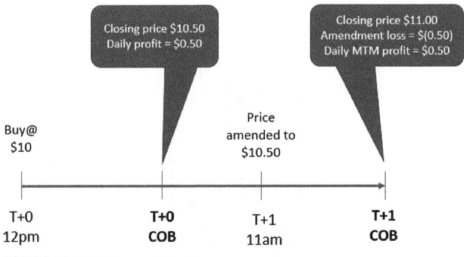

**FIGURE 9.14**   P&L from amended trades

If the confirmation of any of the trade's details are disputed by the counterparty, the discrepancy will be brought to the attention of the person who booked the trade. This person can then check the electronic messaging and taped calls exchanged with the counterparty to establish the facts.

Where there are discrepancies between the trade booking and the confirmation, it is extremely important that those discrepancies are resolved as soon as possible. Why? If the trade has been booked incorrectly, the trader might have then hedged the wrong underlying exposure, which could result in unlimited losses for the bank.

There is another type of front office input error. If the desk execute a trade in the market which was an error, known as a bad trade, they risk having to keep the resulting position and P&L. The trade will be accepted in the RMS as a new trade and although the desk would like the ability to cancel the trade, it is not possible in all situations. Such an error occurred in the trading of HSBC shares on 31st January 2014, as is detailed in the following example (Figure 9.15).

## EXAMPLE

### HSBC Price Spike

In January 2014, a large buy order for HSBC was placed on the London Stock Exchange (LSE). The single trade was for 18,049 shares, a large enough volume to send prices surging 10% as nearly 1.9 million HSBC shares traded before the LSE shut down HSBC trading. Experts blamed the spike on human error—either in the form of a faulty algorithm, miskeyed order or forgotten limit. The unknown trader responsible likely lost about 400,000 pounds for the so-called *fat-finger* mistake.[1]

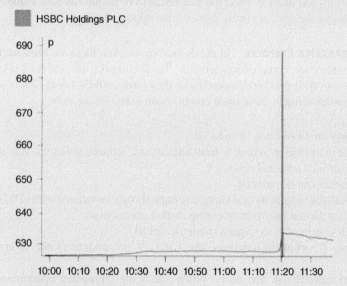

**FIGURE 9.15**   HSBC Share price
Source: ©CITY AM

**TABLE 9.15**  Fund allocation of bond purchase

| Fund | Nominal |
|------|---------|
| European Growth Ltd | $30m |
| Global Diversified Ltd | $10m |
| Enhanced Income Ltd | $40m |
| Total | $80m |

**2. Counterparty Not Known at the Time of Booking**  In some instances, the trader or sales person needs to book a trade with an interim counterparty as the final counterparty is not always known at the time of the booking. This is more common when transacting with a fund or asset manager as it is not until after the trade has been executed that the fund manager will provide the bank with the nominal allocations by fund.

For example, ABC Fund Managers puts in an order to buy $80m of Unilever 4% 2020 bonds. The bank takes the order and fills it at $95.10, recording the trade with counterparty "Temporary." By the end of the business day, ABC Fund Managers have sent the allocation of the $80m by fund to the bank, which is listed in Table 9.15.

At this time, the trade which has already been booked against the counterparty "Temporary" can be cancelled and rebooked to reflect the new counterparties and nominals. This change should have no P&L impact.

Please note that the use of dummy or special counterparties needs to be strictly controlled, as rogue traders use these counterparties to hide their fraudulent activities. They have been able to do this as there has not been a robust set of controls in place.

Each special counterparty needs to have its use approved by senior management in the business, operations and finance. Their use also needs to be monitored both intraday and at the end of day to ensure the desk are using them for the approved purpose.

**3. Trade Compression Exercise**  In the derivatives market, there are firms such as TriOptima which provide trade compression services. Trade compression enables banks to significantly reduce the overall number of open trades they have on their books. There are multiple benefits from participating in these trade compression exercises, namely:

- Counterparty credit risk can be reduced.
  Multilateral termination removes transactions and reduces collateral requirements by keeping portfolios trimmed down.
- Capital charges can be reduced.
  Reduces both the regulatory and economic capital costs associated with OTC derivatives, especially for capital intensive emerging market transactions.
- Improved leverage ratio as required under Basel III.
- By reducing notional outstandings, the CRD IV component of the leverage ratio is improved.
- Reduce operational risk and costs. When trades are eliminated operational costs and risks decline because there are no more payments to settle or potential errors to resolve.[2]

## HOW ARE TRADE COMPRESSIONS REFLECTED IN THE RMS?

Trade compressions result in a portfolio of trades, which may face multiple counter-parties, being cancelled and replaced by only one or two trades to reflect the residual risk or cash to be settled. Product control need operations to provide the list of trade cancellations and the new trades created by the trade compression exercise.

If the desk has used accurate prices to mark their portfolio and the compression exercise has been processed correctly, there should be minimal P&L resulting from the exercise.

**4. Close Out or Partial Close Out**    Instances arise where the trader or the counterparty want to close out their trade. A close out is when a trade is unwound so that it no longer exists on the bank's books. The close out can be for the full notional of the trade or a portion of the notional, which is known as a partial close out.

When executing this close out, both counterparties will agree upon whether a fee needs to be paid or received. A fee will be required when the net present value (NPV) of the trade does not equal zero at the time of the close out (not at the end of day). The fee will be paid by the counterparty whose side of the trade has an NPV<0.

The total P&L reported on the close out will be the difference between the fee and the NPV on T-1 (Figure 9.16).

In Figure 9.16, a trade has been closed out at 12pm on T+0 where a fee for $100,000 will be paid by the counterparty to the bank. The total P&L reported on the close out will be a loss of $30,000, which is due to the changes in the market from T-1 to the time of the close out.

**5. Novation of the Trade to a Different Counterparty**    A novation arises where a coun-terparty to a pre-existing trade is changed to a third party. Even though this can involve the bank or counterparty stepping into or out of a trade, amendments are only concerned with those trades already on the bank's books, which means either the bank or counterparty steps out of the trade.

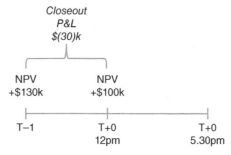

**FIGURE 9.16**    P&L reporting of a close out

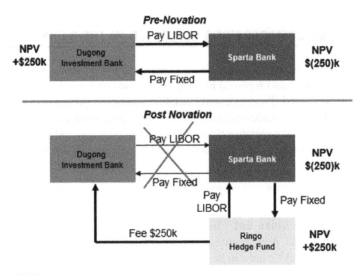

**FIGURE 9.17**  Novation of an interest rate swap

Some of the drivers behind a novation may be:

■ Banks revisiting their target sectors/products, for example, a number of Irish banks looked to exit the UK market immediately post-global financial crisis (GFC), and therefore novated out of such existing trades.
■ If a corporate is refinancing its debt, it may look to revisit which bank it has its related interest rate swaps with.
■ A large corporate may have a number of banks as counterparties to their derivative transactions and wishes to replace those banks with deteriorating credit ratings.

When a novation occurs and the NPV of the trade is not equal to zero, the new counterparty will need to exchange a fee with the previous counterparty. In Figure 9.17, a vanilla interest rate swap between Sparta Bank and Dugong Investment Bank has been novated, which requires Dugong Investment Bank to *step out* of the trade and Ringo Hedge Fund to *step in* to face Sparta Bank. As Ringo Hedge Fund is stepping into a trade that has an NPV of $250,000 in their favour, they are required to pay the value of the NPV back to Dugong Investment Bank in the form of a fee.

If the bank is stepping out of a trade, the reported P&L impact will be the change in market prices between T-1 and the time at which the trade was exited. However, if the bank is stepping into an existing trade, the novation will show as a new deal.

**6. Novation of a Trade to a Central Clearing Counterparty**   According to the International Monetary Fund (IMF):

> *In an effort to improve market infrastructure following the crisis (GFC), central counterparties (CCPs) are being put forth as the way to make over-the-counter (OTC) derivatives markets safer and sounder, and to help mitigate systemic risk.[3]*

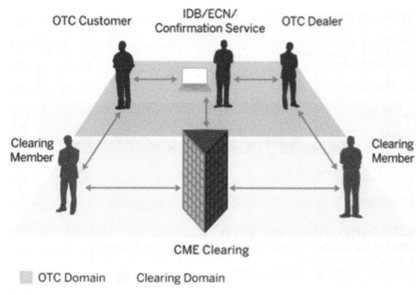

**FIGURE 9.18** CME Group acting as a central clearing counterparty
Source: CME Clearing Europe

Two examples of CCPs are SwapClear (LCH.Clearnet) and CME Clearing. When viewed together, these companies cover a range of instruments including OTC interest rate swaps, forward rate agreements (FRAs), variable notional swaps, inflation swaps and commodity swaps. Figure 9.18 shows a high-level illustration of the CME's CCP process.

In Figure 9.18 the OTC customer and dealer agree terms of the trade. As both these parties are members of CME Clearing, they submit the trade to CME Clearing, which now acts as the counterparty to both the customer and the dealer.

A bank's trade booking system will have inbuilt logic to recognize when a counterparty and financial instrument make it eligible to be cleared through a CCP. Banks also rely on services such as MarkitServ, which performs the trade processing for derivatives that includes checking for CCP eligibility. Figure 9.19 illustrates at a high level MarkitServ's role for buy side clients when clearing through a CCP.

As a result of the introduction of OTC CCP clearing and vendor trade processing software, the executed trade will progress through various statuses as it proceeds from the initial booking to final confirmation. Through this process, product control may see several versions of the trade flow through to the RMS.

**7. Change of Book** Books, also known as portfolios (e.g., in Murex), are used by the front office to store a collection of trades. In some cases, trades are recorded in an incorrect book which needs correcting, or the desk transfers risk amongst their trading books.

Although the P&L impact for the legal entity should be zero across all affected books, product control should be aware of the reason for the transfer. This is important as traders may be transferring P&L to take advantage of differing bonus agreements.

Regulatory processing workflow

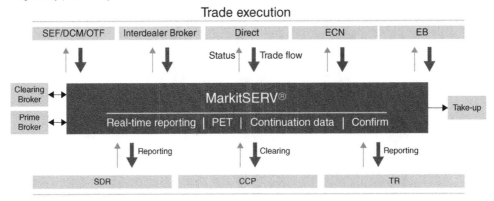

**FIGURE 9.19** Overview of MarkitServ's process
Source: Copyright ©2014 Markit Group Limited. "MarkitSERV for Clearing"
MKT_MS_Clearing_factsheet.pdf

**8. Rogue Trading** When a trader is executing their rogue trading, one of the methods used to conceal the P&L and risk arising from unauthorized trading is to book fictitious trades and then cancel and rebook that trade to mask the audit trail. We will look further at rogue trading concealment mechanisms in Chapter 23.

## Avoidable vs. Unavoidable Amendments

Banks are keen to reduce the number of trade amendments occurring on their trading floor. One of the reasons for this has been the encouragement of regulators, who see high levels of amendments as a source of operational risk.

To assist with this, banks can categorize amendments as avoidable or unavoidable. Using amendment data presented earlier in Table 9.14, Table 9.16 categorizes those causes as avoidable or unavoidable.

**TABLE 9.16** Classifying an amendment as avoidable or unavoidable

| Item | Reason for amendment | Avoidable | Unavoidable |
|------|----------------------|-----------|-------------|
| 1. | Front office input error | X | |
| 2. | Counterparty not known at the time of booking | | X |
| 3. | Trade compression exercise | | X |
| 4. | Close out or partial close out of a trade | | X |
| 5. | Novation of the trade to a different counterparty | | X |
| 6. | Novation of the trade to a CCP | | X |
| 7. | Change of book | X | |
| 8. | Rogue trading | X | |

The bank will divide amendments into avoidable or unavoidable so that it can decide which types of amendments should be allocated resources for remediation. If an amendment is considered avoidable, the bank will want the frequency of amendments to be reduced to nil. If an amendment is considered unavoidable, the bank will consider the amendment as necessary in the running of its business.

For those amendments that management have deemed avoidable, chief operating officers (COO) should spend some time establishing why the amendments are required. To do this, the business will perform a root cause analysis, which will bring to light exactly why the amendments are required and pinpoint what can be done to remove the need for these in the future.

**The Importance of Good Data**   To help reduce the time spent on amendments, product control should be provided with two things from the RMS:

1. Which field has changed and what was the value before and after the change.
2. The reason for the change.

For item 2, the RMS can only provide the data that was input by the desk or middle office.

For each change that is made to a trade there should be a reason code applied to the instance. For example, if a counterparty was not known at the time of the booking then the reason code could be "counterparty not known." By applying a reason code, the firm can then perform root cause analysis, track the size of the issue over time and provide focus and resources to assist in removing the need for the amendment.

**Trends**   Valuable insight can be drawn when data is collated into a time series. A time series enables trends to be identified, which can illuminate unusual events when they occur. When a spike in the number of amendments is identified, it can indicate that something is wrong with either trader behaviour or the performance of the bank's systems.

Each business head and COO will review the trade amendment statistics on a periodic basis to understand and resolve the root causes. The business will focus on those categories which are their biggest cause for concern. This review can occur in a meeting just with product control or in a control forum, where each of the support areas (product control, risk and operations) present their statistics on control weaknesses. For example, in the monthly meeting for April, the following amendment data in Table 9.17 and Figure 9.20 was presented to the business.

## Presentation of P&L from Amended Trades

The P&L resulting from trade amendments should be reported separately from the market movements P&L (Table 9.18). Amendments P&L can be consolidated with new trade P&L under the banner of "Trading Activity" or it can be reported separately. Whatever the choice, the most important thing is to report it separately from market movements P&L, as if it is included it will cause a breach in the VaR backtesting results and a variance in the risk tie run by product control.

That concludes our review of new trades and amendments.

**TABLE 9.17**   Trade amendments update

| Credit Desk | |
|---|---|
| Trend | Trade input errors are up on last month. |
| Area of concern | Duplicate trades are the biggest cause for concern for avoidable amendments. |
| Root cause | During April the desk took on the portfolio of 60 vanilla trades from the structured credit desk. During this transfer 10 trades were entered twice (duplications). |
| Resolution | The portfolio transfer was a one-off event and so we do not expect this level of duplicate bookings to become a trend. |
| **Equities Desk** | |
| Trend | Trade input errors are up on last month. |
| Area of concern | Trade price errors are the biggest cause for concern. |
| Root cause | There is no one factor causing the spike in errors. The errors are spread across several traders and days. |
| Resolution | The desk head has reminded her traders of the importance in getting trades booked correctly the first time. |
| **FX Desk** | |
| Trend | Trade input errors are up on last month. |
| Area of concern | Duplicate trades are the biggest cause for concern. |
| Root cause | There was an error with the RMS risk stripping functionality which resulted in duplicate trades being created between the sales and FX spot desks. The error resulted from a system upgrade which was rolled out over the preceding weekend. |
| Resolution | IT corrected the issue within 10 minutes. Fortunately, the error occurred on a US public holiday which resulted in much lower than average trading. |
| | IT have submitted a paper to the head of FX outlining why the system release testing did not pick this up and what measures will be put in place to prevent this from reoccurring. |
| **Rates Desk** | |
| Trend | Trade input errors are down compared with the prior month. |
| Area of concern | Incorrect product type is the biggest cause for concern. |
| Root cause | The desk incorrectly booked sell buy backs as outright sales and outright buys of German government bonds. The desk were trying to minimize internal liquidity charges by using the incorrect product type. |
| Resolution | Product control have advised the trader and desk head of the seriousness of misrepresenting the true nature of their trade bookings. |
| **Treasury** | |
| Trend | Minimal booking errors this month and in the prior month. |
| Area of concern | N/A |
| Root cause | As there are minimal booking errors a root cause analysis was not performed. |
| Resolution | N/A |

**TABLE 9.18** Presentation of P&L from amendments

Daily P&L

| | Trading Activity | | | | Other | | | | | Grand Total |
|---|---|---|---|---|---|---|---|---|---|---|
| | New Trades Entry P&L | Intraday Market Moves | Amendments | Total Trading Activity | Market Moves | Funding | Valuation adjustments | Fees and charges | Total Other | |
| Trading | 125,000 | 55,000 | 17,000 | 197,000 | 729,000 | –23,000 | –1,000 | 15,000 | –9,000 | 917,000 |
| Sales | 630,000 | 0 | | 630,000 | 0 | 0 | 0 | 0 | 0 | 630,000 |
| Total | 755,000 | 55,000 | 17,000 | 827,000 | 729,000 | –23,000 | –1,000 | 15,000 | –9,000 | 1,547,000 |

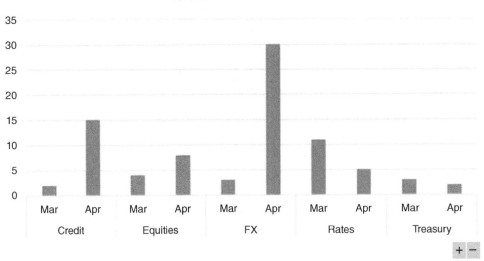

**FIGURE 9.20** Avoidable amendments

## NOTES

1. Wallace, Tim, "Fat finger mistake pushes HSBC shares up 10pc in just 30 seconds," CityAM.com, 31st January 2014.
2. TriOptima, "triReduce Key Benefits," TriOptima.com, 2017.
3. The International Monetary Fund (IMF), "Global Financial Stability Report, Meeting new challenges to stability and building a safer system, Chapter 3 Making Over-the-Counter Derivatives Safer: The Role of Central Counterparties." April 2010. http://www.imf.org/external/pubs/ft/gfsr/2010/01/pdf/chap3.pdf.

# CHAPTER 10

# Review of Mark-to-Market P&L

I n the previous chapter we reviewed the controls over trading activity. We will now move on to look at those controls which validate the profit and loss (P&L) generated from existing positions, which is known as mark-to-market (MTM) or market moves P&L.

This chapter does not apply to portfolios which are accounted for on an amortized cost basis.

## DEFINING MARK-TO-MARKET P&L

When the desk executes a new trade, the P&L generated on day one is ring-fenced and reported as new trade P&L. From T+1 until maturity, the P&L generated will be reported as MTM P&L. This is illustrated in Figure 10.1.

It is important that we ring-fence the MTM P&L as:

- Market risk rely upon an untainted MTM P&L to perform their VaR back testing.
- It enables a comparison back to a risk-based P&L estimate.
- It enables the desk to compare the MTM P&L in their estimate to product control's view.
- The Volcker rule requires MTM P&L to be reported separately.
- It informs the firm's senior management and regulators how much of the bank's P&L is attributable to risk-taking.

Product control employ several methods to validate the MTM P&L (Figure 10.2). These methods include:

- Attributing the MTM P&L to its underlying drivers
- Performing a risk-based P&L estimate
- Understanding price changes in the financial markets.

We will now look at these methods in more detail.

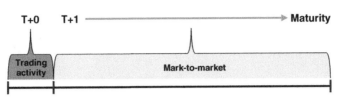

**FIGURE 10.1**   Defining MTM P&L

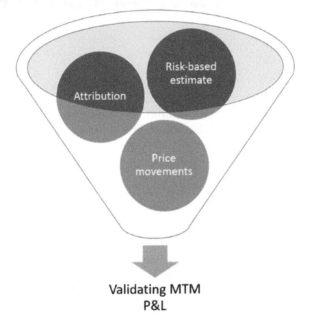

**FIGURE 10.2**   Validating MTM P&L

## ATTRIBUTING MTM P&L

Within the MTM P&L category the P&L can be further attributed (or sub-attributed) into their underlying drivers. These drivers are a mix of the desk's positions and the changes in market prices (Figure 10.3).

These price movements can be attributed using the underlying pricing inputs of the financial instruments in the desk's portfolio. Table 10.1 highlights the sub-attributes expected for some of the most common financial instruments.

**FIGURE 10.3**   Driver of MTM P&L

**TABLE 10.1**   Sub-attribution of MTM P&L

| Financial Instrument | MTM attribute | | | | |
|---|---|---|---|---|---|
| | **Rates** | **Credit** | **FX** | **Volatility** | **Equity** |
| FX Spot | | | X | | |
| FX Forward | X | | X | | |
| FX Swap | X | | | | |
| FX Option | X | | X | X | |
| Interest Rate Swap | X | | | | |
| Cross Currency Swap | X | | X | | |
| Overnight Index Swap | X | | | | |
| Forward Rate Agreement | X | | | | |
| Swaption | X | | | X | |
| Stocks | | | | | X |
| Government Bonds and Paper | X | X | | | |
| Corporate Bonds and Paper | X | X | | | |
| Credit Default Swap | X | X | | | |

In this table I have omitted P&L from time decay, which measures the gain or loss a bank will experience as time gets one day closer to maturity. Most derivatives will be sensitive to changes in time, especially short-dated options. I have also omitted counterparty credit risk.

There are two ways in which the MTM P&L can be sub-attributed, which we will look at now.

## Waterfall Method

The waterfall method to sub-attribute the MTM P&L is popular as it explains all the MTM P&L, resulting in zero unattributed P&L. This approach requires each pricing input to be updated from T–1 (prior close of business (COB)) to T+0 (current COB) in a pre-defined sequence. Figure 10.4 illustrates the waterfall method for sub-attributing the MTM P&L for an FX option. We are using an FX option as it incorporates multiple pricing inputs.

The starting point for determining the sub-attribution of the MTM P&L is the closing value of the FX option for the prior business day, which in Figure 10.4 is $100,000. Subsequently, the following occurs:

- The COB date is moved forward by one business day from T-1 to T+0. This captures time decay (or theta) and results in a profit of $3,500.
- Spot FX rates are then updated for the current business day, which generates a profit of $81,700.
- Volatility surfaces are updated for the current business day which generates a profit of $64,800.
- Interest rates are updated for the current business day which generates a loss of $(12,000).
- Fixings are then updated for today, but in this instance there is no P&L impact.

All components are now up to date for the current business day and the trade's closing value is $238,000.

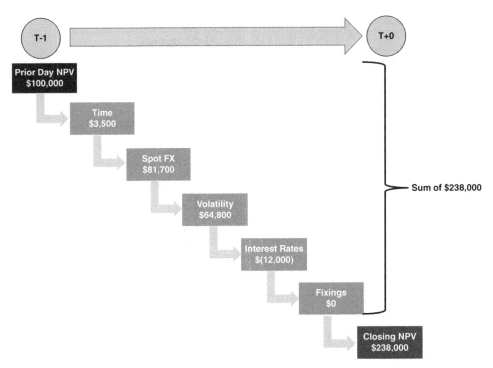

**FIGURE 10.4**   Using the waterfall method to sub-attribute an FX option's MTM P&L

The order in which the pricing inputs are updated can vary by bank. I think it is better to change those components that have the biggest input on the valuation first, which will vary the sequence by business.

For example, for an FX book, after time you would shift spot FX rates first and for a rates book, the yield curves. This business by business approach to attribution will need to be weighed up against achieving consistency across the bank.

It is important to keep in mind that when using this attribution method, the P&L from each pricing input will not exactly tie back to a risk-based estimated P&L. This is because each pricing input is not updated in isolation; that is to say, they are updated after another input has already been updated. This results in second order effects, such as gamma, being mixed in with first order effects, such as delta, in the attributed P&L.

## Restored Method

The second approach for sub-attributing MTM P&L is the restored method, whereby a pricing input is updated from T–1 to T+0, is then reset back to the T–1 and the next pricing input is updated from T–1 to T+0 and so on and so forth. Figure 10.5 sub-attributes the MTM P&L for an FX option.

In Figure 10.5, the following steps are taking place:

1. The COB date is moved forward by one business day from T-1 to T+0. This results in a profit of $3,500.

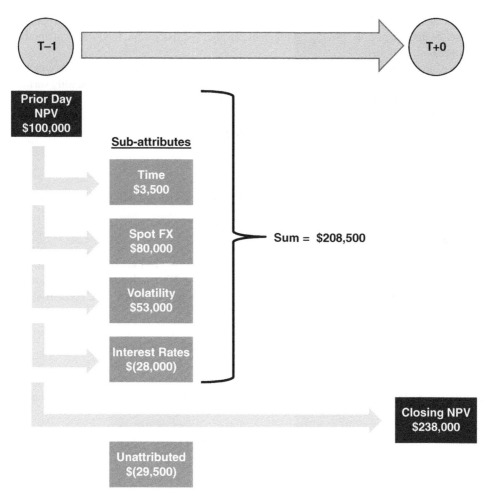

**FIGURE 10.5** Using the restored method to attribute an FX option's MTM P&L

2. *The trade's value is restored to the prior business day.*
3. Spot FX rates are updated for the current business day, which generates a profit of $80,000.
4. *Spot FX rates are restored to the prior business day.*
5. Volatility surfaces are updated for the current business day, which generates a profit of $53,000.
6. *Volatility surfaces are restored to the prior business day.*
7. Interest rates are updated for the current business day, which generates a loss of $(28,000).

Once the P&L from each of the individual pricing inputs has been recorded, all pricing inputs are then updated to generate a closing trade value. During this step, the P&L from fixings (if any) can be quantified. In Figure 10.5 the trade's closing value is $238,000 but the sum of the prior day's MTM value and individual pricing updates totals only $208,500, leaving an unattributed profit of $29,500.

This unattributed P&L comes about due to second order effects such as cross-gamma because the updating of one pricing component can alter the risk profile (and P&L) of another component.

For example, when FX rates are updated, there will be a shift in the trade's delta (which is measured by gamma). This change in delta will also affect the point along the volatility surface (and therefore the volatility) that the trade is revalued off. This is also the reason why the P&L from each pricing input in the waterfall method differs to the restored method and why most banks will use the waterfall method as their primary sub-attribution report.

## Other Sub-attributes

There are two other common sub-attributes of MTM P&L which we will now touch upon.

## FX Revaluation

FX revaluation is the P&L impact from the change in the value of the opening portfolio due to changes in the value of the reporting currency. Given this, FX revaluation only exists when a trade's NPV is in a currency that is different to the reporting currency. The P&L from FX revaluation is calculated as follows:

$$\text{FX revaluation P\&L} = \text{NPV}_{T-1} \times (\text{FX rate}_{T+0} - \text{FX rate}_{T-1})$$

For example, the P&L reporting currency is USD and the trade's NPV is in GBP. On T–1 the NPV was £1,000,000 and the FX rates were 1.51 (T–1) and 1.50 (T+0). The FX revaluation P&L would be:

$$\text{FX revaluation P\&L} = £1,000,000 \times (1.50 - 1.51)$$
$$= \$(10,000)$$

## Fixings

During a trade's lifecycle, it may be exposed to a floating index such as LIBOR or a currency fixing (for resettable cross currency swaps or non-deliverable forwards). When these fixings occur they usually do so during the business day, such as at 11am for LIBOR, rather than at the end of day when the bank captures its market rates. As the fixing event will have a P&L impact that isn't captured by another sub-attribute, its quantum needs to be captured and reported as an additional attribute. We will look at how to quantify this P&L impact in the risk-based P&L estimate section of this chapter.

## RISK-BASED P&L ESTIMATES

MTM P&L is a function of both the size of the desk's open position/market risk exposures and the fluctuations in the pricing inputs. Whereas the bank's market risk function is responsible for the quantification, monitoring and reporting of market risk exposures, product control is responsible for validating the MTM P&L arising from these market risk exposures.

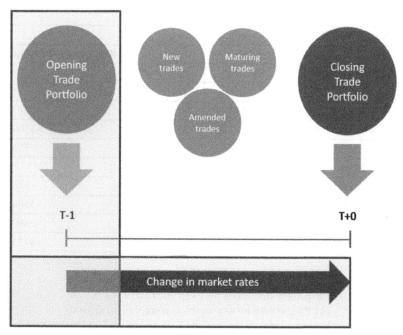

**FIGURE 10.6**   Quantifying a risk-based P&L estimate

The MTM P&L is validated through a number of methods, one of which is a risk-based P&L estimate (it can also be called a risk tie, risk estimate or P&L predict). This process uses the opening market risk exposures (T–1 COB) and applies these exposures to the changes in market rates from T–1 to T+0. This is illustrated in Figure 10.6.

The reason T–1 exposures are used is to exclude new trades or amendments and include maturing trades in the risk parameters. The resulting MTM P&L estimate is then compared back to the actual MTM P&L and any differences that exceed a pre-agreed variance threshold are investigated.

For linear portfolios (i.e., there is no optionality), the risk-based estimate will usually be closely approximated using delta and theta. For example, in Table 10.2 we have the sub-attribution report for the interest rate swap desk. This has been prepared using the waterfall method.

We are now going to validate the MTM P&L using a DV01 and changes in the swap yield curve. This is illustrated in Table 10.3. In Table 10.3 we have several columns which are used to derive a risk based P&L estimate.

**TABLE 10.2**   Interest rate swaps desk MTM sub-attribution report

| Market Moves – Attribution (waterfall method) | | | |
|---|---|---|---|
| Interest Rates | Time decay | Fixings | Total Market Moves |
| −123,950 | 1,200 | 100,000 | **−22,750** |

**TABLE 10.3**   Bucketed USD DV01 (per 1bp shift up)

| Interest Rates – USD | | | | | |
|------|------|--------|--------|-------------|------------------------|
| **Tenor** | **DV01** | **Rate T+0** | **Rate T–1** | **Change (bps)** | **Risk based P&L estimate** |
| O/N | $7,000 | 0.30% | 0.30% | 0.00 | $0 |
| 1M | −$3,500 | 0.50% | 0.49% | 1.00 | −$3,500 |
| 2M | $9,000 | 0.55% | 0.54% | 1.50 | $13,500 |
| 3M | $100,000 | 0.60% | 0.61% | −1.00 | −$100,000 |
| 6M | $50,000 | 0.70% | 0.70% | 0.50 | $25,000 |
| 9M | $20,000 | 0.90% | 0.90% | 0.00 | $0 |
| 1Y | −$24,000 | 1.10% | 1.08% | 2.00 | −$48,000 |
| 2Y | −$50,000 | 1.75% | 1.73% | 2.00 | −$100,000 |
| 3Y | $30,000 | 2.10% | 2.07% | 3.00 | $90,000 |
| **Total** | **$138,500** | | | | **−$123,000** |

| | |
|---|---|
| Tenor | The point in time along the swap yield curve |
| DV01 | The P&L sensitivity to a one basis point shift up in yields |
| Rate | The swap yield for the current (T+0) and prior (T−1) business days |
| Change (bps) | The movement in yield measured in basis points. To convert a yield into basis points, multiply the yield by $10^4$ *or* 10,000. |

Using this data, we can derive our risk based P&L estimate. For example, for the 1Y tenor:

$$\text{Risk based P\&L estimate} = \text{DV01} \times \text{Change in yield} \times 10,000$$
$$= -\$24,000 \times 0.02\% \times 10,000$$
$$= -\$48,000$$

By repeating this process for the remaining tenors, we arrive at an estimated loss of $123,000, which differs to the $123,950 loss reported under interest rates in Table 10.2. There is a reason the two amounts will not tie:

- Second order effects: Second order effects such as gamma may arise if there is a significant change in swap yields.
- Use of discrete tenor points: In the risk-based MTM P&L estimate we are segregating the delta exposures into discrete tenors (1M, 2M etc.) rather than using risk sensitivities for every date they reside on (29 days, 63 days etc.).

For example, if we have a swap with a floating fixing occurring at $2\frac{1}{2}$ years, the DV01 for this fixing may be allocated by the market risk model into either the 2-year tenor or the 3-year tenor. If movements in the $2\frac{1}{2}$-year yield are not the same as either of these tenors, then it will generate a discrepancy between the risk-based estimate and the sub-attribution report.

However, when differences are considered unusual or exceptional, they will be escalated to product control management and raised with market risk, who can investigate whether the risk sensitivities being used require recalibrating or whether certain risk sensitivities are missing.

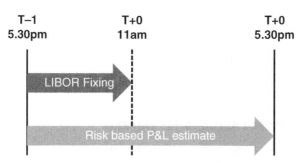

**FIGURE 10.7**   Fixings vs risk based P&L estimate

## Fixings

We are now going to quantify the P&L impact from a LIBOR rate fixing that wasn't captured in the risk based P&L estimate in Table 10.3 or the rates P&L attribute within Table 10.2.

In Figure 10.7, the risk-based P&L estimate uses a swap yield curve which changes from 5.30 p.m. on T−1 to 5.30 p.m. on T+0. As LIBOR fixes at 11 a.m. on T+0, any estimated P&L impact from a change in yields between 11 a.m. and 5.30 p.m. on T+0 needs to be reversed.

For example, in Table 10.4 a DV01 of $100,000 is exposed to a 3-month LIBOR fixing on T+0. The risk-based P&L estimates this DV01 will expect a loss of $100,000 as yields have fallen by one basis point. As 3-month LIBOR has fixed at 0.61%, rather than 0.60%, the P&L impact of the fixing needs to be incorporated to explain the full MTM P&L. In Table 10.2 a profit of $100,000 ($0–$100,000) is added as a fixing attribute of MTM P&L.

## CHANGES IN THE END OF DAY PRICES

The end of day prices used to revalue the portfolio will be a mix of trader and independently sourced prices. A good product controller will monitor the markets on T+0 and, with their knowledge of the trading portfolio, form an opinion of the expected impact on the desk's P&L, which will be reported the following day.

Although there are more formal and in-depth checks around these rates, such as monthly IPV, product control require a level of assurance that the prices reflect the changes in the external market.

**TABLE 10.4**   Differences caused by fixings

| Tenor | dv01 | T+0 | T−1 | Change (bps) | Risk based P&L estimate |
|-------|------|-----|-----|--------------|-------------------------|
| 3m | $100,000 | 0.60% | 0.61% | −1 | −$100,000 |

| Tenor | dv01 | Fixing | T−1 | Change (bps) | Estimated P&L |
|-------|------|--------|-----|--------------|---------------|
| 3m | $100,000 | 0.61% | 0.61% | 0 | $0 |

There are two aspects to this check:

1. Do the end of day prices agree to the market?
2. What has driven the change in prices?

## Do the End of Day Prices Agree to the Market?

This check, referred by some banks as benchmarking, is mainly for trader sourced prices and can only be performed where readily observable prices are available from the market.

Benchmarking is less detailed and accurate than IPV as larger price variances are tolerated. This comes about as fewer price sources are used and fewer staff are available to look into price variances.

Nonetheless, for large MTM P&L this check provides additional assurance that the end of day price is in line with the market.

For illiquid positions, when the desk execute a new trade with an external counterparty, the price at which the trade was executed can be considered the market price. So, if the end of day price is materially different to the traded price, further investigation is required.

## What Has Driven the Change in Prices?

Understanding the driver behind price movements is another important control to validate the MTM P&L.

To gain this assurance product control can consult financial news and price services such as Reuters and Bloomberg. These resources can in most cases provide information not only on current market prices, but also on the daily and intraday changes, volumes, bid and offer prices and the relevant news stories behind those changes.

Figure 10.8 contains an array of rates and stock market data which can be further drilled into.

If the desk were carrying a long AUD/USD spot FX position and the MTM P&L showed a loss due to a fall in the spot FX rate, we could consult Bloomberg to review the changes in the market and understand the underlying drivers of that change.

Figure 10.9 shows a graph of the changes in the AUD/USD spot FX rate. If product control were validating the change in the spot FX rate on the 19th August, they could firstly identify that AUD has fallen from 93.25 U.S. cents to 92.87 U.S. cents or 0.41%.

The next step is to understand why AUD fell on the day. Bloomberg provides news and economic headlines which can assist with this. On this day, the RBA (Reserve Bank of Australia) made a statement expressing uncertainty regarding future growth in the Australian economy, which undermined the currency and led to its weakening.

By following these two steps, product control has validated the movement in rates.

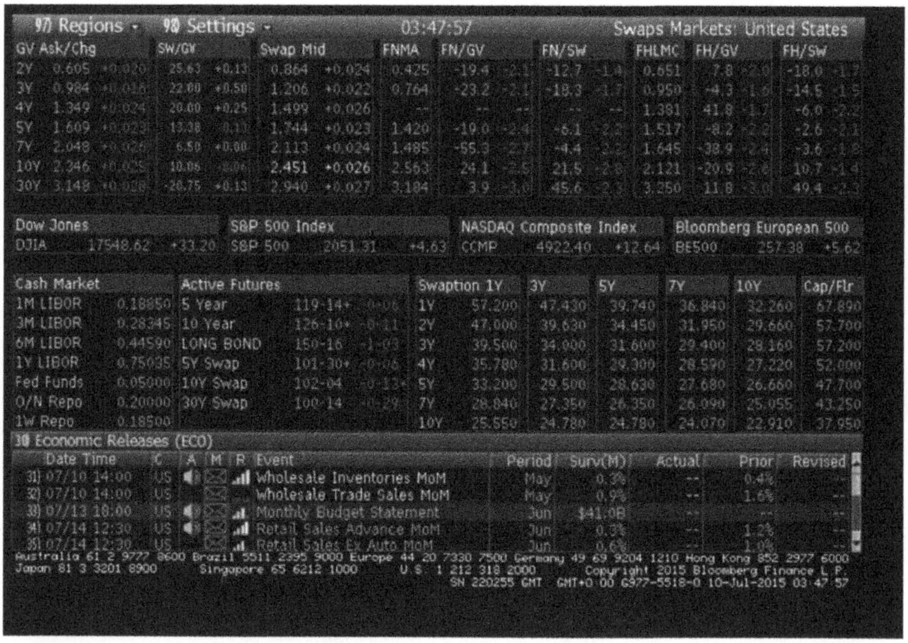

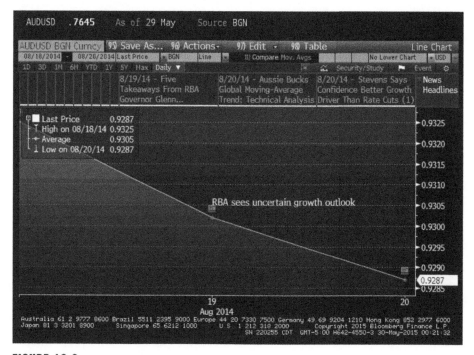

**FIGURE 10.8** U.S. markets in Bloomberg
Source: Used with permission of Bloomberg L.P. Copyright © 2015. All rights reserved.

**FIGURE 10.9** AUD/USD price changes
Source: Used with permission of Bloomberg L.P. Copyright © 2015. All rights reserved.

## WHEN TO VALIDATE THE MTM P&L

Like other P&L controls, MTM P&L doesn't need to be validated if the results are not considered material, unusual or exceptional. Thresholds for validation can be implemented at the total MTM P&L level or at the sub-attribute level, in a similar fashion to what was introduced for the new trades P&L.

# CHAPTER 11

# Funding, Fees and Charges

Funding, fees and charges are a core component of the desk's P&L. In this chapter we will identify the funding requirements of the desk and explore the related P&L components. We will also review the most common types of fees and charges and understand how they are reported in the P&L.

## FUNDING

### Drivers of Funding

The desk's portfolio has an array of financial instruments, all of which generate cash flows during their life cycle. Excess funds will be lent to generate income whilst deficits will require the desk to borrow funds to meet the shortfall. The typical drivers of funding are illustrated in Figure 11.1 and examples are provided in Table 11.1.

### How a Desk Funds Itself

The desk is funded by internal departments which manage the funding needs for the bank. Each bank will structure their funding teams differently, but a typical structure is illustrated in Figure 11.2.

In this figure the trading desks source funding internally from three different functions. The STIR desk (short-term interest rate trading) meets the desk's short-term funding requirements; for example, up to two weeks. The collateral desk (or repo desk) provides secured financing and treasury provide long-term funding to the desk (greater than two weeks). These functions, that may also lend and borrow with each other, will transact with the market to meet the bank's overall funding requirements.

Internal unsecured funding is usually conducted through a mix of term loans and the residual funding mechanism. The residual funding mechanism is usually calculated in the general ledger, where the imbalance in the trial balance is identified as the desk's funding requirement. You can also think of the imbalance as the overall nostro record for the profit centre.

Residual funding balances will attract an interest charge or benefit, with the rates being set by STIR/treasury. Although these yields are levied on the overnight funding balance, the yield

**FIGURE 11.1**   Drivers of funding
Note: CSA denotes a credit support annex and is relevant for the funding of OTC
derivatives

will typically resemble three-month LIBOR, as three-month money is typically more liquid
than overnight money for substantial borrowing.

Treasury/STIR will have other incentives and penalties in place to discourage the desk
from running a funding or tenor mismatch and from trying to arbitrage internal funding rates.

**Example of Funding**   In Figure 11.3, Sparta Bank has purchased a bond from Bilbo Asset
Management for a consideration of $10,000,000. To fund this purchase, Sparta Bank has lent
the bond, via a repo, to Waldo Bank in exchange for $9,500,000. This involves simultaneously
selling the bond to Waldo Bank and agreeing to repurchase the bond at a later date. Legally a
repo is a sale and purchase, but in substance it is a secured financing agreement.

The reason Waldo Bank hasn't lent the full $10,000,000 is because repos embed a haircut
to protect the lender from a price drop in the underlying bond. If they were to lend the full
$10,000,000 and the value of the bond fell to say $9,800,000, Waldo Bank would be exposed
to a $200,000 credit loss if Sparta Bank failed to repay the loan. This leaves Sparta Bank
with a shortfall of $500,000 to pay for the bond, which is funded through the residual funding
mechanism.

Table 11.2 illustrates the trial balance report for the bond trading desk which should be
balanced after summing all the debits and credits in the P&L and balance sheet. However, the

**TABLE 11.1** Funding drivers by financial instrument

| Financial instrument | Principal exchanges | Coupons | Dividends | Premium | CSA | Variation Margin and Initial Margin |
|---|---|---|---|---|---|---|
| Bonds and discount securities | X | X | | | | |
| Repo and Reverse repo | X | X | | | | |
| FX Derivatives (FX Spot, Forward, Swap) | X | | | | X | |
| Options | | | | X | X | |
| Interest rate swaps | | X | | | X | |
| Cross currency swap | X | X | | | X | |
| Credit default swap | | | | X | X | |
| Stocks | X | | X | | | |
| Futures and exchange traded options | | | | | | X |
| Derivatives settling through a central clearing counterparty (CCP) | | | | | | X |

net balance is not zero because the nostro or cash balance is not reported in this profit centre (nostros are usually recorded in a central profit centre). This leaves an imbalance of $500,000 which will need to be offset via the residual funding mechanism.

Once the residual funding mechanism has taken effect in the general ledger (GL), the trial balance report will resemble Table 11.3. As the residual funding is a credit balance, it will generate an interest expense for the desk, which makes sense given the desk are borrowing money to pay for their bond purchase.

## Analysis of Funding P&L

Funding P&L is composed of those items which are interest in nature. This can include all those items listed in Figure 11.4.

Banks will not be consistent in their inclusion of items in interest, so it is important that you are aware of what is and isn't reported in your firm's funding P&L. For instance, time decay and amortization of premiums and discounts may not be included by some banks.

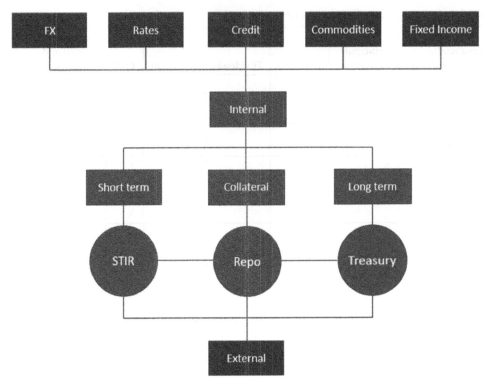

**FIGURE 11.2**  Sourcing funding

Funding is a very simple attribute of the P&L to analyse; unless the structure and strategy of a desk's portfolio changes significantly, the funding requirements should remain similar from one day to the next.

What this means for product control is that the funding P&L should also remain consistent with the prior day's result. If the funding P&L does change materially, the driver of the change needs to be identified and validated, which will require a review of the assets and liabilities on the balance sheet and the yields being applied to each.

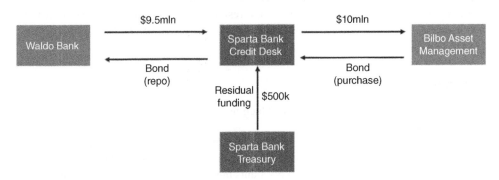

**FIGURE 11.3**  Funding a bond purchase

**TABLE 11.2**  Trial balance report

| Trial Balance | | | |
|---|---|---|---|
| | **Debit** | **Credit** | **Net Total** |
| P&L | | | |
| Unrealized P&L | | $0 | |
| Interest Income | | $0 | |
| Interest Expenses | $0 | | |
| **Total P&L** | **$0** | **$0** | **$0** |

| Balance sheet | | | |
|---|---|---|---|
| Trading Securities | $10,000,000 | | |
| Repo | | $(9,500,000) | |
| **Total Balance sheet** | **$10,000,000** | **$(9,500,000)** | **$500,000** |
| **Total Trial Balance** | **$10,000,000** | **$(9,500,000)** | **$500,000** |

Let's look at the funding profile and P&L for a credit desk which has purchased a GE bond, listed in Table 11.4.

The desk has funded their purchase primarily through a repo, but as the repo counterparty has taken a haircut, the desk is funding the residual $9 million through a term deposit with treasury.

| Bond funding needs | $(99,000,000) |
|---|---|
| Repo funds | $90,000,000 |
| Term borrowing | $9,000,000 |

The funding P&L will therefore be constructed of coupon income, accretion income, repo interest expense and term funding interest expense. Let's look at each of these now.

**TABLE 11.3**  Trial balance report with residual funding

| Trial Balance | | | |
|---|---|---|---|
| | **Debit** | **Credit** | **Net Total** |
| P&L | | | |
| Unrealized P&L | | $0 | |
| Interest Income | | $0 | |
| Interest Expenses | $0 | | |
| **Total P&L** | **$0** | **$0** | **$0** |

| Balance sheet | | | |
|---|---|---|---|
| Trading Securities | $10,000,000 | | |
| Repo | | $(9,500,000) | |
| Residual funding | | $(500,000) | |
| **Total Balance sheet** | **$10,000,000** | **$(10,000,000)** | **$0** |
| **Total Trial Balance** | **$10,000,000** | **$(10,000,000)** | **$0** |

**FIGURE 11.4** Funding P&L

**TABLE 11.4** Bond purchases impacting the desk's funding profile

| Security | GE 5% S/A 31/12/2017 |
|---|---|
| Buy/Sell | Buy |
| Trade Price | 99.00 |
| Trade date | 13/11/2015 |
| Value Date | 18/11/2015 |
| Closing Mkt price | 99.00 |
| Nominal | 100,000,000 |
| Consideration | 99,000,000 |
| Currency | USD |
| Maturity Date | 18/11/2016 |
| Coupon | 5% |
| Payment | Semi-annual |
| Day count basis | ACT/360 |
| Counterparty | Nashberries |

**Coupon**   The coupon income on a bond accrues on a straight line basis as soon as the purchase transaction reaches its value date. For the bonds in Table 11.4, the value date is 18 November, which is the date that Sparta Bank pays the counterparty and receives title for the bond.

The calculation for the coupon is as follows:

$$\text{Daily coupon income} = \text{Nominal} \times \text{coupon\%} \times \frac{days}{basis}$$

$$= \$100,000,000 \times 5\% \times \frac{1}{360}$$

$$= \$13,889$$

**Amortization/Accretion of Premiums and Discounts**   Unless a bond is purchased through a primary issuance at par, as bond yields change daily, most bonds will be purchased at a premium or discount to par.

Discount:   Price < 100
Premium:   Price > 100

Most banks treat the difference between par (100) and the purchase price, as a component of funding P&L. This price difference is reported through funding P&L over the remaining life of the bond.

For the GE bond, the purchase price is 1% less than par so the desk will accrete this difference into the funding P&L over the remaining 12 months of the bond's life. A simple way to calculate this is to use the following formula.

$$\text{Daily accretion income} = \text{Nominal} \times \text{price difference} \times \frac{days}{basis}$$

$$= \$100,000,000 \times 1\% \times \frac{1}{360}$$

$$= \$2,750$$

Alternatively, you can calculate the YTM (or EIR) and apply that to the purchase consideration to derive the overall interest income to accrue. Chapter 4 illustrates this method.

**Repo**   As a repo is a secured financing transaction, it usually carries a lower interest rate than an unsecured loan. In this example, the cost of the repo is 3%.

$$\text{Daily repo interest expense} = \$(90,000,000) \times 3\% \times \frac{1}{360}$$

$$= \$(7,500)$$

**Unsecured Term Borrowing**   Treasury has charged 4.5% on the unsecured loan.

$$\text{Daily term funding interest expense} = \$(9,000,000) \times 4.5\% \times \frac{1}{360}$$

$$= \$(1,125)$$

In Table 11.5 is one week of daily interest income and expenses. You will notice that on Friday there are three days of interest, as this incorporates the interest for Friday, Saturday and Sunday.

**TABLE 11.5** Daily funding P&L

|  | Business Date | | | | |
|---|---|---|---|---|---|
|  | Mon 23/11/15 | Tue 24/11/15 | Wed 25/11/15 | Thu 26/11/15 | Fri 27/11/15 |
| Coupon | $13,889 | $13,889 | $13,889 | $13,889 | $41,667 |
| Accretion | $2,750 | $2,750 | $2,750 | $2,750 | $8,250 |
| Repo | $(7,500) | $(7,500) | $(7,500) | $(7,500) | $(22,500) |
| Term borrowing | $(1,125) | $(1,125) | $(1,125) | $(1,125) | $(3,375) |
| Net interest income | $8,014 | $8,014 | $8,014 | $8,014 | $24,042 |

**Time Decay** Time decay is another component which can be included in funding P&L. Time decay is the P&L resulting from moving time from T-1 to T+0. In a positive yield curve environment, where yields further away from today are higher than those closer to today, this will result in a negative NPV becoming more negative and a positive NPV becoming more positive.

Table 11.6 illustrates this point, where future cash flows of $1,000,000 and $(1,000,000) occur in 365 days on T–1 and 364 days on T+0. By moving these cash flows one day closer to today, each NPV has increased by $77.

For weekend time decay on a swap portfolio, three days of time decay will come through the P&L for Monday rather than Friday.

## Rogue Trading Control

Funding is also a rogue trading control. The reason for this is that when rogue trading occurs, it can involve substantial losses, which need to be funded by the bank.

The strategy of Barings Futures Singapore (BFS) was to execute client orders and engage in arbitrage trading between the Osaka and Singapore stock exchanges. As clients are meant to fund their own margins and arbitrage trading should only require limited funding to cover margin calls from the price differences between the two exchanges, the funding requirements for BFS should have been negligible.

Instead, to fund his rogue trading losses, Nick Leeson was having to draw in hundreds of millions of dollars from local lines of credit and from treasury in Barings' head office. In just one week at the beginning of February 1995, Nick Leeson needed over $100 million in funding for margin calls for BFS. By the middle of February Nick Leeson required circa £300 million to fund his losses.[1]

**TABLE 11.6** Time decay P&L

|  | T+0 | T-1 | P&L |
|---|---|---|---|
| Swap yield | 3% | 3% | |
| Days | 364 | 365 | |
| Discount factor | 0.9710 | 0.9709 | |

| Future cash flow | NPV | NPV | |
|---|---|---|---|
| $1,000,000 | $970,951 | 970,874 | $77 |
| $(1,000,000) | $(970,951) | $(970,874) | $(77) |

With this in mind, it is important for a controller to understand the root cause of significant changes in the funding profile for their desk.

## FEES AND CHARGES

In an environment of declining revenues and increasing capital requirements, banks are very focused on reducing their expenses. There are two types of expenses that a bank reports, as illustrated in Figure 11.5.

1. Above the line expenses: These expenses directly relate to trades executed by the desk and include items such as brokerage and clearing fees.
2. Below the line expenses: These expenses do not directly relate to trades executed by the desk. These expenses include the cost of renting office space, staff costs, IT costs, and so forth.

In the P&L produced by product control, only above the line expenses are reported, which means that they do not typically focus on below the line expenses. This analysis is usually left to a management reporting team.

### Above the Line Expenses

There are a large number of brokers in the financial markets (e.g., ICAP, BGC and Tullet Prebon) whose job it is to facilitate a transaction between a buyer and a seller. When the desk uses a broker to execute a trade, they will incur a brokerage fee which is usually levied on

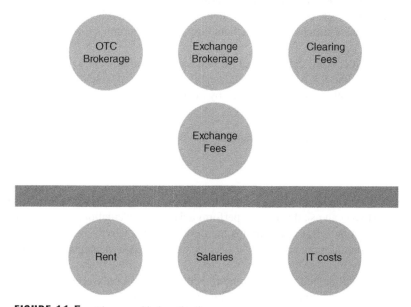

**FIGURE 11.5** Above and below the line expenses

individual transactions. Alternatively, the two parties can agree a fixed monthly fee to cover all broker-related activity.

> **OTC brokers** specialize in financial instruments like interest rate swaps, forwards and FX, which are not traded on an exchange. OTC broker fees are not cheap and if the desk uses them enough, they can form a material portion of the P&L. In the "good old days" of banking, brokers were known to offer some great perks for traders who frequently used their services, including overseas trips to Formula One Grands Prix.
> In my experience these fees make up the bulk of the expenses in the trading P&L, which is why heads of the business will monitor trends and where possible, actively manage them.
>
> **Exchange brokers** are those firms who are members of an exchange and have the right to execute trades on the stock or futures exchange. Not all banks will have membership with the exchange they want to trade on so they will need to use a broker who does. These brokers charge a fee for every transaction the bank executes.
>
> **Exchange clearing fees** are also incurred when a trader executes a trade on the exchange as that trade needs to be settled. The bank will have a relationship with a clearing bank who will arrange for the settlement of all its exchange transactions and the maintenance of initial and variation margin. The bank will transfer cash to and from this clearing bank who then manages all the daily and intraday settlements with the exchange.
>
> **Exchange fees** are not brokerage fees, these fees are incurred when a trader uses an exchange. These fees are paid to the exchange rather than the brokers who have executed or cleared your trades.

**Accounting for Brokerage and Other Trading Fees**   The most common way to account for these fees in the P&L is to accrue for them on a straight line basis. If you choose this method, you can take a simplistic approach and use the prior month's total fees as a baseline for the new month's accrual.

For example, it is April and the total trading fees for March were $100,000. Using this number as our baseline for April we would report an expense of $4,545 in the daily P&L, which is the total month's brokerage divided by the number of trading days in the month.

$$\text{Daily brokerage expense} = \frac{\$(100,000)}{22}$$
$$= \$(4,545)$$

Alternatively, if you have trading fee data included in all of your RMS trade tickets (where a fee is relevant) you can use this data to perform a daily fee calculation. Although this daily fee amount will not be linear each day (as the desk's trading activity is not congruent each day) this method should more accurately reflect the trading expenses incurred from the desk's trading activity.

No matter which method you select, both methods are still only accruals (or estimates) and need to be "trued up" to the actual trading fees that the bank has paid. On a monthly or quarterly basis, brokers will issue invoices to the bank which need to be paid. When Operations settle these invoices (after the chief operating officer (COO) has reviewed and approved them) product control can use this information to "true up" their P&L reporting.

For example, say we accrued for $100,000 of trading fees for the rates desk for March. In April invoices totalling $115,000 were paid for March's trading activity, which results in an under accrual of $15,000. Product control would then deduct $15,000 from the desk's P&L to reflect this "true-up" and use $115,000 as the new baseline to accrue for April's trading fees.

## NOTE

1. Nick Leeson, *Nick Leeson's Rogue Trader*, Page 265, Hachette Digital, 1995.

CHAPTER **12**

# Profit and Loss Adjustments

In a perfect world, there would be no need for P&L adjustments, but due to system deficiencies and human error, product control is required to intervene to ensure the bank's financials are reported accurately. In this chapter, we will explore how to control P&L adjustments effectively.

## THE NEED FOR P&L ADJUSTMENTS

Adjustments to the P&L are required when the GL or P&L reporting system is reporting an incorrect P&L. These amounts will typically remain as open entries on the balance sheet until the issue, which is causing the adjustment, is rectified.

As P&L adjustments weaken the control framework, the management of P&L adjustments is important. P&L adjustments need to be independently validated, recorded, reported and escalated on a timely basis, as losing sight or control of an adjustment can lead to quite serious consequences, including significant trading losses (e.g., the UBS rogue trading event). In Table 12.1 is a list of some of the common incidences which create the need for adjustments.

- Trade input: Adjustments in this category will usually be caused by trade booking errors or delays.
- Marking: This category will usually be caused by traders who fail to update their end of day prices, or they update their prices incorrectly.

    An adjustment is required as the fair values being reported are inaccurate. There may also be a small number of incidents where an external data feed, such as Reuters, could fail, but the vast majority of errors will come from trading staff.
- System feed: The firm will have a number of processes where systems interact with each other (f2b system flow) that create intersystem dependencies. The higher the complexity of a system's infrastructure the more likely that failures in the f2b feeds and calculations could occur.
- Trade or security events: During the life of a trade or security holding, there will be events that require intervention by middle office or operations. Coupon fixings, notional resets, stock splits and dividends are all examples of life cycle events. If the intervention is untimely or incorrect, a P&L adjustment may be required.

**TABLE 12.1**    Items giving rise to P&L adjustments

| P&L adjustment category | Cause | |
|---|---|---|
| | **System** | **Human** |
| **Trade input** | | |
| – Trade input error | | X |
| – Trade missed system end of day cut | | X |
| – Trade booking incomplete | | X |
| **Marking** | | |
| – Stale price | | X |
| – Incorrect price updated | | X |
| – Price update missed end of day cut | | X |
| **System feed** | | |
| – RMS system has not fed P&L reporting system/GL | X | |
| – RMS system feed is incomplete | X | |
| – Residual Funding mechanism hasn't run correctly | X | |
| – FX Revaluation and restatement hasn't run correctly | X | |
| **Trade and Security events** | | |
| – Corporate actions not input correctly | | X |
| – Trade fixings not updated correctly | | X |
| **Manual accruals** | | |
| – Fees and charges | | X |
| – Internal allocations | | X |

- Manual Accruals: There are fees, charges and internal allocations which are not automatically included in the P&L reporting system or GL, which means the P&L needs to be included via an adjustment.

## CONTROLLING P&L ADJUSTMENTS

Before making an adjustment, product control needs to:

1. Independently quantify and verify the need for the adjustment
2. Record the P&L adjustment in the appropriate system/s
3. Report the adjustment to the front office and other stakeholders
4. Escalate the adjustment where appropriate.

### Independent Verification

If the desk is asking product control to make a P&L adjustment, the controller must ascertain whether the adjustment is necessary and if so, is the amount accurate.

In the UBS rogue trading event, the Swiss regulator FINMA identified that the desk influenced the P&L adjustments made by product control which product control processed without challenge.[1] Challenge and professional scepticism is therefore critical to a healthy independent control function.

## Recording

P&L adjustments need to be recorded in the system specified by management, as unrecorded adjustments cannot be reported, interrogated or escalated. When recording a P&L adjustment, the following fields should be completed as a minimum:

- Value date of P&L adjustment
- Amount
- Ccy
- USD equivalent
- Reason – detailed description
- Category of P&L adjustment
- Action required to remove the need for the P&L adjustment
- Action owner
- Expected date of resolution.

For example, an adjustment is required if the P&L reporting system has incorrectly reported a profit of $3.44 million on a GE bond due to a trader's mismark.

### Definition of fields in P&L adjustment example:

- Value date: This is not today's date; it is usually the P&L date. Using the example in Table 12.2, on 15 March 2015, the P&L for 14 March 2015, is being prepared and reported, so the date entered would be 14 March 2015.
- Amount: Transaction currency amount.
- Ccy: The currency in which the P&L adjustment is being made. P&L adjustments should be made in the appropriate underlying transaction currency to avoid creating an FX exposure for the firm.

    For example, using the example in Table 12.2, if the adjustment was made in USD, rather than GBP, and it was carried over month-end (which required a financial accounting journal to be passed in the GL), the USD adjustment (loss) and the GBP profit would each be sold down at the month-end FX rate, thereby creating an erroneous but real long GBP/USD FX position for the desk.

**TABLE 12.2** P&L adjustment example

| | |
|---|---|
| Value date of P&L adjustment | 14/03/2015 |
| Amount | (2,250,000) |
| Ccy | GBP |
| USD equivalent | (3,442,500) |
| Reason – detailed description | Trader mismarked £75 mln GE 3% 2020 bond. Priced at 100 but should have been 97. |
| Category of P&L adjustment | Mismark |
| Action required to remove the need for the P&L adjustment | Desk to remark position correctly today 15/03/2015 |
| Action owner | Trader – Will Smith |
| Expected date of resolution | 15/03/2015 |

- USD equivalent: The USD equivalent (or the currency the P&L is being reported in) of the transaction currency amount using the spot FX rate as of the P&L date. This facilitates consistent reporting of all adjustments.
- Reason: A detailed description explaining the reason for the P&L adjustment. The data in this field should be detailed enough to enable someone who is unfamiliar with the situation to understand why the P&L adjustment is required.
- Category of P&L adjustment: Categorizing the type of P&L adjustment facilitates meaningful management information (MI) for management. It provides management with information regarding which groups of P&L adjustments – for example, mismarks, trade booking errors, RMS system feed delays, and so forth – cause the most additional work for product control. Management can then organize remediation of these issues.
- Action required to remove the need for the P&L adjustment: As with the "Reason" field, the data in this field should be detailed enough to enable someone not familiar with the situation to understand what action is required to remove the need for this P&L adjustment.
- Action owner: The action owner should be explicitly listed as this determines who is responsible for taking away the need for the P&L adjustment. For example, position mismarking would be owned by the trader, whilst system feed issues would be owned by IT.

  Although product control are not the action owner in all circumstances, they do need to be the point guard for ensuring the issue causing the adjustment is resolved.
- Expected date of resolution: It is important that management is aware of how long a P&L adjustment is expected to be carried for, as those with far-dated resolutions may require some attention to bring that date forward.

The P&L adjustments need to be recorded in a system that allows stakeholders timely and relevant access to the data to report on and escalate amounts as necessary.

For example, if the system used to record P&L adjustments could only be accessed monthly to retrieve data then that would hamstring the bank's ability to maintain a strong control environment.

## Reporting

The benefit of recording P&L adjustments is that they can be reported to the front office, management and affected stakeholders. The reported P&L sent to the desk should contain the P&L adjustments being carried. By having this visibility, when the desk sign off their P&L, they are confirming the P&L, inclusive of the P&L adjustments, is accurate. P&L adjustments will also be reported to product control management, who are acutely aware of the risks they pose to the control framework.

## Escalation

Escalating aged or material P&L adjustments is important, as it draws more senior staff in to the controls. In the UBS rogue trading scandal, it was discovered that UBS had no policy to escalate P&L adjustments, even when the P&L adjustments reached $1 billion.[2] We know how that approach to controls ended for them.

The escalation of P&L adjustments should follow the firm's pre-determined escalation matrix. An example of this matrix is supplied in Table 12.3. If a product control manager considers the thresholds too high for their business, it may be appropriate to view the main

**TABLE 12.3** P&L adjustment escalation matrix

| P&L Adjustment Escalation Matrix | | | | | | | | | | | |
|---|---|---|---|---|---|---|---|---|---|---|---|
| | Product control | | | Front Office and COO | | | Operations | | | Market Risk | | |
| USD | Supervisor | Regional Head | Global Head | Trader/Sales/COO | Regional Head | Global Head | Supervisor | Regional Head | Global Head | Supervisor | Regional Head | Global Head |
| $0–$1mln | | | | | | | | | | | | |
| 1 day | X | | | X | | | X | | | X | | |
| 1 week | | X | | | X | | | X | | | X | |
| 1 month | | | X | | | X | | | X | | | X |
| $1mln–$5mln | | | | | | | | | | | | |
| 1 day | X | | | X | | | X | | | X | | |
| 3 days | | X | | | X | | | X | | | X | |
| 1 week | | | X | | | X | | | X | | | X |
| >$5mln | | | | | | | | | | | | |
| 1 day | X | | | X | | | X | | | X | | |
| 3 days | | | X | | | X | | | X | | | X |

matrix as the minimum standard that can be applied and individual businesses can opt to apply lower thresholds where it is deemed appropriate to do so.

The escalation matrix includes four functions: product control, front office (including COO), market risk and operations. Including these other support and control functions in the escalation matrix can have a positive effect on the control environment, as collaboration presents a united front which should lead to control issues being identified and resolved in a timely manner.

For example, when the operations supervisor becomes aware of P&L adjustments being carried for a corporate action error, the supervisor can firstly ensure that the error is corrected immediately. Secondly, they can review the root cause to prevent similar errors from reoccurring.

As the escalation matrix underlines a significant control, it is important to record the instances where an escalation has taken place in an appropriate location (e.g., a shared drive or a shared point on the Intranet), to satisfy reviews conducted by audit and regulators.

You may have noticed that the only function in finance that is made aware of the escalated adjustments are product control. Product control will, through their sign off on the financials at month-end and quarter-end, provide financial control with a list of material P&L adjustments that are being carried.

That completes our review of P&L adjustments.

# NOTES

1. Swiss Financial Market Supervisory Authority, "Investigation into the Events surrounding Trading Losses of USD 2.3 billion incurred by the Investment banking Division of UBS AG in London," 21 November 2012, p. 7. https://www.finma.ch/en/news/2012/11/mm-ubs-london-20121126.
2. Ibid.

# CHAPTER 13

# Profit and Loss Commentary

The daily P&L commentary is produced leveraging all the analytical reviews conducted by product control, in the execution of their daily controls. The commentary is an important control, as it provides the reader with an insight into how the desk generated their P&L for the day.

The reader is particularly interested in product control identifying instances where the desk's P&L is considered unusual. It is on these unusual days that product control provides more value to the reader, as it illustrates that this function has a good grasp on the financial results, their drivers and validity.

As a guide, the commentary should be constructed to focus on the following primary drivers of P&L, which are illustrated in Figure 13.1.

We will reference the P&L results in Table 13.1 in examples throughout this chapter. The terms MTM P&L and market moves P&L will be used interchangeably.

## Day One P&L

Day one P&L is the total P&L earned from new trades, which can be split into P&L earned from client margins and P&L earned from intraday MTM.

**Margin**   Margin is earned by both the sales and trading desks when transacting with clients. For sales margin, it is helpful to consider the following:

- Expected sales pipeline: A sales desk will generally know well in advance if they are transacting a deal with a very large P&L implication. Being informed on business expectations of future deals is an important aspect to consider when understanding and providing commentary on P&L movements related to sales.
- Margin size: A control to consider would be whether the margin charged is outside the range historically charged for the instrument and duration.
- Volume: Is the volume of trades passing through the books up or down on the daily average?

For example, using the P&L data in Table 13.1 and the sales data in Table 13.2, the following is a sample commentary. New trades generated $810k in profits, $630k of which was

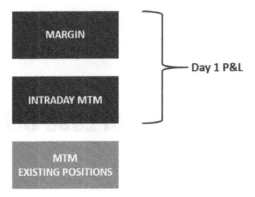

**FIGURE 13.1**  P&L commentary segments

earned through client margins on the sales desk. Trade volumes were up 6% on the daily average which accounts for the slightly higher than usual profit. There were no big ticket items.

**Intraday MTM**   Intraday MTM (mark-to-market) P&L is the portion of day one P&L over and above any margin earned, which is illustrated in Figure 13.2.

On a portfolio level, intraday MTM P&L will only arise if a client trade is left unhedged and, as the market can move favourably or unfavourably, can result in either profits or losses for the trading desk.

When the intraday MTM is a material driver of the day one P&L, a commentary should be provided to explain the position, changes in market rates and why those market rates changed. For example, using the P&L data in Table 13.1, the following is a sample commentary. Intraday MTM of $100k was lost from a long AUD/USD vega position. The desk built up a 200k vega position on an AUD/USD FX option client trade which suffered as volatility fell by 0.50% due to lower demand for downside protection.

**MTM P&L on Existing Positions**   P&L generated on existing positions arises because the portfolio is not fully hedged. In the past, this has been a significant component of a desk's P&L, but since the introduction of the Volcker rule, this significance has diminished.

When the MTM P&L is a material driver of the P&L, product control should consider the following when preparing their commentary:

- How much P&L was generated from market risk exposures
- Which market risks generated material P&L
- What the movements were in market prices that generated this P&L
- What the underlying reasons were for the market prices to change in this manner.

For this component of commentary, it is important that product control understands the drivers of the financial markets. For example, using the P&L data in Table 13.1 and the risk-based P&L estimate in Table 13.3, the following is a sample commentary.

MTM P&L generated a profit of $729k, most of which was from the desk's long AUD/USD $52.5m spot FX position, which benefitted from a rise in AUD of 1.4 US cents.

**TABLE 13.1**  Daily P&L

| | Trading Activity | | | | | Other | | | | | Grand Total |
|---|---|---|---|---|---|---|---|---|---|---|---|
| | New Trades Entry P&L | Intraday Market Moves | Amendments | Total Trading Activity | Market Moves | Funding | Valuation adjustments | Fees and charges | Total Other | | |
| Trading | 125,000 | −100,000 | 17,000 | 42,000 | 729,000 | −23,000 | 0 | −15,000 | −38,000 | | 733,000 |
| Sales | 630,000 | 0 | | 630,000 | 0 | 0 | 0 | 0 | 0 | | 630,000 |
| Total | 755,000 | −100,000 | 17,000 | 672,000 | 729,000 | −23,000 | 0 | −15,000 | −38,000 | | 1,363,000 |

**TABLE 13.2** The daily sales volume results vs. the trend

| Daily Sales Volumes | | |
|---|---|---|
| | **Trades** | **Notional (mln)** |
| **Volume** | 53,000 | 398,000 |
| **Daily average** | 50,000 | 375,000 |
| **% Variance** | 6% | 6% |

AUD strengthened due to better than expected employment numbers, which reduced the likelihood of an early rate cut by the Reserve Bank.

## WHO IS THE READER?

The content of the P&L commentary is often determined by who is going to be reading it. Whilst the quality of the commentary will not be reduced, the recipients will influence the breadth and depth of the commentary that is published.

The recipients can be the desk and their management, management reporting, market risk, regulators, product control and finance management. Usually, the more senior the audience, the less detail that is required. Therefore, product control need to have the skills to not only write a detailed commentary, but also present it in a more summarized format for management.

## WHEN IS P&L COMMENTARY REQUIRED?

The P&L commentary explains a theme rather than an entire story. As every dollar of P&L doesn't need explaining, there has to be a cut-off at some point where the P&L commentary is deemed unimportant. But how should that cut-off be determined?

Firstly, it should be noted that product control is not the only function to determine when P&L commentary is required. The management reporting team, who are responsible for publishing management information internally and externally, will usually set P&L thresholds at

**FIGURE 13.2** Intraday MTM P&L

**TABLE 13.3** AUD/USD Risk-based estimate

| AUD/USD Risk-based P&L estimate | | | | |
|---|---|---|---|---|
| | | Revaluation Prices | | |
| Ccy Pair | Delta | T+0 | T–1 | Risk-based estimate |
| AUD/USD | A$52,500,000 | 0.9640 | 0.9500 | $735,000 |

which they require commentary from product control. These thresholds can be set in regard to requests from the bank's senior management and regulators. Ideally though, product control and management reporting should work together to establish these commentary thresholds so that product control feel they have buy in to thresholds that impact their workload.

With this in mind, one method is to establish commentary thresholds at two levels. For example:

Desk P&L
Level 1    Total P&L
Level 2    Attributed P&L
           (Trading Activity, Market Moves, Other)

The thresholds at both levels can be set using historical P&L data and those thresholds deemed important for senior management and regulators. Hopefully though, the thresholds that product control want to apply are below or equal to those of senior management and regulators.

For example, let's assume the firm's regulators and senior management want to receive commentary when the P&L exceeds a broad dollar threshold of $1 million, rather than a desk-specific threshold. With this in mind, the P&L commentary at Level 1 could be set as the lower of $1,000,000 and one standard deviation.

The point of using one standard deviation as a threshold is because this statistic tells product control what P&L can be considered normal and abnormal for the desk. Two desks can have the same average P&L but their standard deviations can be wildly different. It is these instances of abnormal P&L that require further analysis to determine the reasons for the result and whether the result is valid.

In reality, a whole prior year's, prior month's or prior quarter's P&L would be used as a reference point to calculate the mean and standard deviation of the daily P&Ls. However, for this example let us just use the daily P&L results in Table 13.4 to establish thresholds.

The FX desk has an average total daily P&L of $1,164,000 and a standard deviation of $731,000. This results in a lower level threshold of $433,000 and an upper threshold of $1,896,000. As the lower threshold is below the general $1m threshold, the commentary requirement thresholds for FX product control will be:

P&L is either less than $433,000 or greater than $1,000,000

Although the upper commentary threshold in this example is well below the $1,896,000, product control still need to be cognizant of the standard deviation and average when analysing the desk's P&L, as this statistical information helps shape product control's approach to their analysis of the desk's P&L.

Commentary thresholds at Level 2 apply to each individual attribute; namely, Trading Activity, MTM and Other. These thresholds can be set in a similar manner to Level 1, for example, the lower of $500,000 and one standard deviation.

For Trading Activity, the lower threshold is $690,000 and upper threshold is $930,000. As both thresholds are above $500,000, the commentary thresholds will be $500,000. And so on and so forth for the remaining attributes.

**TABLE 13.4**   Averages and standard deviations of the daily P&L results

| Date | *$000s* Trading Activity | Market Moves | Other | Total |
|---|---|---|---|---|
| 2/01/2014 | 827 | 706 | 14 | 1,547 |
| 3/01/2014 | 900 | 770 | 200 | 1,870 |
| 6/01/2014 | 677 | (500) | (10) | 167 |
| 7/01/2014 | 988 | 900 | 55 | 1,943 |
| 8/01/2014 | 770 | (250) | 50 | 570 |
| 9/01/2014 | 698 | 150 | 40 | 888 |
| **Standard deviation** | **120** | **585** | **74** | **731** |
| **Average** | **810** | **296** | **58** | **1,164** |
| | | | | |
| **Upper Threshold** | **930** | **881** | **132** | **1,896** |
| **Lower Threshold** | **690** | **(289)** | **(15)** | **433** |

Other thresholds may also exist which trigger the need for commentary, such as consecutive losses. This commentary threshold is triggered when the sum of the daily P&L's for a specified time period exceeds the consecutive loss threshold. For example, if the rates desk had a 30-day consecutive loss limit of $(1,000,000) and the sum of the daily P&L's for those 30 business days is $(2,500,000), a commentary is required to explain the nature of the losses. Breaches of this nature are discussed by the trading desk, product control and market risk to understand the risk positions generating the losses and how they will be managed going forward.

## Escalating P&L and the Related Commentary

It is important that front office management (e.g., desk heads), risk management and product control management are not inundated with too much information but are kept adequately informed of significant P&L events. Referring P&L and their commentaries to these stakeholders using two standard deviations can help walk this fine line and maintain an effective control environment.

## Other P&L Commentary

Product control not only provide daily P&L commentaries, they also prepare weekly, monthly and quarterly commentaries. Although different reporting periods are being commented on, the same principles will apply in shaping the commentary and for determining the thresholds that apply.

When preparing these less frequent commentaries, it would be appropriate to consider the following items:

- Analyse trends over time in revenue, margin and volume
- Compare results to a benchmark, which can be a prior period or plan
- Assess general market themes (e.g., market volatility) and its impact on overall performance, volume, margin and opportunity for earning P&L from risk-taking.

That concludes our review of P&L commentary.

# CHAPTER 14

# Profit and Loss Reconciliations and Sign-Offs

T here are two primary P&L reconciliations performed by product control. These are the comparison of the front office estimate to product control's P&L and the comparison of the P&L in the general ledger (GL) to that reported by product control. This chapter will look at both these reconciliations and will also review the front office P&L sign off, which is another important control which product control interact with.

## FLASH VS. ACTUAL

One of the key controls maintained by product control is the comparison of the flash to the actual P&L produced by product control. An accurate flash is important as it shows the desk understand their book, which includes its trading activity, existing risk and the market rates used to revalue their portfolio.

When the desk persistently publish an inaccurate flash it indicates something is wrong. The issue could be due to a range of reasons such as trader laziness, a genuine misunderstanding of how their P&L is measured or system error. Given the importance of this control, any issues rendering it ineffective should be identified and remediated.

At most banks, if the product control P&L is materially different to the flash, the desk will come under a lot of pressure from their management. It is therefore important that product control informs the desk on T+0 if they intend to adjust the desk's P&L by a material amount; for example, for changes in valuation adjustments.

### Apples to Apples

When you have two sets of data to compare, the comparison is made more difficult if there are no common attributes to use. Conversely, the task is made easier when there is a 100% match in attributes.

For example, if the flash only provides one number but the product control P&L is broken down into several attributes, product control would not be able to perform a detailed reconciliation between their P&L and the flash. This could result in material variances not being understood, which ultimately weakens the control framework.

**TABLE 14.1**   T0 Flash vs. Actual P&L

| FX desk P&L | | | |
|---|---|---|---|
| **Attribute** | **Product control P&L** | **T0 Flash** | **Variance** |
| New trades | $65,000 | | $65,000 |
| Modified trades | ($12,000) | | ($12,000) |
| MTM P&L | $845,000 | | $845,000 |
| Funding | ($77,000) | | ($77,000) |
| Fees and charges | ($40,000) | | ($40,000) |
| Reserves | $0 | | $0 |
| Total Day's P&L | $781,000 | $659,000 | $122,000 |

Table 14.1 illustrates the scenario where the flash is unhelpful as it only reports P&L at the total level.

In Table 14.2, the desk has provided a more detailed breakdown of how they generated a profit of $659,000. With the benefit of this detail, product control can now focus their attention on the major driver of the variance, namely, why the EUR MTM P&L is showing a $150,000 variance.

This could be due to one of the following reasons:

1. The end of day revaluation rates used by both functions are not consistent; for example, the desk has forgotten to update the end of day rates in its estimate.

**TABLE 14.2**   Flash vs. product control P&L with further detail from the desk

| FX desk P&L | | | |
|---|---|---|---|
| **Attribute** | **Product control P&L** | **T0 Flash** | **Variance** |
| New trades | $65,000 | $70,000 | ($5,000) |
| Modified trades | ($12,000) | ($11,000) | ($1,000) |
| | | | |
| **MTM P&L** | **$845,000** | **$717,000** | **$128,000** |
| AUD | $645,000 | $645,000 | $0 |
| CAD | ($33,000) | ($18,000) | ($15,000) |
| EUR | $800,000 | $650,000 | $150,000 |
| GBP | ($567,000) | ($560,000) | ($7,000) |
| | | | |
| Funding | ($77,000) | ($77,000) | $0 |
| Fees and charges | ($40,000) | ($40,000) | $0 |
| Reserves | $0 | $0 | $0 |
| | | | |
| **Total P&L** | **$781,000** | **$659,000** | **$122,000** |

**2.** There is a difference in the portfolio of trades used by each function; for example, the desk booked trades after the end of day cut-off, which are not in product control's P&L but are included in the desk's estimate.

**3.** A function has made an error in preparing their P&L.

Material variances can result in the trader not signing off their P&L until they see the variance reversed in a subsequent day's P&L.

If the variances between flash and actual P&L are material and occur frequently, the issue should be escalated in product control and the front office so the root cause can be identified and remediated.

## DESK P&L SIGN-OFF

Although product control is an independent function, it is important that the desk is given an opportunity to challenge product control's P&L. The desk can articulate their approval or rejection of the P&L via the bank's P&L sign-off tool, which can come in the form of:

- Email, where product control must file away the response for future audits or when the desk wish to retract their approval in subsequent P&Ls.
- The P&L reporting system.
- A standalone supervisory system where all the reports that the desk must approve are listed and tracked.

The P&L sign-off is an important internal control as any late, missing or rejected sign-offs could indicate that there is a problem with the P&L. These incidents are identified and tracked by the COO and product control management.

In my experience it has been rare for the desk to reject the P&L in the sign-off tool as most of the issues raised by the desk would have been closed out during the production of the P&L.

Let's look at what the P&L production and sign-off process could look like in a summarized format, which is illustrated in Figure 14.1.

**On T+0** the desk produce their flash at the end of the trading day

**On T+1:**
- Product control commence with the production of the actual P&L.
- Product control compare the actual P&L to the flash and, with the help of the desk, resolve material discrepancies.

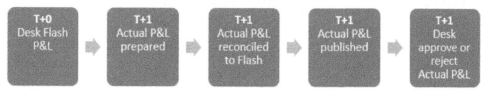

**FIGURE 14.1** P&L sign off

**TABLE 14.3**   Credit desk, flash vs. product control P&L

| Credit desk P&L | | | |
|---|---|---|---|
| **Attribute** | **Actual P&L** | **Flash** | **Variance** |
| New trades | 560,000 | 560,000 | 0 |
| Amended trades | (43,000) | (43,000) | 0 |
| MTM P&L | 197,000 | 205,000 | (8,000) |
| Funding | 35,417 | 60,000 | (24,583) |
| Fees and charges | (40,000) | (40,000) | 0 |
| Reserves | 0 | 0 | 0 |
| **Total P&L** | **709,417** | **742,000** | **(32,583)** |

- Product control publish the P&L.
- The desk approve or reject the P&L in the P&L sign-off tool.

It is through steps 2 and 3 that any material issues between the two P&Ls are identified and resolved. Although it is rare for the desk to reject the product control P&L, there will be instances where this occurs. When disputes cannot be resolved by the two initial parties, escalation through the relevant lines of management may be required.

Product control should also remember that a trader's remuneration is linked to their P&L so it is understandable that traders can become quite excited when presented with a P&L that is lower than they expected. During these instances it is important that product control stick to the facts and ensure their P&L is supported by constructive data.

For example, in Table 14.3 is the P&L comparison for the credit desk. The credit trader does not accept that the funding P&L is $25k worse than their flash and raises this issue with product control during steps 2 and 3. Product control double checks the funding P&L and provides the trader a breakdown of the positions and interest rates that account for the funding P&L. This is displayed in Table 14.4.

In this instance the trader still disagrees with the P&L but cannot provide additional data to support the higher funding P&L. Consequently, the trader rejects the P&L and the issue is escalated through both lines of management to resolve the dispute.

**TABLE 14.4**   Funding breakdown

| Funding | Nominal | Yield | Interest Income or (Expense) |
|---|---|---|---|
| Apple 3% 2025 bond | 300,000,000 | 4.00% | 33,333 |
| GE 4% 2020 bond | 250,000,000 | 5.00% | 34,722 |
| GM 7% 2019 bond | 100,000,000 | 7.00% | 19,444 |
| Repos | (500,000,000) | 3.00% | (41,667) |
| Term borrowings from treasury | (150,000,000) | 2.50% | (10,417) |
| | | **Total** | **35,417** |

## P&L RECONCILIATION

In addition to reconciling the actual P&L to an estimated P&L, there is another important reconciliation which product control also need to perform where the P&L is not reported directly from the GL.

Historically, the P&L reported by product control was reported from the risk management system (RMS) via either Microsoft Excel/Access or a P&L reporting system. As the bank's financial statements emanate from the GL, the GL was seen as the source of truth which meant the RMS P&L needed to be reconciled to the GL P&L.

This reconciliation process, which is most often performed at month-end, can consume hundreds to thousands of hours every time it is performed. Such work is necessary but it is also not adding any value to the bank.

As product control has matured, the industry has recognized the value in reporting the P&L directly from the GL and a number of banks have adopted this approach. Although the work required to build the necessary reporting from the GL is extensive, the benefit of adopting this approach is significant as the thousands of hours spent each year reconciling differences can be saved or redirected to more value added work.

Figure 14.2 illustrates simplistically, the two different approaches to P&L reporting. In Approach 1, product control report the P&L from the RMS which they then need to reconcile to the GL P&L.

The amount of time spent reconciling the two systems and the ability to identify reasons for the variances is dependent on the quality of the bank's system infrastructure. Banks with a poor system infrastructure can result in product control not being able to determine why there

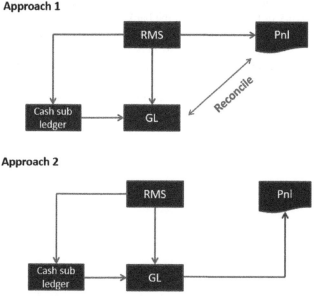

**FIGURE 14.2**  Approaches to P&L reporting and the impact on reconciliations

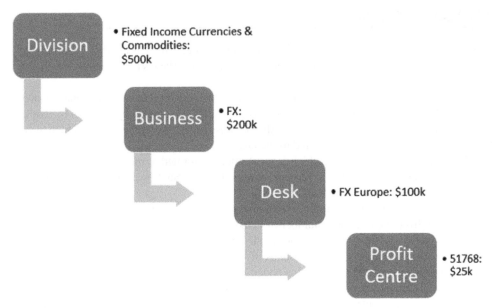

**FIGURE 14.3**   Establishing P&L variance thresholds

are material differences between the two sources, which is not only an operational risk, but a source of frustration for the controllers concerned.

In Approach 2, product control report the P&L directly from the GL. This means that there is no need to reconcile the RMS P&L to the GL P&L, which frees up resources to focus on more analytical work or be released from the bank's payroll.

On a risk and reward basis, thresholds are usually applied to the differences between the two P&Ls, with investigations and resolutions only being required if the differences breach that threshold. The thresholds may be levied at multiple levels, which I have illustrated an example of in Figure 14.3.

That completes our review of P&L reconciliations and sign-offs.

# Four

# Valuations

When a bank's risk management system (RMS) revalues a portfolio of trades, the valuations produced by the RMS may be inconsistent with the fair values required by IFRS and U.S. GAAP. To ensure the valuations are aligned to fair value, product control or valuation control (from here on valuation control) will validate the prices used to revalue the portfolio and if necessary construct the necessary valuation adjustments. In Part Four of the book we will look at the work valuation control perform to align the desk's portfolio to fair value.

CHAPTER **15**

# Independent Price Verification

In Chapter 8 we learnt that a bank can source their end of day rates (or pricing inputs) from both independent providers and the trading desk. When a rate is sourced from the trading desk, valuation control need to ensure that the rate is aligned to the market. This validation process is known as independent price verification or IPV.

IPV of all fair valued assets and liabilities is performed at every month end and a smaller version of IPV is also usually run mid month. Pricing variances can arise due to genuine differences of opinions regarding the fair value of a position and they can also arise due to deliberate mismarking by a trader.

Traders can mismark their prices to manipulate the value of their portfolio, which has a direct impact on their P&L performance. A trader may choose to inflate the value of their trading portfolio (and P&L) to earn a higher bonus and guarantee future employment, which can occur when they are behind on their budget and want to conceal their true trading performance. This type of pricing is known as an aggressive marking.

Mismarking can also be used to deflate the value of a trading portfolio (and P&L), which may occur in the lead up to year end when the trader has made their budget for the year and wants to roll forward some of their unrealized profits into the next financial year. This type of pricing is known as a conservative marking.

Mismarking can often be used for a trader to achieve a smoothed P&L, which aims to report a consistent daily P&L and take away unnecessary P&L volatility. When this occurs, the mismarking can switch between aggressive and conservative marking to achieve the desired P&L outcome. This practice is illustrated in Figure 15.1. When the firm line is below the dashed line, the trader would mark his positions aggressively to inflate the P&L. Using an example of a long bond, the trader would mark the bond above the market's price.

Any form of deliberate mismarking is dishonest and traders can not only face the loss of employment, they may also face being banned from the City. For example:

*The FSA gave Alexis Stenfors a Decision Notice ... prohibiting him from performing any function in relation to any regulated activity carried on by any authorised or exempt person or exempt professional firm on the grounds that Mr Stenfors is not fit and proper.*

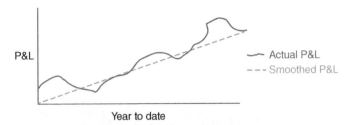

**FIGURE 15.1**   P&L smoothing

*This Notice is issued to Mr Stenfors in light of his conduct ... when Mr Stenfors was a trader on the Short Term Interest Rate Trading ("STIRT") desk of the London branch of Merrill Lynch International bank Limited ("MLIB") and the head of Scandi Swaps Trading at Merrill Lynch.*

*During the relevant period, Mr Stenfors deliberately mismarked positions on his trading books. Mr Stenfors estimates that his positions were overvalued by approximately $100 million ... Mr Stenfors' conduct demonstrated a lack of integrity and he is therefore considered not fit and proper to perform any function in relation to regulated activities.*

*In the FSA's view, Mr Stenfors' misconduct is serious because he was a senior and experienced trader who was fully aware of his responsibilities to mark to market his positions and of the consequences of failing to do so ...*[1]

## COMPONENTS TO IPV PROCESS

There are four components to the IPV process which are illustrated in Figure 15.2.

### 1. Identifying the Fair Valued Financial Assets and Liabilities

IPV is only concerned with those financial assets and liabilities which are accounted for on a fair value basis, which will include not only those financial assets and liabilities accounted for at fair value through P&L, but also those financial assets accounted for at fair value through other comprehensive income.

**FIGURE 15.2**   IPV process

**TABLE 15.1** Fixed income securities

| Security | Nominal | Trader Price | Fair Value |
|---|---|---|---|
| GE 5% 31/12/2017 | 17,000,000 | 99.4 | 16,898,000 |
| Rolls Royce 7% 31/12/2017 | 30,000,000 | 99.1 | 29,730,000 |
| Lloyds TSB 5.25% 31/12/2017 | 5,000,000 | 99.9 | 4,995,000 |
| Unilever 4.75% 31/12/2017 | 6,000,000 | 98.2 | 5,892,000 |

When sourcing the population of fair valued financial assets and liabilities, the data will come from either the general ledger (GL) or the RMS and be in one of two forms, depending on the type of financial instrument. Securities and loans will usually be displayed in nominals, whilst derivatives will be displayed in their relevant Greek sensitivities.

In Table 15.1 are a list of bonds and the trader prices used to derive their fair values.

In Table 15.2 are a list of U.S. interest rate sensitivities and the trader swap yields used to derive their fair values.

Tables 15.1 and 15.2 are just two examples of fair valued populations that require independent price testing. The same approach could be taken with the rest of the bank's trader marked prices such as credit and FX derivatives.

## 2. Price Discovery – Sourcing Fair Values from the Market

Price discovery is the term used to describe a bank's search for fair value of an asset or liability, which requires valuation control to source prices from the market.

The approach taken to sourcing prices needs to be a consistent one to preserve the integrity of the IPV process. A consistent IPV process uses agreed market pricing sources for each asset class on an ongoing basis and does not deviate from these sources unless there is proper due diligence carried out on the new or additional source, which include bringing significant changes through a valuations committee.

**TABLE 15.2** US interest rate risk presented as DV01s by tenor

| Interest Rates – USD | | |
|---|---|---|
| Tenor | DV01 | Rate |
| O/N | 7,000 | 0.090% |
| 1MTH | (3,500) | 0.150% |
| 3MTH | 31,500 | 0.230% |
| 6MTH | 102,000 | 0.330% |
| 9MTH | 20,000 | 0.400% |
| 1YR | 25,000 | 0.560% |
| 2YR | (23,000) | 0.630% |
| 3YR | 20,000 | 0.700% |
| **Total** | **179,000** | |

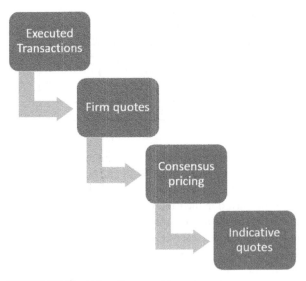

**FIGURE 15.3** Price discovery hierarchy

Due diligence helps ensure the new price is a true and fair view of the underlying market and that the trader is not significantly influencing prices published by the new source. Failure to conduct this due diligence could result in the bank misreporting the value of the P&L and balance sheet.

Valuation control will usually have a hierarchy of pricing sources in their search for fair value. The hierarchy will look something like that shown in Figure 15.3.

Figure 15.3 shows four pricing sources, which the valuation control team have ranked from most preferred to the least preferred.

**Executed Transactions**    These are transactions that the bank has executed with market participants. This is explicit proof of the exit price for the asset or liability.

Ideally the transactions should take place on the measurement date and be as close to the end of day rate snap as possible. For more illiquid instruments, which trade infrequently, the distance from the end of day snap should matter less than for liquid instruments.

**Firm Quotes**    Firm quotes are those bids and offers published by market participants for a specific parcel size, which if hit, a transaction is executed between both parties.

**Consensus Pricing**    Consensus pricing is a service run by companies such as Markit (Totem) where market participants submit indicative prices to the service provider and receive back an average market price based upon the contributions of all participants. As these prices are indicative the bank cannot execute trades at the published price. Aside from that, the consensus prices are usually received one day in arrears which makes them a historic reference point. Therefore, these prices are only an indication of fair value.

For example, Sparta bank submitted quotes for a swap yield curve, which are illustrated in Table 15.3.

**TABLE 15.3**  Consensus pricing results

| Tenor | Your submission | Accepted/Rejected | Consensus price |
|-------|-----------------|-------------------|-----------------|
| Mar-17 | 1.070% | Accepted | 1.070% |
| Jun-17 | 1.170% | Accepted | 1.173% |
| Sep-17 | 1.270% | Accepted | 1.275% |
| Dec-17 | 1.370% | Accepted | 1.370% |
| Mar-18 | 1.470% | Accepted | 1.472% |
| Jun-18 | 1.570% | Accepted | 1.570% |
| Sep-18 | 1.670% | Accepted | 1.670% |
| Dec-18 | 1.770% | Rejected | 1.780% |

| Submitters |
|------------|
| JP Morgan |
| Sparta bank |
| HSBC |
| UBS |
| Citibank |
| Barclays |

In total there were six banks who submitted yields into the consensus price service. Although Sparta bank submitted eight quotes, not all the quotes which they submitted were included in deriving the consensus yield. The Dec-18 yield was rejected because it was deemed too far away from the other bank's submissions. As it is only the second bad yield that the bank has submitted, the bank still gets to view the consensus yield for this month.

**Indicative Quotes**    Quotes provided by pricing services (and some market participants not wanting to commit to a price), such as ICE data services, are usually only indicative prices, which again means that the price is only an indication of fair value and not an executable exit price.

If valuation control were to request quotes from a broker, the broker would provide indicative prices so that they're not obliged to execute a trade at those prices. Traders can also publish indicative prices to let the market know they are willing to provide a firm price if asked. This firm price can deviate from the indicative quote once lot sizes, counterparty (if a derivative) and current market conditions are factored in.

As you can see from the pricing preferences, the greatest weight is given to executed or executable prices, whilst the least weight is given to indicative prices.

**Types of Market Data**    There are different types of market data that will be tested in the IPV process, including:

- Interest rates
- Interest rate tenor spreads
- Cross currency basis spreads
- Prices

- Volatilities
- Spot FX and forward points
- Credit spreads.

We will now look at each of these in more detail.

**Interest Rates**     Conducting IPV on positions with interest rate risk can become quite complex as interest rates can be presented in a variety of ways, such as par rates (coupon bearing), zero coupon rates (bullets) or forward rates (a rate for a period that starts in the future). On top of this, par rates have different compounding frequencies which need to be factored into the IPV process.

It is also market practice post the global financial crisis to use separate yield curves for forecasting and discounting cash flows in swap transactions. For example, an interest rate swap requires a LIBOR-based swap curve to forecast future cash flows and a separate yield curve to discount those cash flows to today. If the swap is collateralized it will use an overnight index swap (OIS) curve and if it is uncollateralized it will most likely use a LIBOR-based yield curve. Consequently, the IPV function is now more complex than it used to be which means that valuation control needs to be clear about the nature of the yields they are testing and the nature of the independent yields that they are sourcing.

*Interest Rate Tenor Spreads*     Swaps are traded with different coupons, which can have compounding frequencies of daily, monthly, quarterly, semi-annual or annual. When generating a forecast yield curve, the firm's valuation engine will need to select the matching forecast curve for the coupon frequency of the swap.

Some valuation engines will be fed multiple swap yields, such as daily, monthly, quarterly, semi-annual and annual to ensure that the valuation is accurate. Others, however, may only be fed, say, a quarterly swap yield curve and then require tenor spreads to derive the relevant forecasted rates. For example, if the base curve uses a quarterly yield but there are trades with 1-month floating fixings, the RMS will need to use the quarterly swap yield and the 3Mv1M spreads to forecast accurate cash flows. On the right hand side of Figure 15.4, there are quotes for 3-month vs. 1-month basis for AUD swaps.

For IPV it is important to understand how the RMS valuation process operates as it will not only determine which yield curves to price test, but it will also influence whether valuation control need to quantify a tenor valuation adjustment.

*Cross Currency Basis Spreads*     When the desk trade cross currency swaps, one of the currency legs needs its future cash flows to be discounted using its native swap yield curve + the cross currency basis. As these spreads impact on the fair value of a swap, they will need to be independently verified in the IPV process. Figure 15.4 shows a Bloomberg screen which provides quotes for both AUD/USD and AUD/EUR cross currency basis across the curve.

**Prices**     Prices are generally far more straightforward to validate and can be sourced to IPV a wide range of instruments including:

- Securities such as bonds, bank bills, treasury notes and stocks
- Loans
- Exchange traded instruments such as futures, options and warrants.

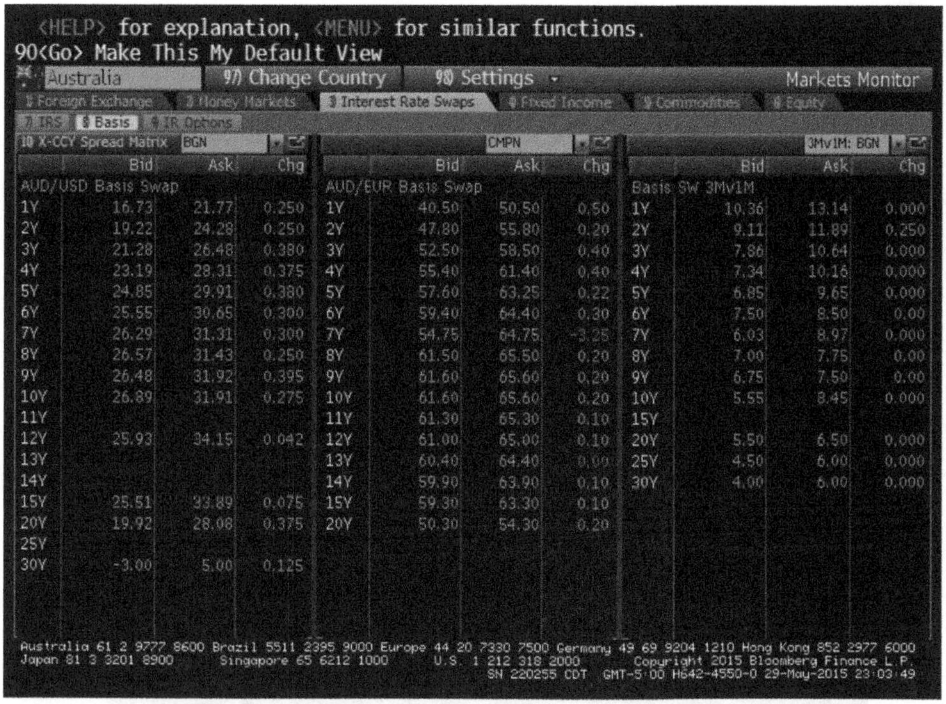

<HELP> for explanation, <MENU> for similar functions.
90<Go> Make This My Default View
Australia | 97) Change Country | 98) Settings | Markets Monitor
Foreign Exchange | Money Markets | Interest Rate Swaps | Fixed Income | Commodities | Equity
7) IRS | 8) Basis | 9) IR Options
10) X-CCY Spread Matrix BGN | CMPN | 3MV1M: BGN

| AUD/USD Basis Swap | Bid | Ask | Chg | AUD/EUR Basis Swap | Bid | Ask | Chg | Basis SW 3MV1M | Bid | Ask | Chg |
|---|---|---|---|---|---|---|---|---|---|---|---|
| 1Y | 16.73 | 21.77 | 0.250 | 1Y | 40.50 | 50.50 | 0.50 | 1Y | 10.36 | 13.14 | 0.000 |
| 2Y | 19.22 | 24.28 | 0.250 | 2Y | 47.80 | 55.80 | 0.20 | 2Y | 9.11 | 11.89 | 0.250 |
| 3Y | 21.28 | 26.48 | 0.380 | 3Y | 52.50 | 58.50 | 0.40 | 3Y | 7.86 | 10.64 | 0.000 |
| 4Y | 23.19 | 28.31 | 0.375 | 4Y | 55.40 | 61.40 | 0.40 | 4Y | 7.34 | 10.16 | 0.000 |
| 5Y | 24.85 | 29.91 | 0.380 | 5Y | 57.60 | 63.25 | 0.22 | 5Y | 6.85 | 9.65 | 0.000 |
| 6Y | 25.55 | 30.65 | 0.300 | 6Y | 59.40 | 64.40 | 0.30 | 6Y | 7.50 | 8.50 | 0.00 |
| 7Y | 26.29 | 31.31 | 0.300 | 7Y | 54.75 | 64.75 | -3.25 | 7Y | 6.03 | 8.97 | 0.000 |
| 8Y | 26.57 | 31.43 | 0.250 | 8Y | 61.50 | 65.50 | 0.20 | 8Y | 7.00 | 7.75 | 0.00 |
| 9Y | 26.48 | 31.92 | 0.395 | 9Y | 61.60 | 65.60 | 0.20 | 9Y | 6.75 | 7.50 | 0.00 |
| 10Y | 26.89 | 31.91 | 0.275 | 10Y | 61.60 | 65.60 | 0.20 | 10Y | 5.55 | 8.45 | 0.000 |
| 11Y | | | | 11Y | 61.30 | 65.30 | 0.10 | 15Y | | | |
| 12Y | 25.93 | 34.15 | 0.042 | 12Y | 61.00 | 65.00 | 0.10 | 20Y | 5.50 | 6.50 | 0.000 |
| 13Y | | | | 13Y | 60.40 | 64.40 | 0.00 | 25Y | 4.50 | 6.00 | 0.000 |
| 14Y | | | | 14Y | 59.90 | 63.90 | 0.10 | 30Y | 4.00 | 6.00 | 0.000 |
| 15Y | 25.51 | 33.89 | 0.075 | 15Y | 59.30 | 63.30 | 0.10 | | | | |
| 20Y | 19.92 | 28.08 | 0.375 | 20Y | 50.30 | 54.30 | 0.20 | | | | |
| 25Y | | | | | | | | | | | |
| 30Y | -3.00 | 5.00 | 0.125 | | | | | | | | |

Australia 61 2 9777 8600 Brazil 5511 2395 9000 Europe 44 20 7330 7500 Germany 49 69 9204 1210 Hong Kong 852 2977 6000
Japan 81 3 3201 8900 Singapore 65 6212 1000 U.S. 1 212 318 2000 Copyright 2015 Bloomberg Finance L.P.
SN 220255 CDT GMT-5:00 H642-4550-0 29-May-2015 23:03:49

**FIGURE 15.4** Cross currency basis
Source: Used with permission of Bloomberg L.P. Copyright © 2015. All rights reserved

The benefit of testing a price is that it is usually a one for one comparison. For example, the trader marked Bank of China stock price recorded in the RMS can be compared to the price from Reuters (Figure 15.5).

Figure 15.6 lists market prices for corporate bonds.

**Volatilities** Volatility (vol) is used as a pricing input into instruments with embedded optionality like options and swaptions (Figure 15.7). Vol measures the fluctuations of the underlying asset's value (price) and is typically presented by delta or by strike. Simplistically, options with a 50 delta have a 50% probability that they will expire in the money and are known as *at the money* (ATM) options, which means they are neither in the money nor are they out of the money.

When the vol surface is independently verified, reference needs to be made to the desk's vega risk by delta. If the desk has vega risk away from the ATM, then the full surface should be tested. The reason for this is volatilities are not typically the same for a 10 delta option as they are for a 50 delta option. Consensus pricing services such as Super Derivatives can provide the full vol surface for FX options.

**FX Spot and Forward Points** In the FX market there are several types of market data that are used to revalue trading positions and foreign currency balance sheet exposures:

- Spot FX: Spot FX rates are used to revalue open FX trades that mature on the spot date (usually T+2) and foreign currency assets and liabilities on the bank's balance sheet. Spot

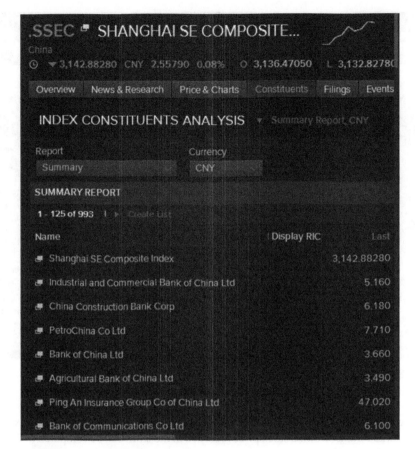

**FIGURE 15.5** Stock prices
Source: Thomson Reuters

FX rates are very easy to source from market providers such as Reuters (Figure 15.8) and Bloomberg.

- FX forward points: FX forward points measure the interest rate differential between the two currencies in an FX forward or FX swap transaction. The FX forward points are used in conjunction with FX spot rates to revalue FX forward trades and the far leg of an FX swap (if the near leg settles at spot). FX forward points are also easy to source using Reuters (Figure 15.9) or Bloomberg.

**Credit Spreads**   Credit Default Swap (CDS) spreads reflects the number of basis points that a trader would have to pay to insure themselves against the default (and other specified credit events) of a reference entity. In Figure 15.10, the 5year CDS quote for Transocean Inc. is 565.907 basis points.

Using this quote and a notional of $1mln, the buyer of a CDS would need to pay a premium of 5.66% or $56,590 per annum to receive protection from default and other specified credit events.

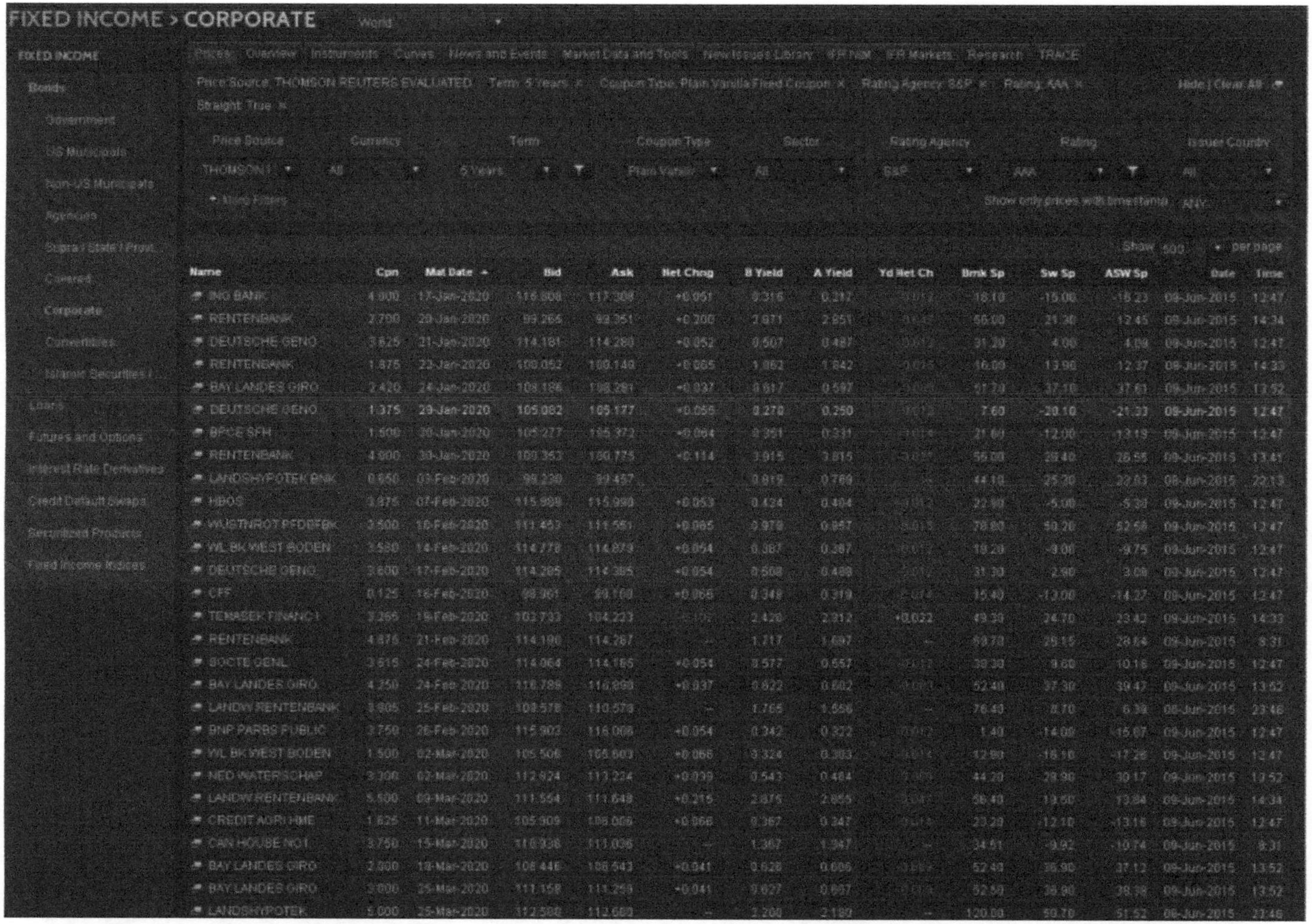

**FIGURE 15.6** World corporate bond prices

Source: Thomson Reuters

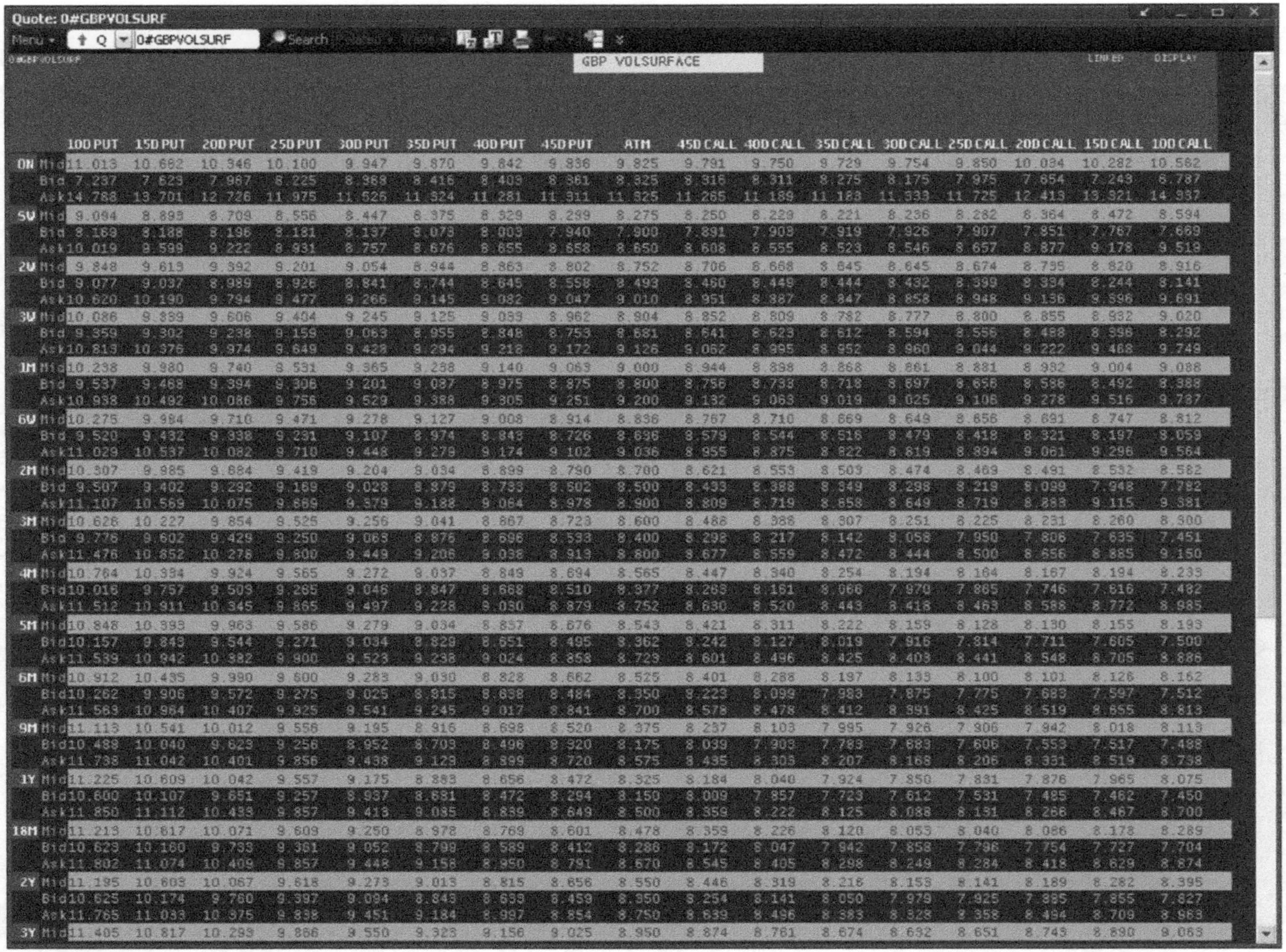


| | | 10D PUT | 15D PUT | 20D PUT | 25D PUT | 30D PUT | 35D PUT | 40D PUT | 45D PUT | ATM | 45D CALL | 40D CALL | 35D CALL | 30D CALL | 25D CALL | 20D CALL | 15D CALL | 10D CALL |
|---|---|---|---|---|---|---|---|---|---|---|---|---|---|---|---|---|---|---|
| ON | Mid | 11.013 | 10.682 | 10.346 | 10.100 | 9.947 | 9.870 | 9.842 | 9.836 | 9.825 | 9.791 | 9.750 | 9.729 | 9.754 | 9.850 | 10.034 | 10.282 | 10.582 |
| | Bid | 7.237 | 7.623 | 7.987 | 8.225 | 8.388 | 8.416 | 8.403 | 8.361 | 8.325 | 8.316 | 8.311 | 8.275 | 8.175 | 7.975 | 7.654 | 7.243 | 6.787 |
| | Ask | 14.788 | 13.701 | 12.726 | 11.975 | 11.526 | 11.324 | 11.281 | 11.311 | 11.325 | 11.265 | 11.189 | 11.183 | 11.333 | 11.725 | 12.413 | 13.321 | 14.337 |
| 1W | Mid | 9.094 | 8.893 | 8.709 | 8.556 | 8.447 | 8.375 | 8.329 | 8.299 | 8.275 | 8.250 | 8.229 | 8.221 | 8.236 | 8.282 | 8.364 | 8.472 | 8.594 |
| | Bid | 8.169 | 8.188 | 8.196 | 8.181 | 8.137 | 8.073 | 8.003 | 7.940 | 7.900 | 7.891 | 7.903 | 7.919 | 7.926 | 7.907 | 7.851 | 7.767 | 7.669 |
| | Ask | 10.019 | 9.599 | 9.222 | 8.931 | 8.757 | 8.676 | 8.655 | 8.658 | 8.650 | 8.608 | 8.555 | 8.523 | 8.546 | 8.657 | 8.877 | 9.178 | 9.519 |
| 2W | Mid | 9.848 | 9.619 | 9.392 | 9.201 | 9.054 | 8.944 | 8.863 | 8.802 | 8.752 | 8.706 | 8.668 | 8.645 | 8.645 | 8.674 | 8.735 | 8.820 | 8.916 |
| | Bid | 9.077 | 9.037 | 8.989 | 8.926 | 8.841 | 8.744 | 8.645 | 8.558 | 8.493 | 8.460 | 8.449 | 8.444 | 8.432 | 8.399 | 8.334 | 8.244 | 8.141 |
| | Ask | 10.620 | 10.190 | 9.794 | 9.477 | 9.266 | 9.145 | 9.082 | 9.047 | 9.010 | 8.951 | 8.887 | 8.847 | 8.858 | 8.948 | 9.136 | 9.396 | 9.691 |
| 3W | Mid | 10.086 | 9.839 | 9.606 | 9.404 | 9.245 | 9.125 | 9.039 | 8.962 | 8.904 | 8.852 | 8.809 | 8.782 | 8.777 | 8.800 | 8.855 | 8.932 | 9.020 |
| | Bid | 9.359 | 9.302 | 9.238 | 9.159 | 9.063 | 8.955 | 8.848 | 8.753 | 8.681 | 8.641 | 8.623 | 8.612 | 8.594 | 8.556 | 8.488 | 8.398 | 8.292 |
| | Ask | 10.813 | 10.376 | 9.974 | 9.649 | 9.428 | 9.294 | 9.218 | 9.172 | 9.126 | 9.062 | 8.995 | 8.952 | 8.960 | 9.044 | 9.222 | 9.468 | 9.749 |
| 1M | Mid | 10.238 | 9.980 | 9.740 | 9.531 | 9.365 | 9.238 | 9.140 | 9.063 | 9.000 | 8.944 | 8.898 | 8.868 | 8.861 | 8.881 | 8.932 | 9.004 | 9.088 |
| | Bid | 9.537 | 9.468 | 9.394 | 9.306 | 9.201 | 9.087 | 8.975 | 8.875 | 8.800 | 8.756 | 8.733 | 8.718 | 8.697 | 8.656 | 8.586 | 8.492 | 8.388 |
| | Ask | 10.938 | 10.492 | 10.086 | 9.756 | 9.529 | 9.388 | 9.305 | 9.251 | 9.200 | 9.132 | 9.063 | 9.019 | 9.025 | 9.106 | 9.278 | 9.516 | 9.787 |
| 6W | Mid | 10.275 | 9.984 | 9.710 | 9.471 | 9.278 | 9.127 | 9.008 | 8.914 | 8.836 | 8.767 | 8.710 | 8.669 | 8.649 | 8.656 | 8.691 | 8.747 | 8.812 |
| | Bid | 9.520 | 9.432 | 9.338 | 9.231 | 9.107 | 8.974 | 8.843 | 8.726 | 8.636 | 8.579 | 8.544 | 8.518 | 8.479 | 8.418 | 8.321 | 8.197 | 8.059 |
| | Ask | 11.029 | 10.537 | 10.082 | 9.710 | 9.448 | 9.279 | 9.174 | 9.102 | 9.036 | 8.955 | 8.875 | 8.822 | 8.819 | 8.894 | 9.061 | 9.296 | 9.564 |
| 2M | Mid | 10.307 | 9.985 | 9.684 | 9.419 | 9.204 | 9.034 | 8.899 | 8.790 | 8.700 | 8.621 | 8.553 | 8.509 | 8.474 | 8.469 | 8.491 | 8.532 | 8.582 |
| | Bid | 9.507 | 9.402 | 9.292 | 9.169 | 9.028 | 8.879 | 8.733 | 8.602 | 8.500 | 8.433 | 8.388 | 8.349 | 8.298 | 8.219 | 8.099 | 7.948 | 7.782 |
| | Ask | 11.107 | 10.569 | 10.075 | 9.669 | 9.379 | 9.188 | 9.064 | 8.978 | 8.900 | 8.809 | 8.719 | 8.658 | 8.649 | 8.719 | 8.888 | 9.115 | 9.381 |
| 3M | Mid | 10.628 | 10.227 | 9.854 | 9.525 | 9.256 | 9.041 | 8.867 | 8.723 | 8.600 | 8.488 | 8.388 | 8.307 | 8.251 | 8.225 | 8.231 | 8.260 | 8.300 |
| | Bid | 9.776 | 9.602 | 9.429 | 9.250 | 9.063 | 8.876 | 8.696 | 8.533 | 8.400 | 8.298 | 8.217 | 8.142 | 8.058 | 7.950 | 7.806 | 7.635 | 7.451 |
| | Ask | 11.476 | 10.852 | 10.278 | 9.800 | 9.449 | 9.206 | 9.038 | 8.913 | 8.800 | 8.677 | 8.559 | 8.472 | 8.444 | 8.500 | 8.656 | 8.885 | 9.150 |
| 4M | Mid | 10.764 | 10.384 | 9.924 | 9.565 | 9.272 | 9.037 | 8.849 | 8.694 | 8.565 | 8.447 | 8.340 | 8.254 | 8.194 | 8.164 | 8.167 | 8.194 | 8.233 |
| | Bid | 10.016 | 9.757 | 9.509 | 9.265 | 9.046 | 8.847 | 8.668 | 8.510 | 8.377 | 8.263 | 8.161 | 8.066 | 7.970 | 7.865 | 7.746 | 7.616 | 7.482 |
| | Ask | 11.512 | 10.911 | 10.345 | 9.865 | 9.497 | 9.228 | 9.030 | 8.879 | 8.752 | 8.630 | 8.520 | 8.443 | 8.418 | 8.463 | 8.588 | 8.772 | 8.985 |
| 5M | Mid | 10.848 | 10.393 | 9.963 | 9.586 | 9.279 | 9.034 | 8.857 | 8.676 | 8.543 | 8.421 | 8.311 | 8.222 | 8.159 | 8.128 | 8.130 | 8.155 | 8.193 |
| | Bid | 10.157 | 9.843 | 9.544 | 9.271 | 9.034 | 8.829 | 8.651 | 8.495 | 8.362 | 8.242 | 8.127 | 8.019 | 7.916 | 7.814 | 7.711 | 7.605 | 7.500 |
| | Ask | 11.539 | 10.942 | 10.382 | 9.900 | 9.523 | 9.238 | 9.024 | 8.858 | 8.723 | 8.601 | 8.496 | 8.425 | 8.403 | 8.441 | 8.548 | 8.705 | 8.886 |
| 6M | Mid | 10.912 | 10.435 | 9.990 | 9.600 | 9.283 | 9.030 | 8.828 | 8.662 | 8.525 | 8.401 | 8.288 | 8.197 | 8.133 | 8.100 | 8.101 | 8.126 | 8.162 |
| | Bid | 10.262 | 9.906 | 9.572 | 9.275 | 9.025 | 8.815 | 8.638 | 8.484 | 8.350 | 8.223 | 8.099 | 7.983 | 7.875 | 7.775 | 7.683 | 7.597 | 7.512 |
| | Ask | 11.563 | 10.964 | 10.407 | 9.925 | 9.541 | 9.245 | 9.017 | 8.841 | 8.700 | 8.578 | 8.478 | 8.412 | 8.391 | 8.425 | 8.519 | 8.655 | 8.813 |
| 9M | Mid | 11.113 | 10.541 | 10.012 | 9.556 | 9.195 | 8.916 | 8.698 | 8.520 | 8.375 | 8.237 | 8.103 | 7.995 | 7.926 | 7.906 | 7.942 | 8.018 | 8.113 |
| | Bid | 10.488 | 10.040 | 9.623 | 9.256 | 8.952 | 8.703 | 8.496 | 8.320 | 8.175 | 8.039 | 7.903 | 7.783 | 7.683 | 7.606 | 7.553 | 7.517 | 7.488 |
| | Ask | 11.738 | 11.042 | 10.401 | 9.856 | 9.438 | 9.129 | 8.899 | 8.720 | 8.575 | 8.435 | 8.303 | 8.207 | 8.168 | 8.206 | 8.331 | 8.519 | 8.738 |
| 1Y | Mid | 11.225 | 10.609 | 10.042 | 9.557 | 9.175 | 8.883 | 8.656 | 8.472 | 8.325 | 8.184 | 8.040 | 7.924 | 7.850 | 7.831 | 7.876 | 7.965 | 8.075 |
| | Bid | 10.600 | 10.107 | 9.651 | 9.257 | 8.937 | 8.681 | 8.472 | 8.294 | 8.150 | 8.009 | 7.857 | 7.723 | 7.612 | 7.531 | 7.485 | 7.462 | 7.450 |
| | Ask | 11.850 | 11.112 | 10.433 | 9.857 | 9.413 | 9.085 | 8.839 | 8.649 | 8.500 | 8.359 | 8.222 | 8.125 | 8.088 | 8.131 | 8.266 | 8.467 | 8.700 |
| 18M | Mid | 11.213 | 10.617 | 10.071 | 9.609 | 9.250 | 8.978 | 8.769 | 8.601 | 8.478 | 8.359 | 8.226 | 8.120 | 8.053 | 8.040 | 8.086 | 8.178 | 8.289 |
| | Bid | 10.623 | 10.160 | 9.733 | 9.361 | 9.052 | 8.798 | 8.589 | 8.412 | 8.288 | 8.172 | 8.047 | 7.942 | 7.858 | 7.796 | 7.754 | 7.727 | 7.704 |
| | Ask | 11.802 | 11.074 | 10.409 | 9.857 | 9.448 | 9.158 | 8.950 | 8.791 | 8.670 | 8.545 | 8.405 | 8.298 | 8.249 | 8.284 | 8.418 | 8.629 | 8.874 |
| 2Y | Mid | 11.195 | 10.603 | 10.067 | 9.618 | 9.273 | 9.013 | 8.815 | 8.656 | 8.550 | 8.446 | 8.319 | 8.216 | 8.153 | 8.141 | 8.189 | 8.282 | 8.395 |
| | Bid | 10.625 | 10.174 | 9.760 | 9.397 | 9.094 | 8.843 | 8.633 | 8.459 | 8.350 | 8.254 | 8.141 | 8.050 | 7.979 | 7.925 | 7.885 | 7.855 | 7.827 |
| | Ask | 11.765 | 11.033 | 10.375 | 9.838 | 9.451 | 9.184 | 8.997 | 8.854 | 8.750 | 8.639 | 8.496 | 8.383 | 8.328 | 8.358 | 8.494 | 8.709 | 8.963 |
| 3Y | Mid | 11.405 | 10.817 | 10.293 | 9.866 | 9.550 | 9.323 | 9.156 | 9.025 | 8.950 | 8.874 | 8.761 | 8.674 | 8.632 | 8.651 | 8.743 | 8.890 | 9.063 |

**FIGURE 15.7** Outright GBP volatilities by delta
Source: Thomson Reuters

Quote List

| | Name | Bid | Ask | Time | Date | Contributor |
|---|---|---|---|---|---|---|
| EUR= | Euro | 1.0967 | 1.0969 | 18:36 | 25/05/2015 | CBA |
| GBP= | British Pound | 1.5483 | 1.5487 | 18:36 | 25/05/2015 | RBS |
| CHF= | Swiss Franc | 0.9428 | 0.9440 | 18:36 | 25/05/2015 | DANSKE BANK |
| JPY= | Japanese Yen | 121.62 | 121.64 | 18:36 | 25/05/2015 | RBS |
| AUD= | Australian Dollar | 0.7822 | 0.7826 | 18:36 | 25/05/2015 | RBS |
| NZD= | New Zealand $ | 0.7302 | 0.7308 | 18:36 | 25/05/2015 | RBS NY |
| CAD= | Canadian Dollar | 1.2293 | 1.2299 | 18:36 | 25/05/2015 | RBS |

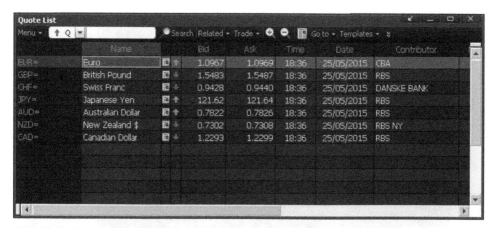

**FIGURE 15.8** Spot FX rates
Source: Thomson Reuters

## Calculating Price Variances

Once the risk and independent prices have been sourced it is now possible to determine the IPV variance in monetary terms. If the variance indicates that the desk are undervaluing their asset or overvaluing their liability, then this is considered to be a conservative variance. If the opposite is true and the asset is overvalued or the liability is undervalued, then this is considered to be an aggressive variance.

Desk heads are far more concerned with aggressive variances as it indicates their trader is inflating his P&L artificially. However, as accountants, we need to be mindful that the bank is required to mark to fair value, which is theoretically agnostic regarding an aggressive or conservative variance.

**Bond Prices** In Table 15.4, the desk have four bonds whose prices have been independently verified using data from Bloomberg.

Quote List

| | Bid | Ask | Tenor | Reference | Contributor | Ccy | Loc | Time |
|---|---|---|---|---|---|---|---|---|
| GBPON= | -0.0200 | 0.0400 | ON | Calc Outrights | STANDCHART | USD | NYC | 18:39 |
| GBPTN= | 0.0800 | 0.0950 | TN | Calc Outrights | STANDCHART | USD | NYC | 18:39 |
| GBPSW= | -0.87 | -0.82 | SW | Calc Outrights | ZUERCHER KB | USD | ZUR | 18:39 |
| GBP1M= | -3.98 | -3.62 | 1M | Calc Outrights | NATIXIS | USD | PAR | 18:39 |
| GBP3M= | -10.77 | -10.32 | 3M | Calc Outrights | BOA | USD | LON | 18:39 |
| GBP6M= | -19.30 | -18.60 | 6M | Calc Outrights | STANDCHART | USD | NYC | 18:39 |
| GBP9M= | -23.78 | -22.38 | 9M | Calc Outrights | STANDCHART | USD | NYC | 18:39 |
| GBP1Y= | -27.76 | -22.36 | 1Y | Calc Outrights | NATIXIS | USD | PAR | 18:39 |

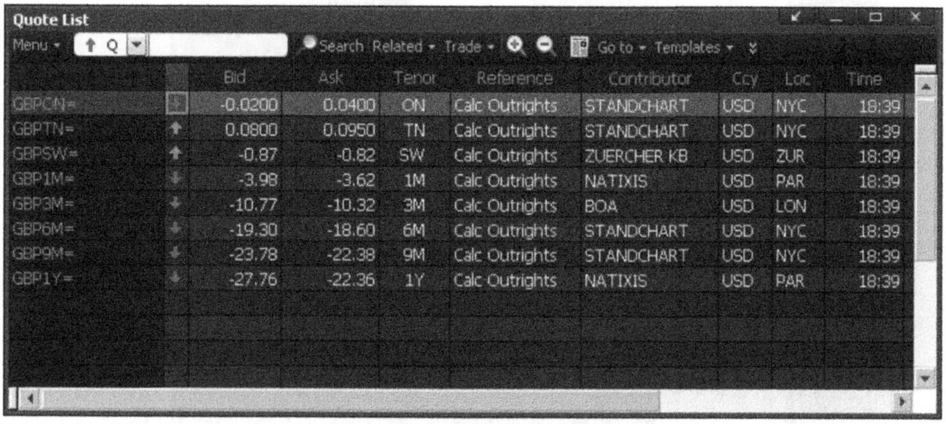

**FIGURE 15.9** GBPUSD FX forward points
Source: Thomson Reuters

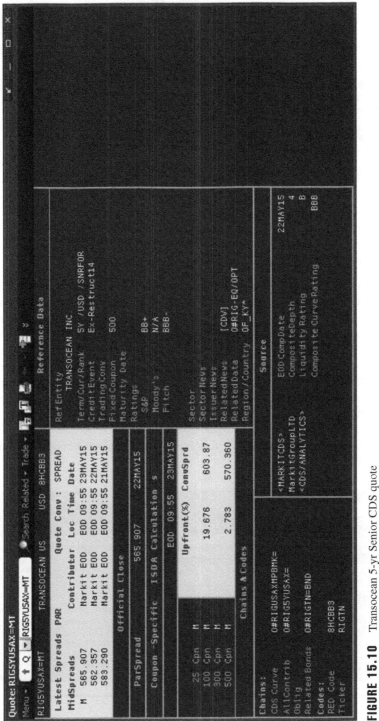

**FIGURE 15.10** Transocean 5-yr Senior CDS quote

Source:: Thomson Reuters

**TABLE 15.4** Bond IPV variance

| Security | Nominal | Trader Price | IPV Price | IPV Source | IPV Market Value | Trader Market Value | IPV Variance |
|---|---|---|---|---|---|---|---|
| GE 5% 31/12/2017 | $17,000,000 | 99.4 | 99.3 | Bloomberg | $16,881,000 | $16,898,000 | ($17,000) |
| Rolls Royce 7% 31/12/2017 | $30,000,000 | 99.1 | 99.25 | Bloomberg | $29,775,000 | $29,730,000 | $45,000 |
| Lloyds TSB 5.25% 31/12/2017 | $5,000,000 | 99.9 | 99.915 | Bloomberg | $4,995,750 | $4,995,000 | $750 |
| Unilever 4.75% 31/12/2017 | $6,000,000 | 98.2 | 98.36 | Bloomberg | $5,901,600 | $5,892,000 | $9,600 |
| Total | $58,000,000 | | | | $57,553,350 | $57,515,000 | $38,350 |

The market value of a bond is derived by multiplying the nominal by its price, which is then divided by 100. For example, the IPV market value for GE 5% 31/12/2017 is:

$$\text{Market value} = \$17,000,000 \times \frac{99.30}{100}$$
$$= \$16,881,000$$

After subtracting the trader market values from the IPV market values, an overall conservative variance of $38,350 arises. If there are no IPV variance thresholds, product control will add $38,350 into the Desk's P&L for the month being tested. The accounting entries in Table 15.5 would be made in the GL to reflect the variance. In this table, the balance sheet is debited via the trading securities account and the P&L is credited.

**Swap Yield Curve**   In Table 15.6, the trader swap yield curve is compared to an independently sourced curve. The differences in yield are applied to the desk's risk (dv01) to derive the dollar IPV variance (the dv01 is the P&L sensitivity to a one basis point change in yields). For example, in the overnight tenor (O/N) is a dv01 of 7,000 with a yield variance of −0.5 basis points or −0.005%. To derive the dollar IPV variance we do the following:

$$\text{IPV variance} = \$7,000 \times -0.5$$
$$= -\$3,500$$

Repeating this process for the remaining tenors, we arrive at an aggressive variance of $39,250, which will result in a loss being taken to P&L. The accounting entries in Table 15.7 would be made in the GL to reflect the variance. In this table, the balance sheet is credited via the derivatives fair value account and the P&L is debited.

**TABLE 15.5**   Accounting entries for the Bond IPV variance

| Trading securities | | Unrealized P&L | |
|---|---|---|---|
| $38,350 | | | $38,350 |

**TABLE 15.6** U.S. swap rates consumed in IPV testing

| | | | Interest Rates | | |
|---|---|---|---|---|---|
| **Time** | **dv01** | **Trader curve** | **IPV curve** | **Variance bps** | **Variance $** |
| O/N | 7,000 | 0.090% | 0.085% | (0.50) | (3,500) |
| 1MTH | (3,500) | 0.150% | 0.145% | (0.50) | 1,750 |
| 3MTH | 31,500 | 0.230% | 0.220% | (1.00) | (31,500) |
| 6MTH | 102,000 | 0.330% | 0.330% | 0.00 | 0 |
| 9MTH | 20,000 | 0.400% | 0.410% | 1.00 | 20,000 |
| 1YR | 25,000 | 0.560% | 0.530% | (3.00) | (75,000) |
| 2YR | (23,000) | 0.630% | 0.600% | (3.00) | 69,000 |
| 3YR | 20,000 | 0.700% | 0.690% | (1.00) | (20,000) |
| **Total** | **179,000** | | | | **(39,250)** |

When product control adjusts the desk's P&L, they will make the accounting entries in Table 15.7 in the GL. In Table 15.7 the P&L is reduced by $39,250 and the balance sheet is credited by the same amount.

The same process that we have just walked through for bonds and interest rates will be mirrored across all pricing inputs that are trader marked, i.e., are not independent.

**Alternate Approach** If the RMS has the appropriate functionality, there is an alternative way to calculate an IPV variance. For systems like Murex, portfolio simulations can be run using the original trade portfolio that is revalued using the new independent rates sourced by valuation control. The independent portfolio value can then be compared to the trader marked portfolio value to derive the IPV variance.

Through this method, valuation control will be able to quantify the impact of any second order impacts, such as gamma, in the IPV variance. This can be seen as a more accurate method for calculating IPV variances for derivative portfolios.

**Proxy Testing** Independent prices cannot always be obtained for all fair valued positions. This can occur for example, when the desk hold an illiquid position, i.e., trades are not being executed in the market, or when the desk purchase an entire issuance of a security so that a market for the security does not exist. In some cases, alternative methods can be employed to provide an opinion on the marks ascribed by the desk, such as proxy testing. Let's assume the desk held the bond shown in Table 15.8.

Valuation control could make reference to the yield on a security with similar features, i.e., they would look for a 2020 bond that has been issued by a construction firm with a BBB credit rating. If they could not find an exact match, the team could then start to modify the

**TABLE 15.7** The accounting entries for interest rate derivatives IPV variance

| Derivatives fair value | | Unrealized P&L | |
|---|---|---|---|
| | $39,250 | $39,250 | |

**TABLE 15.8**   Sample bond held by the Desk

| Issuer | BuildersrUs |
|---|---|
| Type | Senior unsecured |
| Maturity | 2020 |
| Coupon | 8% |
| Payment | Semi |
| Credit rating | BBB |

search parameters, although doing this will mean the proxy testing provides less assurance regarding the fair value of the tested bond.

Although proxy testing is not the best source for price testing, it can still provide the firm with a level of assurance around the trader's mark.

**Untested Positions**   Even after attempting to source a proxy price, it is possible that valuation control are not able to test the price on all positions, which results in a position being classified as untested. When this occurs, it is important that management (business, finance and risk) are made aware of this, as a risk averse bank will not want to be exposed to a large number untested positions. Untested positions would typically be reported in Level 3 of the fair value hierarchy which is reserved for assets and liabilities with significant unobservable pricing inputs.

**IPV Variance Thresholds**   It is common for banks to set IPV variance thresholds, above which variances will be taken to P&L, but below which the variance will not be taken to P&L. Thresholds can be set at a product and/or business level. When setting the thresholds, consideration is given to:

- The size of the portfolio;
- The nature of the products; and
- The volatility of the IPV variances.

**The Size of the Portfolio**   Let's compare two scenarios at Sparta bank.

> **Scenario 1:** Sparta's Global Proprietary Trading Business has 1 trading portfolio, which is constructed of a small number of bonds, futures and FX spot trades. The trades have a combined market value of $10mln.
>
> **Scenario 2:** Contrast this with Sparta's Global Credit business which has 20 trading portfolios, constructed of thousands of credit derivatives, corporate bonds and commercial paper, credit linked notes and CDO's. These trading portfolios have a combined market value of $1bn.

Considering that the size of each business are galaxies apart, it would not make a lot of sense to have the same threshold for the small proprietary business as it would for the larger and more complex credit business. Valuation control and the business need to be mindful of such differences when establishing thresholds.

**The Nature of the Products**   The nature of the products being verified also matters. You wouldn't say, have the same threshold for a highly liquid US Treasury note, as you would for an illiquid complex derivative such as a bespoke CDO. Not only is liquidity and observability yards apart, the bespoke CDO also has far more valuation complexity than a US treasury note.

**The Volatility of the IPV Variances**   The firm may not want to be adjusting for every single IPV variance so it is helpful for valuation control to build in a buffer to allow for the normal and un-alarming variances to exist and be reported without the need for the P&L to be adjusted for every single variance.

## Reporting on the Outcomes of the IPV Process

Once completed, the results of the IPV process need to be communicated to the relevant stakeholders. The IPV pack will include details pertaining to:

- The population of tested positions (including independent sources)
- The population of untested positions
- What proxies (or other indirect testing methods) needed to be used, the methodology employed and the assurance regarding each; for example, how were the proxies established?
- The dollar variances resulting from the testing.

  Management will be particularly interested in at least the following.

- Large pricing variances: Which trader's and positions have the largest variances.
  Is there a visible trend to trader mismarking (e.g., has Trader A materially mismarked aggressively for the past 3 months)?
- Untested positions: Which positions have been untested and for how long they have remained untested.
- Indirect testing methods.

Similarly to the control forum, most banks will have one or several valuation forums where the monthly valuation results and other valuation items are discussed and approved each month. This meeting gives each of the key stakeholders an opportunity to get up to speed on which business has material valuation issues. It also affords stakeholders the opportunity to approve (or not) proposed changes in the valuation methodologies across the investment or institutional bank. Those participating in this forum would be product control, market risk and the business.

In addition to this central forum, it is also quite common in larger banks for each business line to have its own valuation forum, where the valuations results are discussed and approved. These forums would still have their results and any change proposals feed up to the central valuation forum.

## NOTE

1. FSA (FCA). "Final Notice." 16/03/2010. http://www.fsa.gov.uk/pubs/final/alexis_stenfors.pdf.

# CHAPTER 16

# Valuation Adjustments

I n this chapter, we will look at why valuation adjustments are required and will explore some of the more common valuation adjustments that are applied to trading desks.

## WHY VALUATION ADJUSTMENTS ARE REQUIRED

In an ideal world, the trade valuation generated by the risk management system (RMS) would be the financial asset's or liability's fair value, but due to system limitations this rarely happens. Valuation adjustments (VAs), which are also known as *reserves*, are necessary adjustments to bring the RMS valuations, of financial assets or liabilities, to their fair value (see Chapter 4 for a definition of fair value).

Figure 16.1 illustrates how a financial asset's or liability's valuation transforms into an exit price. In Figure 16.1, the bank executes a trade at the market price, which is then fed into the RMS, where it is typically revalued at a mid-market price.

To transform the mid-market price to an exit price, several VAs need to be applied. In Figure 16.1 I have listed the most common types of VAs which we will look at in more detail shortly.

When these VAs are applied, in most cases they will lower the value of the financial asset and increase the value of the financial liability (i.e., make it a larger liability), which results in a loss for the desk.

VAs can be taken when trades requiring adjustments are brought on to a bank's books and records and they are often recalibrated monthly. When the VA is recalibrated, both the risk sensitivities and market spreads are refreshed to the current measurement date. The desk will be informed of the results and should be given the opportunity to challenge the result. This approach helps ensure that the most accurate VAs are being applied to the trading portfolio.

We will now explore the different VAs which were illustrated in Figure 16.1.

## BID–OFFER

Bid–offer spreads reflect the difference in price between what the buyer is willing to pay and what the seller is willing to receive if a trade is executed. The bid–offer spread is a cost the trading desk incurs when they need to hedge or close out a trading position.

## The path to fair value

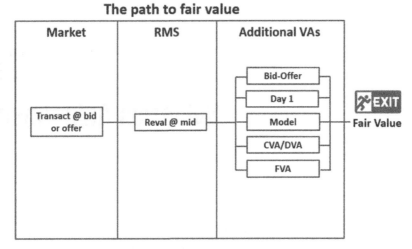

**FIGURE 16.1**   Aligning valuations to their exit price

For example, the Sparta Banks swaps desk enters an interest rate swap with a client where they receive fixed and pay floating. The desk want to hedge their market risk, so they enter the interbank market and execute a pay fixed receive floating swap with another bank, as is illustrated in Figure 16.2. There is a difference in yield on a receive fixed swap, which is known as a bid–offer spread. So, by crossing the market, the desk have incurred a cost.

In Figure 16.2 the desk has incurred a cost of 1.5 basis points to trade on a fully hedged basis with the client. In reality, the cost of this bid–offer spread would be built into the price the desk give the client, so that each client trade is profitable for the bank.

The width of the bid–offer spread is influenced by the liquidity of the instrument and the volatility of the market. Higher liquidity denotes a larger number of buyers and sellers competing to trade that instrument, which lowers the spread. For example, GBP/USD FX forward contracts are highly liquid and have a substantially narrower bid–offer spread than an illiquid instrument such as a USD/NGN non-deliverable forward.

Bid–offer spreads also vary by tenor, as some points along a curve are less liquid than others. For example, as seen in Figure 16.3, for the currency pair GBP/USD, the bid–offer spread for the one-month forward points are narrower than the spread for the one-year forward points.

The volatility of the market also influences the width of the bid–offer spread. The reason for this is that market makers, who are publishing simultaneous bids and offers into the market, will need to build in a wider spread during periods of volatility to protect themselves from large swings in prices.

Figure 16.4 illustrates the need for wider bid–offer spreads during volatile markets. Within a 20-second period at the start of trading, the market is moving by up to 10 cents every

**FIGURE 16.2**   Crossing the bid–offer spread

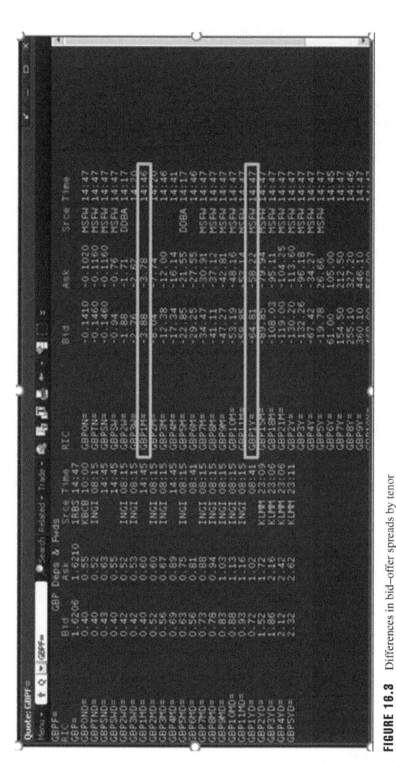

**FIGURE 16.3** Differences in bid–offer spreads by tenor

Source: Thomson Reuters.

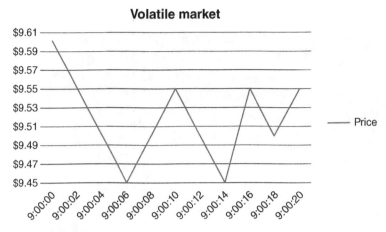

**FIGURE 16.4**   Volatile market

2 seconds, which means that the bid and offer quotes need to be wide enough (e.g. 10–15 cents) to absorb these swings and not lead to losses for the market maker.

Figure 16.5 illustrates the need for narrower bid–offer spreads as this market is not volatile. Within a 20-second period at the start of trading the market is only moving by up to 1 cent every 2 seconds, which means that the bid and offer quotes can be a lot narrower than the volatile market quotes.

## Quantifying the Bid–Offer Valuation Adjustment

When it comes to the accounting standards, IFRS 13 requires the price within the bid–ask spread that most represents fair value to be used. Using bid prices for assets and ask prices for liabilities is permitted but not required, and using mid-prices as a practical expedient isn't

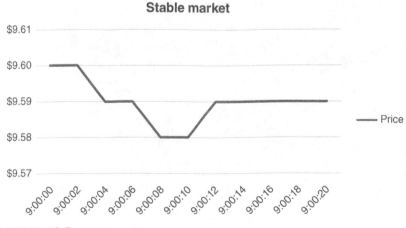

**FIGURE 16.5**   Stable market

**TABLE 16.1** UK Treasury bond

| Instrument | Position | Bid | Mid | Ask |
|---|---|---|---|---|
| UK Treasury bond 1.25% 31/12/2017 | 100,000,000 | 98.99 | 98.995 | 99.00 |

precluded (IFRS 13:71-72).[1] In practice, most banks will not use the practical expedient for the fair value reporting and will instead use bid prices for assets and ask prices for liabilities.

As most RMSs will value assets and liabilities using mid-market prices, the way that the bid or offer prices are adjusted to, is by taking half the bid–offer spread and applying that to the bank's positions. By approaching the calculation in this way, it doesn't matter if you have an asset or liability, the spread can be applied to both underlying positions.

The only situation where a bid–offer VA would not be taken is where the desk can demonstrate that they do not incur the cost of the bid–offer spread to exit their positions, for example if they are a market maker.

A simple example of a typical bid–offer VA is as follows. A UK Treasury bond is held by Sparta Bank, which is laid out in Table 16.1.

If Sparta Bank were to sell the bond they would, in theory, execute the trade at the buyer's bid price. However, Sparta Bank's RMS uses a mid-market price from the Debt Management Office, which is used to revalue all the bank's UK Treasury bond positions, whether they are long or short. Subsequently, a bid–offer VA is required to align the value of the bond to its exit price.

The spread from bid to offer is 0.01% ($\frac{99.00 - 98.99}{100}$) or one basis point. Therefore, the bid–offer VA for the UK Treasury bond would be calculated as follows:

$$\text{ABS(Position)} \times \frac{bid\ offer\ spread}{2}$$

$$= £100,000,000 \times \frac{(0.01)\%}{2} = £(5,000).$$

As you can see in this formula, the bid–offer VA is a factor of the size of the spread and the position. Additionally, it doesn't matter whether the position is long or short, we take the absolute value of the position, which means that the desk does not benefit from the VA; it always results in a loss.

The reason we take only half the full bid–offer spread is that to exit the position, the trader will need to go from either the RMS mid to bid or RMS mid to offer. This means that the P&L is overstated by £5,000 which will be corrected when product control take the bid–offer VA at month-end. Obviously, product control can take a bid offer VA each day, but the cost of doing so usually outweighs the benefit.

**How Should the Risk Sensitivities Be Aggregated?** In Chapter 4, we looked at IFRS 13 and we learnt that if the entity manages its market risk on a net basis, it is permitted to derive the fair value for that group of financial assets and liabilities using its net position. The duration and type of market risk needs to be materially the same and if a basis is appropriate then this needs to be factored in to derive the fair value (IFRS 13:54).[2] What this means for valuation adjustments like bid–offer, is that the firm can maximize its use of netting similar risk to achieve a more efficient adjustment.

**FIGURE 16.6** Rates desk risk aggregation

**At What Level in the Bank's Hierarchy Should the Risk Be Aggregated?** The risk sensitivities can be aggregated at various levels in the bank's hierarchy. The hierarchy to choose from could be the division, business, desk, profit centre or trader. When choosing an approach, the bank wants to take advantage of the netting of risk across portfolios (so the VA is not excessive) but also needs to be granular enough to identify potential issues in the calculation. A common approach is to calculate the VA at desk level. For example, in Figure 16.6 the rates business is illustrated, which has three desks:

1. **Europe:** The desk has six traders who are responsible for managing the interest rate risk in the region. Countries covered are United Kingdom, European Union, Scandinavia and Turkey.
2. **Americas:** The desk only covers North American interest rate risk; namely, US and Canada. The desk has three traders.
3. **Asia:** The Asia desk has three traders to cover the interest rate markets in Hong Kong, Singapore and Australia.

As these desks manage the interest rate risk of different regions, there would be a low risk of taking an excessive VA.

An example of the benefit of netting is as follows. On the Americas desk, two of the three the traders have the following USD interest rate risk (Table 16.2):

**TABLE 16.2** Americas Rates desk USD DV01

| Tenor | DV01 | | Net |
|---|---|---|---|
| | Trader 1 | Trader 2 | |
| 1 year | 10,000 | −8,000 | **2,000** |

If the VA was taken at trader level and netting wasn't taken into account, the VA would be applied to the $18,000 gross exposure (ABS 10,000 + ABS 8,000). However, if the VA was taken at the desk level, both interest rate exposures would be netted and the VA would apply to a net exposure of $2,000.

**How Should the Risk Be Aggregated into Tenor Points?** The second consideration on risk aggregation relates to the time bucketing of risk. The use of appropriate time bucketing is critical to achieving an efficient VA. In a similar vein to the risk-based P&L estimate, the rule of thumb is to use observable and liquid data points. The time bucketing for the VA calculation will be aligned to the bucketing used by market risk, which should also be aligned to how the market trades.

**TABLE 16.3**   USD Interest Rates DV01

| Interest Rates – USD | | | |
|---|---|---|---|
| **Time** | **DV01** | **Bid–Offer Spread** | **VA** |
| O/N | 7,000 | 0.01% | 3,500 |
| 1MTH | (3,500) | 0.01% | 1,750 |
| 3MTH | 31,500 | 0.01% | 15,750 |
| 6MTH | 102,000 | 0.01% | 51,000 |
| 9MTH | 20,000 | 0.01% | 10,000 |
| 1YR | 25,000 | 0.01% | 12,500 |
| 2YR | (23,000) | 0.01% | 11,500 |
| 3YR | 20,000 | 0.01% | 10,000 |
| **Total** | **179,000** | | **116,000** |

Table 16.3 represents the desk's DV01 exposures (sensitivity to a one basis point change in yields) which are aligned to how the desk trade and how market risk monitor interest rate risk. In this example, the bid-offer spread is 1 basis point or 0.01% (to convert a percentage to basis points multiply the percentage by 10,000). To quantify the bid-offer VA we use the following formula:

$$\text{ABS (exposure)} \times \frac{bid\ offer\ spread}{2}$$

Applying this to the 1 month tenor (1 MTH) we arrive at the following adjustment:

$$\text{VA} = \text{ABS} (-3,500) \times$$
$$\text{VA} = 1,750$$

After repeating this for the remaining tenors, we arrive at a total bid-offer VA of $116,000, which is deducted from the P&L and credited to the balance sheet.

Now, if we used a generic risk report from the RMS to calculate the VA, with no regard for how the market trades, it might look like the data in Table 16.4. The DV01 data in this table is too granular and doesn't reflect how the desk manage their risk. By using this risk data, it results in a punitive VA of $308,000, which is $192,000 in excess of where it should be.

**Bid–Offer Spreads**   Spreads can be sourced from providers such as:

■ Brokers
■ Interbank traders
■ Bloomberg
■ Reuters
■ ICE data services (IDS).

Market participants (traders and brokers) can publish their prices into Bloomberg and Reuters. Bloomberg will also publish its own prices which are derived from the data it has received and modelled itself.

**TABLE 16.4** USD Interest Rate DV01 with excessive bucketing

| Interest Rates – USD | | | |
|---|---|---|---|
| Time | DV01 | Bid–Offer Spread | VA |
| O/N | 7,000 | 0.01% | 3,500 |
| 1WK | 6,000 | 0.01% | 3,000 |
| 2WK | (4,000) | 0.01% | 2,000 |
| 3WK | (1,000) | 0.01% | 500 |
| 1MTH | (4,500) | 0.01% | 2,250 |
| 2MTH | 3,500 | 0.01% | 1,750 |
| 3MTH | 9,000 | 0.01% | 4,500 |
| 4MTH | 19,000 | 0.01% | 9,500 |
| 5MTH | (16,000) | 0.01% | 8,000 |
| 6MTH | 110,000 | 0.01% | 55,000 |
| 7MTH | 8,000 | 0.01% | 4,000 |
| 8MTH | 90,000 | 0.01% | 45,000 |
| 9MTH | 50,000 | 0.01% | 25,000 |
| 10MTH | (120,000) | 0.01% | 60,000 |
| 11MTH | (50,000) | 0.01% | 25,000 |
| 1YR | 75,000 | 0.01% | 37,500 |
| 2YR | (23,000) | 0.01% | 11,500 |
| 3YR | 20,000 | 0.01% | 10,000 |
| **Total** | **179,000** | | **308,000** |

These bid and offer prices, from which spreads are derived, can be either executable (firm) or indicative. An *executable* quote is a firm price which, if a counterparty wants to trade at that level can hit the quote and a trade will be executed. As we are adjusting our prices to the exit price, executable prices are obviously more reliable than indicative prices.

An *indicative* quote is not a firm price where the other party who publishes the price is willing to trade. An indicative quote lets the market know that the publisher is in the market and could trade if another participant is interested in doing so. In Table 16.5, the broker Delphi Derivatives have emailed their indicative quotes to product control.

For market data providers such as Reuters and Bloomberg, product control will usually retrieve the data via Excel. These companies provide Excel add-in tools, which make the extraction of data very fast and more efficient than manually capturing the data by going through each relevant Reuters or Bloomberg page.

**Recalibrating the Bid–Offer Spreads** In a perfect world, bid–offer spreads should be updated daily to reflect the market's exit price on that day. However, given the large cost and little benefit to sourcing spreads daily, this option is not usually feasible, so most banks update the spreads on a monthly cycle.

Spreads will not remain static from month to month; however, a judgement call can be made (similarly to not updating the spreads daily) as to whether it is appropriate and materially beneficial to update the spreads less frequently, such as quarterly.

**TABLE 16.5** Broker quotes for Base Metals Vols

Wednesday 11 June

| | ATM Option Volatility Indications | | | | | | | | | | |
|---|---|---|---|---|---|---|---|---|---|---|---|
| | Copper | | Aluminium | | Zinc | | Nickel | | Lead | | |
| | Indic. | Val. | Indic. | Val. | Indic. | Val. | Indic. | Val. | Indic. | Val. | |
| Jul-14 | 19/20 | 20.11 | 18/19.5 | 18.38 | 15.5/17 | 16.09 | 30/32 | 30.57 | 16/17 | 16.22 | Jul-14 |
| Aug-14 | 19/20 | 19.92 | 17/18 | 17.84 | 15.5/16.5 | 15.83 | 29/31 | 29.86 | 16/17 | 16.36 | Aug-14 |
| Sep-14 | 18.75/19.75 | 19.72 | 16.75/17.75 | 17.47 | 15.5/16.5 | 15.77 | 28/30 | 29.04 | 16/17 | 16.54 | Sep-14 |
| Oct-14 | 18.5/19.5 | 19.44 | 16.75/17.75 | 17.28 | 15.5/16.5 | 15.75 | 28/30 | 28.76 | 16/17 | 16.67 | Oct-14 |
| Nov-14 | 18.25/19.25 | 19.22 | 16.5/17.5 | 17.17 | 15.5/16.5 | 15.73 | 27/29 | 28.27 | 16.25/17.25 | 16.79 | Nov-14 |
| Dec-14 | 18/19 | 19.08 | 16.25/17.25 | 17.05 | 15.5/16.5 | 15.73 | 27/29 | 27.99 | 16.25/17.25 | 16.87 | Dec-14 |
| Dec-15 | 18/19 | 18.85 | 16/17 | 16.83 | 15.5/16.5 | 15.76 | 26.5/28.5 | 27.66 | | | Dec-15 |
| Dec-16 | 18/19 | 18.88 | 16.25/17.25 | 16.96 | | | | | | | Dec-16 |

Source: Delphi Derivatives Ltd.

**TABLE 16.6**   Client trade

| Buy/Sell | Buy |
|---|---|
| Call/Put | Call |
| Type | European |
| Currency pair | GBP/ZAR |
| Strike | 11.5 |
| Maturity | 10 years |

**TABLE 16.7**   Pricing information

| Pricing input | Observability |
|---|---|
| Time | Yes |
| Strike | Yes |
| Spot | Yes |
| FX swap points | 3 years |
| Volatility | 18 months |

## DAY 1 RESERVES

IFRS 13 requires us to maximize the use of observable pricing inputs when deriving a fair value. When pricing inputs are unobservable and the resulting fair value has a significant element of uncertainty, it is necessary to take a day 1 reserve (under U.S. GAAP, it is not necessary to take a day 1 reserve for unobservable pricing inputs).

For example, the desk sell the following currency option in Table 16.6 to a client. We are given the information in Table 16.7 to assist with our review. As the volatility surface for GBP/ZAR is only observable out to 18 months and the FX swap points out to 3 years, the day 1 profit (total profit less any existing model and bid/offer reserves) is too uncertain to report. We therefore need to withhold the day 1 P&L until either those unobservable pricing inputs become observable or the desk hedges the market risk on the trade.

A linear amortization of the reserved P&L is only appropriate if you can observe that the risk to the unobservable parameters decreases linearly over time. If the risk reduction of the trade is non-linear then it may be more appropriate to say release the day 1 reserve as a bullet amount at the end of the trade or when the desk hedge the market risk on the trade. In this example, it would be very reasonable not to release the profit on a linear basis, as all of the vega risk is in the 10-year bucket.

When taking a day 1 reserve it is important that the impact on the fair value hierarchy (FVH) is also considered. Any financial assets or liabilities with a day 1 reserve should be reported into level 3 of the FVH. We will look at the FVH in Chapter 21.

## MODEL VALUATION ADJUSTMENT

Model VAs are required when there is a material degree of uncertainty in the valuations generated by the financial model in the RMS.

Quantitative risk validate the models used to derive the trade valuations in the RMS. Where possible, models need to be calibrated to market prices on a periodic basis, say quarterly, to ensure the valuations output by the model are accurate.

Model VA's are usually quantified through running simulations. For example, given that correlation is not observable for all asset pairs, if the desk are exposed to the unobservable correlations of two or more assets, the financial model will need to make assumptions regarding these correlations in order to generate a valuation. In this case, it may be appropriate to take a VA for the correlation uncertainty. This reserve could comprise of, say, a 10% shock of the correlation parameter each way, with a reserve of max [abs(x−10), abs(x+10)] taken to account for this uncertainty.

# XVA AND COLLATERAL AGREEMENTS

XVA, the acronym that has generated so much excitement across the industry since the GFC, refers to the numerous VAs made to capture the impact of funding and credit risk on a derivative's value. Whilst there are many VAs that we could cover, we will focus our attention on CVA, DVA and FVA, which are now an embedded set of valuation adjustments in most banks.[3] Before we look further at CVA, DVA and FVA, let's first understand CSAs and collateral which impact these adjustments.

## CSA

OTC interbank derivatives, and some client derivatives, are traded with the support of a credit support annex (CSA). A CSA is an agreement which regulates and defines the credit support (collateral) for OTC derivative transactions like swaps. A CSA mitigates the credit risk arising from in-the-money positions by defining the terms and conditions under which collateral is posted/transferred between the counterparties of the swap transaction. These terms and conditions mainly specify parameters like:

- Threshold Amount: This amount is the reference value of the mark-to-market of the swap above which collateral has to be posted. For example, if the threshold amount is €5.0m for a party, this party is required to post collateral only when their negative mark-to-market of the swap is above €5.0m.
- Frequency: Both parties need to agree on the frequency of collateral postings. Often applied frequencies are daily, weekly and fortnightly.
- Eligible Collateral: The assets that classify as eligible collateral need to be negotiated. Cash and government bonds are the most common eligible instruments. If securities are to be used, it is necessary to define a set of eligible instruments along with the associated haircuts.
- Minimum Transfer Amount: If the difference between the mark-to-market and the value of the collateral position is in excess of the minimum transfer amount (MTA), extra collateral needs to be posted. The MTA provides operational efficiency as it prevents small amounts having to be paid/received.
- One-way: A standard CSA will operate on a two-way basis, where each counterparty pledges collateral on a symmetrical basis. In some cases, counterparties will enter into a one way CSA, which makes provision for only one of the parties to post collateral when the trade is out of the money.

- Rehypothecation: This clause determines whether the party who receives the collateral can reuse it for its own purposes (i.e., to fund business activities) or whether the collateral must be segregated.
- Downgrade Triggers: These aim to protect both parties from a fall in the counterpart's creditworthiness during the life of a CSA. In the event that one of the parties experiences a downgrade past a predefined rating in their external credit rating (e.g., A−), they will be required to post higher levels of collateral.

An example of how a CSA operates is as follows: Bank HBC enters a 10-yr EUR/USD cross-currency swap with Sparta Bank, whereby Sparta Bank pays a fixed USD coupon and the Bank HBC pays a fixed EUR coupon. The swap is documented under a CSA with the following terms and conditions.

| | |
|---|---|
| Threshold Amount: | €5.0m |
| Frequency: | Weekly |
| Eligible Collateral: | EUR cash only |
| Minimum Transfer Amount: | €1.0m |

As illustrated in Table 16.8, on day 1 the value of the swap is zero, but after two weeks the value changes to €6.5 million in Sparta Bank's favour. The value is above the threshold amount, so a collateral amount equal to €6.5 million needs to be posted by Bank HBC to Sparta Bank.

After three weeks, the value of the trade increases from €6.5 million to €7.0 million. As the €0.5 million change is smaller than the minimum transfer amount €1.0million, no additional collateral needs to be posted.[4]

If your bank is a party involved in the exchange of collateral, there will be implications for your funding position and P&L for both parties. When collateral is pledged by one party to another, the recipient of the collateral will pay interest to the party who pledged the collateral. The interest is based on an overnight funding rate which, for EUR, GBP and USD, are listed in Table 16.9. These funding rates are aligned with the Overnight Index Swap (OIS) yields, which banks will use to discount a collateralized derivative's future cash flows. For uncollateralized derivatives banks most commonly use a LIBOR-based swap curve to discount future cash flows.

For the pledger of collateral, before they can post the collateral they first need to source the funds to pay for the collateral. Consequently, the pledger of collateral will have a funding P&L equal to the difference between the income from the CSA funding rate and the rate at which the bank can fund itself.

For the recipient of the collateral, the funding P&L will be the difference between the cost of the CSA funding rate and the benefit they can gain from using the cash or securities pledged by the counterparty.

**TABLE 16.8** NPV of trade

| Date | NPV |
|---|---|
| T+0 | €0 |
| T+2weeks | €6.5 million |
| T+3weeks | €7.0 million |

**TABLE 16.9** Funding rates applicable for collateral underpinning OTC derivative transactions

| Ccy | Index | Description |
|------|-------|-------------|
| EUR | Euro Overnight Index Average (EONIA) | The weighted average interest rate on unsecured overnight lending transactions denominated in euros, which are sourced from a panel of contributing banks.[5] |
| GBP | Sterling Overnight Interbank Average (SONIA) | SONIA is the weighted average rate of all unsecured sterling overnight cash transactions of £25 million and above, which are brokered in London by contributing members of Wholesale Markets Brokers' Association.[6] |
| USD | Fed Funds Rate | The weighted dollar average interest rate at which depository institutions lend reserve balances to other depository institutions overnight.[7] |

## Credit Value Adjustment (CVA) and Debit Value Adjustment (DVA)

Credit risk is the risk that the counterparty may default on its obligations to the bank. The VA is made to incorporate the possibility of this occurring it is known as CVA. When the bank has a two-way CSA in place, with no minimum posting thresholds, unless the counterparty is very risky and the underlying market is highly volatile, there would be no need to make an adjustment for CVA as the credit risk is limited to intraday market movements on the portfolio of related trades.

DVA refers to the bank's credit riskiness for the counterparty and is often referred to as *own credit*. As a bank can have many trades with a single counterparty, the CVA or DVA will be levied based upon the net profile of those trades. In simple calculations, DVA and CVA are mutually exclusive at a single point in time. However, more complex simulations (e.g., Monte Carlo) can allow both a DVA and CVA to be recognized. Jon Gregory's *The xVA Challenge* covers this topic in more detail and is recommended reading.

A simple method to illustrate the quantification and impact of CVA is to use a risk-adjusted yield curve to discount the trade's future cash flows. To apply the market's view of credit riskiness, the counterparty's single name quoted CDS spreads or relevant quoted sector level CDS spreads can be used. In Table 16.10 we have an example of how to derive the CVA on an interest rate swap.

**TABLE 16.10** Impact of CVA on an interest rate swap

| Impact of CVA | | | | | | |
|------|------|------|------|------|------|------|
| Tenor | Cash flow | Swap yield | Discounted cash flow | CDS Spread | CVA impact | CVA adjusted discounted cash flow |
| | | | | | | |
| 1Y | 100,000 | 1.10% | 98,912 | 2.00% | (1,919) | 96,993 |
| 2Y | 50,000 | 1.75% | 48,295 | 2.10% | (1,933) | 46,361 |
| 3Y | 20,000 | 2.10% | 18,791 | 2.20% | (1,164) | 17,627 |
| Total | 170,000 | | 165,998 | | (5,016) | 160,982 |

In Table 16.10 we have the forecasted cash flows for the trade which amount to $170,000. These cash flows are then discounted back to today using the swap yield curve (yields are p.a.), which gives us an NPV of $165,998.

To get a credit risk-adjusted yield we then reference the single name CDS for this counterparty, which tells us that to protect the bank against a credit event on this counterparty it costs 200 basis points, 210 basis points and 220 basis points per annum for one, two or three years respectively. We then apply these spreads (in addition to the swap yield) to the future cash flows to derive a new NPV, which reduces the NPV by a further $5,016 to $160,982. The CVA impact for this counterparty and trade is $5,016.

For DVA, the bank will need to discount all applicable OTC derivatives and unsecured funding liabilities (where the firm elects to apply the fair value option) using a risk-adjusted yield curve that reflects the bank's own credit risk.

To assess its own credit risk the bank can refer to the CDS market (similarly to CVA) or the debt funding market. It should also be pointed out that the Basel Committee on Banking Supervision (BCBS) disallows recognition of DVA for regulatory capital purposes and IFRS 9 does not allow changes in the bank's fair valued funding liabilities due to own credit (where the fair value option has been selected) to be passed through the P&L. Such changes need to go through other comprehensive income (OCI).

A bank will usually manage credit risk through a dedicated desk, which we will call the XVA desk. For every trade that the various sales and trading desks execute, the XVA desk may charge those desks a credit risk premium. This premium provides protection to those desks in the event of a counterparty default.

## Funding Value Adjustment (FVA)

When a bank trades with a client, it will usually hedge the risk arising from that trade with the interbank market, as is illustrated in Figure 16.7. When the trade with the client and the interbank counterparty are not both collateralized or uncollateralized, a funding cost or benefit arises. FVA, therefore, is the cost or benefit arising from funding uncollateralized derivatives over the life of the trade, present valued to today.

Where the bank has loss-making collateralized trades, which are not offset by in-the-money collateralized trades, it gives rise to a funding cost (FCA) for the bank. When the opposite is true, it gives rise to a funding benefit (FBA) for the bank.

In Figure 16.7, Sparta Bank has entered an interest rate swap with Fly Airlines where they receive a fixed coupon and pay the floating 3-month LIBOR coupon. The interest rate risk from this trade is then hedged with Bank HBC, which leaves Sparta Bank with a 15-basis-point client margin (2.05% less 1.90%).

During the life of the trades, the swap facing Bank HBC becomes an out-of-the money trade whilst the swap facing Fly Airlines becomes an in-the-money trade. An FVA arises

**FIGURE 16.7** Back-to-back interest rate swap

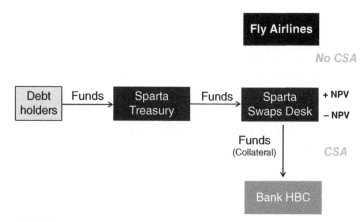

**FIGURE 16.8**   FCA on a back-to-back interest rate swap

because whilst the Bank HBC trade is covered by a CSA, the Fly Airlines trade is not. Consequently, collateral needs to be provided to Bank HBC without Sparta Bank receiving collateral from Fly Airlines.

As illustrated in Figure 16.8, Sparta Bank now needs to go and source funds to pledge the collateral to Bank HBC, which usually occurs through the treasury department. Treasury will not have spare cash lying around, so they will need to raise the funds from retail depositors or from the wholesale funding market. This funding has a cost attached to it, and it is the difference between this cost and the rate of return earned on the collateral being pledged that generates a FCA.

For banks that account for XVAs and choose to disclose relevant information in their earnings updates and financial statements, their reporting is a constructive resource for assessing the impact XVA has on the bank's overall performance. These updates will also highlight changes to methodologies and terminology that the market is adopting.

## RECORDING AND REPORTING OF VAs

When recording VAs in the GL it is better to isolate each type of VA in its own balance sheet account. The reason for this is that it makes substantiating the GL balances much simpler.

Every valuations control team will produce valuation packs, which contain information regarding the size and movements of the VAs (including IPV adjustments). Similar to the P&L, commentary is attached to significant or notable changes in VAs. This information is usually distributed to the business and market risk. In some cases, the regulator may also wish to view these packs.

## NOTES

1. IFRS Foundation. IFRS 13 Fair Value Measurement, paragraphs 70–71.
2. IFRS Foundation. IFRS 13 Fair Value Measurement, paragraph 54.

3. There is an outstanding text book on XVA written by Jon Gregory, *The xVA Challenge*. I'd recommend you secure a copy of this book if you wish to get a far more in-depth understanding of XVA.

4. Treasury Services, "Credit Support Annex and OTC Pricing." http://www.treasuryservices.be/blog/credit-support-annex-and-otc-pricing/.

5. European Central Bank, "Glossary," 2017. https://www.ecb.europa.eu/home/glossary/html/glosse.en.html#189.

6. © 2011 WMBA, Wholesale Markets Brokers' Association. Sterling Overnight Index Average ("SONIA"). https://www.wmba.org.uk/pages/index.cfm?page_id=31.

7. Board of Governors of the Federal Reserve System. https://www.federalreserve.gov/monetarypolicy/bst_openmarketops.htm.

# Balance Sheet Controls

In this part of the book we will explore the controls a bank will have in place to protect their balance sheet. We will look in detail at how to substantiate and analyze the balance sheet, what is dividending and FX selldown and how nostros can be controlled.

# CHAPTER 17

# Balance Sheet Substantiation and Analysis

**F**or many years, when capital and liquidity were cheaper and more plentiful in the markets, a bank's balance sheet was the running mate of the P&L. The size and construction of a bank's balance sheet was somewhat important, but it wasn't high on the desk's list of priorities. The main function that monitored the balance sheet was Treasury and the trading desks preferred to devote their time to managing their P&L performance.

Since the global financial crisis (GFC) however all this has changed. The balance sheet has climbed out of the shadows and into the spotlight to get the attention it deserves. Banks are now very concerned with the size and shape of their balance sheet, as an oversized and inefficient balance sheet can result in higher capital requirements, government fees and ultimately a lower P&L. These days, the desk's performance is not only scrutinized from a P&L perspective, but also from a balance sheet perspective.

It is with this in mind that product control can provide real value to the bank, through assisting the business in maintaining an optimal balance sheet. Not only this, but as changes in the balance sheet generate the P&L, it is vital that the balance sheet is substantiated. In this chapter, we will look at the typical controls a bank will maintain over its balance sheet.

## SUBSTANTIATING THE BALANCE SHEET

Balance sheet substantiation can be viewed by some as a mind numbing tick and bash exercise and if the process is manual, it can certainly feel like that. Value can however be salvaged through this process, as a controller can reach a more informed view of the business drivers, market influences and systems which constitute the shape and movement of the balance sheet. This process will also highlight whether there are any systemic issues, such as defective feeds from sub systems, into the general ledger (GL).

To properly substantiate the balance sheet, product control is required to:

1. Identify an appropriate source that supports the account's balance
2. Confirm that the account used to record the amount is appropriate
3. Confirm the balance and movement are in line with the activities of the business.

## 1. Identify an Appropriate Source that Supports the Account's Balance

In most cases, the support for the account balance will be found in the systems which feed the GL, which can be known as sub systems, sub ledgers or source systems. The most common forms of sub systems are the risk management system (RMS) and the cash sub ledger.

Additionally, as systems are imperfect, product control may need to post manual accounting journals into the GL to correct system feed issues or account for offline processes such as IPV or VAs. These accounting journals result in an accurate balance sheet and the evidence underpinning the journal will be referenced during the substantiation process.

To rely on the sub systems in the substantiation process, the integrity of the sub systems needs to be ensured. Each sub system should have a sub system owner who monitors and manages the feed into the GL. These sub system feeds should have controls that highlight if there are any control breaks that require remediation. In Figure 17.1 you can observe the flow of substantiation back from the GL through to the feeder systems and on to the external source of truth. Table 17.1 lists several substantiation examples.

Although product control may not be the sub system owner, it is important that they are aware of what controls exist for each sub system feed and how control breaks are communicated to the affected parties.

For example, a derivative fair value account can contain trades which have not yet been confirmed with the counterparty. This means that the trader has entered the trade into the RMS, which has also fed the GL, but the counterparty has not yet acknowledged that they agree the trade. For product control, it is important to understand what portion of the account balance relates to these unconfirmed trades as it will impact on whether it is appropriate to start recognizing the asset or liability. The operations team should be able to provide product control with a list of these trades which includes a risk assessment of each outstanding trade.

For any accounts which have assets and liabilities recorded at their fair value, the valuation control team should be consulted so they can confirm that the positions have been considered in the IPV and VA process. It is also worth consuming information regarding the fair value which has been tested, the fair value which cannot be independently verified and the IPV variance which should have been adjusted by product control.

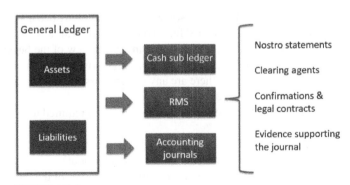

**FIGURE 17.1**   Substantiating the GL

**TABLE 17.1**   Account category substantiation support and sub system integrity checks

| Account Type | Sub System | | | Sub System Checks |
| | RMS | Cash | Other | |
|---|---|---|---|---|
| Nostro | | X | | **Operations:** Nostro balances agree to external bank statement. TLM reconciliation referred to for risk assessment. |
| Bond fair value | X | | | **Operations:** Bond nominals agree to Clearing statement.<br>**Valuation Control:** Fair values validated using IPV and VAs made where required. |
| Derivative fair values | X | | | **Operations:** Trade particulars confirmed.<br>**Valuation Control:** Fair values validated using IPV and VAs made where required. |
| Repo Liability | X | | | **Operations:** Trade particulars confirmed by Operations. Clearing agent used as sources of truth where relevant. |
| Internal Funding Balance (TP) | | | X | **Finance shared service:** Centrally owned accounts validated at entity level |
| Loan Receivable | X | | | **Operations:** Trade particulars confirmed |
| Interest Receivable | X | | | **Operations:** Trade particulars confirmed |
| Deposit Payable | X | | | **Operations:** Trade particulars confirmed |
| Interest Payable | X | | | **Operations:** Trade particulars confirmed |
| FX Position Accounts | X | | X | **Finance shared service:** Re-stated account balance should = 0 in functional ccy.<br>**product control:** The individual transaction ccy balances should agree to the Trader's RMS FX position balances |
| Notionals | X | | | **Operations:** Trade particulars confirmed |

## 2. Confirm that the Account Used to Record the Amount is Appropriate

Now that we have identified where the GL balance has emanated from, we now need to ensure that the GL account used to record the balance is appropriate. Before we can do this we first need to understand the nature of the account balance. For example, if you are reviewing a derivative asset account for the commodities business, the nature of the account will be:

- The fair values of all open (un-matured) derivative contracts (OTC forwards, OTC swaps etc…) that the desk have executed up to the reporting date.
- The fair value balances have been generated by fluctuations in market prices (Soft Commodities, Base Metals, Precious Metals and Energy) in relation to the individual trade prices of each of the contracts.

Confirming that the account is appropriate is a critical step in the substantiation process as if the correct balance is being reported, but in the wrong account, it can have a significant

**TABLE 17.2** Gold Lease transaction

| Gold Lease | |
|---|---|
| Counterparty | Gold R US |
| Principal (oz) | 2,000 |
| Interest (pa) | 0.09% |
| Payment Freq | PA |
| Effective date | 15/01/2015 |
| Maturity | 15/01/2016 |

impact on the financial results that the bank publishes. This error can lead to investors and management making investment decisions on poor data.

Ideally the firm's accounting rule engine will be rock solid and will direct each trade type to the correct accounts in the general ledger. However, depending upon the state of the bank's system infrastructure, it is very possible that this rock solid state does not exist and trades are automatically populated into the incorrect accounts in the RMS to GL interface.

When an error does occur, it is product control's responsibility to identify these errors and either arrange for IT to reverse and repost the RMS feed correctly or, if that is not an option, post correcting accounting journals to remedy the situation.

To identify these errors, it is important that product control has an intimate understanding of their desk's trade portfolio and how it should be represented on the balance sheet. This is where product control's accounting training and relationship with accounting policy and financial reporting will come in handy. For example, the precious metals (PM) desk enters into gold loans with a gold jewellery wholesaler. The PM desk book the gold loan (also known as a gold lease) as a swap in the Commodities RMS (Table 17.2).

The Accounting Rules Engine has been configured to treat gold swaps as derivative transactions, with the P&L and balance sheet accounting entries outlined in Table 17.3.

The only correct accounting entry in Table 17.3 is the nostro credit which reflects the gold ounces leaving the bank's bank account. The remaining entries are not appropriate for a loan (excluding instances where the fair value option has been elected by the bank) as the accounting entries are in line with how you would account for a derivative rather than a loan. The accounting rules engine should have populated the accounts and amounts (view as of 6months into the trade) in Table 17.4.

**TABLE 17.3** Gold lease accounted for as a derivative

| Unrealized P&L – Gold swaps | | Realized P&L – Gold swaps | |
|---|---|---|---|
| | 1,998.20 | −2,000.00 | |
| | 1,998.20 | −2,000.00 | |
| **Balance Sheet – Gold nostro** | | **Balance Sheet – Gold swaps fair value** | |
| −2,000.00 | | | 1,998.20 |
| | −2,000.00 | 1,998.20 | |

**TABLE 17.4**  Gold lease accounted for as a loan

| P&L Interest Income | | Balance Sheet Interest Receivable | |
|---|---|---|---|
| 0.9 | | 0.9 | |
| 0.9 | | 0.9 | |
| **Balance Sheet Gold Nostro** | | **Balance Sheet Gold Loans Receivable** | |
| −2,000.00 | | 2,000.00 | |
| −2,000.00 | | 2,000.00 | |

## 3. The Balance and Its Movement are in Line with the Activities of the Business

In order to answer this question, the product controller has to be familiar with the desk's portfolio for the prior month and the current month, understanding what has changed and why. Although product control can observe the changes in the portfolio, such as increased lending or a reduction in open derivative positions, they will often need to consult the desk to glean the business rationale for such changes. Such interaction usually best occurs intra-month when product control is reviewing the new and amended trade reports and notices changes in the desk's portfolio.

For example, during the month the desk may have participated in a tri-optima compression exercise which has resulted in the tear up of hundreds of derivative transactions. As a result of this, the positive and negative derivative fair values and notionals have dropped by 20%. During the daily review of the amended trades report product control should have spotted this and made a note of the impact this would have for the monthly balance sheet review.

Another example, the bank wants to increase their capital ratio to match the ratios of their peers. One of the strategies to do this is to reduce the bank's risk weighted assets (RWAs). The bank has asked the Corporate Lending business to cut their RWAs by 20% over the course of the next year.

Prior to this reduction strategy, product control would see a fairly consistent lending portfolio month on month, where, as deals matured and rolled off, new trades would roll on leaving the balance sheet materially the same. During the course of the year, within the new trade review and the funding P&L review, product control could see one or more of the following movements:

- A reduction in the number of new trades being put on as deals mature
- A reduction in the principals attached to new trades
- The trading out of loans which have high RWAs
- An increased number of CDS trades being booked.

This type of analysis takes substantiating the balance sheet away from the factory floor and into the head office. Smart banks will automate the checking of balances between the GL and RMS so that product control can expend most of their resources on analyzing the size and movements in the balance sheet, which provides the most value to the bank.

## FREQUENCY OF THE BALANCE SHEET SUBSTANTIATION

Ideally substantiation of the balance sheet will be performed daily, but most commonly it is performed monthly. As a guide, when the bank has achieved a system architecture where all sub systems feed the GL daily, the bank is in a strong position to substantiate the balance sheet daily. However, the frequency of the substantiation will also depend upon the cost required to perform it and the perceived benefits of performing the work more frequently.

There are two main benefits to performing the substantiation daily:

- The peak workload at month end should reduce as system feed issues can be identified and resolved intra-month. Additionally, significant changes in the balance sheet can be identified and investigated intra-month.
- Stakeholders will have more confidence in the daily balance sheet data, which means that they can access the balance sheet data for decision making purposes more frequently.

The cost to the bank will vary throughout the industry, as the costs are influenced by the state of the bank's system infrastructure. For example, Deutsche Bank recently (May 2016) noted that they had under invested in their systems. Under investing in systems can appear to save the bank money, but it usually carries a cost. That cost can involve having to hire additional staff to perform manual processes to support the bank's objectives. It can also mean that banks have an opportunity cost through not being able to access accurate data regarding their financial position on a speedy and consistent basis.

With regard to the balance sheet, this opportunity cost can arise as follows. For example, if there are 10 systems feeding the GL and only 7 of them feed the GL daily, extra work will be required by product control to simulate and substantiate the missing system feeds (or a call can be made to accept that gap and only substantiate the 7 feeds).

Additionally, the timing of these system feeds needs to be appropriate so that the GL can produce the necessary reports that are consumed for substantiation and the substantiation output (or system) is made available early enough during the product control working day so that the necessary work can be performed.

For example, as outlined in Table 17.5, out of the 10 feeder systems 1 is the futures system, Futurama. Futurama does not run its end of day until the U.S. has closed. As a result of this the GL cannot run its end of day until Futurama has supplied its end of day batch files.

In this example, product controllers based in London will have no issues substantiating their balance sheet daily as the GL and substantiation system are made available as the London working day commences. If Sydney, Australia were reliant on the Futurama U.S. close feed then it will be a different outcome, as the substantiation system would not be made available until 17.00 which is at the end of the Sydney day.

Management could implement a number of measures to work around this, such as by having staff start later in the day, use futures prices that are one day in arrears or get Futurama

**TABLE 17.5**  System timings for end of day batch runs

| Batch description | Time |
| --- | --- |
| Futurama runs end of day | BST 22.30 (Chicago 16.30) |
| Futurama end of day batch files produced | BST 00.30 |
| GL runs end of day | BST 01.00 |
| GL end of day completed | BST 05.00 |
| Substantiation system runs end of day | BST 06.00 |
| Substantiation system end of day completed | BST 08.00 |

to run a Sydney end of day, but these all need to be factored into the cost of substantiating the balance sheet daily.

## EVIDENCING THE BALANCE SHEET SUBSTANTIATION

In order to facilitate supervisory, internal audit and operational risk reviews and to comply with the Sarbanes-Oxley Act, it is necessary to evidence the balance sheet substantiation. Generally, the following are evidenced:

- Reporting date being substantiated
- Account details and closing balance
- Supporting items including balance, system and description
- Variances between the two numbers and commentary as to why there is a variance
- Evidence of a supervisory review.

The evidence can be recorded in the document that contains the substantiation or in the substantiation system. For example, Table 17.6 shows an example of the type of information that could be expected for the substantiation of a balance sheet account used to record the external CDS fair values.

The amount of detail and data included in the evidence should facilitate a review by a 3rd party who has experience in product control but is unfamiliar with the business being accounted for.

## UNSUPPORTED BALANCES

During the substantiation process, there will be some amounts that cannot be supported. These amounts arise due to human or system error and need to be investigated and remediated. There are two types of unsupported balances on the balance sheet:

1. Amounts which were unsupported at the time of the reconciliation but have since been resolved.
2. Amounts which were and are still unsupported.

**TABLE 17.6** CDS balance sheet substantiation

| CDS fair value – 31.03.2014 | | | | CDS Population | | | | | | |
|---|---|---|---|---|---|---|---|---|---|---|
| **GL** | | | | | | | | | | |
| Profit Centre | Account | Account Description | Balance (USD eq) | Book | Trade no | Instrument | Buy/ Sell | Counterparty | MTM (USD eq) | Balance under investigation |
| 51111 | 1000001 | CDS MTM | $2,631,900 | USCREDIT1 | Total | | | | 2,631,900 | – |
| | | | | USCREDIT1 | 756111 | CDS | Buy | Majestic Banks | –120,000 | |
| | | | | USCREDIT1 | 756112 | CDS | Sell | Bank ABC | 17,000 | |
| | | | | USCREDIT1 | 756113 | CDS | Sell | Jeesters Hedge Fund | 2,800,000 | |
| | | | | USCREDIT1 | 756114 | CDS | Sell | Might Bank | 77,000 | |
| | | | | USCREDIT1 | 756115 | CDS | Buy | Swissey Bank | –480,000 | |
| | | | | USCREDIT1 | 756116 | CDS | Buy | Corporate Junk | 93,000 | |
| | | | | USCREDIT1 | 756117 | CDS | Buy | US Savings Bank | 46,500 | |
| | | | | USCREDIT1 | 756118 | CDS | Buy | ABC Hedge Fund 1 | 109,000 | |
| | | | | USCREDIT1 | 756119 | CDS | Buy | ABC Hedge Fund 1 | 11,000 | |
| | | | | USCREDIT1 | 756120 | CDS | Buy | ABC Hedge Fund 1 | 5,000 | |
| | | | | USCREDIT1 | 756121 | CDS | Buy | ABC Hedge Fund 1 | 5,500 | |
| | | | | USCREDIT1 | 756122 | CDS | Sell | ABC Hedge Fund 1 | 2,800 | |
| | | | | USCREDIT1 | 756123 | CDS | Buy | ABC Hedge Fund 1 | 2,300 | |
| | | | | USCREDIT1 | 756124 | CDS | Buy | ABC Hedge Fund 1 | –3,200 | |
| | | | | USCREDIT1 | 756125 | CDS | Sell | Mutual Fund Returns | 66,000 | |
| | | | | USCREDIT1 | 756126 | CDS | Sell | Uncle Sam Hedge Fund | 40,000 | |
| | | | | USCREDIT1 | 756127 | CDS | Sell | Bona Fide Bank | 28,000 | |
| | | | | USCREDIT1 | 756128 | CDS | Buy | Kanagroo bank | –33,000 | |
| | | | | USCREDIT1 | 756129 | CDS | Sell | Platypus Industries | –35,000 | |

**TABLE 17.7**  Risk ratings for unsupported balances

| Amount (USD) | <1 month | <3 months | <6 months | >6 months |
|---|---|---|---|---|
| 0–$100k | G | A | R | R |
| $100k–$500k | A | A | R | R |
| $500k–$1mln | A | R | R | R |
| >$1mln | R | R | R | R |

The second instance is of more concern for management and escalation matrices will reflect this.

When balances are identified as being unsupported, it is important that these amounts are investigated and if they have breached agreed materiality thresholds, escalated.

The materiality thresholds can be set as a function of their dollar size and age. As the validity of the account balances affects more than just product control, the escalation thresholds should be agreed amongst product control, financial reporting and operational risk.

Table 17.7 represents the product control escalation matrix. In the month-end substantiation system, operational risk and financial reporting are made aware of the risk ratings of each unsupported balance.

When a balance is unsupported, one of the questions management will ask is whether it will impact the bank's financials. By setting out an escalation matrix, the bank can come to a decision regarding this more effectively, as the riskier the balance, the more senior the staff that will be reviewing and opining on the matter (Table 17.8).

In order for management to opine on this they need to have enough information to make a decision. When a balance is unsupported, the following information should accompany the escalation and reporting:

- The business, profit centre, account, account description, account balance, unsupported balance, age and the nature of the support (e.g., Murex fair value trade report)
- What actions are required to investigate the unsupported balance
- Who is responsible for those actions
- When are those actions expected to be completed.

For example, the CDS fair value account balance could not be fully substantiated for the following reporting date (Table 17.9).

In this instance, given that the unsupported balance is $150k, it needs to be escalated to the country head of product control. The product controller escalates the following email.

**TABLE 17.8**  Risk ratings and levels of management

| Risk Rating | Position | Rank |
|---|---|---|
| Green | Line product control manager | VP |
| Amber | Country product controller | Director |
| Red | Global product control | Managing Director |

**TABLE 17.9** CDS Balance Sheet substantiation

CDS fair value – 30.04.2014

| GL | | | | CREDIT DERIVATIVES RMS | | | | | | GL v RMS (USD eq) | Balance under investigation | Comments |
|---|---|---|---|---|---|---|---|---|---|---|---|---|
| Profit Centre | Account | Account Description | Balance (USD eq) | Book | Trade no | Instrument | Buy/ Sell | Counterparty | MTM (USD eq) | | | |
| 51111 | 1000001 | CDS MTM | $2,781,900.00 | USCREDIT1 | Total | | | | $2,631,900.00 | 150,000 | 150,000 | Variance to be investigated, see escalation email |
| | | | | USCREDIT1 | 756111 | CDS | Buy | Majestic Banks | $(120,000.00) | | | |
| | | | | USCREDIT1 | 756112 | CDS | Sell | Bank ABC | $17,000.00 | | | |
| | | | | USCREDIT1 | 756113 | CDS | Sell | Jeesters Hedge Fund | $2,800,000.00 | | | |
| | | | | USCREDIT1 | 756114 | CDS | Sell | Might Bank | $77,000.00 | | | |
| | | | | USCREDIT1 | 756115 | CDS | Buy | Swissey Bank | $(480,000.00) | | | |
| | | | | USCREDIT1 | 756116 | CDS | Buy | Corporate Junk | $93,000.00 | | | |
| | | | | USCREDIT1 | 756117 | CDS | Buy | US Savings Bank | $46,500.00 | | | |
| | | | | USCREDIT1 | 756118 | CDS | Buy | ABC Hedge Fund 1 | $109,000.00 | | | |
| | | | | USCREDIT1 | 756119 | CDS | Buy | ABC Hedge Fund 1 | $11,000.00 | | | |

| | | | | | |
|---|---|---|---|---|---|
| USCREDIT1 | 756120 | CDS | Buy | ABC Hedge Fund 1 | $5,000.00 |
| USCREDIT1 | 756121 | CDS | Buy | ABC Hedge Fund 1 | $5,500.00 |
| USCREDIT1 | 756122 | CDS | Sell | ABC Hedge Fund 1 | $2,800.00 |
| USCREDIT1 | 756123 | CDS | Buy | ABC Hedge Fund 1 | $2,300.00 |
| USCREDIT1 | 756124 | CDS | Buy | ABC Hedge Fund 1 | $(3,200.00) |
| USCREDIT1 | 756125 | CDS | Sell | Mutual Fund Returns | $66,000.00 |
| USCREDIT1 | 756126 | CDS | Sell | Uncle Sam Hedge Fund | $40,000.00 |
| USCREDIT1 | 756127 | CDS | Sell | Bona Fide Bank | $28,000.00 |
| USCREDIT1 | 756128 | CDS | Buy | Kanagroo bank | $(33,000.00) |
| USCREDIT1 | 756129 | CDS | Sell | Platypus Industries | $(35,000.00) |

## EXAMPLE: EMAIL ILLUSTRATING AN ESCALATION INCIDENT

**From:** Product controller
**Sent:** Tuesday, 06 May 2014 3:12 PM
**To:** Country head of product control
**CC:** Product control – Credit VP; Operational risk; Financial reporting
**Subject:** Escalation: Unsupported Balance 30Apr14

*Dear Country Head of Product Control*

*Following the substantiation of the balance sheet for April month end I am escalating the following item to you:*

| | |
|---|---|
| Business | European Credit Trading desk |
| Profit Centre | 51111 |
| Account | 1000001 |
| Account Description | CDS fair value |
| Account Balance | $2.78mln |
| Unsupported Balance | Dr $150k |
| Nature of Support | Full trade extract of the book USCREDIT1 from Murex, the Credit RMS |

### What actions are required to investigate the unsupported balance?

*Currently the GL report used for substantiation does not include trade level balances. Product control will extract these trade level balances from another report in the GL and reconcile them to the Murex output.*

### Who is responsible for these actions?

*The European credit product controller*

### When are those actions expected to be completed?

*15/05/2014*
*Kind regards*
*European credit product controller*

In the above example an email was used to illustrate an escalation incident. It is however very common now for balance sheet substantiations to be recorded in purpose built software. The software would record whether the balance has been confirmed or not and enable variances to be identified and escalated appropriately.

## LINES OF RESPONSIBILITY

Within the substantiation process there will usually be three lines of review:

1. The person performing the reconciliation or substantiation (e.g., Junior product controller).
2. The supervisor who reviews the work performed by Line 1 (e.g., Senior product controller).
3. The product control manager for the business line or country (or equivalent) who reviews the business' or country's overall balance sheet.

There are several reasons for having multiple lines of review, all of which should add to the effectiveness of the control. Primarily, though, the reasons can be grouped as follows:

- **Four eyes review:** As humans we are susceptible to error and prone to making honest mistakes. By having additional reviews of our work, the bank increases the probability of catching any material errors.
- **Additional paradigms:** Managers can identify potential material issues that Line 1 or 2 have not considered to be an issue, which is due to three reasons:
  - Firstly, judgement plays a part in controlling trading desks and more experience typically results in better judgement. Managers have usually been controlling for longer and have experienced more control exceptions.
  - Secondly, the manager has not performed the substantiation so their mind is freed up to spend more time considering what could cause a material issue for the bank.
  - Thirdly, as the manager is more senior in the bank they recognize that the buck stops with them. This understanding translates into the manager wanting to identify all material control exceptions as early as possible.

This completes our review of balance sheet substantiation and analysis.

CHAPTER **18**

# Dividending of Profit and Loss and FX Selldown

**D**ividending and FX selldown are two very important processes that impact the desk's trial balance each month. As these processes impact both the funding and FX profiles of the desk, it is imperative that product control understand both processes and their impact.

FX selldown is also the most common area where I have seen product control incur losses for their bank, where incorrect FX exposures are sold down. Consequently, it is important that each controller understands their roles and responsibilities regarding these processes to avoid the bank hedging the incorrect P&L exposures.

The profits and losses made by the sales and trading desks need to be dividended on a periodic basis, which usually occurs on a monthly basis. Dividending involves debiting (for profits) and crediting (for losses) the retained earnings accounts within each profit centre, with contra entries being made into treasury or the corporate centre.

As the profits and losses made by the sales and trading desks across the bank will eventually need to be remitted to the head office, the foreign currency P&L is usually sold down and converted into the functional currency of head office. The functional currency will typically be the currency of the country in which the head office is located; for example, EUR for the eurozone, USD for USA and GBP for British banks. However, some entities will have specific local or regulatory drivers that mean it wouldn't always be the functional currency of the head office that the P&L is sold into. By doing this the bank has hedged the FX exposure emanating from P&L across the firm, thereby avoiding any potential adverse movements in FX rates. These amounts are then repatriated to head office periodically.

Figure 18.1 is a high-level overview of the dividending, FX selldown and repatriation of profits to head office.

1. On the top left hand side, we have the P&L (both realized and unrealized), which has been generated in various currencies.
2. This P&L is passed through to treasury via the retained earnings account.
3. Treasury will now go to the spot FX desk and convert the foreign currency via FX trades. It is up to the spot FX desk to manage this FX risk.
4. Once treasury has converted the P&L into the functional currency, the P&L can be repatriated to head office in the functional currency.

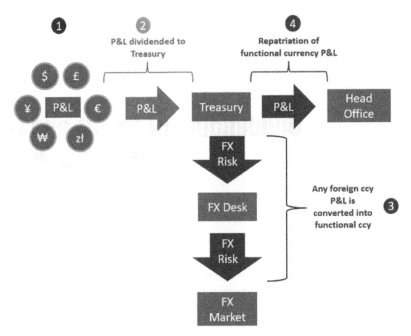

**FIGURE 18.1**    Overview of dividending, FX selldown and repatriation of P&L

In Table 18.1 we have an example of the credit desk's trial balance undergoing dividending and FX selldown.

The desk has made $12m in January from derivatives trading that will need to be sold down into euros, which is the functional currency of head office.

In Table 18.2 we can see that the trial balance report for the credit desk has changed in the following ways:

- An entry has been made across the retained earnings account. This amount of $12m reflects the repatriation of profits to treasury.
- As a result of the repatriation, the credit desk's funding needs have increased by $12m.

We can also see in this table that treasury's retained earnings account has been credited by $12m, which is the contra side to the debit entry made by the credit desk's retained earnings

**TABLE 18.1**    Trial balance report

| Credit desk | | | |
|---|---|---|---|
| Trial Balance Report 31st January 2015 | | | |
| **P&L** | Ccy | Dr | Cr |
| Trading income | USD | | 12,000,000 |
| | | | |
| **Balance Sheet** | | | |
| Derivative fair values | USD | 12,000,000 | |
| | | | |
| **Total Trial Balance** | **USD** | **12,000,000** | **12,000,000** |

**TABLE 18.2**   Dividending the P&L

| Credit desk | | | |
|---|---|---|---|
| **Trial Balance Report 31st January 2015** | | | |
| **P&L** | Ccy | Dr | Cr |
| Trading income | USD | | 12,000,000 |
| | | | |
| **Balance Sheet** | | | |
| Derivative fair values | USD | 12,000,000 | |
| Internal borrowings | USD | | 12,000,000 |
| | | | |
| **Equity** | | | |
| Retained earnings | USD | 12,000,000 | |
| | | | |
| **Total Trial Balance** | **USD** | **24,000,000** | **24,000,000** |

| Treasury | | | |
|---|---|---|---|
| **Trial Balance Report 31st January 2015** | | | |
| | Ccy | Dr | Cr |
| **Balance Sheet** | | | |
| Internal lending | USD | 12,000,000 | |
| | | | |
| **Equity** | | | |
| Retained earnings | USD | | 12,000,000 |
| | | | |
| **Total Trial Balance** | **USD** | **12,000,000** | **12,000,000** |

account. As treasury fund the trading desk, their internal lending account has also been credited by $12m.

Now that treasury has the $12m retained profit, it is their responsibility to hedge the P&L into the functional currency. Treasury will, via the FX trading desk, enter the interbank market to exchange $12m for the equivalent in euros (in reality the FX risk from all desks will be consolidated before executing a trade with the market).

One further step that occurs outside of the awareness of product control is the repatriation of profits to the head office. The frequency of this step may differ within a banking group depending on type and materiality of the entity. For example, subsidiaries are typically semi-annual, in line with the shareholder's dividend policy, and branches are quarterly. Entities with material P&L may repatriate to head office monthly.

The frequency of the repatriation doesn't necessarily change the frequency of the FX selldown, which is monthly, as the aim of the two processes is different.

## Additional Items to Consider

There are four additional items I would like you to consider.

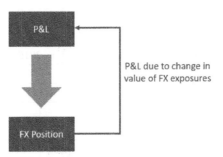

**FIGURE 18.2**   In non-selldown centres, foreign currency P&L is transferred to the FX position accounts

**Trader-Managed FX Exposures**   In some banks, desks will be given the opportunity to manage the FX exposures arising from their P&L. Where this is the case, these profit centres will be excluded from the selldown process and their foreign currency P&L will be transferred to their FX position accounts.

The FX position accounts will restate the desk's FX exposures into the entity's functional currency (or another major currency such as U.S. dollars), which means changes in the value of the desk's foreign currency exposures will be reported back through the P&L in the entity's functional currency. This is illustrated in Figure 18.2.

Chapter 4 has an example of FX restatement in action.

**Estimating the FX Selldown**   Secondly, treasury will usually request an estimate of foreign currency P&L prior to the general ledger (GL) processes taking effect. The purpose of this estimate is to allow treasury to hedge the foreign currency P&L as near to the month-end close as possible and therefore reduce the possibility of trading losses from changes in market rates.

Given this, it is important that product control provide an accurate P&L estimate (by currency). Any differences between the estimate and final P&L will need to be hedged by treasury (via FX desk) in a final clean up.

**P&L from FX Selldown**   The way in which the FX selldown process operates means that the GL will assume that all the P&L has been sold down at the prevailing month-end FX rate in the GL. In reality, the spot FX desk has to execute a real trade, which most probably will not equal the month-end FX rate. This means that the residual P&L, whether a profit or loss, needs to be absorbed by a profit centre. It is up to management to determine which business absorbs this P&L.

**Currency Restrictions**   The final point I would like to make is with regard to currency restrictions. Some foreign currency P&L may be recorded in a currency that is not able to be settled offshore (CNY – Chinese Yuan) or is restricted (NGN – Nigerian Naira).

When this is the case, the foreign currency exposures will not be sold down by the treasury/FX desk and will be left in the FX position accounts of the profit centre driving the balances.

# CHAPTER 19

# Controlling Nostros

**A**s every bank needs nostros to settle their transactions, well-controlled nostros are a key ingredient for a successful bank. In this chapter, we will explore what a nostro is and examine the controls a bank has in place to safeguard their cash.

## INTRODUCTION TO NOSTROS

Nostros for banks are akin to the savings accounts that you and I have, to receive our salary payments into and pay our living expenses from. A bank will require a nostro for each currency they trade in, which will be held with depository institutions (other banks). These accounts are known as vostros from the depository institution's side.

Nostros attract interest and fees which vary depending on the balance. When nostros have surplus funds (and interest rates are not negative), interest is usually paid to the customer by the depository institution. When nostros are overdrawn, interest and possibly overdraft fees are levied against the customer.

As the interest received on surplus funds is generally very low, the bank's treasury will fund nostros in a way that avoids being overdrawn, whilst not leaving too much surplus cash that attracts a low interest rate.

Table 19.1 illustrates a collection of nostros for Sparta Bank, which has six bank accounts in six different currencies. As Sparta Bank has a legal entity and banking licence in the United Kingdom, they can hold their GBP cash within their own bank. There are three sources of nostro account balances, which are illustrated in Figure 19.1.

> **Real world:** This is the bank account which exists at the depository institution. For example, Sparta Bank holds AUD cash in an account with Kangaroo Bank. This is the source of truth for Sparta Bank's AUD cash balance.
>
> **Cash subledger:** This is the bank's internal cash system which records the cash balance and its movements.
>
> **General Ledger (GL):** This is the asset account in the GL which records the cash balance and its movements. This balance is presented in the bank's financial reporting.

**TABLE 19.1**   Sparta Bank's nostros

| Sparta Bank Nostros | | |
|---|---|---|
| **Depository Institution** | **CCY** | **Amount** |
| Kangaroo Bank | AUD | 1,200,350 |
| Montreal Beaver Bank | CAD | 785,000 |
| German National Bank | EUR | −332,000 |
| Sparta Bank | GBP | 85,900 |
| Singaporean Value Bank | SGD | 20,000,000 |
| Yankee Doodle Bank | USD | 2,750,115 |

## CONTROLLING NOSTROS – CASH BREAKS

As the bank's nostro accounts are usually controlled in a central finance team, for example, treasury product control or the finance shared service, most product controllers will not come into contact with the nostro accounts. Consequently, they will not be aware of how nostros function nor what controls exist over them. We will now look at how cash breaks are controlled.

There is an old saying in life: Cash is king! The bank needs to ensure that the funds being drawn from their bank accounts are for valid purposes and the amounts are accurate.

A nostro reconciliation checks that the amounts being paid into and out of a bank's nostro agrees with the bank's expectations. The bank will extract the following data (as a minimum) from its internal systems and reconcile these attributes to the entries in the external nostro accounts:

1. Amount
2. Currency
3. Value date.

The internal data is known as "ledger debits and ledger credits." A ledger debit represents cash being paid into the nostro and a ledger credit represents cash being paid out of the nostro (Figure 19.2).

The external data extracted from the depository institutions are known as "statement debits and credits." Statement debits represent cash being paid out of the nostro and statements credits represent cash being paid into the nostro. In the most basic terms, for each statement credit there will be a ledger debit and vice versa.

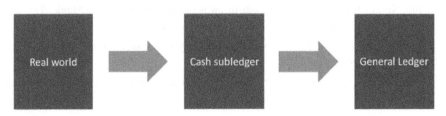

**FIGURE 19.1**   Nostro record keeping

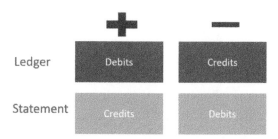

**FIGURE 19.2** Ledger and statement entries

As the volume of daily settlement postings will stretch into the thousands or millions at each bank, the nostro reconciliation needs to be automated. One of the most popular types of reconciliation software that is used in the market is TLM. "TLM has the industry leading automatic match rates in reconciliations. They tend to achieve above 95% auto match rates which is important as this lessens the work load in resolving any dispute process for the reconciliation. TLM's standard matching capabilities include matching on tolerance (e.g., x%, +−2 days, 10 dollars or x% etc.), 1-to-1 matching, 1-to-many, many-to-many reconciliations."[1]

Figure 19.3 depicts the reconciliation workflow for cash settlements using TLM. In the top left corner is the external settlement data, denoted by the SWIFT box (SWIFT is a transaction payment system used by banks and other market participants) and the internal settlement data (this will be the bank's cash sub ledger) flowing into TLM.

Once in TLM the internal and external settlement entries are either matched off with each other or are identified as exceptions. When an item is *matched* it signifies that the expected cash settlement (ledger) agrees to the external cash settlement (statement). When a ledger entry

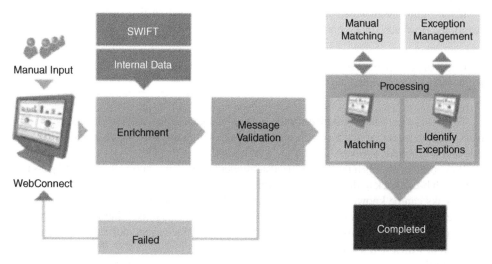

**FIGURE 19.3** TLM reconciliation workflow
Source:© Smartstream Technology. All rights reserved.

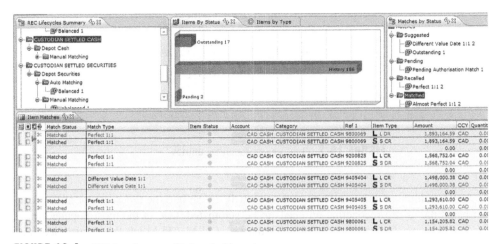

**FIGURE 19.4**   TLM cash reconciliation dashboard
Source: © Smartstream Technology. All rights reserved.

cannot be matched with a statement entry, the unmatched items are considered exceptions and are known as *cash breaks*.

In Figure 19.4 there are five sets of settlement entries which have been matched. In the column *Item Type* the *L* signifies a ledger entry and the *S* signifies a statement (or external) entry.

Ledger entries can only be matched off with statement entries and vice versa. It appears that in the third set of entries, the *L* and *S* entries have different value dates, which means operations would have had to manually match the two entries, as the automatic matching would have initially identified these two entries as exceptions.

If the items are matched in TLM there is no further action that needs to be taken by operations. However, for exceptions, operations will need to:

a) Understand why the break has arisen; and
b) Work to clear the break.

To do this, operations will identify the trade causing the break and check for any obvious errors with the ledger or statement entries. Operations will liaise with the desk that booked the trade and if required, check with the trade's counterparty.

If operations establish that the internal settlement entries are incorrect, they will pass that nostro cash break back to the profit centre which is causing the break. Once in the profit centre, these breaks can be known within finance as actual vs. expected breaks (AVE), cash breaks, settlement breaks or suspense items. Whatever the bank wishes to call them is irrelevant, but what *is* relevant is that this break will usually sit on the balance sheet of the profit centre until it is cleared, which will usually be to P&L.

Using the bond purchase in Table 19.2 as an example, we can review a nostro and AVE break.

It has been discovered that the desk made a booking error and the trade price should be 91.55 rather than 91.50. This results in TLM identifying that the nostro account is breaking on

**TABLE 19.2**   A bond purchase

| Trade | 16589238 |
|---|---|
| Trader | Neil Mclauchlan |
| Trade Date | 16/01/2015 |
| Product Type | Corporate Bond |
| Instrument | GE 3.50% 31/12/2017 |
| Buy/Sell | Buy |
| Trade Price | 91.50 |
| Nominal | 10,000,000 |
| Ccy | USD |
| Value Date | 19/01/2015 |
| Maturity Date | 31/12/2017 |
| Day count basis | 30/360 |
| Payment freq | Semi-annually |
| Counterparty | Melrose trading Inc |

the expected cash settlement of $9,150,000 (LC) vs. the actual settlement of $9,155,000 (SD) that was paid to the counterparty. This is depicted in Figure 19.5.

Where the bank's systems accept backdated cash postings, when the trader rebooks the trade, the cash break will remove itself. Alternatively, operations will arrange for the break to be moved back to the profit centre causing the break.

In Figure 19.6, the systems cannot accept backdated cash postings, so operations have transferred the nostro break to the cash control account (AVE) in the credit profit centre. From here, the balance is transferred to the P&L, resulting in a $5,000 loss for the credit desk.

In this example, the identification and resolution of the cash and AVE break were straight-forward, but due mainly to the complexities of a bank's systems, the identification and clearance of breaks is not always as straightforward. Sometimes, for example, AVE breaks are created through bad system feeds, which has nothing to do with a real nostro break.

Additionally, the ownership of AVE accounts may not rest with operations; product control or the finance shared service may be the owners. It is my view that cash-related breaks should always reside with operations, as this is their forte and bread and butter responsibility.

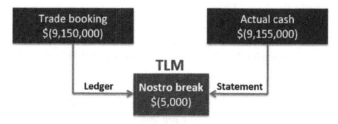

**FIGURE 19.5**   Cash break identification

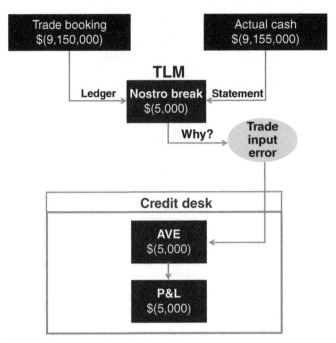

**FIGURE 19.6**   Cash break transfer to the credit desk

Whether AVE ownership resides with product control or not, when assessing the financial health of their business, product control need to understand how the breaks are created, cleared, and what risk the balances pose to their business.

## RISK-WEIGHTING CASH AND AVE BREAKS

Both nostro and AVE breaks should be, but are not always, cleared in a timely manner. This may be due to the complexity of the cash breaks, a lack of resources or a lack of proper attention required from operations, product control or the desk.

As guardians of the bank's financials, product control need to be aware of the risk attached to each of the breaks. For this reason, product control should be able to rely on a RAG rating from operations.

RAG ratings indicate to the stakeholders what risk the nostro and AVE breaks pose to the firm. The risk can be in the form of how old the breaks are, their dollar size and/or their risk of having a high probability of being taken to P&L.

Table 19.3 illustrates the RAG ratings for Sparta Bank, which factors in the dollar amount and the age of the break. Each bank will establish its own set of RAG ratings based upon their risk appetite.

Ideally, the RAG ratings will be generated in the reconciliation system where the breaks are identified, monitored and resolved (e.g., TLM). The benefit of this approach is that all the data and information pertaining to the breaks are stored in a one-stop shop, which facilitates management or stakeholders drilling from the dashboard into the underlying break data.

**TABLE 19.3**  Risk ratings for nostro and AVE breaks

| Age | Amount – USD equivalent | | |
|---|---|---|---|
| | <$500k | $500k–$1mln | >$1mln |
| 0–1 week | G | G | A |
| 1–2 weeks | G | A | A |
| 2 weeks–1 month | A | A | R |
| >1 month | A | R | R |
| >3 months | R | R | R |

In Table 19.4 is product control's escalation matrix for cash and AVE breaks. As product control are primarily responsible for the financial reporting of the business, they need to be aware of any significant risks, which includes nostro and AVE breaks. As a nostro account is used by all businesses, when being notified of nostro breaks, operations need to stipulate which businesses are the cause of the breaks.

A similar matrix would exist for operations management. As with other escalation matrices that we have looked at, their purpose is to bring control exceptions to the attention of appropriate management as and when required.

## PROVISIONING FOR NOSTRO AND AVE BREAKS

At each quarter end, product control should receive, from their operations counterpart, an update regarding the riskiness of each break, which usually comes in the form of RAG ratings and additional commentary for the riskier items. This is an important step in the review and sign off of the bank's financials as product control can assess whether any breaks warrant a provision being taken. Per IAS 37, an entity must recognize a provision if:

- As a result of a past event a present obligation exists;
- It is probable that an outflow of resources will be required to settle the obligation; and
- The obligation can be reliably estimated (IAS 37:14).[2]

As the recording of a provision affects the desk's P&L, it is very important that the desk are kept abreast of the decision-making process regarding the provision. The desk should not be told after the event; they should be informed of all the details product control and operations have regarding the break so that if a provision is required it is not a surprise.

**TABLE 19.4**  Product control escalation matrix for nostro and AVE breaks

| Risk Rating | Position | Rank |
|---|---|---|
| Green | Product control manager | VP |
| Amber | Regional product control manager | Director |
| Red | Global head of product control | Managing Director |

When recording a provision, the balance sheet is credited, creating a liability, and the P&L is debited, creating a loss. These entries would then be reversed once the nostro or AVE break is cleared to P&L.

## NOTES

1. SmartStream. RECS Premium screenshots.doc. © Smartstream Technology. All rights reserved.
2. © IFRS Foundation. IAS 37 Provisions, Contingent Liabilities and Contingent Assets, paragraph 14.

# Six

# Financial Accounting and Reporting

**F**inancial accounting and reporting are important aspects of the product control role as they capture the financial performance of the trading desk in accordance with the relevant accounting principles. Part Six of the book will commence with a review of financial accounting entries and systems used by banks to control and process these entries. We will then go on to explore financial reporting and those components which are most relevant to product control.

# CHAPTER 20

# Financial Accounting Entries

In Chapter 4 we established how to recognize and measure financial assets and liabilities in the trading books. We now need to understand what financial accounting entries are required so that we adhere to IAS 39 and IFRS 9. In this chapter, we will look at financial accounting entries for financial instruments, a typical chart of accounts and the role of an accounting rules engine.

## FINANCIAL ACCOUNTING ENTRIES

Financial accounting is a double entry system which stipulates that whenever there is a debit entry there also needs to be a corresponding credit entry and vice versa. Debits and credits have the following impact on the financials:

- P&L and equity accounts are debited for losses and credited for profits.
- Balance sheet accounts, conversely, are debited for assets and credited for liabilities.

Figure 20.1 illustrates a typical trial balance report for a bank. In the top section you have the profit and loss entries where fair value losses and interest expenses are recorded as debits on the left-hand side whilst fair value gains and interest income are reported as credits on the right-hand side.

Below the dotted line we have those amounts which make up the balance sheet and statement of equity. On the left-hand side, we represent our assets as debits and on the right-hand side we represent our liabilities and equity as credits. By making double-sided accounting entries, the accounting trial balance report should be balanced.

We will now go through the financial accounting entries for some of the financial instruments that you will deal with. It is worth noting that the financial accounting entries related to the revaluation of open positions (fair value gains and losses) and the accrual of interest are usually made on a post and reverse basis, rather than incrementally. This is the method that has been used in the following financial accounting examples.

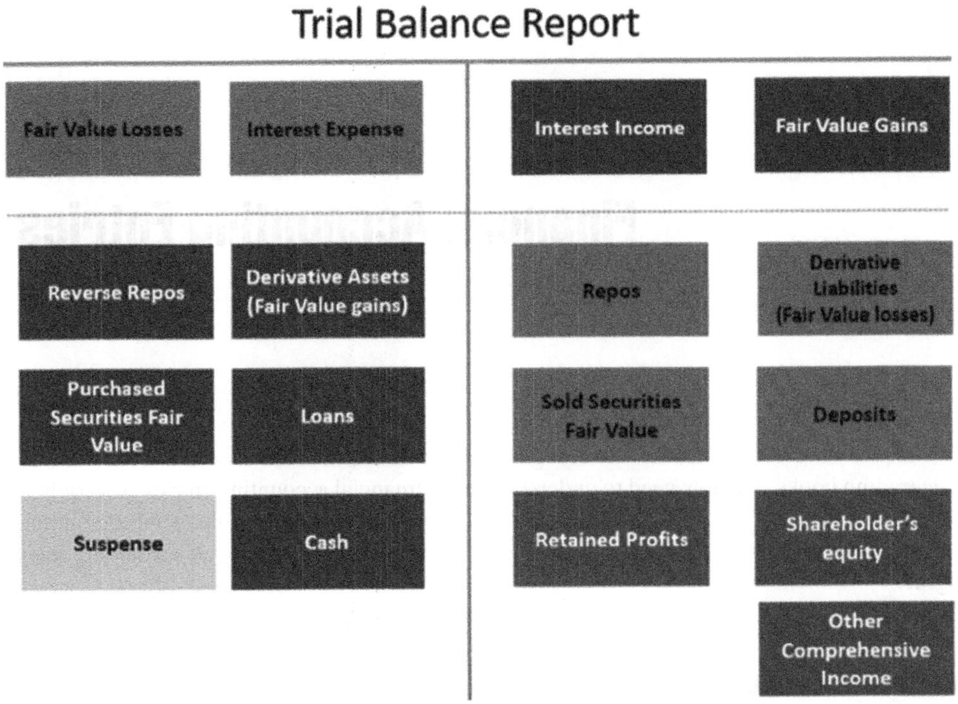

## Trial Balance Report

| Fair Value Losses | Interest Expense | | Interest Income | Fair Value Gains |
|---|---|---|---|---|
| Reverse Repos | Derivative Assets (Fair Value gains) | | Repos | Derivative Liabilities (Fair Value losses) |
| Purchased Securities Fair Value | Loans | | Sold Securities Fair Value | Deposits |
| Suspense | Cash | | Retained Profits | Shareholder's equity |
| | | | | Other Comprehensive Income |

**FIGURE 20.1**    A trial balance report

## Stock

Sparta Bank has purchased stock (or shares) in the mining company ABC. The details of the purchase are displayed in Table 20.1. For simplicity we have assumed the purchase settles on T+0.

To account for the stock, we first need to:

1. Establish how we will categorize and measure the stock, which requires us to reference IAS 39/IFRS 9.
   **IAS 39**
   The stock purchased is:
   ▪ Held primarily to sell in the short term; and

**TABLE 20.1**    ABC stock purchase

| Shares | ABC |
|---|---|
| Quantity | 1,000 |
| Buy/Sell | Buy |
| Price | $10.00 |
| Cash | $(10,000) |
| Settlement | T+0 |

- On initial recognition is part of a portfolio of instruments with an actual pattern of short-term profit taking.

    Therefore, the stock is held for trading and is measured at fair value with changes recorded in the P&L.

    **IFRS 9**

    The stock purchased is:
- Not a debt instrument so cannot undergo the business model and cash flow test;
- Will be held for trading; and
- The firm does not elect fair value through OCI.

    Therefore, the stock will be measured at fair value with changes recorded in the P&L.

2. We now need to identify those attributes of the stock which need to be accounted for:
    - Purchase consideration
    - Changes in fair value
    - Dividends.

**T+0**   At the close of business on T+0 (trade date), the stock price had increased in value to $11.00. On the day of purchase (T+0), the following accounting entries need to be made, which are illustrated in Table 20.2:

- A credit of $10,000 in the nostro account and a corresponding debit of $10,000 into the trading securities account, which represents the purchase consideration and initial fair value of the stock.
- A debit of $1,000 into the trading securities account and a corresponding credit of $1,000 into the unrealized P&L account, which represent the change in the stock's fair value on T+0.

This completes one day of financial accounting entries for a purchase of stock.

**T+180**   On T+180, ABC stock goes ex dividend, which means that the holders of stock on that date will be entitled to receive a dividend of $1.50 per share, which ABC has already declared. As the dividend is not being paid for two more weeks, we need to accrue for that dividend.

On T+180 as the stock is now ex-dividend, the price has fallen from $12 to $10.40, which is primarily due to the $1.50 dividend no longer being included in the stock's price. On T+180 the following accounting entries need to be made, which are illustrated in Table 20.3.

- A credit of $2,000 into the trading securities account and a corresponding debit of $2,000 into the unrealized P&L account, which represents the reversal of the prior day's fair value entries.

**TABLE 20.2**   Accounting for the purchase of ABC stock

| | Trading securities | |
|---|---|---|
| T+0 | $10,000 | |
| | $1,000 | |

| | Nostro | |
|---|---|---|
| T+0 | | $10,000 |
| | | |

| | Unrealized P&L | |
|---|---|---|
| T+0 | | $1,000 |

**TABLE 20.3**  Accounting for the dividend on ABC stock

|        | Trading securities |          |
| ------ | ------------------ | -------- |
| T+0    | $10,000            |          |
| T+179  | $2,000             |          |
| T+180  |                    | $2,000   |
|        | $400               |          |

|        | Unrealized P&L |          |
| ------ | -------------- | -------- |
|        |                |          |
| T+179  |                | $2,000   |
| T+180  | $2,000         |          |
|        |                | $400     |

|        | Dividend receivable |   |
| ------ | ------------------- | - |
| T+180  | $1,500              |   |

|        | Dividend income |        |
| ------ | --------------- | ------ |
| T+180  |                 | $1,500 |

- A debit of $400 into the trading securities account and a corresponding credit of $400 into the unrealized P&L account, which represent the stock's fair value gains as of T+180.
- A debit of $1,500 into the dividend receivable account and a corresponding credit of $1,500 into the dividend income account, which represents the accrual of dividend income which Sparta Bank will receive in two weeks.

When the dividend is paid, Sparta Bank will credit their dividend receivable account and debit their nostro account.

## Loan

Sparta Bank lends a client, Masters Motors, $1 million for a term of one year at a rate of 10% per annum. The loan is part of a non-trading portfolio where assets are held to collect their contractual cash flows. The cash flows pertaining to the loan are illustrated in Figure 20.2.

To account for the loan, we first need to:

1. Establish how we will categorize and measure the loan, which requires referencing IAS 39/IFRS 9.
   **IAS 39**
   A loan is defined as:
   - Non-derivative financial assets;
   - With fixed or determinable payments; and
   - Not quoted in an active market.[1]

**FIGURE 20.2**  Loan agreement

**TABLE 20.4**   Accounting for a loan

| Nostro | | |
|---|---|---|
| T+0 | | $1,000,000 |

| Interest income | | |
|---|---|---|
| T+0 | | $274 |

| Loan receivable | | |
|---|---|---|
| T+0 | $1,000,000 | |

| Interest receivable | | |
|---|---|---|
| T+0 | $274 | |

The loan in this example meets this definition and is not held by the desk for trading and has not been classified as AFS. Therefore, the loan will be measured at amortized cost using the effective interest rate of 10%.

**IFRS 9**

- As a loan is a debt instrument, it will be subject to the business model and SPPI test.
- Business model – the loan is not held for trading and is within a business model which holds assets to collect their contractual cash flows.
- SPPI test – the loan is a basic lending arrangement and is solely payments of principal and interest.

Therefore, the loan will be measured at amortized cost using the effective interest rate of 10%.

2. We need to identify those attributes of the loan which need to be accounted for:
   i) Principal: There are principal exchanges at the start of the loan and upon maturity.
   ii) Interest: Interest income needs to be recognized throughout the life of the loan, using the EIR.

**T+0**   On the day of purchase (T+0), the following accounting entries need to be made, which are illustrated in Table 20.4:

- A credit of $1 million in the nostro, which represents the payment of money to Masters Motors.
- A corresponding debit of $1 million into the loan receivable account, which represents the principal amount owed to Sparta Bank by Masters Motors.
- A credit of $274 in the interest income account and a corresponding debit of $274 in the interest receivable account, which represents one day's accrual of interest income ($1,000,000 \times 10\% \times \frac{1}{365}$).

Throughout the life of the loan we will continue to recognize the incremental interest accrual. For example, on day 31 we will have accrued $8,493 in the interest income and interest receivable accounts ($1,000,000 \times 10\% \times \frac{31}{365}$).

**Maturity**   At maturity, when Masters Motors repays Sparta Bank the principal plus interest, we will need to:

- De-recognize the loan and interest receivable assets.
- Recognize the cash received from Masters Motors.

The accounts will look like those displayed in Table 20.5.

**TABLE 20.5** Accounting for a loan

|  | Nostro | |
|---|---|---|
| T+0 | | $1,000,000 |
| Maturity | $1,100,000 | |

|  | Interest income | |
|---|---|---|
| T+0 –> Maturity | | $100,000 |
| | | |

|  | Loan receivable | |
|---|---|---|
| T+0 | $1,000,000 | |
| Maturity | | $1,000,000 |

|  | Interest receivable | |
|---|---|---|
| T+0 –> Maturity | $100,000 | |
| Maturity | | $100,000 |

## Bond

The next instrument we are going to look at is a bond, which is a debt instrument. In the example illustrated in Table 20.6, Sparta Bank has purchased a bond at par, which pays a coupon of 10% on a semi-annual basis and matures in 1 year.

Figure 20.3 illustrates the cash flows of the bond which Sparta Bank has purchased.

To account for the bond, we first need to:

1. Establish how we will categorize and measure the bond, which requires referencing IAS 39/IFRS 9.

   **IAS 39**
   - The bond is held primarily to sell in the short term; and
   - On initial recognition is part of a portfolio of instruments with an actual pattern of short-term profit taking.

     Therefore, the bond is considered as being held for trading and so is measured at fair value with changes recorded in the P&L.

   **IFRS 9**
   - As a bond is a debt instrument, it will be subject to the business model and SPPI test.
   - Business model – the bond is held for trading.
   - SPPI test – not applicable as the bond is held for trading

     Therefore, the bond will be measured at fair value with changes recorded in the P&L.

2. We need to identify those attributes of the bond which need to be accounted for:

   i) Purchase consideration

      The bond purchase requires an upfront payment to the seller or issuer.

**TABLE 20.6** Example of a bond purchase

| Issuer | Muster Inc |
|---|---|
| Coupon | 10% |
| Frequency | Semi-annual |
| Maturity | 1 year |
| Principal | $1,000,000 |
| Price | 100 |
| Settlement | T+1 |
| Day count | Act/365 |

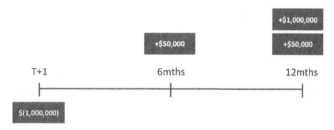

**FIGURE 20.3**   Cash flows for $1m Muster Inc. 10% S/A bond

**ii)** Interest

If the bond is part way through a coupon period when it is purchased, the buyer will pay for, and receive, the coupon which has been accrued up until settlement date. After the purchase is settled, the holder will proceed to accrue for any subsequent coupon income.

For this example, the bond is not part way through a coupon period.

**iii)** Fair value of the bond.

**T+0**   On T+0 (trade date) the market price of the bond has reduced from 100 to 99. On the day of the purchase (T+0), the following accounting entries need to be made, which are illustrated in Table 20.7:

- A debit of $1 million in the trading securities account, representing the bond's purchase consideration.
- A corresponding credit of $1 million in the securities payable account, representing the purchase consideration to be paid.
- A credit of $10,000 in the trading securities account and a corresponding debit of $10,000 in the unrealized P&L account, which represents the fair value loss.
- Note, we do not recognize any coupon on T+0 as the bank does not become eligible to coupon until the bond purchase settles on T+1.

On the day the purchase settles (T+1), the bond's market price has increased from 99 to 102. The accounting entries in Tables 20.8 and 20.9 need to be made:

- A debit of $10,000 in the trading securities account and a corresponding credit of $10,000 in the unrealized P&L account, which represents the reversal of the prior day's fair value loss.

**TABLE 20.7**   Accounting for a bond

|  | Trading securities | |
|---|---|---|
| T+0 | $1,000,000 | |
|  | | $10,000 |

|  | Securities payable | |
|---|---|---|
| T+0 | | $1,000,000 |
|  | | |

|  | Unrealized P&L | |
|---|---|---|
| T+0 | $10,000 | |

**TABLE 20.8**   Accounting for a bond

| | Trading securities | | | Unrealized P&L | |
|---|---|---|---|---|---|
| T+0 | $1,000,000 | | | | |
| | | $10,000 | T+0 | $10,000 | |
| T+1 | $10,000 | | T+1 | | $10,000 |
| | $20,000 | | | | $20,000 |

- A debit of $20,000 in the trading securities account and a corresponding credit of $20,000 in the unrealized P&L account, which represents the current day's fair value gain.

As shown in Table 20.9, the following accounting entries should be made to reflect the settlement of the purchase:

- A credit of $1 million in the nostro account and a corresponding debit of $1 million in the bond payable account, representing the settlement of the bond purchase.

Now that the bond purchase has settled, the desk can start to recognize interest income (bond coupon), which is illustrated in Table 20.10 and is constructed of the following accounting entries:

- A debit of $274 in the Interest receivable account and a corresponding credit of $274 in the interest income account, which represents one day's bond coupon ($1,000,000 $\times$ 10% $\times \frac{1}{365}$).

When the bond redeems at par, the bond asset is de-recognized and a cash asset is recorded in the nostro, which reflects the repayment of the principal and any accrued coupon.

## Interest Rate Swap

We are now going to look at the financial accounting for the most common OTC interest rate derivative, an interest rate swap (Table 20.11).

**TABLE 20.9**   Accounting for a bond

| | Nostro | | | Securities payable | |
|---|---|---|---|---|---|
| | | | T+0 | | $1,000,000 |
| T+1 | | $1,000,000 | T+1 | $1,000,000 | |

**TABLE 20.10**   Accounting for a bond

| | Interest receivable | | | Interest income | |
|---|---|---|---|---|---|
| T+1 | $274 | | T+1 | | $274 |

**TABLE 20.11** An interest rate swap

| Principal | $100,000,000 |
|-----------|--------------|
| Pay | 3.00% |
| Receive | LIBOR + 1.0% |
| Payment | Qrtly |
| Calculation | Qrtly |
| Day count | 30/360 |
| Maturity | 1 yr |

In this example, Sparta Bank has entered into a USD interest rate swap with a notional of $100 million, paying a fixed rate of 3% and receiving floating LIBOR + 1.0%. Interest is calculated and settled quarterly in arrears. This means that the floating rate fixes at the start of the coupon period and the interest is settled three months later (at the end of the coupon period). The swap cash flows are illustrated in Figure 20.4.

To account for the interest rate swap, we first need to:

1. Establish how we will categorize and measure the interest rate swap, which requires referencing IAS 39/IFRS 9.
   - The interest rate swap is a derivative, therefore under IAS 39 and IFRS 9 it is measured at fair value with changes recorded in the P&L.
2. We need to identify those attributes of the interest rate swap which need to be accounted for:
   - **i)** Principal: The principal is not exchanged in an interest rate swap as it is only used as a reference to calculate interest cash flows. Derivative notionals are published by most banks as a disclosure in the notes to their accounts. We will ignore notionals in this accounting example.
   - **ii)** Interest: The settlement of interest on the floating and fixed legs.
   - **iii)** Fair value of the interest rate swap.

**T+0** By close of business on T+0 (trade date), swap yields have risen, causing the net present value (NPV) of the interest rate swap to be $100,000 in Sparta Bank's favour. We need to make the following accounting entries which are illustrated in Table 20.12.

- A debit of $100,000 in the derivative assets account and a corresponding credit of $100,000 in the unrealized P&L account, which represents the fair value gain.

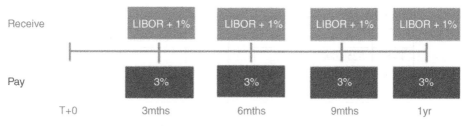

**FIGURE 20.4** Accounting for an interest rate swap

**TABLE 20.12**   Accounting for an interest rate swap

| | Derivative assets | | | | Unrealized P&L | |
|---|---|---|---|---|---|---|
| T+0 | $100,000 | | | T+0 | | $100,000 |

**Day 90**   On day 90, the first interest settlement occurs. Sparta Bank is due to receive $200,000 and the closing NPV of the trade is $10,000 (Table 20.13). Table 20.14 has the relevant accounting entries:

- A credit of $250,000 in the derivative assets account and a corresponding debit of $250,000 in the unrealized P&L account, which represents the reversal of the prior day's fair value gain.
- A debit entry of $10,000 in the derivatives assets account and a corresponding credit of $10,000 in the unrealized P&L account, which represents the current day's fair value gain.
- A debit of $200,000 in the nostro account and a corresponding credit of $200,000 in the realized P&L account, which represents the receipt of the net interest amount. Realized interest amounts from interest rate swaps are not recorded in interest income and expense lines.

Did you notice on the interest settlement date, that the NPV of the swap reduced by an amount similar to the interest Sparta Bank received? If the swap curve doesn't move a great deal on the settlement date, you should see the change in cash and NPV almost offset.

**TABLE 20.13**   Interest settlement

| | |
|---|---|
| LIBOR fix | 2.80% |
| Spread | 1.00% |
| **Pay** | **3.00%** |
| **Receive** | **3.80%** |
| | |
| Notional | $100,000,000 |
| Pay | −$750,000[1] |
| Receive | $950,000[2] |
| Net | $200,000 |

[1]$(100,000,000) \times 3\% \times \frac{90}{360}$

[2]$100,000,000 \times 3.80\% \times \frac{90}{360}$

**TABLE 20.14**   Accounting for an interest rate swap

| | Derivative assets | | | | Unrealized P&L | |
|---|---|---|---|---|---|---|
| T+89 | $250,000 | | | T+89 | | $250,000 |
| T+90 | | $250,000 | | T+90 | $250,000 | |
| | $10,000 | | | | | $10,000 |

| | Nostro | | | | Realized P&L | |
|---|---|---|---|---|---|---|
| T+90 | $200,000 | | | T+90 | | $250,000 |

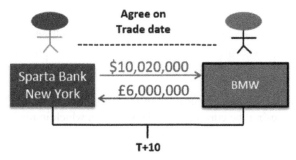

**FIGURE 20.5**  Accounting for an FX forward

## FX Forward

An FX forward is the simultaneous purchase of one currency and sale of another currency at a date other than spot (which for most currencies is T+2). In this example, as illustrated in Figure 20.5, Sparta Bank New York is purchasing £6,000,000 in exchange for selling $10,020,000, which will be exchanged 10 days after the trade date. These currency amounts imply a trade price of 1.67.

To account for the FX forward, we first need to:

1. Establish how we will categorize and measure the FX forward, which requires referencing IAS 39/IFRS 9.
   i) An FX forward is a derivative, therefore under IAS 39 and IFRS 9 we are required to measure the FX forward at fair value with changes recorded in P&L.
2. We need to identify those attributes of the FX forward which need to be accounted for:
   i) Principal: Both currencies are settled on maturity.
   ii) Fair value of the FX forward.

**T+0**  By close of business on T+0 (trade date) the FX forward price in the market has increased to 1.68, which gives rise to a fair value gain of $60,000. We need to make the following accounting entries, which are illustrated in Table 20.15. A debit of $60,000 in the derivative assets account and a corresponding credit of $60,000 in the unrealized P&L account, which represents the current day's fair value gain.

**Maturity**  On maturity of the FX forward (T+10), the market FX rate for GBP/USD is 1.6755. The following accounting entries need to be made, which are illustrated in Table 20.16.

- A credit of $50,000 in the derivative assets account and a corresponding debit of $50,000 in the unrealized P&L account, which represents the reversal of the prior day's fair value gain.

We now need to make accounting entries reflecting the settlement of the trade. To effect this, we will be using an FX position account, which is used by most banks to capture and account for settled currency trading positions. The FX positon account restates the foreign

**TABLE 20.15**  Accounting for an FX forward

|  | Derivative assets | |  |  | Unrealized P&L | |
|---|---|---|---|---|---|---|
| T+0 | $60,000 | |  | T+0 | | $60,000 |

**TABLE 20.16** Accounting for an FX forward

| | Derivative assets | |
|---|---|---|
| T+9 | $50,000 | |
| T+10 | | $50,000 |

| | Unrealized P&L | |
|---|---|---|
| T+9 | | $50,000 |
| T+10 | $50,000 | |

currency amount into the functional currency of the bank (which for a U.S. bank would be United States Dollars) using the current day's FX spot rate, which in this example is 1.6755. These accounting entries are reflected in Table 20.17.

- A debit of $10,020,000 in the FX position account and a corresponding credit of $10,020,000 in the nostro account, which represents the settled sale of USD.
- A credit of £6,000,000 in the FX position account and a corresponding debit of £6,000,000 in the nostro account, which represents the settled purchase of GBP.
- A debit of $33,000 in the FX position account and a corresponding credit of $33,000 in the FX P&L account, which reflects the restatement of £6,000,000 from the traded price of 1.67 to the current day's GBP/USD Spot FX rate 1.6755 (£6,000,000 × (1.6755−1.67)).

In this accounting example, you would have noticed that the entries from the FX restatement of the settled currency position replaces the fair value postings that were being made prior to settlement.

One of the key controls a bank has over its FX position account is to ensure the balance in functional currency equivalent, in this case USD as it is a U.S. company, equals zero. When the balance is zero, it shows that the foreign currency balances are being restated correctly to the current day's FX rate. In this example, in Table 20.20 the debit column sums to $10,053,000 and the USD equivalent of the £6,000,000 credit balance is also $10,053,000.

## Futures

Future contracts are executed and settled with an exchange. When it comes to maturity, the contract can either be physically settled (e.g., the commodity is delivered from the sellers to buyers) or financially settled (the difference between settlement price and trade price is cash settled). We will use the trade in Table 20.18 as an example.

1. Establish how to categorize and measure the futures contract, which requires referencing IAS 39/IFRS 9.
   i) The futures contract is a derivative, therefore under IAS 39 and IFRS 9 we are required to measure the futures contract at fair value with changes recorded in P&L.

**TABLE 20.17** Accounting for an FX forward

| T+10 | FX position | |
|---|---|---|
| Principal | $10,020,000 | £6,000,000 |
| FX Restatement | $33,000 | |

| T+10 | Nostro | |
|---|---|---|
| Principal | £6,000,000 | $10,020,000 |
| | | |

| T+10 | FX P&L | |
|---|---|---|
| FX Restatement | | $33,000 |

**TABLE 20.18**  A purchase of futures contracts

| Contract | Eurodollar Future |
|----------|-------------------|
| Maturity | March 2018 |
| Exchange | CME |
| Buy or Sell | Buy |
| Contracts | 100 |
| Trade Price | 99.00 |

2. We need to identify those attributes of the future that need to be accounted for.

For futures there are two primary attributes we need to account for:

i) Initial margin: The initial margin is a deposit provided to the exchange when a contract is bought or sold. The amount covers the maximum probable one-day move in the price of the futures contract.[2]

ii) Variation margin: Variation margin is the fair value of the futures position and is derived from the difference between the daily settlement price and the traded price (mark-to-market). Variation margin is settled daily with the exchange. If your position has a mark-to-market (MTM) profit, the exchange will pay that amount to you. Conversely, if your position generates a MTM loss, you will need to pay that amount to the exchange.

**T+0**  On T+0 (trade date), the closing settlement price is 98.99, which implies a fair value loss of $2,500 (100 contracts × (98.99 − 99.00) × 100 × $25). Note that to derive the fair value of a futures contract you need to use the tick value of the contract. The tick value is unique to that type of futures contract and can be found in the contract specifications section of the exchange's website.

For the initial margin, we will assume in this example that we need to pay $400 per contract or $40,000 (100 × $400). Initial margin is a balance sheet entry and does not have an impact on the P&L. The following accounting entry in Table 20.19 will be made for the initial margin on T+0.

- A debit of $40,000 in the initial margin account and a corresponding credit of $40,000 in the nostro account, which represents the initial margin paid to the exchange. The initial margin is an asset for the bank.

We now move on to the variation margin postings, which are illustrated in Table 20.20.

- A credit of $2,500 in the variation margin account and a corresponding debit of $2,500 in the futures P&L account, which represents the MTM loss on the futures contract.

**TABLE 20.19**  Accounting for a future

| | Initial margin | | | Nostro | |
|---|---|---|---|---|---|
| T+0 | $40,000 | | T+0 | | $40,000 |

**TABLE 20.20**   Accounting for a future

| | Variation margin | |
|---|---|---|
| T+0 | | $2,500 |
| T+S | $2,500 | |

| | Futures P&L | |
|---|---|---|
| T+0 | $2,500 | |
| | | |

| | Nostro | |
|---|---|---|
| T+S | | $2,500 |

- When the bank settles the variation margin with the exchange (T+S), the variation margin liability is extinguished. This is reflected through a credit of $2,500 into the nostro and a corresponding debit of $2,500 into the variation margin account.

As this futures contract is financially settled at maturity, there is no material difference between the daily accounting entries and those at maturity. At maturity, the initial margin of $40,000 would be returned to the bank, which is illustrated in Table 20.21.

That completes our review of financial accounting entries.

# CHART OF ACCOUNTS

In addition to financial accounting entries, you also need to be aware that there are different types of accounts in the general ledger (GL) which are used to record these debits and credits.

To assist with financial accounting and reporting, each bank will have their own chart of accounts which is a static table showing the accounts, their descriptions and which part of the balance sheet or P&L they map into. For example, Table 20.22 illustrates Sparta Bank's chart of accounts.

As you can see from this illustration, the chart of accounts is broken up into many segments.

- Accounts numbering 1000000 through to 1899999 record details of the bank's assets. This distinction is necessary to aid with calculations including risk-weighted assets, capital ratios and other performance ratios such as return on assets.
- Accounts 1900000 through to 1999999 record details of the bank's intra-entity implicit or explicit transactions. This distinction is important for two main reasons. Firstly, these underlying transactions will not feature in the bank's external financial reporting as the transactions are equal and offsetting within the same legal entity. Secondly, these accounts act as a control as the sum of the accounts for the entire legal entity should net to zero.
- Accounts 2000000 through to 2999998 record details of the bank's liabilities.

**TABLE 20.21**   Accounting for a future

| | Initial margin | |
|---|---|---|
| T+0 | $40,000 | |
| Maturity | | $40,000 |

| | Nostro | |
|---|---|---|
| T+0 | | $40,000 |
| Maturity | $40,000 | |

**TABLE 20.22** Sparta Bank's chart of accounts

| Account | Account description | Classification | Category |
|---------|---------------------|----------------|----------|
| 1000000 | Bond MTM | Asset | Balance Sheet |
| 1899999 | Derivative asset MTM | Asset | Balance Sheet |
| 1900000 | Internal residual funding | Intra-entity assets and liabilities | Balance Sheet |
| 1999999 | Intra entity loans | Intra-entity assets and liabilities | Balance Sheet |
| 2000000 | Loan payable | Liability | Balance Sheet |
| 2999998 | Derivative liability MTM | Liability | Balance Sheet |
| 2999999 | FX Positions | FX Restatement | Balance Sheet |
| 3000000 | Brokerage – Bonds | Expense – "above the line" | Profit & Loss |
| 3999999 | Clearing fees – Exchange traded derivatives | Expense – "above the line" | Profit & Loss |
| 4000000 | Rent – premises | Expense – "below the line" | Profit & Loss |
| 4999999 | IT maintenance fees | Expense – "below the line" | Profit & Loss |
| 5000000 | Unrealized P&L – FX derivatives | Income | Profit & Loss |
| 5999999 | Realized P&L – FX derivatives | Income | Profit & Loss |
| 6000000 | Interest income – secured lending | Interest income | Profit & Loss |
| 6499999 | Interest income – corporate loans | Interest income | Profit & Loss |
| 6500000 | Interest expense – secured lending | Interest expense | Profit & Loss |
| 6999999 | Interest expense – corporate loans | Interest expense | Profit & Loss |
| 7000000 | Interest income – intra entity loans | Intra-entity income and expenses | Profit & Loss |
| 7999999 | Trading P&L – intra entity transactions | Intra-entity trading P&L | Profit & Loss |
| 8000000 | Shareholder's equity | Equity | Equity |
| 8999999 | Retained earnings | Equity | Equity |
| 9000000 | Notionals – Interest rate derivatives | Notionals | Off Balance Sheet |
| 9999999 | Notionals – Sell interest rate derivatives | Notionals | Off Balance Sheet |

- Account 2999999 records FX positions and restates the positions into the relevant functional currency.
- Accounts 3000000 through to 4999999 record expenses. For a sales and trading desk, there are two groups of expenses for management reporting purposes: "above the line" and "below the line." The "above the line" expenses are those items of expense which are directly related to the desk's sales and trading activities, such as broker's fees, clearing fees and exchange fees.

   The "below the line" expenses are those items of expense which are not directly related to the desk's sales and trading activities, such as IT costs, premises charges and personnel costs that have been allocated to the desk. Product control will typically only focus their reviews on above the line expenses.

- Accounts 5000000 through to 5999999 record sales and trading income that has been generated by the desk. Examples of the sorts of amounts feeding these accounts are P&L from trading derivatives such as interest rate swaps and spot FX and forward contracts. They also include the MTM and realized P&L from securities such as bonds but would not include the coupon income from bonds.
- Accounts 6000000 through to 6999999 record the interest income and expenses associated with products such as loans and deposits, repos and coupon-bearing instruments such as bonds. Interest income and expenses are recorded in separate accounts for financial reporting purposes and to facilitate more detailed analysis of the gross interest returns and expenses for assets and liabilities.
- Accounts 7000000 through to 7999999 record the P&L and interest income and expenses associated with internal transactions. In the same vein as the intra-entity balance sheet accounts, the P&L from intra-entity transactions will not be reported in the external financial statements as across the entire legal entity the P&L in these accounts should net to zero. These accounts also act as a control as the sum of the accounts for the entire legal entity should net to zero.
- Accounts 8000000 through to 8999999 record those amounts which are classed as equity such as prior year's profits, other comprehensive income and shareholder's equity.
- Accounts 9000000 through to 9999999 record those amounts that need to be reported in the financial statements as note disclosures. The notionals relating to derivatives are an example of such disclosures.

Now that we know what types of accounts exist, we then need to be able to determine which debits and credits should be passed into which accounts. This job is typically performed by a centrally maintained accounting rules engine.

## ACCOUNTING RULES ENGINE

The accounting rules engine (ARE) is a central source for determining the financial accounting entries that make their way into the GL. The ARE will have inbuilt logic which uses the data sent to it by the feeder systems (risk management systems (RMSs) and cash sub ledger) in order to determine the appropriate accounting entries that should populate the GL. The goal of the ARE is to account for the financial assets and liabilities in such a way that the entity is compliant with the relevant GAAP.

AREs will not cover all accounting entries, such as manual accounting journals that are entered directly into the GL, but they will cover all the accounting entries that are generated by the feeder systems which populate the GL (Figure 20.6).

The bank's feeder systems will send to the ARE all the data that is necessary to prepare the double-sided accounting entries. For example, using an interest rate swap, the following fields will be used by the ARE to generate the necessary accounting entries and populate the necessary fields within the GL (Table 20.23).

The reasons that a bank will set up an ARE is twofold. Firstly, rather than have each RMS maintain and generate their own set of accounting rules, a single ARE means that there is only

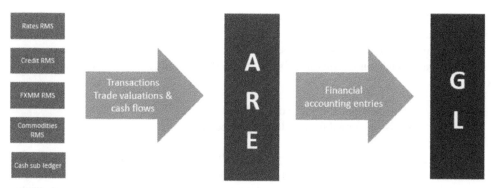

**FIGURE 20.6** Accounting rules engine flows

**TABLE 20.23** How an ARE uses trade data

| RMS | RMS | How does ARE use this data (aside from populating a matching field in the GL)? |
|---|---|---|
| Financial instrument | Interest Rate Swap | Determines Product Code and which P&L and balance sheet accounts will be used |
| Trade date | 26/08/2014 | |
| Value date | 28/08/2014 | For a firm electing value date accounting, this field determines when the trade begins to be accounted for in the financial statements. This field isn't relevant for derivatives as they are accounted for from trade date. |
| Counterparty type | Bank | Determines the grouping of transactions and balances in the financial statements |
| Counterparty | Rayner Prince Bank | Determines whether the trade is consolidated (internal or intercompany counterparties) or not |
| Maturity | 26/08/2015 | Determines when the deal ceases to be accounted for in the financial statements |
| Notional | 10,000,000 | Used in the derivative note disclosures |
| Floating leg | Receive | |
| Fixed leg | Pay | |
| Notional exchange | No | Determines if the notional will generate cash and realized P&L entries |
| Coupon | 2% | |
| NPV | 10,000 | Determines fair value gains and losses to be reported |
| Coupon frequency | Qrtly | |
| Transaction currency | GBP | Determines the amount to be populated in functional currency |
| Book | Swaps UK | |
| Profit centre | 71111 | |
| Company | Sparta London Ltd | Determines which GAAPs are applied |

one source of accounting rules, which adds a control layer for the financial accounting logic within the bank.

For example, at some firms, it is possible to book the same trade type into two or more RMSs. In Sparta Bank, an internal loan between two desks has been booked in two different RMSs.

RMS1    Loan is accounted for as a derivative
RMS2    Loan is accounted for as a lending agreement.

In Table 20.24, you can observe that because RMS1 is accounting for the loan as a derivative, the necessary on balance sheet entries are not being generated. The firm is missing the loan principal and interest receivable entries along with the interest income in the appropriate balance sheet and P&L accounts.

The fallout from this is that the GL will, if not corrected, publish incorrect information in the firm's financial statements, which could lead to investors making decisions based on poor financial data.

The second reason a bank will choose to set up a central ARE is with regard to change. Once the bank establishes the accounting rules for a new product, these rules will not change unless new pronouncements are released by the various accounting bodies. When these pronouncements occur, it is much simpler and less onerous for the banks to amend one set

**TABLE 20.24**   RMS posting asymmetry

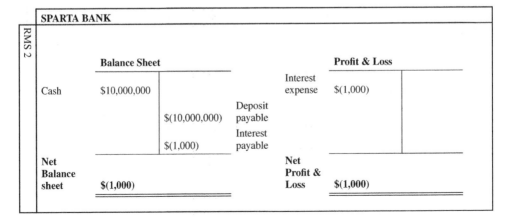

of accounting rules rather than several. A bank will also ensure that when changes are made to the ARE, there will be a set of robust controls to ensure that the ARE's integrity remains intact.

That concludes our review of financial accounting entries.

## NOTES

1. IFRS Foundation. IAS 39 Recognition and Measurement, Definitions.
2. ASX, "Index Derivative: Futures Margins," ASX.com.au, 2017. http://www.asx.com.au/products/index-derivatives/futures-margins.htm.

# CHAPTER 21

# Financial Reporting and Note Disclosures

**E**arnings updates and financial statements are published periodically to provide the market with information on the bank's performance and statement of financial position. The frequency and depth of reporting differs by jurisdiction, with U.S. banks, such as Citigroup, having to publish financial statements each quarter, whilst U.K. banks, such as HSBC, publish earnings updates quarterly and financial statements semi-annually.

There is a dedicated team within a bank, financial control or financial reporting, who review and publish the financial reports. Their existence, however, does not absolve product control from understanding their business' results from a financial reporting perspective. On the contrary, product control are required to provide their financial reporting colleagues with the business rationale for the results presented in the financial statements.

## CONTEXT OF FINANCIAL REPORTING

It is important to consider the context of financial reporting and how it may differ to product control's context. We will look at some of the key items to consider within this subject.

### Legal Entity View

Financial reporting present and analyse financial results from an alternate paradigm to that which product control are familiar with. Whereas product control will focus on a collection of trading books forming a trading desk and business, financial reporting's focus is on the legal entity view of that business. Figure 21.1 illustrates this difference in paradigms.

Legal entity view is important as each entity will have its own set of published accounts for standalone financial reporting, presented in accordance with their country's generally accepted accounting principles (known as local GAAP). These results will also need to be consolidated into the parent entity's financial reporting, which will be prepared in accordance with the parent entity's local GAAP. For example, Sparta Bank Australia is a subsidiary of Sparta Bank Holding Inc., which means their standalone financial report is prepared in alignment with Australian GAAP and their consolidated accounts are prepared in accordance with U.S. GAAP.

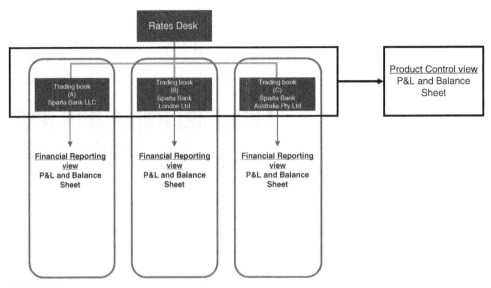

**FIGURE 21.1** Different paradigms

Banks will try to automate the transition from standalone GAAP to consolidated GAAP within their general ledger.

## Intercompany and Intracompany Transactions

When product control reviews the desk's P&L and balance sheet, they will be aware that there will be a mix of intracompany, intercompany and external trades that flow through the desk's books, generating an overall P&L and risk position.

Intracompany transactions are those trades between two desks within the same entity. For example, using Figure 21.1, if the rates desk executes a trade with the FX desk and both desks use trading books within Sparta Bank London Ltd, this will be identified as an intracompany transaction.

An intercompany transaction is a trade between two entities with the same parent company or an entity and its parent company. For example, if Sparta Bank Holding Inc were the parent company of both Sparta Bank London Ltd and Sparta Bank Australia Pty Ltd, trades between these U.K. and Australian entities would be considered intercompany transactions.

As the consolidated financial statements net down these related party trades, product control need to be familiar with the transition from an internal view to an external view. This translates into viewing the P&L and balance sheet by counterparty type.

## Timings

Product control will review their desk's financial reporting each month, but as the bank publishes financial information to the market on a quarterly basis, it is at these reporting dates that product control conducts deeper and broader analytical reviews of their desk's financial statements, including note disclosures, to flag and correct material reporting errors.

You will also encounter the "champing at the bit" by senior management to compress their financial reporting timelines so they can deliver information to the market before their peers. It is my view that the race to report early must be weighed against the personal cost to staff who are expected to work very late nights and weekends to meet these tight deadlines.

## Labelling

Finally, the terms banks use in their financial statements are inconsistent across the industry. For example, for P&L associated with fair value gains and losses on financial assets and liabilities classified as fair value through P&L, some of the terms I have seen used in the market are:

- Principal transactions
- Net trading income
- Gains less losses on financial instruments at fair value
- Other operating income.

It is therefore important to understand the chart of accounts at your bank and how they feed into the financial reports. You can also read the accompanying notes in the annual report, which provide a plethora of mostly useful information and ask questions of your financial reporting colleagues when and where required.

## PROFIT AND LOSS

There are some differences between the product control view of the P&L and the standalone financial reporting view. A lot of product controllers will view their P&L on a net basis, whilst the financial statements report interest on a gross basis and separately from trading income. As interest represents more stable income than the highly volatile trading income, the bank's management, investors and analysts alike, rely on the interest data to quantify what net interest margin the bank is generating on its balance sheet and whether it is improving or declining. It is, therefore, important that product control understand how their financial instruments will be presented in the financial statements.

An example of an instrument that has P&L feeding multiple lines in financial statements is a bond. A bond which is held for trading will have P&L that is attributed to interest income and expense as well as trading income. Table 21.1 illustrates the P&L components resulting from the purchase of a bond.

The bond has coupon income of $1, which will be a consistent source of income until the bond is sold or is redeemed. Interest income will also be affected if the bond was purchased at a premium or discount, as the difference between par and the purchase price will be dripped into the net interest income over the remaining life of the bond. Chapters 4 and 11 provide examples and discussions around this.

If the bond is funded by a repo that is rolled daily (the repo's maturity is 1 day which means the desk enter a new repo transaction each day at potentially different yields every time), the cost of borrowing funds via a repo is presented as an interest expense.

As most repos don't lend 100% of the bond's fair value, there may be a residual funding component from treasury. This would be reported as intra-entity borrowings and the cost of

**TABLE 21.1**    Presentation of the bank's P&L

| Interest income | Jun-15 | Jul-15 | Aug-15 |
|---|---|---|---|
| Coupon | 1 | 1 | 1 |
| | | | |
| **Interest expense** | | | |
| Repo interest | (0.7) | (0.75) | (0.73) |
| Intra-entity borrowings | (0.05) | (0.06) | (0.05) |
| | | | |
| **Trading income** | | | |
| Fair value gains and losses | (0.1) | 0.5 | 0.65 |

this would be recorded as an interest expense. As this is an intracompany transaction, from an entity view this cost will offset to zero with the income amount being reported in treasury.

Finally, as the bond is classified and measured at fair value through P&L, any changes in the fair value of the bond would need to be reported into trading income. Table 21.2 illustrates how a typical income statement (i.e., P&L) will be presented in the financial statements for a bank.

Companies are required by their local accounting standards to provide comparative data in their financial statements. IFRS and U.S. GAAP both require two years of comparative data for earnings and one for balance sheet.

**TABLE 21.2**    Presentation of the bank's P&L

| Income Statement<br>*For the year ended 30 June 2015* | | | | | |
|---|---|---|---|---|---|
| | | **Financial Year ended** | | | **Change from** |
| | Note | 2015 | 2014 | 2013 | 2014 |
| | | $ million | $ million | $ million | % |
| Interest income | 3 | 10,000 | 9,890 | 9,000 | 1.11% |
| Interest expense | 3 | −8,500 | −8,490 | −8,000 | 0.12% |
| **Net interest income** | | **1,500** | **1,400** | **1,000** | **7.14%** |
| | | | | | |
| Net fees & commissions income | 4 | 2,500 | 2,450 | 2,300 | 2.04% |
| Net trading income | 5 | 4,400 | 5,400 | 6,000 | −18.52% |
| **Other Income** | | **6,900** | **7,850** | **8,300** | **−12.10%** |
| | | | | | |
| **Total net operating income before impairment & operating expenses** | | **8,400** | **9,250** | **9,300** | **−9.19%** |
| | | | | | |
| Loan impairment expense | 6 | −50 | −40 | −42 | 25.00% |
| Operating expenses | 7 | −1,200 | −1,100 | −1,320 | 9.09% |
| **Net profit before tax** | | **7,150** | **8,110** | **7,938** | **−11.84%** |

**TABLE 21.3**  Derivate assets and liabilities

| Trades | Fair value |
|---|---|
| FX Forward | 10 |
| Interest rate swap | (5) |
| Credit default swap | 5 |

Next to each of the components in the income statement is a note number. These notes reference where readers can find more information regarding that component of income. For example, if an investor or analyst wants to find out more information about the $4,400 million in trading income, they would refer to note 5.

# BALANCE SHEET

The balance sheet is also a central part of a bank's financial statements and earnings updates.

## Derivative Assets and Liabilities

Aside from related party transactions, the main difference between the product control view and the financial reporting relates to the reporting of derivatives. Product control typically views derivative assets and liabilities as a net number, rather than gross, and tend to place more emphasis on the desk's risk sensitivities to understand how the desk's derivative profile has changed over time.

In financial reporting, the fair values of the derivative portfolios are presented as gross assets and gross liabilities after counterparty netting has been factored in. We will look at netting shortly.

For example, let's suppose we have the following three externally traded derivative trades in our portfolio, which are illustrated in Table 21.3

Without considering counterparty netting, the trades would be reported as follows in Table 21.4.

What this means for product control, is that we need to consider both derivative assets and liabilities when reviewing changes in our balance sheet. It also means that we need to be cognizant of the impact that netting can have on the presentation of derivative fair values.

**TABLE 21.4**  Presentation of derivate assets and liabilities

| Trades | Derivative asset | Derivative liability |
|---|---|---|
| FX forward | 10 | |
| Interest rate swap | | (5) |
| Credit default swap | 5 | |

## Counterparty Type

Another less significant difference is that the financial statements report some balances by counterparty type. For example, in Table 21.5, cash deposited with the Bank of England will be reported under "Cash with central banks," whilst cash deposited with interbank counterparties,

**TABLE 21.5**   Presentation of the bank's balance sheet

| Balance Sheet | | | | |
|---|---|---|---|---|
| *For the year ended 30 June 2015* | | | | |
| | | **Financial Year ended** | | **Change from** |
| | **Note** | **2015** | **2014** | **2014** |
| Assets | | $ million | $ million | % |
| Cash with central banks | 8 | 50,000 | 49,500 | 1.01% |
| Cash and due from banks | 9 | 40,000 | 39,800 | 0.50% |
| Trading assets | 10 | 16,000 | 15,480 | 3.36% |
| Derivative assets | 11 | 42,950 | 43,000 | −0.12% |
| Available for sale investments | 12 | 16,000 | 15,900 | 0.63% |
| Loans, bills and other receivables | 13 | 5,000 | 5,900 | −15.25% |
| Deferred tax assets | 14 | 490 | 560 | −12.50% |
| **Total assets** | | **170,440** | **170,140** | **0.18%** |
| | | | | |
| Liabilities | | $mln | $mln | % |
| Deposits | 15 | −37,000 | −36,445 | 1.52% |
| Due to other banks | 15 | −44,000 | −43,560 | 1.01% |
| Trading liabilities | 16 | −29,000 | −28,855 | 0.50% |
| Derivative liabilities | 17 | −15,000 | −15,475 | −3.07% |
| Debt issuance | 18 | −5,000 | −4,900 | 2.04% |
| Tax liabilities | 19 | −760 | −433 | 75.52% |
| Other provisions | 20 | −120 | −433 | −72.29% |
| **Total liabilities** | | **−130,880** | **−130,101** | **0.60%** |
| | | | | |
| **Net assets** | | **39,560** | **40,039** | **−1.20%** |
| | | | | |
| Shareholders' equity | | | | |
| Share capital | | | | |
| − Common stock | 21 | −36,710 | −37,369 | −1.76% |
| − Preferred stock | 22 | −750 | −720 | 4.17% |
| Reserves | 23 | −500 | −550 | −9.09% |
| Retained earnings | 24 | −1,600 | −1,400 | 14.29% |
| | | | | |
| **Total shareholder's equity** | | **−39,560** | **−40,039** | **−1.20%** |

such as Barclays, will be reported as cash and due from banks. This reinforces the need for product control to be familiar with their balance sheet by counterparty type.

# NETTING

Within the accounting standards, if certain conditions are met, an entity is required (required under IFRS but is optional under U.S. GAAP) to offset financial assets and liabilities and present the net amount in their financial statements.

The benefit of netting is that the entity can report a lower asset base, which in turn improves performance ratios, such as return on assets, and will also reduce the amount of capital a bank needs to hold.

When an entity does apply netting, it is not derecognizing the asset or liability; it just affects the presentation of the balance sheet. The two most common categories of financial assets and liabilities in which a trading desk will apply netting, are derivatives and repos (liability)/reverse repos (asset).

## IFRS

The international accounting standard which deals with netting is IAS 32 Financial Instruments: Presentation. Under IAS 32, a financial asset and liability should be offset and the net amount presented in the statement of financial position when:

1. There is a legally enforceable right to set off the amounts; and
2. The two parties intend either to settle on a net basis, or to realize the asset and settle the liability simultaneously[1] (IAS 32:42).

Figure 21.2 summarizes the conditions for netting under IAS 32.

### Legally Enforceable Right to Set-Off if Either Party Defaults and in the Normal Course of Business The first condition requires the entity to have a legal agreement in place with a counterparty which specifies that any amounts owed by the entity can be offset against amounts the counterparty owes the entity[2] (IAS 32:45).

An example of such a contract is a master netting agreement which exists within ISDA master agreements for OTC derivative transactions and Global Master Repo Agreements (GMRA), which applies to repos and reverse repos. It is imperative that these contracts can be enforced by the courts in the relevant legal jurisdiction.

Under these agreements there are two types of netting arrangements:

1. **Close out netting:** Amounts owed between parties are netted into one single amount upon default of either party or termination of the contract due to an event like bankruptcy[3] (IAS 32:50).

    Close out netting is important, as it mitigates the risk of administrators cherry picking assets. If an entity has an enforceable master netting agreement in place, it has satisfied this condition.

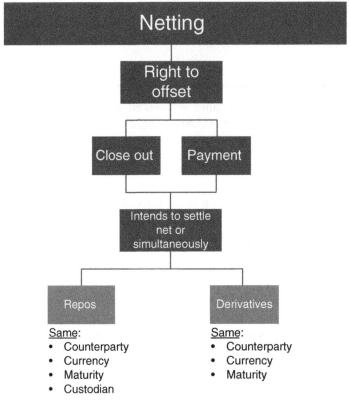

**FIGURE 21.2**    Netting – a summary of IAS 32's criteria
Note: Illustration based upon IAS 32:42-50[4]

2. **Payment netting:** In the ordinary course of business, amounts owed between parties which are settling on the same date and in the same currency can be settled in a single amount.[5,6] This incorporates life cycle settlements such as CDS premiums and interest settlements on interest rate swaps.

**Intends to Settle Net**    Even if the entity has the enforceable right to offset, it must also have the intention to settle net or realize the financial asset and liability simultaneously[7] (IAS 32:46). This applies to both settlement upon close out and during the normal course of business (payment netting).

**Derivative Netting**    The criteria for derivatives netting is:

- Same counterparty
- Same currency
- Same maturity.

**TABLE 21.6**  Presentation of derivate assets and liabilities

|  | Asset | Liability |
|---|---|---|
| Derivatives | 15 | (5) |
| Amounts offset which are subject to a master netting agreement | (5) | 5 |
| Total | 10 | 0 |

For OTC derivative transactions, which are not cleared through a CCP, it is very difficult for banks to satisfy this condition in IAS 32 as most trades will not satisfy the condition to net payments in the normal course of business.

I believe this failure is due to a logistical hurdle, as it would be challenging for a bank to consolidate all payment information by counterparty, across hundreds or thousands of trades, which also span several different risk and settlement systems.

Let's assume the derivatives in Table 21.4 are with the same counterparty, which trade under a master netting agreement, they also settle all life cycle payments on the same day and in the same currency and they all mature on the same day. If we subject these transactions to netting, we are presented with the following result in Table 21.6.

After netting, the financial liabilities of the entity have been reduced to nil and the entity is left with a derivative asset of 10, which is 5 less than before netting was applied.

**Central Clearing Counterparties (CCP)**  Trades which settle through a CCP, such as CDS trades facing LCH CDSClear, would qualify for netting. However, the entity would not usually be able to offset financial assets and liabilities which are settled through different clearing units within LCH.

For example, interest rate swaps which are settled through LCH SwapClear could not be offset with CDS trades settling through LCH CDSClear, as the settlement cycles are not synchronized to satisfy the net settlement aspect of IAS 32.

**Collateral**  A financial instrument, for example, cash, which has been pledged or received as collateral can also be set off against the related financial asset or liability if it meets the IAS 32 netting criteria. However, due to being unable to meet the payment netting test, it is difficult to net cash collateral under IAS 32.

**Repo Netting**  For repos and reverse repos, IAS 32 conditions are satisfied if the financial asset and liability have the same:

- Counterparty
- Maturity
- Currency
- Custodian.

Custodians are the party who settles the securities and cash for the bank.

For example, in Table 21.7 Sparta Bank London Ltd have the following transactions with Bank Giro Italia outstanding as of 30th June, which have been executed under a GMRA.

In Table 21.8 is the gross view of the balance sheet before any netting is applied.

**TABLE 21.7**   Repo and reverse repo transactions with Bank Giro Italia

| Instrument | Repo | Reverse repo |
|---|---|---|
| Amount lent/(borrowed) | (1,000,000) | 1,500,000 |
| Currency | GBP | GBP |
| Maturity | 1st July | 1st July |
| Custodian | LCH RepoClear | LCH RepoClear |

**TABLE 21.8**   Gross presentation of repos and reverse repos

| 30th June | | |
|---|---|---|
| | Asset | Liability |
| Reverse repo | 1,500,000 | |
| Repo | | (1,000,000) |

In Table 21.9 is the view of the balance after netting has been applied.

As IAS 32 includes financial assets and liabilities which are settled simultaneously, it raises the possibility for an entity to offset trades which are settled through a CCP, where settlement may take place over a number of hours.

## U.S. GAAP

Under U.S. GAAP, the entity has the option rather than the requirement to apply netting. U.S. GAAP criteria for netting are also less stringent than IFRS. Under U.S. GAAP, netting can be applied when the following criteria are met:

- **Each party owes determinable amounts:** These determinable amounts, which are owed between the two parties, are the fair values of the respective financial assets and liabilities.
- **A right to set-off exists:** Akin to IFRS, this right is established through master netting agreements.
- **Intend to set-off:** Derivatives are not required to meet these criteria, as having an enforceable master netting agreement is satisfactory.[8]
- **Set-off is enforceable at law:** As with IFRS, a master netting agreement needs to have the support of the law in the relevant legal jurisdiction (FASB, ASC 210-20-45-1).[9]

**TABLE 21.9**   Net presentation of repos and reverse repos

| 30th June | | |
|---|---|---|
| | Asset | Liability |
| Reverse repo | 1,500,000 | |
| Repo | | (1,000,000) |
| Amounts offset which are subject to a master netting agreement | (1,000,000) | 1,000,000 |
| Total | 500,000 | 0 |

**TABLE 21.10** Net presentation of derivatives

| Criteria | IFRS | U.S. GAAP |
|---|---|---|
| Payment netting | X | |
| Close out netting | X | X |
| Currency | Same | All |
| Maturity | Same | All |
| Counterparty | Same | Same |

**Derivatives Netting** Fin 39 (FASB Interpretation No.39) provides further application guidance for derivatives. The main differences between IFRS and U.S. GAAP are listed in Table 21.10.

Under U.S. GAAP, derivative netting is not restricted by the bank's ability and intention to net payments in the normal course of business, nor by the maturity or currency of the transactions.

**Collateral** Under U.S. GAAP, cash collateral that is pledged or received in relation to a financial asset or liability under the master netting agreement can also be set off on the balance sheet. For example, using the data in Table 21.6, as the fair value of the trades is in the money to the bank, the counterparty posts cash collateral of 10. The financial reporting result of this is presented in Table 21.11.

Because we have received this cash collateral, we need to recognize a cash asset of 10 and a corresponding liability of (10), as the cash will need to be repaid to the counterparty in the future (unless they default). These entries increase our assets to 20 and our liabilities to (10). Under U.S. GAAP we can net other liabilities with the derivative assets, which results in the following balances illustrated in Table 21.12.

In Table 21.12, the effect of netting the cash collateral has reduced the assets from 20 back down to 10 and the liabilities have been reduced to nil.

**Repos Netting** U.S. GAAP is materially the same as IFRS for offsetting repos and reverse repos. Further reading can be found in FIN 41 (FASB Interpretation No.41).

Repos and reverse repos can be offset if the transactions:

- Have the same counterparty.
- Have the same maturity date.

**TABLE 21.11** Presentation of cash collateral

| | Asset | Liability |
|---|---|---|
| Derivatives | 15 | (5) |
| Amounts offset which are subject to a master netting agreement | (5) | 5 |
| Cash | 10 | |
| Other liabilities | | (10) |
| Total | 20 | (10) |

**TABLE 21.12** Netting cash collateral

|  | Asset | Liability |
|---|---|---|
| Derivatives | 15 | (5) |
| Amounts offset which are subject to a master netting agreement | (5) | 5 |
| Cash | 10 | |
| Other liabilities | | (10) |
| Netting of cash collateral | (10) | 10 |
| Total | 10 | 0 |

- Have been executed under a master netting agreement.
- The securities underlying both the repo and reverse repo exist in electronic book entry form and can only be transferred via a market transfer system, such as LCH RepoClear.
- Use the same bank account with the clearing bank to settle the cash outflows (repo) and inflows (reverse repo) (FASB, ASC 210-20-45-11).[10] The consequence of this is that the repo and reverse repo will need to be in the same currency.

## Disclosures Relating to Netting

Where IAS 32 lays out the criteria for netting, IFRS 7 Financial Instruments: Disclosures, lays out disclosure requirements for netting. IFRS 7 is broader than just netting disclosures as it requires entities to provide information in their financial statements which enable users to evaluate:

- The significance of financial instruments for the entity's financial position and performance; and
- The nature and extent of risks arising from the financial instruments the entity is exposed to and how the entity manages those risks (IFRS 7:1).[11]

As the breadth of IFRS 7 is so wide this chapter will only provide an illustration of IFRS 7 and how it relates to netting. In Table 21.13 is an example of a typical note disclosure for netting. In the disclosure, the entity is required to disclose what amounts subject to a netting arrangement have and have not been set off.

On the left hand side of Table 21.13 are the gross financial assets and liabilities of the firm which are subject to netting arrangements (assets 24,666 and liabilities −23,789). Moving from left to right, the firm presents those amounts which are subject to a netting arrangement and have been offset. This reduces the total assets and liabilities reported down by 8,381 to 16,285 and −15,408 respectively.

Table 21.13 then discloses those assets and liabilities which are subject to a netting arrangement but have not been offset on the balance sheet. If these amounts could have been offset it would have reduced assets by 13,077 to 3,208 and liabilities by 12,218 to −3,190.

Moving further to the right, the firm discloses the quantum of assets and liabilities which are not subject to a netting arrangement. By adding these amounts to the net amounts presented under netting arrangements, you arrive at the total balance sheet amount for derivatives and repos/reverse repos. For assets, this is the sum of 16,285 and 1,700 and for liabilities it is the sum of −15,408 and −1,700.

**TABLE 21.18** Offsetting financial assets and financial liabilities

| | Amounts subject to enforceable netting arrangements | | | | | | Amounts not subject to netting arrangements | Total balance sheet |
| | Amounts which have been offset | | | Amounts which have not been offset | | | | |
| | Gross amounts | Amounts offset | Net amounts presented | Financial instruments | Cash and other financial collateral | Net amounts that would be presented if offset | | |
|---|---|---|---|---|---|---|---|---|
| | $mln | $mln | $mln | $mln | $mln | $mln | $mln | $mln |
| **Assets** | | | | | | | | |
| Derivatives | 22,115 | (7,121) | 14,994 | (10,617) | (2,432) | 1,945 | 1,000 | 15,994 |
| Reverse repurchase agreements | 2,551 | (1,260) | 1,291 | (28) | 0 | 1,263 | 700 | 1,991 |
| **Total assets** | 24,666 | (8,381) | 16,285 | (10,645) | (2,432) | 3,208 | 1,700 | 17,985 |
| **Liabilities** | | | | | | | | |
| Derivatives | (21,042) | 7,121 | (13,921) | 10,617 | 1,573 | (1,731) | (1,200) | (15,121) |
| Repurchase agreements | (2,747) | 1,260 | (1,487) | 28 | 0 | (1,459) | (500) | (1,987) |
| **Total liabilities** | (23,789) | 8,381 | (15,408) | 10,645 | 1,573 | (3,190) | (1,700) | (17,108) |

## FAIR VALUE HIERARCHY

The fair value hierarchy is a fair value disclosure which the bank needs to incorporate into its financial reporting. The requirement is embedded within IFRS 13 and ASC 820 and seeks to allocate an asset or liability and its fair value into one of three levels depending upon the observability of its pricing inputs (Figure 21.3).

As a fair valued asset or liability can only be allocated into one level of the hierarchy, where the item's pricing inputs would have it allocated into two or more levels, the lowest pricing input that is significant to the entire measurement will determine which level is appropriate[12] (IFRS 13:73).

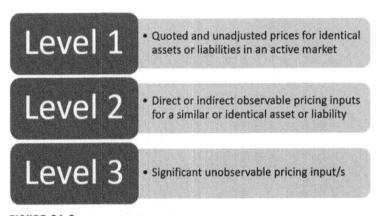

**FIGURE 21.3**   Fair value hierarchy
Note: Illustration based upon IFRS 13:72-90[13]

It is usually the responsibility of the valuations team to determine fair value hierarchy classifications; however, product control can also provide input on the levelling where it is appropriate. Two areas where classifications can be determined are through independent price verification (see Chapter 15) and the new trade review (see Chapter 9).

## Level 1

The fair value for level one assets and liabilities is very certain, as not only is a quoted (unadjusted) price for an identical asset or liability available from the market, the market is active, meaning trades are executed frequently and with sufficient volume to provide ongoing price information[14] (IFRS 13:Appendix A). The entity will need to have access to the market at the measurement date.

In *Insights into IFRS* (KPMG, 2016/17), the author makes the point that OTC derivatives would not typically be allocated to level 1 as these are individual contracts between specific parties and as such there is unlikely to be an active market for an identical instrument.[15]

Examples of level 1 items would be the short-dated March, June, September and December contracts for CME Eurodollar futures, US Treasury bonds and GE stock.

**TABLE 21.14** FX option

| | |
|---|---|
| Buy/Sell | Buy |
| Call/Put | Call |
| Type | European |
| Currency pair | GBP/ZAR |
| Strike | 11.5 |
| Maturity | 10 years |

## Level 2

If an asset or liability doesn't meet the requirements for level one, we now need to consider if level two is appropriate. Level two items have their fair values derived using:

- Quoted prices for similar financial assets or liabilities in a market that is active;
- Quoted prices for an identical or similar asset or liabilities;
- Indirectly via pricing inputs which are observable for most of the asset or liability's life; or
- Indirectly via pricing inputs that rely on correlation with observable market data[16] (IFRS 13:82)

Indirect pricing can include inputs such as implied volatilities, interest rates (observable at commonly quoted intervals), credit default swaps (CDS) spreads and FX swap points, which are fed into a financial model that generates a market value for the asset or liability[17] (IFRS 13:82).

Examples of level two items are a 3-year USD interest rate swap, a 5-year CDS referencing a liquid name like HSBC, a 1-year GBP/USD European FX call option and a EUR/USD spot FX contract, all of which have observable pricing inputs for most of the asset's life.

## Level 3

Level 3 assets and liabilities have their fair values derived from pricing input(s) which are unobservable and that unobservable pricing input has a significant impact on the fair value of the asset or liability. An example of a level 3 asset is the following option listed in Table 21.14.

Table 21.15 lists the pricing inputs which will be used by the financial model to determine the fair value of the FX option. As the FX swap points and volatility inputs are unobservable

**TABLE 21.15** Observability of pricing inputs

| Pricing input | Observability |
|---|---|
| Time | Yes |
| Strike | Yes |
| Spot FX | Yes |
| FX swap points | Up to 3 years |
| Volatility | Up to 18 months |

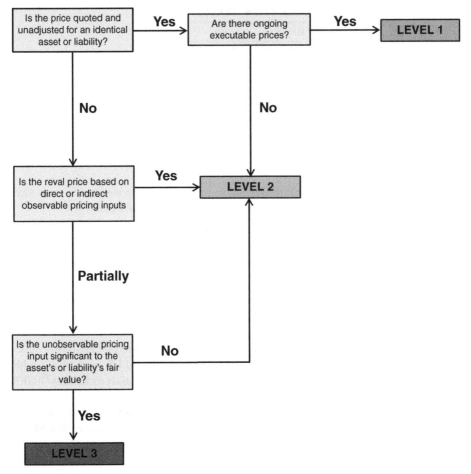

**FIGURE 21.4**   FVH decision tree
Note: Illustration based upon IFRS 13:72-90[18]

for most of the trade's life, this trade needs to be considered for level 3. As both these pricing inputs, but especially volatility, have a significant impact on the financial asset's fair value, it would be appropriate to allocate this asset into level 3.

As the financial impact from the unobservability of level 3 assets is significant, under IFRS (not required for U.S. GAAP) these items need to be considered for reserving. This is discussed in Chapter 16.

Figure 21.4 illustrates a simplified decision tree for determining which level of the hierarchy an asset or liability should reside in.

Once the classifications have been assigned, the bank can publish these classifications to the market. The published information will lay out the balances for the current financial year (Table 21.16 and 21.17), the previous financial year (Table 21.18) and the movements in each level (Table 21.19).

For level 3 assets and liabilities, the entity will need to provide further information regarding the unobservable pricing input. For example, a portfolio of mortgage-backed securities

**TABLE 21.16**   Note – Fair Value Hierarchy (current financial year)

| Note 30 Disclosures on fair values | 30 June 2015 | | | |
| --- | --- | --- | --- | --- |
| | **Fair Value** | | | |
| | **Level 1** | **Level 2** | **Level 3** | **Total** |
| Financial assets measured at fair value | $ million | $ million | $ million | $ million |
| Trading assets | 12,800 | 3,200 | 0 | 16,000 |
| Derivative assets | 17,180 | 21,475 | 4,295 | 42,950 |
| Available for sale investments | 3,200 | 11,200 | 1,600 | 16,000 |
| Bills | 4,050 | 450 | 0 | 4,500 |
| Total financial assets measured at fair value | 37,230 | 36,325 | 5,895 | 79,450 |
| | | | | |
| Liabilities | $ million | $ million | $ million | $ million |
| Trading liabilities | (23,200) | (5,800) | 0 | (29,000) |
| Derivative liabilities | (6,000) | (7,500) | (1,500) | (15,000) |
| Debt issuance | (500) | (4,500) | 0 | (5,000) |
| Total financial liabilities measured at fair value | (29,700) | (17,800) | (1,500) | (49,000) |

(MBS) unobservable bond prices which range from 5 to 95 with a weighted average price of 65. The P&L and other comprehensive income (OCI) on these items is also disclosed.

In Table 21.17, the bank has provided a breakdown of the asset classes making up the derivative assets balance for each of the three levels. As you can see in this table, the primary driver of the level 3 balance are interest rate derivatives.

## U.S. GAAP

Under this topic, the only significant differences under US GAAP relate to level 3 financial assets and liabilities. Under U.S. GAAP, unlike IAS 39/IFRS 9, a day 1 reserve is not required

**TABLE 21.17**   Note – Fair Value Hierarchy, breakdown of derivative asset balances

| Note 30 Disclosures on fair values | 30 June 2015 | | | |
| --- | --- | --- | --- | --- |
| | **Fair Value** | | | |
| | **Level 1** | **Level 2** | **Level 3** | **Total** |
| Derivative assets | 17,180 | 21,475 | 4,295 | 42,950 |
| – Foreign exchange contracts | 5,154 | 4,295 | 0 | 9,449 |
| – Credit derivatives | 0 | 1,074 | 430 | 1,504 |
| – Interest rate derivatives | 859 | 10,738 | 3,436 | 15,033 |
| – Equity derivatives | 9,449 | 4,295 | 0 | 13,744 |
| – Commodity derivatives | 1,718 | 1,074 | 430 | 3,222 |

**TABLE 21.18**   Note – Fair Value Hierarchy (prior financial year)

| Note 30 Disclosures on fair values | 30 June 2014 | | | |
|---|---|---|---|---|
| | Fair Value | | | |
| | Level 1 | Level 2 | Level 3 | Total |
| Financial assets measured at fair value | $ million | $ million | $ million | $ million |
| Trading assets | 12,384 | 3,096 | 0 | 15,480 |
| Derivative assets | 17,200 | 21,500 | 4,300 | 43,000 |
| Available for sale investments | 3,180 | 11,130 | 1,590 | 15,900 |
| Bills | 4,779 | 531 | 0 | 5,310 |
| Total financial assets measured at fair value | 37,543 | 36,257 | 5,890 | 79,690 |
| | | | | |
| Liabilities | $ million | $ million | $ million | $ million |
| Trading liabilities | (23,084) | (5,771) | 0 | (28,855) |
| Derivative liabilities | (6,190) | (7,738) | (1,547) | (15,475) |
| Debt issuance | (490) | (4,410) | 0 | (4,900) |
| Total financial liabilities measured at fair value | (29,764) | (17,919) | (1,547) | (49,230) |

for those financial assets or liabilities with significant unobservable pricing inputs. A bank only needs to disclose the P&L earned on those financial assets.

If you would like to learn more about financial reporting, there is a treasure trove of information within the earning updates and financial statements which banks publish to their website.

**TABLE 21.19**   Note – Changes in the level 3 balances

| Level 3 movement analysis | Derivative Assets | Available for Sale Investments | Derivative Liabilities | Total |
|---|---|---|---|---|
| | $ million | $ million | $ million | $ million |
| As at 1 July 2014 | 4,300 | 1,590 | (1,547) | 4,343 |
| Purchases | | | | 0 |
| Sales | (100) | | 68 | (32) |
| Gains/(losses) in the period: | | | | 0 |
| – Recognized in income statement | 87 | | (19) | 68 |
| – Recognized in statement of comprehensive income | | 10 | | 10 |
| Transfers in | 10 | | (9) | 1 |
| Transfers out | (2) | | 7 | 5 |
| As at 30 June 2015 | 4,295 | 1,600 | (1,500) | 4,395 |

Note: Banks will also typically provide information on the level 3 balances by financial instrument and describe the valuation technique and significant unobservable input for each instrument.

# NOTES

1. © IFRS Foundation. IAS 32 Financial Instruments: Presentation, paragraph 42.
2. © IFRS Foundation. IAS 32 Financial Instruments: Presentation, paragraph 45.
3. © IFRS Foundation. IAS 32 Financial Instruments: Presentation, paragraph 50.
4. © IFRS Foundation. IAS 32 Financial Instruments: Presentation, paragraphs 42–50.
5. Mengle, David, Derivatives, ©2010 International Swaps and Derivatives Association, ISDA Research Notes, Number 1 2010, "The Importance of Close-Out Netting," Page 2, http://www.isda.org/researchnotes/pdf/Netting-ISDAResearchNotes-1-2010.pdf.
6. Choudhry, Moorad. *An Introduction to Repo Markets, 3rd Edition* John Wiley & Sons Ltd, 2006.
7. © IFRS Foundation. IAS 32 Financial Instruments: Presentation, paragraph 46.
8. Financial Accounting Standards Board, FASB Interpretation No.39, "Offsetting of amounts related to certain contracts, an interpretation of APB Opinion No.10, and FASB Statement No.105." March 1992. http://www.fasb.org/cs/BlobServer?blobcol=urldata&blobtable=MungoBlobs&blobkey=id&blobwhere=1175820930240&blobheader=application%2Fpdf.
9. Financial Accounting Standards Board, Accounting Standards Codification®, Topic 210 Balance Sheet Subtopic 20, Section 45, paragraph 1.
10. Financial Accounting Standards Board, Accounting Standards Codification®, Topic 210-20-45-11.
11. © IFRS Foundation. IFRS 7 Financial Instruments: Disclosures, paragraph 1.
12. © IFRS Foundation. IFRS 13 Fair Value Measurement, paragraph 73.
13. © IFRS Foundation. IFRS 13 Fair Value Measurement, paragraphs 72–90.
14. © IFRS Foundation. IFRS 13 Fair Value Measurement, Appendix A.
15. KPMG. *Insights into IFRS, KPMG's practical guide to International Financial Reporting Standards, 13th Edition* UK: Sweet & Maxwell, 2016/17.
16. © IFRS Foundation. IFRS 13 Fair Value Measurement, paragraph 82.
17. © IFRS Foundation. IFRS 13 Fair Value Measurement, paragraph 82.
18. © IFRS Foundation. IFRS 13 Fair Value Measurement, paragraphs 72–90.

# Seven

# Supplementary Controls

In this final part of the book we will explore the role product control plays when the business launches a new product. We will also review the risk rogue trading poses to a bank, and examine in detail the most recent significant rogue trading event.

# CHAPTER 22

# New Product Proposals

**B**anks, like any firm that provides goods and services to clients, are constantly aware of the need to enhance their product offering in order to meet their clients' needs. Sharia bonds, Chinese Renminbi denominated products and CDOs are just some of the new products I have seen come to life over my career.

When the business wants to introduce a new product, there needs to be a period of due diligence undertaken by both the business and their stakeholders before the product can be traded or marketed. This period of due diligence is usually undertaken within the governance framework known as the New Product Proposal (NPP). It is important that this process has a strong level of engagement from the business's stakeholders as it will need the support of all stakeholders to get the products introduced in a cohesive and controlled manner.

Not every idea that the business conceives will make its way into the NPP, as banks run lean operations and don't want staff, capital and assets being allocated to initiatives which are not going to maximize shareholder value. Consequently, before the NPP is communicated to stakeholders, the proposal will need to meet indicative financial hurdles. These financial hurdles will focus on the key performance indicators for the bank, like profit, balance sheet and capital usage and their returns. It is common for these forecasts to be provided on an annual basis out to three to five years.

If the product is subsequently approved, it is important for the bank to hold the business accountable to those forecasts as new products are often implemented on the promise of glowing returns, only for the actual returns to be mediocre. Such examples do not foster a culture of strategic investing.

## STARTING LINE

When an NPP is launched, it is usually done so by the chief operating officer (COO). However, in some cases a separate team is established purely for launching, coordinating and implementing NPPs. The benefit of having a separate team manage the NPP is that it ensures the bank launches NPPs with the same level of consistency across all businesses. The NPP team can also have leads in each of the bank's functions; for example, finance, operations, risk, etc., who take responsibility for their department during the NPP process. These leads will then interact with the actual people who are reviewing the NPP. For example, the finance lead will interact with the managers for product control, financial control and regulatory reporting.

The NPP should be documented in such a way that the stakeholder's questions have already been answered. Often, though, this will not be the case and so it is up to the stakeholders to draw out more information from the business representatives.

So that the process does not drag on, when the NPP is launched, a deadline for sign-off will be set. This will vary depending upon the complexity of the product and the needs of the business.

## THE REVIEW

When reviewing the NPP, product control should have use of a pre-approval checklist to help them identify those key aspects that need to be reviewed. This checklist should cover all of the key controls that product control maintain. In Table 22.1 is an example of such a checklist.

During the review, it is quite common for the new product to be tested in the systems it will use once approved. The testing is usually carried out by each of the relevant stakeholders in a test system environment, which is often a direct copy of the production environment.

A test environment is used, rather than a production environment, so that the test trades do not interfere with the running of the business. For example, if a test trade was booked in production, the trader's risk reports could become inaccurate, operations may accidentally try to confirm the deal with the counterparty, product control may report the P&L, market risk may flag the trade as a VaR limit breach and financial and regulatory reporting may report erroneous information to shareholders and regulatory bodies.

Product control's testing is performed by the line product control team with the assistance of the finance change team. Whilst product control are the subject matter experts of their business, the finance change team understand how to set up a test up environment, administer testing cycles and perform testing much better than product control. This is a case of two teams having complementary skills, working together to support the business.

Table 22.2 is an example of an NPP that has just been launched by Sparta Bank:

- The NPP is offering clients a product which gives them exposure to Sparta Bank's FX strategy for EUR/USD and GBP/USD baskets.
- The clients will invest the funds for a period of three years.
- Investors may, if they wish, sell their notes back to Sparta Bank before the three-year term. Sparta Bank will purchase the notes at the prevailing market prices less a discount for early redemption.
- In return for their purchase of the note, the investors will receive a fixed coupon equal to the three-year U.S. LIBOR rate less 1.5 basis points, which will be paid annually.
- In addition to the fixed rate coupon, investors will receive back their original investment plus or minus the performance of the fund. For example, an investor purchases the note at a price of $100 and if the note has earned 20% over the 3 years, the investor receives $120 back.
- Investors will be notified quarterly as to the performance of the note.
- The note will be issued on an unsecured basis.

**TABLE 22.1** NPP product control pre-approval checklist

| Category | Systems | P&L New trade review, risk based P&L, P&L attribution, P&L sign-off | Balance Sheet | Financial Reporting | Valuation Control (Valuations and IPV) | Financial Accounting | Tax | Resources |
|---|---|---|---|---|---|---|---|---|
| **Systems** | | | | | | | | |
| In which systems will these products be booked | X | | | | | | | |
| In which books will the desk book these products | X | | | | | | | |
| What static set up is required in the finance layer | X | X | X | X | X | X | | |
| What system testing is required | X | X | X | X | X | X | | |
| **Financial Accounting (incl. Valuations, IPV & Valuation Adjustments)** | | | | | | | | |
| How do we account for this product? | | | | X | | X | | |
| Does the Accounting Rules Engine (ARE) need updating for this product? | X | | | | | X | | |
| How will the desk value this product? | | | | | X | | | |
| Are there any un-modelled risks? | | | | | X | | | |
| Can the pricing inputs be independently verified (IPV)? | | | | | X | | | |
| Are valuation adjustments required, including Day One, Bid–Offer, Model, XVA? | | | | | X | | | |
| What fair value hierarchy level will this product fall into? | | | | | X | | | |

(continued)

**TABLE 22.1** (*Continued*)

| Category | Systems | P&L New trade review, risk based P&L, P&L attribution, P&L sign-off | Balance Sheet | Financial Reporting | Valuation Control (Valuations and IPV) | Financial Accounting | Tax | Resources |
|---|---|---|---|---|---|---|---|---|
| **P&L Controls** | | | | | | | | |
| Can our new trade review incorporate this product? | | X | | | | | | |
| Can our MTM P&L review, including risk based P&L, incorporate this product? | | X | | | | | | |
| Who from the desk will be reviewing the P&L & signing it off? | | X | | | | | | |
| **Balance Sheet controls** | | | | | | | | |
| How will we substantiate the balance sheet? | | | X | | | | | |
| Will the new product be incorporated into the existing cash break controls? | X | | X | | | | | |
| **Cross-Border controls** | | | | | | | | |
| Is a Tax Transfer Pricing Agreement required? | | | | | | | X | |
| **Resourcing** | | | | | | | | |
| How much headcount is required to control this product in 1, 2, 3 years? | | | | | | | | X |

**TABLE 22.2** NPP proposed by Sparta Bank

| What is the Product | FX Note – Return is linked to the performance of Sparta Bank's FX Strategy |
| --- | --- |
| What tenors will be traded? | Up to 3 years |
| What volumes will be generated? | Expected volumes for Year 1 $100m, Year 2 $150m, Year 3 $250m |
| How will revenue be generated? | Investors are charged a management fee of 1.5% per annum |
| How much P&L will it generate? | Expected P&L in Year 1 $1.5m, Year 2 $2.25m, Year 3 $3.75m |
| How much balance sheet will it use? | Expected balance sheet usage in Year 1 $100m, Year 2 $150m, Year 3 $250m |
| What are the performance ratios such as return on equity (ROE) & return on assets (ROA) & do these returns exceed relevant thresholds? | Expected ROA 1.50%, ROE 18.75% |
| Which sales & trading staff will be risk managing this product? | London Sales & London FX & STIR Trading Desks |
| Which markets will the product be traded in? | Europe (including the UK) |
| Which legal entities will be used to book these trades? | Sparta Bank London Ltd |
| Who will be purchasing it? | Investors who want exposure to Sparta Bank's FX strategy |
| What is the F2B workflow? | See flow chart |

We can simulate a product control review by working through the pre-established checklist:

1. Financial Accounting (including Valuations & Reserves)
   a) How do we account for this product?

   The product will be accounted for under the relevant UK and IFRS GAAP. Under IAS 39, the bank will bifurcate (separate) the value of the liability (note) into two components, the fixed yield host contract and the embedded derivative (performance of the strategy). The host contract will be accounted for on an amortized cost basis and the embedded derivative will be accounted for as fair value through P&L.

   b) Does the ARE need to be updated for this product?

   No, the ARE will account for the note in the two components described above. Deposits and FX derivatives are already accounted for through the ARE.

   c) Will all of the economic features be included in the booking (unmodelled risks)?

   Yes, there are no unmodelled economic features.

   d) How will the desk value this product?

   The position is valued in two distinct parts. The fixed coupon is valued at amortized cost using the three-year LIBOR rate at the date of the note issuance. The performance of the fund is valued using the fair value of any open FX positions. These FX positions will be revalued using the market's mid spot FX rate and forward points.

e) Can we IPV these curves and surfaces?

Yes, the spot FX and forward points are sourced independently daily from the relevant FX pages on Reuters.

f) Do we need to take any VAs on this product?

- Day 1 – as the market prices and rates used to revalue the trades are observable, there is no need to take a reserve.
- Bid–Offer – as the prices/points used to revalue the FX trades are at mid-level, a bid offer reserve will need to be applied on a monthly basis.
- Model – no model adjustments are necessary.
- XVA – CVA or DVA will be required on open derivative trades and the unsecured deposit liability. FVA may be required.

g) What fair value hierarchy level will this product fall into?

The FX trades will generally be classed as level two as these are individual contracts between specific parties and there is unlikely to be an active market for an identical instrument in the market.

As the host contract (deposit) is accounted for on an amortized cost basis, the fair value hierarchy is not applicable.

2. P&L Controls

a) Can our new trade review incorporate this product?

Yes, FX derivatives & deposits are already captured by this control.

b) Can our MTM review incorporate this product?

Yes, FX trades and foreign currency cash are already captured by this control.

c) Who from the desk will be reviewing the P&L & signing it off?

The London FX desk head, Usman Khawaja.

3. Balance Sheet Controls

How will we substantiate the balance sheet? The balance sheet will be substantiated using:

- The FX RMS for the MTM value of the spot FX, forward or swap trades.
- The money market RMS for the amortized cost value of the deposit (host contract).
- The cash subledger for any foreign currency cash.

Will the new product be incorporated into the existing cash break controls?

- Yes, any cash breaks arising from the new product will be captured in the existing control framework.

4. Cross-Border controls

Will a Tax Transfer Pricing Agreement be required?

No. The sales team and traders are all based in London. Additionally, the trades, including the note issuance, are all booked in Sparta Bank London Ltd. Consequently, there is no need for a tax transfer pricing agreement.

5. Systems

a) In which systems will these products be booked?

See f2b flow chart.

b) In which books will the desk book these products?

Two new books will be set up to house the deposit (host contract) and FX trades.

c) What static set-up is required in the finance layer?

A new profit centre is required.

d) What system testing is required?

**TABLE 22.3**   Checks made by other departments

| Stakeholder | Checks |
|---|---|
| Senior Management | Reputational risk for the firm. |
| Legal | Legal documentation for note issuance. |
| Tax | Tax transfer pricing agreements. |
| Operations and Middle Office | Ensure that the product can be confirmed and settled and that client valuations can be provided as necessary. This includes having nostros and securities clearing facilities in place and controls including nostro, AVE & securities inventory reconciliations. |
| Risk – Market & Credit | Risk can be reliably measured, monitored and reported. Risk limits are in place and appropriate given the nature of the product. |
| Compliance & Operational Risk | Is the product creating a heightened level of risk (reputational or operational) for the bank? |

As deposits and FX derivatives are already accounted for in the bank's systems, no testing is required.

**6.** Resourcing

How much headcount is required to control this product in one, two, or three years?

Product control should be able to absorb this product in the existing headcount as we estimate the work to be only 1% of a headcount per annum for the next three years.

In addition to product control's review, the other stakeholders will also review the NPP. Let's look at some of the checks that the other main stakeholders will perform in Table 22.3.

## THE SIGN-OFF

Once product control is satisfied that the NPP meets their requirements, sign-off can be provided and usually occurs through the global head of the business line, or by an appropriate delegate.

Another important item to note is that during the testing phase, if all of the systems were unable to be tested, once the product is approved it can be helpful to request a low value test trade to be entered into production. This provides product control with an opportunity to review the booking and confirm the system flows and controls are operating successfully. Once satisfied, product control can give the green light to the business to trade on the scale approved by the stakeholders.

# CHAPTER 23

# Rogue Trading

R ogue trading occurs when a trader engages in unauthorized trading, placing bets on the market in excess of their risk limits or trader mandate. To avoid detection, these bets are often hidden by one or a number of concealment mechanisms.

If we hear about rogue trading in the press it usually means that the losses are so significant that they cannot be swept under the carpet by the affected bank. Given the size of the losses, these events make for fascinating case studies. As most rogue traders incur their losses on the balance sheet of their bank, the rogue trading will eventually come to light but how quickly depends upon the effectiveness of the internal control framework.

In this chapter, we will explore rogue trading, the damage it causes and will look at a rogue trading incident in detail. We will also look at another significant control failure that, although was not rogue trading, created more than a storm in a teacup for one CEO.

## THE FOREFATHERS OF ROGUE TRADING

There have been some high profile and significant rogue trading cases over the past few decades, where traders have risked it all to cover up losses, earn larger profits and preserve or maintain their reputation. Figure 23.1 lists these rogue trading events.

- **Nick Leeson:** In 1995 Nick Leeson managed to wipe out all the capital of Barings Bank and force its collapse whilst trying to recoup losses from operational errors. Leeson lost £827 million[1] of Barings' money through exploiting holes in a very poor control culture.

    The most striking control failure was that Leeson was permitted to be the head of both front office and back office for Barings Futures Singapore. His unauthorized trading was discovered in 1995 and he was sentenced to six and a half years in a Singaporean prison.[2]
- **Toshihide Iguchi:** In 1995 a Japanese bond trader in New York, Toshihide Iguchi, sent a 30-page letter to Daiwa's CEO explaining that he had been concealing trading losses over the past 12 years which had resulted in a final loss of $1.1 billion. Without this letter Daiwa would not have known that this unauthorized trading even existed.[3]

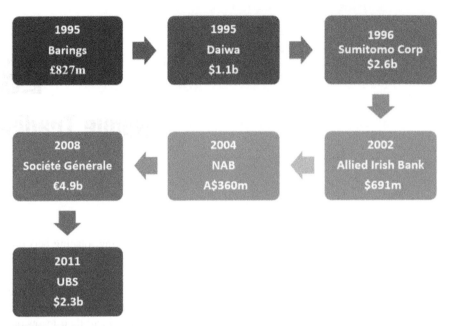

**FIGURE 23.1**   Rogue trading events

Unfortunately for Daiwa, they had delayed informing the U.S. authorities of the rogue trading losses, which resulted in them being kicked out of the U.S.[4] This was the first significant rogue trading event to have occurred on U.S. soil. Iguchi was sentenced to four years in prison and fined $2.6 million.[5] (Both Leeson and Iguchi have published books on their rogue trading, which I recommend you read.)

- **Yasuo Hamanaka:** In 1996 a copper trader, Yasuo Hamanaka or "Mr Five Percent" as he was known in the market, confessed to $2.6 billion of losses which were built up over a decade whilst he inflated the price of copper. Hamanaka was sentenced to eight years in prison.[6]
- **John Rusnak:** In 2002 John Rusnak, an FX Trader for a subsidiary of Allied Irish Bank, bet heavily on the yen only to lose $691 million. At one stage, Rusnak exceeded his risk limits by almost $7.5 billion in his quest for profits. He was sentenced to seven and a half years in prison.[7]
- **FX Options traders, NAB:** In 2004 the FX options traders (that's right, four traders not just one!) lost A$360 million for the National Australia bank.[8] The traders benefitted from weak controls over internal trades, end of day timings and IPV on the volatility surface. They each served varying lengths of incarceration.
- **Jérôme Kerviel:** In 2008 Jérôme Kerviel lost €4.9 billion[9] which wiped out most of Société Générale's 2007 full-year profit and caused the bank to launch a €5.5 billion rights issue.[10]

Although only a junior trader on the Delta One Desk, Kerviel took advantage of poor controls and a lack of supervision to bet heavily on the DAX, EUROSTOXX and FTSE.[11] At one stage in December 2007 Kerviel actually made a profit in excess of €1 billion,[12] but given the size of the profit it would have been inconceivable to report such a sum. Even so, I know what his bosses would have preferred.

Kerviel was sentenced to five years in prison with two years being suspended[13] and was initially ordered to pay his former employer €4.9 billion in damages, which was later reduced to €1 million.[14]

- **Kweku Adoboli:** And in 2011 Kweku Adoboli chalked up $2.3 billion in losses for UBS,[15] which we will look at in more detail later on in this chapter.

## THE FALLOUT FROM ROGUE TRADING – THE BANK

When rogue trading is discovered, all the attention in the media is placed on the rogue trader(s), but it is important to be cognizant of the impact that rogue trading has on the bank and its staff. Not only does the bank have to report the trading losses generated by the rogue trader, they also have a number of other challenges to contend with, which are listed in Figure 23.2.

### Regulators

When a rogue trading incident has occurred, the bank needs to inform the regulator, who will then come in and penalize the bank in a number of ways.

Firstly, they will make the bank pay for an external company to identify the control failures that allowed the rogue trading to occur or prevented it from being detected sooner. This external company is usually one of the big accounting firms who are not the bank's auditor. This raises the costs for the bank which will reduce profits in the short term.

Secondly, the bank will need to put in place a plan to remediate any significant control failings. The timeline for remediation will need to be agreed with the regulator, which may mean the bank needs to hire external consultants or more staff to meet the agreed deadlines. This also raises the costs of the bank which will reduce profits in the short term.

Thirdly, the regulator will raise the required capital base that the bank needs to maintain. This is because the bank has just become riskier and attracted a higher operational risk charge. This extra capital will need to be funded and the cost of this will also reduce the bank's profits.

For example, following the NAB (National Australia Bank) FX option losses, NAB was required to raise its target capital base. From 2003 to 2004 the bank raised their capital base from 9.70%[16] up to 10.60%[17] of risk-weighted assets. On risk-weighted assets of A$287

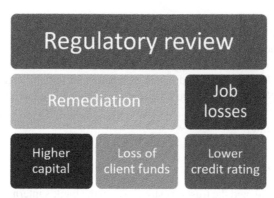

**FIGURE 23.2**  Repercussions of rogue trading

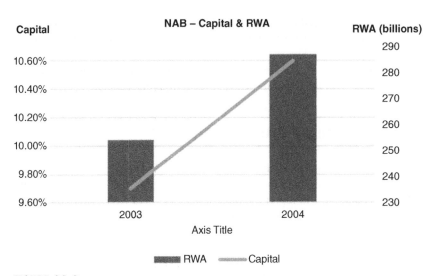

**FIGURE 23.3**    NAB capital increase post rogue trading
Note: The graph makes use of capital and RWA data from: the National, Concise Annual
Report 2004, page 61, and National, Concise Annual Report 2003, page 43.

billion, that extra 90 basis points translates into an additional $2.6 billion in capital to be held
and funded, which the bank did through dividend reinvestment plans, bonus share plans and
debt issuance.[18]

As the cost of capital for NAB was 11% in 2004,[19] this capital increase equates to a capital
charge of $286 million. This increase in capital is illustrated in Figure 23.3.

Fourthly, the regulator may impose restrictions on acquisitions and new products the bank
wants to introduce which can reduce revenue streams. For example, UBS's Swiss regulator
FINMA banned new acquisitions by the investment bank and needed to approve any new
products which materially increased the bank's operational complexity.[20] Finally, the bank
may have to pay a fine to the regulator. In the case of UBS, the FSA fined them £29.7 million
for systems and control failings.[21]

## Job Losses

People will get fired or be asked to resign when a rogue trading incident occurs. The chairman,
CEO, CFO, business heads, desk supervisors and control functions are all "fair game" when a
rogue trading incident occurs.

For example, at UBS the CEO and heads of equities all left the organization following
the rogue trading. At NAB, the CEO and chairman were both forced to resign in the shake up
after the trading losses were announced. At Daiwa, the U.S. authorities made the entire Daiwa
operation leave the country.

## Reputational Losses

The reputation of the bank and the trust investors have in the bank's internal control framework
are damaged through rogue trading. This diminution of trust can result in a lower share price

and the withdrawal of client funds. When client funds are withdrawn, the liquidity profile of the bank is weakened and the asset base from which to generate revenue has just gotten smaller. When the UBS rogue trading incident was announced, UBS's share price fell by 10%.

## Credit Ratings

When a bank loses money from a rogue trading event they become a riskier investment. This riskiness arises from uncertainty regarding what impact the incident will have on future earnings and the lack of assurance investors have in the integrity of the bank's internal control framework. Following the NAB FX options rogue trading incident, S&P downgraded the company's long-term credit rating from AA to AA−.[22]

## THE FALLOUT FROM ROGUE TRADING − THE INDUSTRY

Not only does rogue trading affect the bank involved, it also has an impact on the overall industry, as the bank's peers review their control framework to assess whether the same thing could happen at their bank.

When Jérôme Kerviel's rogue trading came to light in 2008, the Committee of European Banking Supervisors (CEBS), which is now replaced by the EBA, "conducted a stock take with its member authorities on how this event affected other banks, their operational risk practices, governance and internal control environment, and the internal models used for calculating capital requirements for operational risk."[23]

In the executive summary, the report makes an important statement:

> *No operational risk framework or internal control system can be considered completely immune from events like that which occurred at SocGen. However, strong governance, operational risk management and control culture across all businesses, and especially those potentially able to generate high profits, but also big losses, can significantly mitigate such risks.*

What this statement points out is that risks can be mitigated but not removed all together and that all banks are vulnerable to an attack like that which Jérôme Kerviel unleashed on Société Générale. Sometimes though, even when a peer's significant failures provides a lesson in control failures, some banks may become lazy and leave themselves open to similar attacks.

In 2008, post the Société Générale rogue trading incident, UBS initiated its own operational risk review to assess the risk of a rogue trading event. The review identified a number of control weaknesses which are illustrated in Figure 23.4.

Unfortunately for UBS, one of their traders exploited these very control weaknesses to lose $2.3 billion for the bank some three years later.

## GOING ROGUE

When rogue trading is being committed, there will be indications that this criminal activity is transpiring. Yes, these indications can be missed due to real-world imperfections like system

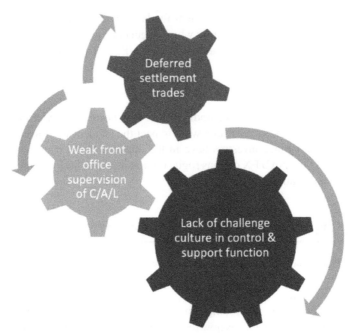

**FIGURE 23.4** Control weakness at UBS not remediated post rogue trading review in 2008
Source: Based on: FINMA. "UBS trading losses in London: FINMA finds major control failures." Pages 11–12. 26th November 2012, http://www.finma.ch/e/aktuell/Pages/mm-ubs-london-20121126.aspx.
Note: C/A/L denotes trades which are cancelled (C), late (L) or amended (A).

failures, a lack of resources, a lack of collaboration, poor management information, etc., but the signs are there, you just need to pay attention to them.

## Why Does a Trader Go Rogue?

The two most common reasons for a trader to go rogue are related to pride and money. The trader wants to maintain or enhance their reputation and they also want to maintain their current salary and bonus or achieve higher levels of compensation. These two factors draw the noose around the trader's neck and lead them into unauthorized activities which will eventually cause significant damage to them, their firm and their industry.

In the case of Nick Leeson, his rogue trading was instigated to cover up the losses from an operational error made by one of his staff. As he was the boss of the Singapore operation, he wanted to be seen as capable of running a successful business.

## How Does a Trader Go Rogue?

A trader goes rogue by deliberately carrying positions which exceed their risk limits or trading mandates. Although these traders don't intend on causing harm to their bank, by exceeding their trading mandate they are exposing the bank to unlimited financial and reputational losses.

In the biggest rogue trading losses at Société Générale and UBS, the traders placed massive bets on the future direction of various stocks and stock market indices such as EUROSTOXX, DAX and S&P 500. As these bets incur losses, the trader keeps on increasing the size of their bets (doubling down) to win back their losses. This will go on and on until the trader is caught or confesses.

## How Does a Rogue Trader Conceal Their Crime?

If acting without an accomplice in a support or control function, there are only two methods a trader can employ to conceal the risk and P&L emanating from their unauthorized trading.

1. **Mismarking:** Firstly, to manipulate the P&L the trader can mismark their trading portfolio to inflate or deflate its value.
2. **Trade bookings:** Secondly, to manipulate the P&L and risk from the unauthorized trading, the rogue trader can manipulate their trade bookings by either failing to book real trades on time or by booking fictitious trades and cancelling and amending these fictitious trades as and when required.

As there will be controls built around both valuations and trade bookings, there needs to be a breakdown in the bank's controls to execute and perpetuate the fraud.

We will now look in detail at the most recent significant rogue trading scandal, Kweku Adoboli at UBS in 2011. Through reviewing this case it is hoped that the control failures can be converted into lessons for the banking industry which can help prevent these same failings from leading to another significant rogue trading incident.

## UBS ROGUE TRADING INCIDENT, 2011

On 15 September, 2011, UBS admitted that one of their traders had caught them with their pants down. After six years with the bank, Kweku Adoboli had managed to circumvent controls to build up enormous risk exposures that culminated in a loss of $2.3 billion.

### Background

Adoboli joined UBS's operations department as a summer intern in 2002 but he didn't remain in the back office for long. In 2005 he transferred to the front office to become an equities trader where he remained until his arrest in September 2011. During that time, he was promoted twice, earning a corporate title of director and large levels of compensation, including a bonus of £250,000 in 2010.[24]

In his final position with the bank, Adoboli was a senior trader on the exchange-traded fund (ETF) desk in London, which was located within the equities division of UBS (Figure 23.5). The ETF desk engaged in both proprietary and client trading, dealing in cash equities, depositary receipts, ETFs and investment trusts. They were also permitted to use exchange-traded options, futures and spot FX to hedge their portfolio.[25] It was on this desk that Adoboli managed to blow $2.3 billion for UBS and lead to the resignations of the bank's CEO and co-heads of equities.

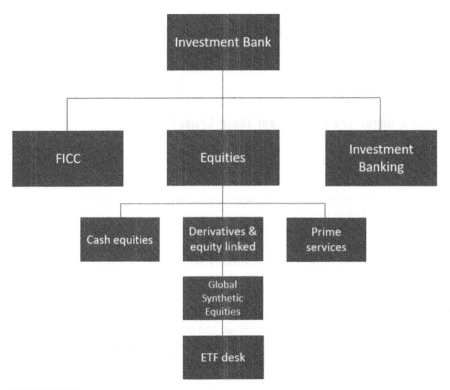

**FIGURE 23.5**   UBS Organizational structure
Source: Structure based upon information sourced from FINMA's summary report and UBS 2011 Annual Report.

## The Trading Activities Which Caused the Losses

Of the $2.3 billion Adoboli lost in trading, $2.1 billion of the losses emanated from large bets on futures positions in Eurostoxx 50 and S&P 500.[26] EURO STOXX 50 and S&P 500 are both share market indices, the former tracking the value of the top 50 stocks across 12 nations in the eurozone and the later tracking the top 500 stocks in the U.S.

Adoboli was positioned long in these indices, with his exposure at one stage reaching $12.1 billion on 8 August 2011, before being closed out on 11 August 2011.[27] (A long position profits from price rises.) Unfortunately for him and UBS, both these indices experienced large devaluations from late June through to early August 2011, losing approximately 20% of their value.

Following the close out of the long position on 11 August, Adoboli then held a short position in the S&P 500 and DAX futures which peaked at $8.5 billion on 15 September when it was closed out by UBS.[28] This final month of Adoboli's trading appear to have cost UBS another $200 million – an extraordinary feat.

Figure 23.6 illustrates the movement in the Euro Stoxx 50 and S&P 500 indices over the period that the rogue trader is alleged to have had a significant exposure.

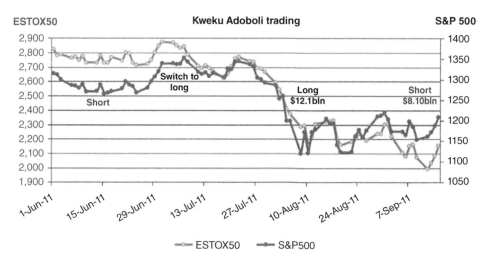

**FIGURE 23.6** EURO STOXX 50 and S&P 500 price history
Sources: FINMA. "Summary Report: FINMA Investigation into the Events Surrounding Trading
Losses of USD 2.3 billion Incurred by the Investment Banking Division of UBS AG in London," 21
November 2012, and Adoboli's email to product control.

## Concealing the Crime and Weak Controls

Whilst appearing on P&L and risk reports to remain within the desk's risk limits, Adoboli was
actually running risk exposures that were grossly in excess of the desk's net delta limits.[29] To
be able to do this Adoboli had to make use of concealment mechanisms to hide his excesses.

Adoboli fooled his colleagues through several concealment mechanisms, which he
employed from as early as 2008 right up to 2011. Although he used these mechanisms from
2008, the effect from these activities was only to conceal approximately $40 million in losses
and $296 million in risk exposures.[30]

FINMA identified the following primary methods used by Adoboli to conceal his unauthorized trading, which are also illustrated in Figure 23.7.

- One-sided internal futures trades.
- Late booking of genuine external futures trades into the front office risk system.
- Fictitious ETF trades with deferred settlement dates.
- Zero-notional bullet cash trades.[31]

Although not considered a primary method of concealment by FINMA, Adoboli also
influenced P&L adjustments being applied to his books, which masked the losses from his
unauthorized trading.[32]

A strong internal control framework could have detected and indeed prevented the trader
from making use of these concealment mechanisms. The problem for UBS was that their internal control framework was not strong and it enabled the rogue trading to carry on for longer
than it should have.

The FINMA report into the rogue trading (which is available for free from the FINMA
website) found "widespread deficiencies across the investment bank's control environment.

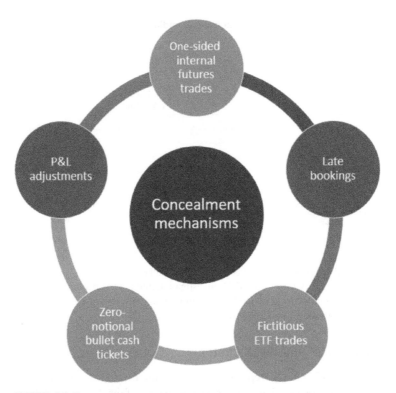

**FIGURE 23.7** Concealment mechanisms used by the rogue trader
Source: FINMA. "Summary Report: FINMA Investigation into the Events
Surrounding Trading Losses of USD 2.3 billion Incurred by the Investment
Banking Division of UBS AG in London," 21 November 2012.

Despite efforts to improve the control framework, significant and sustained control deficiencies remained. This was not recognized or addressed by senior management."[33]

We will now look at each of these concealment mechanisms in more detail.

**One-Sided Internal Futures Trades**   A one-sided internal futures trade is a trade executed between two parties in the same legal entity where only one side of the trade is booked and reported.

For example, in Table 23.1 is an internal trade where the ETF1 book faces an internal counterparty. As only the ETF1 side of the trade is booked and flows into the finance and risk layers, the bank erroneously reports a net $1.5 million profit. In the NAB FX options rogue trading case, the traders also made use of one-sided internal trades to conceal their trading losses.[34]

**Purpose**   These trades were designed to misreport the P&L and risk exposures that were being generated by the unauthorized trading.

**Control weakness**
1. **No confirmations:** Overall these trades were subject to less stringent controls. Usually when a trade is executed it is confirmed with the counterparty, but with these internal

**TABLE 23.1** Cancel and rebook of deferred settlement trades

| Side 1 | | Side 2 | |
| --- | --- | --- | --- |
| Trade date | 1st August 2011 | Trade date | |
| Book | ETF1 | Book | |
| Counterparty | Internal | Counterparty | |
| Instrument | S&P 500 futures | Instrument | |
| Expiry | Sep-11 | Expiry | |
| Buy/Sell | Sell | Buy/Sell | |
| Contracts | 1,000 | Contracts | |
| Price | 1,400 | Price | |
| P&L | $1,500,000 | P&L | |

trades, the other side of the trade was not checked to see if it existed and matched Adoboli's booking.[35]

2. **SCP alerts:** UBS had a supervisory control portal (SCP) for front office supervisors, which generated alerts regarding C/A/L trades on their desk. Front office supervisors would have to investigate and sign off on the alerts.[36] This process is illustrated in Figure 23.8.

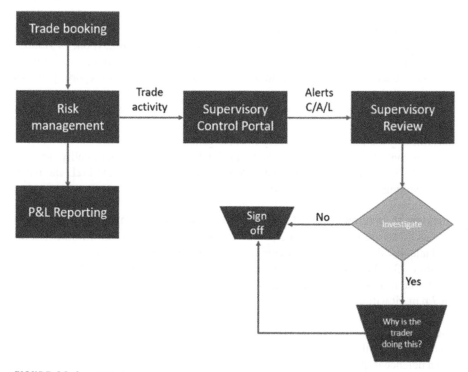

**FIGURE 23.8** SCP alerts

However, futures did not feed the SCP until 26 August 2011, and when the feed was switched on, the ETF Traders, including Adoboli, received these alerts (and signed off) rather than their ETF supervisor.[37] The ETF supervisor was therefore blind to any issues contained within these alerts, deeming the control ineffective.

3. **New and amended trades review:** Product control were not provided with the necessary tools to perform reviews of the P&L at trade level. Consequently, they couldn't see the P&L impact from these fictitious trades.[38]

**Effective Controls**    Several controls, if in place, could have identified these trades.

1. **Line 1 controls:** The risk management system (RMS) could have been built to only permit internal trades if a valid internal counterparty is selected on the trade ticket. The RMS will then automatically generate the necessary risk, P&L and accounting entries for both trading books. The benefit of this approach is that the control is built into the line 1 system architecture.

   For this to be effective, there cannot be trading books which do not have feeds into the downstream risk, finance and settlement systems. Some banks refer to these as dormant books and review their population periodically.

2. **Middle office/operations checks:** Middle office or operations can run end of day reconciliations to ensure every internal trade has an equal and opposite booking in the same legal entity.

   Any exceptions should be identified and then escalated as per the agreed escalation matrix. This would have identified the one-sided bookings on the day they first started to occur.

3. **New and amended trades review:** Product control's new trade review validates the P&L on those trades which have an exceptional or unusual day one P&L. If one of Adoboli's internal futures trades exceeded the review thresholds, product control's investigations could have uncovered the fictitious trade and the fact that no one was reporting the other side of the P&L.

4. **Intra-entity P&L and balance sheet:** The bank will have intra-entity P&L and balance sheet controls in place to capture internal booking or valuation errors. This control is performed by the finance team as they own the general ledger (GL).

   This control checks that the internal trade bookings, known as intra-entity, net to zero in the GL. This check would also have identified an imbalance in the P&L and balance sheet resulting from the internal trades.

### Late Booking of Genuine External Futures Trades into the Front Office Risk System

Late booked trades are those which are booked beyond the end of day cut-off time. If a trade is booked late, it will miss the downstream feeds for risk and P&L reporting.

In Figure 23.9 the trader executes a trade in the market at 2 p.m. on 25 July but doesn't enter it into the bank's systems until 8 p.m. As the trade misses the end of day cut, which is taken at 7 p.m., it will not flow into the risk and P&L reporting until the following day.

**Purpose**    Trades were entered late to misreport the P&L and risk exposures that were being generated by the unauthorized trading.[39] By entering the trades late, he is also providing himself with a defence if queried about the missing trades.

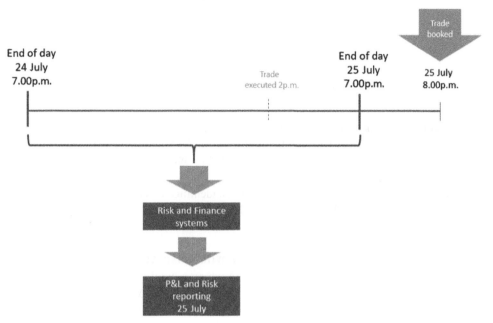

**FIGURE 23.9** Late trades

For example, if queried by operations about trade breaks on the reconciliation between the RMS and futures clearing agent, the trader can assert that he has remediated that break by booking the trade (albeit late), hence, there is no longer a reconciliation exception. This method of concealment bought the trader more time.

**Control Weakness**

**1. SCP Alerts:** As per the first concealment mechanisms, the SCP was not operating effectively. The SCP also let the supervisors down as it provided limited trend analysis. Any detailed trend analysis would need to be performed manually which operations and the front office had no bandwidth for.[40]

**2. Escalation of persistent booking errors:** Support staff did not escalate persistent trade booking issues. Operations were aware of persistent late and mis-booked trades, trades with huge notional values, and frequent and material reconciliation breaks, but these were not identified as significant risk issues and were not appropriately escalated to senior operations management.[41]

**Effective Controls**   Several controls, if in place, could have captured these late bookings:

▪ **SCP alerts:** If the SCP had been operating effectively, the desk supervisor would have been aware that Adoboli was repeatedly booking his futures trades late, which could have identified the unauthorized trading much sooner.

**FIGURE 23.10** Deferred settlements

▪ **Escalation of persistent booking errors:** For exchange-traded bookings, operations will maintain a reconciliation between the trades in the RMS and those with the clearer. A futures clearer settles cash with the exchange on the bank's behalf.

Any differences between the data sets need to be identified and resolved as soon as possible. Persistent late booked trades from a desk and trader, which can be identified through trend analysis, must be escalated within operations and the business.

### Fictitious Exchange-Traded Fund (ETF) Trades with Deferred Settlement Dates  An ETF is a security which tracks the performance of one or a number of stocks or indices. As most securities settle within T+3 business days (where a buyer pays the seller and receives the securities), trades with extended settlement periods pose a greater risk for a bank as it introduces additional operational and credit risk.

Adoboli booked ETF trades into the RMS which were not real and instead of settling within three business days, would settle much later than that, say T+20 business days.

Some of these trades were booked using off-market prices, or initially booked at market but then amended to an off-market price.[42] And it was these trades which ultimately led to his activities being discovered.

**Purpose**  These trades were designed to misreport the P&L and risk exposures being generated by the unauthorized trading.[43] Figure 23.10 is an example of a timeline for an ETF trade.

On T+0 the trade is booked and can be used to misreport P&L and risk up until T+19, one day prior to settlement.

To avoid the risk of operations trying to confirm the trade, the trader cancels the trade five days before settlement date, on T+15. Any resulting P&L and risk arising from this cancellation would then need to be embedded into a new fictitious trade.

**Control Weakness**  There were two control weaknesses noted by FINMA:

1. **Deferred settlement report:** Operations had a report which identified trades with extended settlement dates. The purpose of the report was to let operations know that they needed to confirm the trade with the counterparty.

   This report wasn't working for extended periods, sometimes for as long 10 months. Unfortunately for UBS, these outage periods coincided with the time when significant losses were being masked by such trades.[44]
2. **New and amended trades review:** Product control were not provided with the necessary tools to perform reviews of the P&L at trade level.[45] Consequently, they could not view the individual P&L amounts on new, amended and cancelled trades.

**TABLE 23.2**  Cancel and rebook of deferred settlement trades

| Trade | 1 | 2 | 3 |
|---|---|---|---|
| Trade date | 10-Jul | 27-Jul | 06-Aug |
| Settlement date | 30-Jul | 11-Aug | 23-Aug |
| Actual life to date trading losses | $(499.9)m | $(499.9)m | $(499.9)m |
| Cancelled on | 27-Jul | 06-Aug | |
| New trade P&L | +$500m | +$500m | +$500m |
| Cancel P&L impact | – | $(500)m | $(500)m |
| Net daily P&L | +$100,000 | – | – |

In Table 23.2 you can see that if a trader is inflating his P&L by $500 million in a fictitious trade, when he cancels that trade the P&L impact from doing so (assuming it is still worth $500 million) will be a loss of $500 million.

Now, because he replaces that cancelled trade with a new fictitious trade, a new trade P&L will generate a profit of $500 million, nullifying the impact from the cancelled trade. If product control could see the P&L individually from the cancelled trade and the new trade, it would have been obvious the trader was up to no good.

3. **Off-market trades:** There were no reviews of off market trades.[46] An off-market trade is one where the trade price is different to the market price. These trades should automatically get considered as a suspicious trade.

4. **SCP alerts:** The SCP alerts were not used effectively by the bank. Even though these trades fed the SCP, either the correct supervisor wasn't being applied or the current supervisor didn't know what his responsibilities were regarding the alerts. For example, during August, some deferred settlement ETF trades generated P&L in excess of $500 million but weren't investigated by the supervisor.[47]

The opportunity to identify these fictitious trades existed, but weak controls prevented this from occurring.

**Effective Controls**  There are at least two controls which could have detected this mechanism.

1. **Confirmations:** All OTC trades should be confirmed with the relevant counterparties on the day of the trade booking. If operations had been required to confirm these trades with the counterparty, the unauthorized trading would have been identified much earlier on.

2. **New and amended trades review:** All new and amended trades should be captured by product control and exceptional or unusual trades should be reviewed and validated. Again, if product control were given the tools to see the P&L at trade level for a new or cancelled trade, the game would have been up from Adoboli much earlier.

   If the P&L is being generated from an off-market trade is significant, it should be captured by the new trade exception criteria. A bank may also choose to have a trader surveillance team embedded in their control framework to monitor trader activity. Their remit would include identifying and reviewing off-market trading.

**FIGURE 23.11**  P&L smoothing using fee tickets

3. **SCP alerts:** SCP alerts over suspicious trades. C/A/L trades should be captured and suspicious trades reviewed by the desk supervisor. Trend analysis should also be performed on these statistics so that persistent breaches can identified and acted upon.

**Zero-Notional Bullet Cash Trades**  Zero-notional bullet cash trades were fictitious fee tickets, where the shell of a normal trade ticket was used but only a cash amount was entered. As there was only a cash amount, the notional and price on the ticket will be zero.[48]

**Purpose**  UBS used these trades for legitimate reasons, such as recording the settlement of dividends, but Adoboli's purpose was to misreport the P&L and clear cash breaks generated by other concealment mechanisms.[49]

If a trade is fictitious and it remains live in the RMS over a settlement date, it will auto-generate expected cash settlement entries but have no actual cash settlement entries in the UBS bank account. This asymmetry will create a nostro break and require investigation by operations (see Chapter 19 for more information on nostro breaks).

For Adoboli, these cash tickets were used to smooth his P&L and the rest of the trading desk were aware that P&L was being smoothed.[50][51] For example, let's assume that on 10 August, the desk had a good trading day and made a profit of $1 million, but only wanted to report a profit of $200,000. To achieve this smoothed P&L, they could enter a fee ticket paying $800,000 to a fictitious counterparty (dummy) at a future date, which "stores" the P&L for a rainy day. This is illustrated in Figure 23.11.

When the desk subsequently have a poor trading day, they could use this same counterparty to claw back all or part of the $800,000 and report their desired P&L.

**Control Weakness**
1. **New and amended trades review:** Product control were not provided with the necessary tools to perform reviews of the P&L at trade level.[52] This made it impossible to see how much P&L was being generated by these fictitious trades.
2. **Cash breaks – lack of root cause analysis:** The operations team were too focused on clearing down cash breaks and not focused enough on performing root cause analysis to determine:
   a) Why these breaks were occurring; and
   b) What actions had been taken to clear them (i.e., does what is happening make sense?).[53]

If operations had performed this analysis for Adoboli's cash breaks, they would have noticed that his fictitious trades were not only creating cash breaks, they were also clearing them.

3. **Lack of challenge:** Control functions need to have a good understanding of a desk's mandate and trading activities to understand what impact control exceptions, such as reconciliation breaks, pose to the business.[54]

Operations staff saw themselves as support staff rather than controllers, which led to staff not challenging the trader and his fictitious reasons regarding the cause of the high number of breaks he was generating.[55] The truth is, a support function exists to both support and control the front office. It is important that by supporting the desk you are not infringing on your controlling responsibilities.

**Effective controls**

1. **Cash breaks – root cause analysis:** Cash breaks should be investigated so that the cause of the break is understood properly and when it is cleared, control staff should understand how the break was cleared. This is more appropriate for high value or aged cash breaks, rather than every single cash break.

2. **New and amended trades review:** All new and amended trades should be captured by product control and exceptional or unusual trades should be reviewed and validated. Whenever you see the trading desk book a fee ticket there has to be economic substance to the trade. For example, if a client unwinds an interest rate swap and the NPV of the trade is $250,000 in the client's favour, it would be plausible that the trader would unwind the trade and book a fee paying the client an amount of approximately $250,000.

Product control also need to be curious regarding how the desk generated their P&L. If a desk is smoothing their P&L, the economics or real-world driver of the P&L won't exist and further investigation can illuminate the underlying fraud.

**Trader Influencing P&L Adjustments**   Though not listed as primary concealment mechanism used by Adoboli, P&L adjustments are still worth highlighting in our review of the rogue trading incident.

Adjustments to the P&L are required when the GL or P&L reporting system is reporting an incorrect P&L. Adoboli requested P&L adjustments on more than one occasion to offset the P&L from his actual P&L and other concealment mechanisms. On one day, 11 August, 2011, the P&L adjustments for his desk totalled approximately $1 billion, which offset a loss of $1 billion.[56]

**Purpose**   The purpose of the P&L adjustments was to misreport the P&L.

**Control weakness**

1. **Lack of governance around P&L adjustments:** The FINMA report points out that UBS had no policy for governing P&L adjustments, which meant that P&L adjustments could be made by product controllers without approval from their supervisor.[57]

As the P&L produced by product control was reported on a net basis, there was a lack of transparency regarding what adjustments were being taken. It wasn't until

18 August 2011, that P&L adjustments were reported to the ETF desk supervisor, meaning that prior to this date, he was unaware of what adjustments were being made for his traders.[58]

Although I do not know this, I imagine that from 18 August 2011, this small change resulted in Adoboli using P&L adjustments less frequently to conceal his unauthorized trading.

2. **Lack of challenge:** Product control didn't challenge the desk when they requested adjustments to their P&L.[59]

#### Effective controls

**Governance around P&L adjustments:** As an independent control function, product control are the gatekeepers to the financials, so it is important that any adjustments to the P&L requested by the trader are not accepted without challenge and have the proper level of governance. See Chapter 13 for instruction on how to govern P&L adjustments.

**Other Control Failures**   FINMA identified additional cracks in the internal control framework which contributed to the rogue trading going undetected. Whilst I won't go into each of them in this book, it is worth highlighting the themes regarding several of these.

**Balance Sheet Reconciliations**   The general lack of challenge culture permeated through the internal control framework to render several controls ineffective. Balance sheet reconciliations also became less effective due to control functions not challenging the rogue trader and his activities.

For example, for the July 2011 month-end balance sheet reconciliations, there was an unexplained break across two accounts summing to CHF 209 million, or €4 billion if viewed on a gross basis. The break existed because the trader hadn't booked large futures trades and although being chased by product control and operations to do so, he fobbed them off, telling them they will be booked shortly.[60]

After two weeks, the break was finally escalated to the ETF supervisor and a report prepared by Adoboli, product control and operations, which explained why the break existed. "Despite lacking credibility in many respects, the explanation was not challenged by any of the front office, operations or product control staff who saw it and was accepted by those present at a senior finance committee meeting on 24 August 2011. The conclusion of this meeting was that no amounts were at risk."[61]

**Little Regard for Control Existed in the Front Office**   FINMA identified that the business prioritized profits ahead of control.[62] This resulted in:

- Front office managers tolerating market risk breaches: on one occasion a risk breach resulted in a $6 million profit. The initial response from the supervisor was to congratulate the trader before reminding him he needed authorization in future.[63] When the rogue trader breached risk limits on other occasions, management also took no action.[64]
- Support and control functions were pressured to reduce headcount. Senior management's focus on reducing staffing levels compromised the effectiveness of some controls.[65]

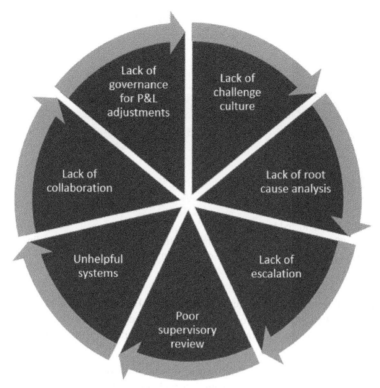

**FIGURE 23.12**   Summary of control weaknesses
Source: FINMA. "Summary Report: FINMA Investigation into the Events
Surrounding Trading Losses of USD 2.3 billion Incurred by the Investment
Banking Division of UBS AG in London," 21 November 2012.

**Summary of Control Weaknesses**   If I could sum up the weakness of the internal control
framework, I would present those seven items in Figure 23.12.

**Lack of challenge culture:** Operations and product control did not challenge the front
office, even when the reason for control exceptions didn't make sense.[66] This lack of
challenge allowed the trader to make use of concealment activities for an extended
period of time.

**Lack of root cause analysis:** Operations failed to understand why cash breaks existed and
how they were cleared, which made the control less effective.[67] Product control also
did not perform root cause analysis of the P&L performance of the desk, especially
the increase in proprietary trading income. In their defence, the systems provided
limited information for them to use.[68]

**Lack of escalation:** Control exceptions identified by product control and operations were
not escalated to supervisors and managers for review or approval.[69] This meant that
junior staff were dealing with complex issues created by the rogue trader.

**Poor supervisory reviews:** The ETF desk supervisor failed to supervise his desk properly,
missing opportunities to spot the rogue trading.

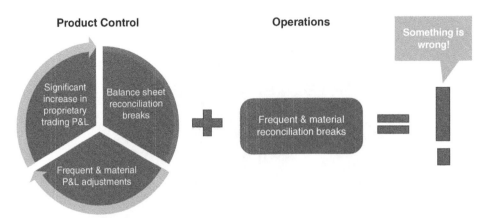

**FIGURE 23.13**   Consolidated lens
Source: FINMA. "Summary Report: FINMA Investigation into the Events Surrounding Trading
Losses of USD 2.3 Billion Incurred by the Investment Banking Division of UBS AG in London,"
21 November, 2012.

**Unhelpful systems:** The UBS systems were unhelpful for the controlling of the ETF desk.
   Product control were not provided with trade level P&L reports, operations' T+14
   report wasn't operational for almost a year and trend analysis couldn't be performed
   on the SCP alerts.[70]

**Lack of collaboration:** A bank is fragmented into multiple departments, all of which need
   to work together to maintain a strong internal control framework. At UBS, there was
   a lack of collaboration amongst the business and support functions, which meant that
   an overall picture of the control exceptions was never created.[71] I refer to this picture
   as a consolidated lens.

   For UBS, a consolidate lens could have highlighted, to the business and senior
   management in operations and finance, the collective control exceptions listed in Figure 23.13. This information would provide management with strong evidence that
   something was seriously wrong with the ETF desk and an immediate collaborative
   investigation could ensue.

**Lack of governance for P&L adjustments:** Product control's lack of controls around
   P&L adjustments allowed material P&L adjustments to be entered at the discretion
   of junior employees with limited control experience.[72] All these shortcomings weakened the control framework and made it more difficult to identify the rogue trading
   that occurred on the ETF desk.

## How Was the Fraud Detected?

By 13 September, 2011, Adoboli's life on the run was fast approaching its end, as senior finance
managers started to question large uncollateralized assets created by the fictitious deferred
settlement ETF trades.

   As these balances were uncollateralized, they exposed UBS to significant amounts of
credit risk, which the finance managers wanted mitigated against by calling collateral from
the counterparties. During a phone call between the financial controller, product control and
Adoboli, the latter was requested to confirm the exposures and counterparties were accurate

so that UBS could go ahead and make the collateral call. Knowing the ruse was finally up, the trader left the office and went home to pen the following email to the product controller he had been misleading.

## CASE STUDY: UBS, KWEKU ADOBOLI

The following email was sent by Adoboli to his product control colleague.

*Dear Will,*

*It is with great stress and disappointment that I write this mail. First of all the ETF [exchange-traded funds] trades that you see on the ledger are not trades that I have done with a counterparty as I previously described.*

*I used the bookings as a way to suppress the PnL (profit and loss) losses that I have accrued through off book trades that I made.*

*Those trades were previously profit making, became loss making as the market sold off aggressively through the aggressive sell off days of July and early August.*

*Initially, I had been short futures through June and those lost money when the first Greek confidence vote went through in mid-June. In order to try and make the money back I flipped the trade long through the rally.*

*Although I had a couple of opportunities to unwind the long trade for a negligible loss, I did not move quickly enough for the market weakness on the back of the first back macro data and then an escalation Eurozone crisis cost me the losses you will see when the ETF bookings are cancelled.*

*The aim had been to try and make the money back before the September expiry date came through but I clearly failed.*

*These are still live trades on the book that will need to be unwound. Namely a short position in DAX futures (which had been rolled to December expiry) and a short position in S and P 500 futures that are due to expire on Friday.*

*I have now left the office for the sake of discretion. I will need to come back in to discuss the positions and explain face to face, but for reasons that are obvious, I did not think it wise to stay on the desk this afternoon.*

*I will expect that questions will be asked as to why nobody else was aware of these trades. The reality is that I have always maintained that these were EFP [exchange for physical] trades to the member of my team, BUC [product control], trade support and John Di Bacco [Adoboli's manager].*

*I take full responsibility for my actions and the s\*\*\* storm that will now ensue. I am deeply sorry to have left this mess for everyone and to have put my bank and my colleagues at risk.*

*Thanks, Kweku.*[73]

That is the one type of email you don't want to get from your trader and it must have sent a chill down the spine of the product controller, whom Adoboli had been misleading to conceal his losses.

Once Adoboli confessed his losses, the City of London Police and FINMA, the Swiss Financial Markets regulator, were notified by UBS. FINMA subsequently issued a press release stating that they would arrange for an independent investigation into the events that led to the trading loss.

Kweku Adoboli was charged by the City of London Police with two counts of fraud by abuse of position and four counts of false accounting. He faced criminal proceedings in Southwark court and on 20 November 2012, was found guilty on two counts of fraud by abuse of position but acquitted of four charges of false accounting. He was sentenced to jail for seven years.

The rogue actions of Adoboli were considered sophisticated and so serious that they almost wiped out UBS. His actions led to many people losing their jobs and damaged the morale of many of the Swiss bank's staff, myself included.

Adoboli has now served his time and I think it's important to give him the liberty to create a new career for himself, which will hopefully include assisting the banking industry to prevent rogue trading from reoccurring on this scale.

## Other Significant Operational Losses

Although not considered to be a case of rogue trading, there has been a trading loss in recent history which is also worth exploring. JP Morgan's "London Whale beaching" in 2012 was a significant event for the company, as within the space of six months the firm had unwittingly walked into more than $6 billion of trading losses.

Bruno Iksil, nicknamed the London Whale, worked with colleagues in the chief investment office (CIO), whose mission was to reduce JP Morgan's risk level. However, instead of reducing risk, the London office engaged in trading complex derivatives to generate trading profits. Sometimes this worked, pulling in huge profits for the bank but, eventually, their strategy failed and became a target for other market participants.

As losses continued to unexpectedly mount in the CIO structured credit portfolio, the firm established a task force to investigate the cause of the losses[74] and the trades also drew the attention of U.S. prosecutors.

Whilst Iksil appears to have made a deal with prosecutors, his supervisor and junior colleague were charged with securities fraud. While the trades weren't illegal, prosecutors acted on the charge that the traders concealed the magnitude of losses from the bank's management. The incident shed light on how oversight can fail, as a U.S. Senate investigation report showed that the bank did not disclose key information to regulators and overlooked risky trading habits, including more than 300 risk-limit breaches in the first four months of 2012. JP Morgan's reputation took a hit and CEO Jamie Dimon took a 50% paycut.

"When the Whale's trading first came to light, Dimon dismissed it as '*a tempest in a teapot.*' Later he was more contrite, calling the trades '*flawed, complex, poorly reviewed, poorly executed and poorly monitored.*'"[75]

In the bank's task force report, all functions within the CIO business drew criticism, including the traders, trading management, risk and finance. These key findings reinforce the notion that all functions need to maintain their lines of defence in order for the overall control framework to be effective. For product control, the report reinforces the importance of having appropriately skilled people in the role who provide transparency into the desk's trading activity through the channels available to them. Frequently I hear senior management in the front office asking for product control to challenge their staff and that is exactly what was required in the CIO function at JP Morgan.

Fraud and trading losses, whether significant or not, will always be a real risk for banks where trading desks exist. A diligent review of incidents in the past can help reduce the risk of history repeating itself. Always be on your guard, remain part of the collective control fabric and remember to remain independent of the front office.

# NOTES

1. Rodrigues, Jason, "Barings collapse at 20: How rogue trader Nick Leeson broke the bank," *The Guardian*, 25 February 2015, https://www.theguardian.com/business/from-the-archive-blog/2015/feb/24/nick-leeson-barings-bank-1995-20-archive.
2. Leeson, Nick, *Rogue Trader*. Little, Brown Book Group. Kindle Edition.
3. Iguchi, Toshihide, *My Billion Dollar Education, Inside the Mind of a Rogue Trader*, 2014.
4. Ibid.
5. Wearden, Graeme, "The biggest rogue traders in history," *The Guardian*, 25 January 2008, https://www.theguardian.com/business/2008/jan/24/europeanbanks.banking.
6. Pignal, Stanley, "Rogue Traders who went off the rails," *FT Magazine*, 24 January 2009, https://www.ft.com/content/2d78785c-e755-11dd-aef2-0000779fd2ac.
7. Wearden, Graeme, "The biggest rogue Traders in history," *The Guardian*, 25 January 2008, https://www.theguardian.com/business/2008/jan/24/europeanbanks.banking.
8. APRA, "Report into Irregular Currency Options Trading at the National Australia Bank," 23 March 2004.
9. Société Générale Group, 2008 registration document.
10. Daneshkhu, Scheherazade, 'SocGen €5.5bn rights issue oversubscribed," *Financial Times*, 11 March 2008, https://www.ft.com/content/10bfb5fe-ef3f-11dc-8a17-0000779fd2ac.
11. Société Générale Group, 2008 Registration document.
12. Société Générale, "General Inspection Department, "Mission Green Summary report," 20 May 2008.
13. Roland, Denise, "Rogue trader Jérôme Kerviel leaves prison less than five months into three-year sentence, Former banker who lost Société Générale nearly €5bn has secured job in IT consultancy firm," *The Telegraph*, 25 March 2017, http://www.telegraph.co.uk/finance/newsbysector/banksandfinance/11081554/Rogue-trader-Jerome-Kerviel-leaves-prison-less-than-five-months-into-three-year-sentence.html.
14. Sebag, Gaspard and Benedetti Valentini, Fabio, "Kerviel Bill Cut to $1 Million from $5.5 Billion by Judges," Bloomberg, 24 September 2016, https://www.bloomberg.com/news/articles/2016-09-23/kerviel-must-pay-socgen-1-million-euros-over-2008-trading-loss.
15. FINMA, "UBS trading losses in London: FINMA finds major control failures," 26 November 2012, https://www.finma.ch/en/news/2012/11/mm-ubs-london-20121126.
16. National, Concise Annual Report 2003, p. 43.
17. Ibid., p. 61.
18. Ibid.
19. National, Annual Financial Report 2004, p. 6.
20. FINMA. "Summary Report, FINMA Investigation into the Events surrounding Trading Losses of USD 2.3 billion incurred by the Investment Banking Division of UBS AG in London," p. 13, 21 November 2012, https://www.finma.ch/en/news/2012/11/mm-ubs-london-20121126.
21. FSA, "FSA fines UBS £29.7 million for significant failings in not preventing large scale unauthorised trading," 26 November 2012, http://www.fsa.gov.uk/library/communication/pr/2012/105.shtml.
22. National, Concise Annual Report 2004, p. 61.
23. Committee of European banking Supervisors, "Reactions to the Société Générale loss event: results of a stock-take," 18 July 2008, https://www.eba.europa.eu/documents/10180/16166/20080718survey.pdf.

24. Fortado, Lindsay, "Kweku Adoboli: A Rogue Trader's Tale," FTfm, 22 October, 2015, https://www.ft.com/content/0fa0b42a-783a-11e5-a95a-27d368e1ddf7.
25. FINMA. "Summary Report: FINMA Investigation into the Events Surrounding Trading Losses of USD 2.3 billion incurred by the Investment Banking Division of UBS AG in London," p. 3, 21 November 2012, https://www.finma.ch/en/news/2012/11/mm-ubs-london-20121126. UBS, Annual Report 2011, Page 43, https://www.ubs.com/global/en/about_ubs/investor_relations/annualreporting/archive.html.
26. FINMA. "Summary Report, FINMA Investigation into the Events surrounding Trading Losses of USD 2.3 billion incurred by the Investment Banking Division of UBS AG in London," page 4, 21 November 2012, https://www.finma.ch/en/news/2012/11/mm-ubs-london-20121126.
27. Ibid., pp. 4–5.
28. Ibid.
29. FINMA. "Summary Report, FINMA Investigation into the Events surrounding Trading Losses of USD 2.3 billion incurred by the Investment Banking Division of UBS AG in London," page 4, 21 November 2012, https://www.finma.ch/en/news/2012/11/mm-ubs-london-20121126.
30. Ibid.
31. Ibid.
32. Ibid.
33. Ibid., p. 12.
34. APRA, "Report into Irregular Currency Options Trading at the National Australia Bank," pp. 17–18, 23 March 2004.
35. FINMA. "Summary Report, FINMA Investigation into the Events surrounding Trading Losses of USD 2.3 billion incurred by the Investment Banking Division of UBS AG in London," p. 5, 21 November 2012, https://www.finma.ch/en/news/2012/11/mm-ubs-london-20121126/.
36. Ibid., p. 6.
37. Ibid.
38. Ibid., p. 10.
39. Ibid., p. 5.
40. Ibid., p. 9.
41. Ibid., p. 11.
42. Ibid., p. 5.
43. Ibid.
44. Ibid.
45. Ibid., p. 10.
46. Ibid.
47. Ibid., p. 6.
48. Ibid., p. 5.
49. Ibid.
50. Although other traders on the desk were aware of this P&L smooth mechanism, there is no evidence that suggests they knew Adoboli was using this mechanism to conceal his unauthorized trading losses.
51. Ibid.
52. Ibid., p. 10.
53. Ibid.
54. Ibid.
55. Ibid.
56. Ibid., pp. 6–7.
57. Ibid.
58. Ibid.
59. Ibid.
60. Ibid.

61. Ibid.
62. Ibid., p. 12.
63. Ibid., p. 6.
64. Ibid.
65. Ibid., p. 13.
66. Ibid., p. 10.
67. Ibid.
68. Ibid.
69. Ibid., p. 11.
70. Ibid.
71. Ibid.
72. Ibid.
73. Rankin, Ben, " 'I take full responsibility for the s∗∗∗ storm that will now ensue': rogue trader's email to colleagues," Mirror.co.uk, 20 November 2012, http://www.mirror.co.uk/news/uk-news/kweku-adoboli-read-bombshell-email-1446637.
74. JP Morgan, "Report of JPMorgan Chase & Co. Management Task Force Regarding 2012 CIO Losses," 16 January 2013, http://files.shareholder.com/downloads/ONE/2272984969x0x628656/4cb574a0-0bf5-4728-9582-625e4519b5ab/Task_Force_Report.pdf.
75. Hurtado, Patricia, "The London Whale." Bloomberg, 23 April 2015. Bloomberg L.P. Copyright© 2015, http://www.bloombergview.com/quicktake/the-london-whale.

Printed and bound by CPI Group (UK) Ltd, Croydon, CR0 4YY

23/04/2025

14660950-0002